GODDESSES WHO RULE

D0224509

# Goddesses Who Rule

Edited by
Elisabeth Benard and Beverly Moon

OXFORD
UNIVERSITY PRESS

2000

OXFORD
UNIVERSITY PRESS

Oxford New York
Athens Auckland Bangkok Bogota Bombay Buenos Aires
Calcutta Cape Town Dar es Salaam Delhi Florence Hong Kong
Istanbul Karachi Kuala Lumpur Madras Madrid Melbourne
Mexico City Nairobi Paris Singapore Taipei Tokyo Toronto

and associated companies in
Berlin Ibadan

Copyright © 2000 by Oxford University Press, Inc.

Published by Oxford University Press, Inc.
198 Madison Avenue, New York, New York 10016

Oxford is a registered trademark of Oxford University Press

All rights reserved. No part of this publication may be reproduced, stored in a retrieval system, or transmitted, in any form or by any means, electronic, mechanical, photocopying, recording, or otherwise, without the prior permission of Oxford University Press.

Library of Congress Cataloging-in-Publication Data
Goddesses who rule / edited by Beverly Moon and Elisabeth Benard.
p. cm.
Includes bibliographical references and index.
ISBN 0-19-512130-9; ISBN 0-19-512131-7 (pbk.)
1. Goddesses. 2. Queens—Mythology. I. Moon, Beverly Ann.
II. Benard, Elisabeth Anne.
BL473.5.G65 2000
291.2'114—dc21 99-047723

9 8 7 6 5 4 3 2 1

Printed in the United States of America
on acid-free paper

# Foreword

Throughout the twentieth century historians of religion have been deeply involved in exploring the dynamics of divine and human sovereignty in the religious and religio-political traditions they study. More recently there has been a movement within many areas of religio-historical research to balance an inherited male-oriented bias by focusing attention on female deities and on the roles of women. In *Goddesses Who Rule* these two very powerful and on-going religio-historical projects are brought together in a way that greatly advances them both.

Past history of religions scholarship has contributed immensely to our understanding of gods associated with sovereignty such as Yahweh, Indra, and the Jade Emperor, as well as our understanding of divine or sacral kings in societies all across the pre-modern world. In contrast, past scholarship on goddesses associated with sovereignty and with the sacrality of royal women has been very weak and scattered. This imbalance has left us with a very inadequate overview of sovereignty as a religio-historical category. It has also left us with a skewed understanding of the very high percentage of particular cases in which the religious dimension of sovereignty is constituted by a complex combination of male and female components.

Recent feminist efforts in history of religions scholarship have made great progress in redressing the imbalance between the volume and quality of studies focused on male deities and sacral figures on the one hand, and the volume and quality of studies focused on female deities and sacred women on the other. Yet it remains the case that the study of female deities and personages associated with sovereignty has not been given anything like the attention it deserves. This has been a very significant factor in preserving a situation in which unfortunately limited, essentially a-political stereotypes of female symbolism and the powers and activities of women have been left largely intact.

In *Goddesses Who Rule* Beverly Moon and Elisabeth Benard have made a major contribution by gathering together fourteen essays that deal with goddesses and sovereignty in many different areas of the world including ancient Greece, Egypt, India, China, Japan, Europe, Meso-America, and Africa. In addition, they have provided an informative introduction; they have developed an intriguing organizational structure; and they have provided some thoughtful concluding reflections. Each reader will have his or her favorite essay or essays. But anyone who has a serious interest in the religious dimensions of sovereignty and/or the richness and diversity of feminine symbolism and power will want to read this book from cover to cover.

—Frank Reynolds

# Preface

In the fall of 1995, a group of Columbia University graduates traveled to New York to pay their final respects to their teacher Wing-tsit Chan. While there, they met with another alumna for breakfast at Ollie's, a Chinese noodle shop across the street from the gates of the university. Sitting around a table, eating congee and talking, we discovered that three of us were doing research on goddesses who were also queens. Frustrated with the fact that scholars and theologians in the West typically identify every goddess as a symbol of motherhood or "fertility," we decided to focus in depth on goddesses who play some kind of political role.

We are grateful to our editor at Oxford University Press, Cynthia Read, for her enthusiasm and support of this project. We want to thank our contributors, who shared so freely of their expertise and precious time. Other thanks go to those who have offered us special assistance during these years of editing: the University of Puget Sound for a Martin Nelson Summer Research Grant and Bart Collopy at Fordham College Lincoln Center. We also thank Stuart Smithers for encouraging us to seek out a publisher and Joseph M. Dunlap for helping us find a title. As for us, collaboration has brought many rewards: Our friendship has grown and we realize that we can rely on each other as editors in future projects.

*Tacoma, Washington* — Elisabeth Benard
*New York City* — Beverly Moon

# Contents

# Contributors

Constantina Rhodes Bailly is chair of the Department of Religious Studies at Eckerd College in St. Petersburg, Florida. Her areas of specialization include Sanskrit poetry, Kashmir Shaivism, and goddess worship in India. She is the author of *Shaiva Devotional Songs of Kashmir: A Translation and Study of Utpaladeva's Shivastotravali* and *Meditations on Shiva* (both from the State University of New York Press). She is coauthor of *Meditation Revolution: A History and Theology of Siddha Yoga Lineage* (Agama Press) as well as the author of numerous articles.

Elisabeth Benard teaches in the Asian Studies Program at the University of Puget Sound, where she is also the director of the Pacific Rim/Asia Study Travel Program. She is the author of *Chinnamasta, the Aweful Buddhist and Hindu Goddess* (1994).

Laurel G. Broughton is a scholar of medieval literature, who teaches at the University of Vermont. For the past twenty years her research has focused on the miracles of the Virgin Mary. Currently she is completing a catalogue of legends about Mary found in England.

Professor of History Emeritus at the University of California, Berkeley, Delmer M. Brown continues to teach a graduate course on Shinto at the Starr King School for Ministry in Berkeley. He has authored *Nationalism in Japan: An Introductory Historical Analysis* (1955) and co-translated *Studies in Shinto Thought* (1964) and *The Future and the Past: A Translation of the Gukanshö, An Interpretative History Written in 1219* (1979). He has also edited and contributed chapters to *The Cambridge History of Japan* (volume 1, 1993).

Suzanne E. Cahill teaches Chinese history at the University of California, San Diego. She is well-known for her study entitled *Transcendence and Divine Passion: The Queen Mother of the West in Medieval China* (1993).

William Harman teaches the history of religions at De Pauw University. He combines expertise in methodology in the study of religion with the Hinduism of Tamil-speaking southern India. Author of *The Sacred Marriage of a Hindu Goddess* (1990), he is currently doing a study of goddesses associated with healing.

Susan Tower Hollis has worked as a senior college administrator as well as a teacher in Massachusetts, California, and Nevada. Her publications and presentations deal primarily with ancient Egyptian goddesses, queens, and women, basing her research on narrative and myth analysis (using the tools available from folklore and anthropology) as well as comparative materials relating ancient Egypt and the history and culture of ancient Israel.

Proinsias Mac Cana is the author of *Celtic Mythology* (1983) and numerous articles on kingship and goddesses in ancient Irish culture. He teaches in the School of Celtic Studies at the Dublin Institute for Advanced Studies.

Beverly Moon has taught the history of religions in Asia and the United States. An associate project director for Mircea Eliade's *The Encyclopedia of Religion* (1987), she is also the editor of *An Encyclopedia of Archetypal Symbolism* (1991), a volume that presents mythical themes expressed in the sacred art of the world's religious traditions.

Vivian-Lee Nyitray teaches in the departments of Religious Studies and Literatures and Languages at the University of California, Riverside, where she is also director of the Asian Languages and Civilizations Program. In addition to continuing research on Mazu devotionalism, she is presently completing a manuscript on the confrontation between Confucianism and feminism.

Jacob K. Olúpọ̀nà is professor of African American and African Studies as well as chair of the Religious Studies Program at the University of California, Davis. A specialist in comparative religions and African religions, his works include *Kingship, Religion, and Rituals in a Nigerian Community* (1991); *Religious Plurality in Africa: Essays in Honor of John Mbiti* (co-edited with Sulayman Nyang: 1993); *African Traditional Religions in Contemporary Society* (1991); *Religion and Peace in Multi-Ethnic Nigeria* (1992); and *African Spirituality* (in press).

Kay A. Read, a scholar of the religions of ancient Mesoamerica and the Native Americans, teaches in the History of Religions and Art and Religion at DePaul University in Chicago. Her publications include articles on Mexica (Aztec) cosmology, sacrifice, ethics, and kingship as well as a volume called *Binding Reeds and Burning Hearts: Mexica-Tenochca Concepts of Time and Sacrifice* (forthcoming from Indiana University Press).

Serinity Young teaches in the Religious Studies Department of Southern Methodist University. The author of *An Anthology of Sacred Texts By and About Women*, she is also the editor of the *Encyclopedia of Women and World Religion* (1998). Her *Dreaming in the Lotus: Buddhist Dream Narrative, Imagery, and Practice*, a study of dreams in Indo-Tibetan Buddhist biography, appeared in print in 1999.

GODDESSES WHO RULE

# Introduction

This volume presents a collection of essays about goddesses and sovereignty, focusing in particular on sacred or divine queens and those goddesses who exhibit a special relationship with an earthly ruler. Sovereign goddesses have been worshipped in numerous cultures, in the past as well as in the present. They are found primarily in complex societies with specialized social roles, where governing is a full-time position and where the ruler serves as a religious focal point binding the community together.

Some of these goddesses are worshipped as divine queens. For example, Minatci, traditionally recognized as a princess of the Pandya kingdom in southern India, grows up to become a queen and a goddess. Her temple in Madurai is her palace, where she rules together with her divine husband, the pan-Indian god Siva. Other divine queens include Mazu (also known as Empress of Heaven) and Xiwangmu (Queen Mother of the West) in Chinese tradition.

As queens, these and other goddesses of sovereignty are often depicted sitting on a throne or bearing a royal headdress: In the Italian city of Siena, Duccio di Buoninsegna's great altarpiece the Maestà, or Virgin in Majesty, celebrates Mary's regal nature, showing her seated on a gothic throne; a statue of Aphrodite from her ancient city of Aphrodisias presents her wearing the *polos*, the royal headdress of Anatolian goddesses.

The Sumerian goddess Inanna appears on a cylinder seal in full regalia: On her head is the crown of the steppes made up of multiple horns, her torso is draped with the flounced gown of royalty, and one foot rests on the back of a lion, an animal often associated with kingship.

Not only are certain goddesses worshipped as queens, a goddess can also be the source of sovereignty. A ruler who receives sovereign powers from a goddess does so by virtue of a special relationship that exists between them: For example, the emperor of Japan is sanctified in his role by his ancestor, the Great Goddess Amaterasu; in ancient Egypt, where the pharoah was typically regarded as having divine parents, the goddess Hathor is often depicted in art as his mother; sometimes the king receives his royal power through union with a goddess, as in the Celtic *banais rígi*, or "wedding-feast of kingship."

## The Study of Goddesses

Until recently, however, Western scholars of religion have dismissed the subject matter of goddesses—sovereign or not—as unworthy of serious study. In the planning of *The Encyclopedia of Religion* (1987) under the general editorship of Mircea Eliade, an effort was made to include discussion of goddess traditions as well as articles on specific goddesses. However, at that time, in the early 1980s, so little up-to-date scholarship was available in this area that the coverage was rather limited. Since then, interest in goddesses has emerged increasingly as a serious topic for consideration in the field of religion.

Two factors have contributed to changing attitudes about goddesses and the study of goddesses. Above all, there has been a shift in religious studies from a focus primarily on Western traditions to an interest in all the world's religions. This is reflected already in *The Encyclopedia of Religion*, whose editors consciously made broad coverage of all traditions a primary goal. Increasingly the polytheistic traditions are receiving attention and are being interpreted within the context of their own cultures, instead of being viewed through the lens of Western monotheism.

Another factor is an increase in the number of women scholars in religious studies. These women sometimes ask different questions than do their male counterparts; many wonder why serious study of goddesses is not respected in academic settings. Further, recognizing the historical fact of goddesses and their importance in living traditions, these women (and some men, too) are less inclined than scholars in the past to accept popular but superficial generalizations about goddesses. As Proinsias Mac Cana points out in his essay on Celtic goddesses, scholars need to look beyond the categories that simplify our understanding of deities and recognize that each is perceived by devotees as an individual: "One suspects that the goddess Brigid would have been as much an individual in the eyes of the average man or woman in pre-Christian Ireland as her Christian avatar Saint Brigid still is for their modern counterparts" (Mac Cana, in this volume, 86)

## The Diversity and Complexity of Goddesses

The picture is complicated further because goddesses usually display more than one kind of symbolism. The Nahua (Aztec) goddess Cihuacoatl is a good example of this: Her name means Snakewoman, and yet as Eagle Woman she is also a goddess of the sky. At times she appears as a female warrior; elsewhere, as a social matron or an inhabitant of the underworld. Ancient Celtic goddesses also exhibited a diversity of roles: "Like other sovereignty-figures, the Morrigán was a multi-functional and many-layered character. War, death, prophecy, guardianship, sexuality, fertility and rulership were all inextricably intertwined in this complex divinity, whose relationship to humans appears to have been capricious and changing, but who was strongly committed to the fortunes of Ireland" (Green 1995, 79).

Over time a goddess may acquire a complex symbolism because her role and symbolism change with the gradual transformation of the culture around her. For example, there is some evidence that Aphrodite was once a sea goddess of Paphos on the western coast of Cyprus. Eventually she was recognized as the local form of Inanna/Ishtar, whose fame had spread throughout the ancient Mediterranean with the spread of kingship as a political institution. Aphrodite, too, became identified with the morning and evening star and was called Queen of Heaven. Her importance continued to grow: Roman emperors looked to her for help on the battlefield and as the source of their divine right to rule.

## Distorted Views of Goddesses

In spite of their great diversity and individual complexity, Western writers typically identify goddesses as symbols for motherhood or fertility. The expressions *fertility goddess* and *mother goddess* are so ubiquitous as to convince the general public, and many scholars, that a necessary relationship exists linking every goddess figure to maternity and the natural processes of reproduction.

### *Mother Goddess*

Everywhere, even in the best studies of mythology and the religions of the non-Western world, goddesses are too quickly labeled "mother goddesses." For example, in Samuel Noah Kramer's account of the Sumerian myth about "The Creation of Man," it is the goddess Ninmah who fashions human beings out of the earth: "Ninmah takes some of the clay which is over the abyss and fashions six different types of individuals, while [the god] Enki decrees their fate and gives them bread to eat" (Kramer 1961a, 71). In Hebrew scripture, Yahweh too makes Adam out of clay, and thus he is known as the Creator. But instead of calling Ninmah a creator, she is referred to as a mother goddess. In the index to Kramer's introduction to Sumerian mythology, Ninmah is a cross-reference to Nintu, who is cited as "Nintu (mother goddess)."

Of course, Kramer most likely was not the indexer; nevertheless, in another of his works (Kramer 1961b, 121) we find him referring to the Sumerian goddess Aruru as the mother goddess Aruru. In *The Epic of Gilgamesh*, Aruru creates a half-man, half-animal creature named Enkidu to subdue the hero Gilgamesh. Once again the expression *mother goddess* distorts our understanding of her role: After all, Aruru is not "the mother" of the monster; she is its creator.

In the same volume, W. Norman Brown suggests that each of the many goddesses of India is a variation of a single primordial Great Mother, who was worshipped by the early inhabitants of the Indus River Valley: "It is considered that in Western Asia these [pottery figurines of pregnant females] are representations of the Mother Goddess, or the Great Mother, or the Earth Mother, whose worship was generally observed throughout all this region, and it is assumed therefore that the same worship existed in the Indus Valley" (Kramer 1961b, 310). The mountain goddess Parvati, the warrior and protector goddess Durga, the goddess of time and death, Kali, even Camunda, the insatiable demon-slayer—all are seen as later manifestations of an ancient Great Mother goddess.

In her article "The Goddess: Fact, Fallacy, and Revitalization Movement" (1990), Joan B. Townsend criticizes the modern Western theory that the mother goddess is somehow the primal form of every goddess. This theory goes hand in hand with the idea that human culture was originally matriarchal, or at least matrifocal, and centered around the worship of a single (mother) goddess, all of which was overthrown later by a patriarchal, warlike development, which introduced male gods and male rule simultaneously. Townsend cites typical sources of this widespread view, which "include the archetype [sic] analysis of the psychological history of humans, especially as discussed by Erich Neumann in *The Great Mother,* and the works of Crawford and James which advocate a kind of 'universal' prehistoric religion focused on the Mother Goddess" (Townsend 1990, 182). In turn, the theoretical bases of these writings are derived from yet earlier writings of anthropologists Robert Briffault (1927), J. J. Bachofen (1861), Lewis Henry Morgan (1877), and Sir Edward Burnett Tylor (1871), as well as the perspective on history set forth by Karl Marx and Friedrich Engels (1978). These thinkers all belong to an intellectual tradition that sees history in terms of a unilinear evolution from matriarchy linked with worship of the Goddess to patriarchy and, eventually, the worship of a single God.

Another factor that has led scholars to associate goddesses with motherhood is the common use of the term *mother* in many traditions as a title of highest respect. After all, mothering does not end with a successful pregnancy and childbirth; on the contrary, that is but the beginning. Not only does the mother feed and clothe the child's body, it is she who teaches the child how to become a human being: language, custom, tradition—all this is the content of the mother's care. A successful mother is a woman who has raised a fully realized adult. Hence, it makes sense that in many cultures respected female elders are called mother, whether or not they actually have given birth to a child.

Lotte Motz shows us, for example, that among the peoples of northern Eurasia numerous deities are addressed as mother: Forest Mother of the Livonians Thunderstorm Mother of the Udmorts, the Mari Mother of Jumo (a god), Earth

Mother of the Mordvins, and Mother of Kaltasa (a village) of the Mansi (Motz 1997, 45). A close examination of these mothers reveals that none are actually maternal deities. Some are rulers of a specific place or a group of living creatures; others are spirits that dwell in elements of nature; many are ancestors of the tribe or clan.

Motz examines the names and roles of goddesses in numerous societies, concluding that the origins of specific goddesses are diverse and that each develops in a unique way due to historical factors. No one archetype sets the pattern for all goddesses. Motz suggests that contemporary belief in "the concept of an all-embracing maternal divinity" (Motz 1997, 5) may have its source in Enlightenment theory rather than in the actual religious experience of any one people: "Such constructions and ideals . . . came to the fore when people turned from the gods of their revealed religions" (Motz 1997, 185).

This collection of essays on goddesses of sovereignty bears out Lotte Motz's discoveries. Some of the goddesses are actual mothers, but the majority are not. For example, the Egyptian goddesses, such as Nekhbet, Nut, Hathor, and Isis, do tend be more maternal. Sometimes they are actually thought to be the pharoah's mother, elsewhere they are depicted nursing him. The Virgin Mary is another sacred mother; not only is she the mother of Christ, she also acts toward her devotees as a loving mother. On the other hand, many goddesses of sovereignty are worshipped as the founders of a royal lineage. For example, the emperors of Japan and the emperors of Rome received their powers from goddesses who were not the personal mother but rather the ancestor. Amaterasu, the sun goddess of Japan, lends her powers to her descendant, the emperor; as a female warrior, Aphrodite guides and protects her descendant Julius Caesar in battle. Many goddesses, although neither mothers nor ancestors, are called mother out of respect. Cihuacoatl (sometimes called Tonan, "Our Mother") and the Queen Mother of the West are not mothers; nor are they maternal in the usual sense. Both are powerful, regal figures generally without connection to matters of pregnancy, birth, and small children. (Cihuacoatl has a role in connection to childbirth, not as a mother but as a warrior.)

Finally, there are numerous goddesses of sovereignty who are neither ancestors nor mothers, not even in name only. They are more likely to be the wife of a king or a ruling god. The Celtic goddesses, the Sumerian Inanna, and Sri-Laksmi grant actual kingship in the context of erotic love. The king is regarded as the husband of the goddess from whom he receives his powers to rule successfully.

### *Fertility Goddess*

Surely the second most common classification assigned by Westerners to any given goddess is that of "fertility goddess." This language is rarely used in reference to gods, even gods associated with life, generation, and sexuality.

Siva, for example, is a Hindu god associated with both sexuality and asceticism. In spite of the fact that two of his central symbols are the bull and the phallus (*lingam*), he is not called a fertility god. Yet the goddess Inanna, one of the three most important deities in the royal cult of Sumer, is introduced often as a "fertility goddess," even in the otherwise careful work of Nanno Marinatos, a contemporary scholar of Minoan religion. According to Marinatos, Inanna is "the goddess of fertility, who appears as both the protector and the recipient of all the wealth of nature" (1993, 194).

Perhaps the key word here is *nature*. There is in Western intellectual history the common assertion that nature (identified with the material aspect of existence) is female, whereas the mind (identified with the formal aspect of existence) is male. This assumption is found already in Greek literature of the classical period. For example, in the *Oresteia* by Aeschylus, Apollo argues that Orestes in killing his mother has not really killed his "parent."

> Apollo:
> Here is the truth, I tell you—see how right I am.
> The woman you call the mother of the child
> is not the parent, just a nurse to the seed,
> the new-sown seed that grows and swells inside her.
> The man is the source of life—the one who mounts. (*The Eumenides* 665–669)

Only the father is the parent of the child, according to this argument, because the father deposits the seed (the form) of the child in the woman's womb where it receives material nourishment so that it can increase in size. The woman is the nurse to the child, feeding it but not creating it.

Philo of Alexandria agrees,[1] and this is important, because it is Philo who first succeeds in harmonizing Greek philosophy (Middle Platonism) and Biblical tradition. Philo's allegorical interpretation of the Septuagint (an early Greek translation of the Hebrew Torah) provided a model for later theologians—whether Jewish, Christian, or Islamic—seeking a way to defend their religious faith in philosophical language. Although a Jew, Philo received a formal Greek education in the highly hellenized city of Alexandria, Egypt. He takes for granted a cosmology that sees matter as female: "For progress is indeed nothing else than the giving up of the female gender by changing into the male, since the female gender is material, passive, corporeal, and sense-perceptible, while the male is active, rational, incorporeal, and more akin to mind and thought" (*Quaestiones et Solutiones in Exodum* 1.8). Not only does Philo's bias link the female to matter but it condemns both (matter and female creatures) as "inferior" to the so-called masculine world of mind. Such gender symbolism—biological processes as female and mental processes as male—supports the seemingly automatic Western conviction that every female deity must necessarily be a fertility goddess.

Another related intellectual tradition contributes to this bias: the allegorical interpretation of polytheistic gods and goddesses as personifications of natural forces, more generally. Not new, this theory was set forth already by Theagenes of Rhegium, a Greek philosopher living during the sixth century BCE. For Theagenes, the gods were allegorical representations of either the elements of nature or abstract spiritual qualities. In his view, Apollo represented the sun, Artemis, the moon, whereas Aphrodite was the personification of desire and Hermes the discerning intellect. The allegorical interpretation of so-called pagan deities as forces of nature continues to pervade much of contemporary scholarship. Any reference to so-called nature worship is built on this conceptual foundation. Instead of seeing individual gods and goddesses as symbols of divinity—as images of the unknowable mystery that confronts all humans—these scholars automatically "interpret" any god or goddess as a personified "natural power." Fertility as a power of nature belongs to this language. It reduces and limits our understanding of religious experience and prevents us from appreciating the diversity and complexity of individual deities.

## The Symbolism of Goddesses

The real problem that arises when we see every goddess in terms of motherhood and fertility is that our understanding becomes myopic. We fail to distinguish the goddesses when we ignore their diversity. The symbolism of a given goddess may derive from any aspect of human experience: It may be based on a mythical geography or on her role in the natural, cultural, or even metaphysical domains. Frequently a goddess has an animal form as well as a human form. The following lists give an indication of the diverse symbolism associated with goddesses:

*Animal Symbols*

Cobra: the Egyptian Wadjet
Cow: the Egyptian Hathor
Frog: the Egyptian Heqet
Goose: the Greek Aphrodite
Kites: the Egyptian Isis and Nephthys
Lion: the Hindu Durga
Snake: the Nahua Cihuacoatl
Spider: the Hopi Spider Woman
Vulture: the Egyptian Nekhbet

*Geographical Symbolism*

The Sky: the Egyptian Nut
The Sun: the Japanese Amaterasu
Wind: the Yoruba Oya
Mountain: the Hindu Parvati
Volcano: the Hawaiian Pele
Planet Venus: the Sumerian Inanna
Moon: the Greek Selene
Stars: the Australian Seven Sisters (Pleiades)
River: the Yoruba Oshun

*Culture Heroines*

Shamanism: the Scandinavian Freyja
Agriculture: the Greek Demeter

Wine Making: the Mesopotamian Siduri
Weaving and Painting: the Nahua Xochiquetzal

*Metaphysical Discernment*

Transcendental Insight: the Buddhist Prajnaparamita
Severing Erroneous Views of a Self: the Hindu and Buddhist Chinnamasta
Wisdom: the Hellenistic Sophia
Knowledge: the Hindu Sarasvati

*Cosmic Roles*

Creation: Old Grandmother of the Shawnee
Ongoing Materialization: the Nahua Coatlicue
Time: the Hindu Kali
Ruler of the Dead: the Greek Persephone
Immortality: the Chinese Queen Mother of the West
Sovereignty: the Hindu Sri-Laksmi

It is this last category of sovereignty, the symbolism that connects certain goddesses with political authority, that is the theme of the chapters in this volume. Sacred and divine queens, such as the Virgin Mary and the Queen Mother of the West, as well as goddesses who support and protect a king, belong to this category. Sacred kingship is a theme that has been explored by historians of religion, but the role of goddesses in sacred kingship has not been the focus of a cross-cultural study.

## Goddesses and Sacred Kingship

The beliefs and rituals that form sacred kingship occur in ancient and contemporary complex societies governed by a centralized ruler. Sacred kingship has flourished in the ancient world and in contemporary societies, in places as diverse as Tibet, South America, and Ireland. Not every king is divine, but the institution of kingship is always sacred in some way. For example, the Akan of Ghana do not perceive their kings to be divine beings, but the office of king, or chief, is sacred because it mediates between the people and their royal ancestors (Opoku 1998, 949).

The study of sacred kingship (see Grottanelli 1987) was influenced during the last century by the publication of James G. Frazer's *The Magic Art and the Evolution of Kings* (1911–1915) and A. M. Hocart's *Kingship* ([1927] 1969). A number of monographs on specific aspects of kingship appeared. For example, Marc Bloch (1924) studied the healing power of kings in medieval Europe, and the sacred authority of royalty was the subject of John Neville Figgis's *The Divine Right of Kings* (1914) and Ernst H. Kantorowicz's *The King's Two Bodies: A Study in Medieval Political Theology* (1957). In 1955, sacred kingship was the topic of the Eighth International Congress for the History of Religions held in Rome. The papers presented at the meeting were published as *The Sacral Kingship* (1959) and provide a comparative view of this widespread phenomenon.

The diverse historical forms of kingship do seem to share a symbolic structure: mediation between human and divine realms. The king is a living *axis mundi* (or center of the world), providing a concrete and accessible connection between the gods and the kingdom—both the land and its people. The king is a man and simultaneously a god, both human and divine. And it is because he combines these two essential natures in his own person that he provides the ongoing mediation between the two realms. The divinity of the king is understood to be rooted in his relationship with a specific deity—a god or a goddess: A king of the Zhou dynasty in ancient China was called Son of Heaven, Heaven being their name for the supreme deity; the Tibetan king is recognized to be an emanation of Avalokitesvara, the bodhisattva of compassion; and in pre-Christian Ireland, the king became the ruler of the land by virtue of his marriage to the goddess of sovereignty, owner of the land or the land itself.

In spite of the attention given to kingship in recent decades, neither the royal goddess nor the divine patroness of kings has been isolated and studied. Exploring the theme of goddesses and sovereignty as it appears in a numerous religious traditions can only enrich our appreciation of the symbolism of kingship while broadening and deepening our understanding of goddess worship.

*Sovereignty* has many connotations. Beginning with the establishment of nation states in Europe during the seventeenth century, *sovereignty* has become a political term that indicates supreme authority within a limited territory, usually an autonomous nation (Philpott 1995). In this book, however, the concept of sovereignty will be understood in much broader terms, so as to apply equally to ancient cultures as well as to present-day societies.

The English term *sovereign* is an Indo-European word related to the Sanskrit expression *sva-raj*. *Sva* is an adjective meaning "autonomous"; while *raj* means "rule" or "king." *Sva-raj* is frequently translated as "self-rule," "self-ruling," or "self-ruler." Another meaning for *raj* is "resplendence" or "radiance." Thus *sva-raj* might also be rendered as "self-resplendent," "self-luminous," or "one possessing radiance." Indeed, according to ancient Sanskrit texts, "the king outshines all beings in *tejas* (luster or majesty)" (Gonda 1969, 35). (See Bailly's essay, in this volume.)

If one looks in English dictionaries for the meaning of *sovereign*, one frequently finds that the term derives from Old French *sovereign*, "one who exercises supreme authority within a limited sphere, an acknowledged leader." The French in turn derives from Latin *superanus* ("over and above"), a broader term that refers to some superlative quality, such as moral excellence. It is noteworthy that the aspect of *sovereignty* that has become obsolete since the mid-seventeenth century is this sense of supreme excellence, whereas the older Latin and Sanskrit terms both suggest some kind of supreme value rather than political power over others.

For most of us today, the word *sovereignty* does not call to mind qualities of excellence, radiance, or moral value. We associate sovereignty with the autonomy of an ethnic, racial, or indigenous group, perhaps within a larger nation, such as various Native American tribes in the United States. We think of the desire for self-rule as something limited to a group of people who want to rid themselves of their colonizers and oppressors, as in the Union of South Africa or Tibet. Such a definition is valid, but in this book our understanding of sovereignty will not be limited to modern political interpretations.

Because we are stressing the relationship between goddesses and sacred kingship, the concept of the sovereign as ruler over a specific territory is central in this book. This focus stresses the vertical axis, embodied by the ruler as intermediary between the earthly community and the heavenly realm, which the goddess represents. This is an exclusive axis accessible only to a proper ruler. The land and its inhabitants depend on the ruler, and through the ruler, the goddess, for protection from external enemies and natural disasters.

At the same time, we explore the concept of sovereignty as it pertains to individual self-rule, or self-realization. A goddess of sovereignty may protect and support one who seeks to attain some kind of transcendence: The yogin attains freedom from reincarnation; the Egyptian is resurrected in the world of the gods; the Taoist adept becomes an Immortal. This focus stresses the horizontal axis, which is available to anyone who seeks the autonomy of the self. Bailly (in this volume) states it well, "Whereas the king seeks sovereignty of the royal kingdom, the goal of the yogin is to acquire sovereignty of the inner Self" (144).

This collection, about goddesses and sovereignty, seeks to integrate the exclusive, vertical axis of royalty with the inclusive, horizontal axis of individual religious experience. Sovereignty thus clarifies patterns that are common to both the political ruler, supreme authority over a limited territory, and the adept, spiritual autonomy and absolute authority over oneself.

## NOTE

1. *De Opificio Mundi* 14: "the male that sows" and "the female that receives the seed."

## REFERENCES

Bachofen, J. J. 1861. *Das Mutterecht*. Basel: Schwabe.

Bloch, Marc. 1924. *Les rois thaumaturges: Étude sur le caractère surnaturel attribué à la puissance royale particulièrement en France et en Angleterre*. Strasbourg: Librairie Istra.

Briffault, Robert. 1927. *The Mothers: The Matriarchal Theory of Social Origins* (3 vols.). New York: Macmillan.

Crawford, Osbert G. S. 1957. *The Eye Goddess*. London: Phoenix House.

Eliade, Mircea, ed. 1987. *The Encyclopedia of Religion* (16 vols.). New York: Macmillan.

Engels, Friedrich. 1978. "The Origin of the Family, Private Property, and the State." Pp. 734–759 in *The Marx Engels Reader* (2nd ed.). New York: W. W. Norton.

Figgis, John Neville. 1914. *The Divine Right of Kings* (2nd ed.). Cambridge: Cambridge University Press.

Frazer, James G. 1911–1915. *The Magic Art and the Evolution of Kings*. Part 1 in his *The Golden Bough: A Study in Magic and Religion* (3rd ed.). London: Macmillan.

Gonda, Jan. 1969. *Ancient Indian Kingship from the Religious Point of View*. Leiden: E. J. Brill.

Green, Miranda. 1995. *Celtic Goddesses: Warriors, Virgins, and Mothers*. New York: George Braziller.

Grottanelli, Cristiano. 1987. "Kingship: An Overview." Pp. 313–317 in vol. 8 of *The Encyclopedia of Religion*, ed. Mircea Eliade. New York: Macmillan.

Hocart, A. M. 1969. *Kingship*. London: Oxford University Press. (Original work published 1927.)

James, E. O. 1959. *The Cult of the Mother Goddess*. London: Thames and Hudson.

Kantorowicz, Ernst H. 1957. *The King's Two Bodies: A Study in Medieval Political Theology*. Princeton, NJ: Princeton University Press.

Kramer, Samuel Noah. 1961a. *Sumerian Mythology: A Study of Spiritual and Literary Achievement in the Third Millenium B.C.* (rev. ed.). New York: Harper & Row.

———. 1961b. "Mythology of Sumer and Akkad." Pp. 93–137 in *Mythologies of the Ancient World*, ed. Samuel Noah Kramer. Garden City, NY: Doubleday.

Marinatos, Nanno. 1993. *Minoan Religion: Ritual, Image, and Symbol*. Columbia, SC: University of South Carolina Press.

Morgan, Lewis Henry. 1877. *Ancient Society*. New York: World Publishing.

Motz, Lotte. 1997. *The Faces of the Goddess*. New York: Oxford University Press.

Neumann, Erich. 1955. *The Great Mother: An Analysis of the Archetype*, trans. Ralph Mannheim. Princeton, NJ: Princeton University Press.

Opoku, Kofi Asare. 1998. Review of Anthony Ephirim-Donkor's *African Spirituality: On Becoming Ancestors*. *Journal of the American Academy of Religion* 66/4 (Winter): 947–949.

Philpott, Daniel. 1995. "Sovereignty: An Introduction and Brief History." *Journal of International Affairs* 48 (Winter): 353–368.

*The Sacral Kingship*, 1959. Leiden: E. J. Brill.

Townsend, Joan B. 1990. "The Goddess: Fact, Fallacy, and Revitalization Movement." Pp. 179–203 in *Goddesses in Religions and Modern Debate*, ed. Larry Hurtado. Atlanta: Scholars Press.

Tylor, Edward Burnett. 1871. *Primitive Culture: Research into the Development of Mythology, Philosophy, Religion, Language, Art, and Custom*. London: John Murray.

# PART I

## Love and War

### Foundations of Sovereignty

The king goes with (eagerly) lifted head
　　to the holy loins,
goes with (eagerly) lifted head
　　to the loins of Inanna.

"O my holy loins! O my holy Inanna!"

After he on the bed, in the holy loins,
　　has made the queen rejoice,
after he on the bed, in the holy loins
　　has made holy Inanna rejoice,
she in turn soothes the heart for him
　　there on the bed:

"Iddin-Dagan, you are verily my beloved!"

—Thorkild Jacobsen
"New Year's Sacred Marriage: Inanna as Bride"

# 1

# Aphrodite, Ancestor of Kings

*Beverly Moon*

In ancient Greek art and literature the goddess Aphrodite is praised for her beauty and her power to awaken love. As the standard of feminine comeliness, many a beautiful woman was compared to her, Helen's daughter, for example, the "rose-lipped Hermione, a girl like the pale-gold goddess Aphrodite" (*Odyssey* 4.14–15). Yet Aphrodite's ability to awaken desire did not depend on beauty alone. She possessed a magical amulet covered with potent symbols that made the bearer irresistible: "the passion of sex is there, and the whispered endearment that steals the heart away, even from the thoughtful" (*Iliad* 14.216–217).

Aphrodite was commonly associated not only with love but also with the sky and the sea. During the historical period of Greek religion, from the age of Homer (ca. 700 BCE) to Theodosius I and the christianization of the Roman empire (381 CE), she was worshipped as Ourania, or Queen of Heaven, appearing to all as the morning and evening star (which we call the planet Venus). Birds were sacred to this celestial queen, and her devotees brought doves as votive offerings to her temples. An Athenian cup attributed to the Pistoxenos Painter depicts Aphrodite riding through the sky on a white goose.[1] There the border of her gown is decorated with a continuous meander pattern, representing the movement of water. As goddess of the sea, Aphrodite was able to protect the sailor on his journey and guide him safely home.

At the same time, Aphrodite's domain was not limited to the natural worlds of love, beauty, sea, and sky. As Queen of Heaven, she was a goddess of royal sovereignty, the begetter of kings. In statues created for her temples, on coins, and in popular art, Queen Aphrodite appears sitting on a throne, bearing a crown, and accompanied by lions, all symbols of royal power. Nor was her role as goddess of sovereignty limited to the Greek-speaking world. Aphrodite was especially prominent during the period of the Roman empire when Julius Caesar and other rulers recognized in her their patron and ancestor, the source of their divinity and kingship.

A fresh look at the religious traditions associated with Aphrodite, from the earliest Greek sources through the Hellenistic period and up until the christianization of the Roman empire, discloses a continuity in her role as a goddess of sovereignty. The literary evidence, beginning with Homer, Hesiod, and the Homeric Hymns, as well as the visual evidence of religious art throughout this period of over a thousand years present Aphrodite as ancestor of kings. In her oldest known myth, her descendants ruled in Asia Minor, while the later development of this myth brings her son Aeneas and his family to Italy to found the Roman civilization. This ancient tradition was revitalized by the rulers of the Roman empire, above all, Julius Caesar. Believing that their divine right to rule rested on an ancestral bond to the Queen of Heaven—known to the Romans both as Aphrodite and as Venus—they continued to build on this foundation of sacred kingship.

## Julius Caesar

In 1969 archeologists discovered at Aphrodisias, the site of an ancient city of Asia Minor, modern-day Turkey, a series of letters from the emperors of Rome inscribed on the so-called Archive Wall (Erim 1986). One early inscription mentions a golden statue of Eros, which Julius Caesar had sent to Aphrodisias as a gift-offering for Aphrodite, the city's patron goddess (Reynolds 1982, 102).[2] In the mind of Caesar, the Roman Venus was identical to the Greek Aphrodite; furthermore, she was the ancestor of his family—a lineage of kings going back to before the Trojan War.[3]

In Latin the word *venus* was originally the neuter noun from which the verb *uenerari* was derived. In ancient times, *uenerari* was restricted to religious contexts and referred to an attitude of hospitality by means of which humans sought to attract the benevolence of the gods. The noun expressed this quality as an abstraction: graciousness or charm. Eventually the term was personified as a goddess: Venus. She was worshipped outside Rome as a protector of gardens, a goddess who ruled over the month of April. When the two goddesses were identified, the Romans simply gave the name and attributes of the Italian Venus to the complex figure of Aphrodite. The merging of the two goddesses is best understood against the dramatic story of the Punic Wars between Carthage and Rome.

During the first Punic War (264 to 241 BCE), Rome came to the aid of the people of Sicily, who were being attacked by the Carthaginians of North Africa. In 263 the Elymi of Sicily, who regarded themselves as descendants of Trojan emigrants, joined ranks with the Romans. Their main temple was on Mount Eryx, a temple dedicated to Aphrodite (which itself had supplanted a Phoenician temple of the goddess Astarte). According to local tradition, the temple was originally built by Aeneas, the son of Aphrodite, when his ship landed in Sicily. The Romans believed that they, too, descended from Aeneas, and so in 248 they took the Elymian sanctuary at Eryx by surprise, holding it until the end of the war, protecting the goddess in whom they saw the divine mother of their ancestor.

However, it was not until the middle of the next Punic War (218–201 BCE) that Venus Erycina (the Roman name for Aphrodite of Eryx) became an official figure in Roman state religion. The second Punic War began when the brilliant Carthaginian general Hannibal took the offensive against the hitherto victorious Romans and led his troops over the Alps into Italy itself. In 217 Hannibal and his army wiped out the opposing Roman army at Lake Trasimene in one of the worst defeats that Rome had ever experienced. As a result of this and other defeats, the Romans turned to Aphrodite for help. Not only did they see themselves as her descendants, but they associated her with the power of victory in war. After the slaughter at Trasimene, a state ceremony was celebrated for three days to appeal to the twelve highest Roman gods, including for the first time Venus. At the same time, consultation of the Sibylline Books, ancient books of prophecy, led the dictator Q. Fabius Maximus to build Venus Erycina a temple on the Capitol. He dedicated the temple two years later on 23 April. The cult was romanized to the extent that sacred prostitution (as practiced on Mount Eryx) was not allowed. Instead, a new ritual, one that had its origins in a Roman festival of victory, was instituted whereby vast quantities of wine were poured from the temple into the surrounding gutter. From this time forth, Venus was simply the Roman name for the mother of Aeneas, and her primary concern, in the Roman view, was the protection of the state through her relationship with its rulers.

By the time of Julius Caesar, the reputation of Venus as a champion of political and military power was well established in Rome. During the war against the Ligurinas in 184, a consul by the name of L. Porcius Licinius vowed if victorious to build for her a second temple in Rome, which he finished and dedicated three years later. Then it was Pompey who gave her the name Venus Victrix, after one of his own great military victories, and in 55, at the height of his reign, he built her a temple above his own magnificent theater in Rome.

Nor was Caesar the first Roman ruler to pay homage to Aphrodite of Aphrodisias in far away Caria. Lucius Cornelius Sulla—during his campaign against Mithridates, the king of Pontus in Asia Minor (87–85 BCE)—received an oracle compelling him to offer sacrifice to Aphrodite of Aphrodisias:

> "To that city bring an ax and you will win for yourself supreme sovereignty." . . . As a result Sulla in fact sent to Aphrodite a golden crown and a golden ax with the following inscription: "Dedicated to you, Aphrodite, is this hatchet belong-

> ing to the autocrat Sulla. I saw myself in a dream how you transversed my troops, fully armed and carrying the weapons of Ares into battle." (Appianos, *Bell. civ.* 1.97)

Indeed, the city of Aphrodisias maintained a special relationship with Rome for centuries, because of the recognized kinship between their patron goddess and the Roman emperors. The inscriptions on the Archive Wall of the city refer again and again to the special status of the city under Roman rule. From 39 BCE on, the city enjoyed the status of a free city: The people were allowed to follow their own traditional laws; they were immune from paying taxes to Rome; and the temple of Aphrodite was declared a place of asylum (Reynolds 1982, doc. 8). The loyalty of the Aphrodisians to Rome is a common theme: They supported Sulla in his war against Mithridates and continued to side with the Romans in other local conflicts. The privileged status of Aphrodisias and the preservation of the close relationship between the city and the rulers in Rome continued into the second and third centuries, as evidenced by a series of letters from emperors—ranging from Trajan to Gordian III and Decius, most of which were inscribed likewise on the Archive Wall.

As a goddess of war Venus appeared in Caesar's dreams, inspiring him to conquer Gaul (Appian, *Bell. civ.* 2.68). By 48 he and Pompey had both become so powerful that a military conflict was inevitable: Their armies met at Pharsalus, in Thessaly. At midnight on the eve of battle, Caesar offered sacrifices to Mars and to his "grandmother" Venus, vowing to raise up a temple to Venus Victrix after his victory. Just then a streak of light burst forth from his camp and flew through the night into Pompey's. Caesar interpreted this phenomenon as a message from the goddess, promising him success. The next morning he led his troops into the fray with shouts of "Venus Victrix!"

Not only Caesar but also Pompey dreamed of the goddess the night before the battle. In Pompey's dream, he saw himself proceeding to the theater at Rome through the applause of a happy crowd and offering all sorts of spoils of war to adorn the temple of Venus Victrix. His counselors interpreted the dream as an augury of victory. But Pompey was less optimistic. He recalled that his opponent, Caesar, was the descendant of the goddess, and further that it is the vanquished who carry the spoils of war offered by the conqueror in rites of victory.

In 46, having subdued Pompey and his followers, Caesar returned to Rome in triumph. The Senate hailed him as the "father of his country." Although publicly he rejected the offer of a royal crown, indirectly Caesar went about consolidating his power as absolute sovereign. On 26 September 46, only a few weeks after his return, he dedicated a gold and marble temple to Venus, not as Victrix but as Genetrix, in what was to be the Forum Iulium. The only temple to bear the name of Julius Caesar, it was the first to be dedicated to the goddess as ancestor. The consecration of the temple was followed by games at the Circus in her honor. Further, a special college of priests was established to ensure the annual performance of the games (Weinstock 1971, 88).

The worship of Aphrodite as Venus Genetrix was not limited to Rome. During his short rule, Caesar founded and dedicated numerous colonies to her (e.g., Colonia Genetiva Iulia Ursonensis in Spain, founded in 44).[4]

Even in death, Julius Caesar was linked to Aphrodite: His funeral bier was placed in a miniature shrine modeled on the Temple of Venus Genetrix. Nor did death signify an end to the relationship between the king and the goddess; through her he was able to gain life eternal. According to Pliny (2.94), when Augustus was celebrating the games in honor of Venus Genetrix, "a comet was seen in the north for seven days; it rose in the sky around the eleventh hour of the day, and its brilliance was to be seen in all parts of the world. According to popular belief, this luminary proclaimed that Caesar's soul was admitted into the company of the immortal gods." In response to this sign, Augustus set up a statue of Caesar in the Forum and placed upon his head the symbol of his immortality, the star. Further, after his consecration as a god two years later (in 42), the Senate decreed that henceforth the image of Julius Caesar was to be carried in procession at the *pompa circensis* together with that of the goddess.

Julius Caesar regarded Aphrodite as the source of his beauty,[5] his military success, and his right to rule. Above all, he saw her as his own grandmother. Caesar's family, the *gens Julia*, had long claimed descent from a son of Aeneas, a certain Ascanius also called Iulus (Serv. *Aen.* 2.166; Livy I.30.2; Dion. *Hal.* 3.29.7). Early in the first century BCE, L. Iulius Caesar, had recorded this family tradition in his account of the origins of Rome (Weinstock 1971, 4f.). At the funeral of his Aunt Julia, Caesar publicly recalled her royal ancestry, the kings on her maternal side (through the Marcii Reges), together with her divine descent from the gods on her paternal side, through Aphrodite (Weinstock 1971, 17f.).

According to Roman tradition, Aeneas was able to flee from the destruction of Troy only because of his mother's help. Varro, a contemporary of Caesar, recounts how Aphrodite in her star form led her son and his ships safely to Italy (Serv. *Aen.* I.382). Ancestor worship was an important aspect of Roman religion. The Iulii worshipped both their ancestor Iulus and his grandmother, the mother of Aeneas, Aphrodite.

## Aeneas

The Roman tradition that links Aphrodite with the rulers of the Roman empire, above all with Julius Caesar, rests on the mythology of Aphrodite and her son Aeneas. Earliest extant sources of this myth include the *Iliad* and the first Homeric Hymn to Aphrodite, both of which may have been recorded around 700 BCE and reflect earlier oral traditions.[6]

In myth it is the judgment of Paris that gives rise to the Trojan War, the subject of the *Iliad*. In a competition that pits three Greek goddesses against one another, the Trojan prince Paris offers the prize apple to Aphrodite rather than to Hera or Athena, because she promises to reward him with the love of the most beautiful woman in the world, Helen, the wife of Menelaus. Paris takes

Helen home with him to Troy, located like Aphrodisias in Asia Minor. Not long thereafter, Menelaus and his brother Agamemnon, together with the Achaean warriors and kings of western Greece, sail east to rescue Helen and avenge their honor.

The story of this war between two groups of Greeks from the east and west shores of the Aegean is related in the *Iliad* from the perspective of the Achaeans, that is, from that of Menelaus, Agamemnon, and their comrades. The gods who support their cause are identified as Poseidon, the god of the sea, together with the two goddesses Hera and Athena, who hate Troy and the Trojans "because of the delusion of Paris who insulted the goddesses when they came to him in his courtyard and he favored" Aphrodite (*Iliad* 24.22–30). From their point of view, Paris was clearly not in his right mind to favor "her who supplied the lust that led to disaster." Throughout the *Iliad*, Aphrodite is associated with human suffering, the miseries brought on by love as well as the death and destruction of war.

Thus the *Iliad* presents an unsympathetic, even hostile picture of Aphrodite, the goddess most closely allied with the Trojans. Athena, on the other hand, appears as the champion of the Achaeans, using her talents in war and her wisdom to guide and protect them. For example, Athena gives the Achaean warrior Diomedes the capacity to see the gods but forbids him to attack any except Aphrodite. In another scene, Athena knocks down Ares, and when Aphrodite comes to his aid, Hera incites Athena to attack her as well:

> "For shame now, [Athena], daughter of Zeus of the Aegis. Here again is that dogfly [Aphrodite] leading murderous Ares out of the fighting and through the confusion. Quick, go after her!" She spoke, and Athena swept in pursuit, heart full of gladness, and caught up with her and drove a blow at her breasts with her ponderous hand, so that her knees went slack and the heart inside her. Those two both lay sprawled on the generous earth. (*Iliad* 21.415ff.)

So it is not surprising that in the *Iliad*, a rather negative view of Aphrodite prevails: She is referred to as a goddess who lacks skill in warcraft (*Iliad* 5.310–430), depicted as a child rushing to the arms of her mother when Diomedes stabs her, and even her father Zeus disparagingly recommends that she stick to overseeing "the lovely secrets of marriage" rather than involve herself in the conflict at Troy. No wonder that some scholars, basing their understanding of Aphrodite on this text, insist that she is a goddess of beauty and sexuality, and nothing more (see, e.g., Nilsson 1976, 523).

Nevertheless, in spite of the bias of the *Iliad* and the depreciation of Aphrodite in her encounters with Athena, some scenes of the poem point to an Aphrodite who is strong, loyal, and unafraid in battle. Throughout the war she stands by Paris, driving away the spirits of death (*Iliad* 4.10–12). When Menelaus does bring him down and begins to drag him by the helmet off the battlefield, the goddess breaks the chin strap, leaving Menelaus with an empty helmet in his hand. She then carries Paris out of battle and back to his own bedroom. When Achilles kills the Trojan hero Hector and threatens to feed him to the dogs, it is Aphrodite who day and night stands over the body, fending off the dogs and anointing him with the rosy oil of immortality (*Iliad* 23.184–187).

Further, it is in the *Iliad* that we have one of the earliest extant texts referring to the myth of Aphrodite and Aeneas: "The strong son of Anchises was leader of the Dardanians, Aeneas, whom divine Aphrodite bore to Anchises in the folds of [Mount] Ida, a goddess lying in love with a mortal" (*Iliad* 2.819–821; also 5.247–248). In fact, it is because of his lineage that Apollo incites him to fight with Achilles, whose mother is a lesser goddess (*Iliad* 20.75–109). Elsewhere when Diomedes takes up a stone and smashes Aeneas's hip so that the latter falls onto one knee losing consciousness, it is his mother, Aphrodite, who rushes to his aid. With her white robe she shields her son from the arrows of the Achaeans as she carries him out of reach.

Aphrodite is not the only one who protects Aeneas. In spite of the fact that he favors the Achaeans, the sea-god Poseidon intervenes when Aeneas fights with Achilles, lifting the former out of the battle altogether. He fears the wrath of Zeus should Aeneas be killed, for he is the Trojan of noble lineage who is foreordained to survive the war: "It is destined that he shall be the survivor, that the generation of Dardanos shall not die, . . . since Dardanos was dearest to Kronides [Zeus] of all his sons that have been born to him from mortal women. For Kronos' son [again Zeus] has cursed the generation of Priam, and now the might of Aeneas shall be lord over the Trojans, and his sons' sons, and those who are born of their seed hereafter" (*Iliad* 20.302–308).

According to Aeneas's paternal lineage (which he recites to Achilles before attacking him with his spear), his ancestor Dardanos, a son of Zeus, founded Dardania in the foothills of Mount Ida before Troy ever existed. Dardanos's son was King Erichthonios, a wealthy lord who sired Tros, the first king of Troy. The three sons of Tros were Ilos (hence Ilium), Assarakos, and Ganymedes. Deemed the most beautiful of all mortals, Ganymedes was lifted up to Olympus to serve there as Zeus' wine pourer. His older brother Ilos became the grandfather of Priam, king of Troy and father of Paris, Hector, and forty-eight other sons. Assarakos became the grandfather of Anchises, Aphrodite's beloved and the father of Aeneas. Thus, the youngest generation to descend from Dardanos at the time of the Trojan War included Paris, Hector, and Aeneas, but only Aphrodite's son is destined to survive.

The birth of Aeneas is likewise the subject of the first and longest Homeric "Hymn to Aphrodite" from the same period. Here the reader learns how the crowned Cytherean[7] came to be the mother of Aeneas and the ancestor of kings. The myth relates that Zeus, out of revenge for all the times Aphrodite had put desire into his heart, causes her to fall in love with the mortal prince Anchises, who grazes his cattle on the highlands of Mount Ida near Troy. Under the spell of desire, the goddess flees to her temple in Paphos, on the island of Cyprus, where the Graces bathe her and anoint her body with fragrant oils. Returning to Mount Ida, Aphrodite appears to Anchises in the form of a mortal maiden. Anchises is so amazed at her beauty that he is convinced she must be a goddess, and so he offers to build an altar and offer sacrifices. But Aphrodite convinces the young prince that she is a Phrygian princess, raised by a Trojan nurse, who was brought to this place by the god Hermes to become Anchises's lawful wife and the mother of his children.

After their love making, Aphrodite reveals her divinity. Anchises turns away in fear, covering his face with his cloak, and begs her to spare him his manhood: "Now at your knees I implore you, in the name of Zeus who carries the aegis, don't permit me to live impotent among men from now on. Pity me. For a man who sleeps with immortal goddesses loses his potency" (Boer 1979, 77). The golden one reassures him that he is loved and blessed by Zeus and all the gods: "You will have a fine son, who will rule among the Trojans, and children will be born forever to his children. . . . And those mortal men whose beauty and form come nearest to the gods will always be from your stock" (Boer 1979, 77).

The story of Aphrodite and Aeneas, found in the *Iliad* and in the first "Homeric Hymn to Aphrodite," is the only myth about the goddess that appears in three separate places in the oldest surviving Greek texts. Even Hesiod in his *Theogony* refers to this story of Aeneas's birth.[8] This suggests that the central myth in the early tradition surrounding Aphrodite is her role as the divine ancestor of a lineage of kings at home in the eastern Greek culture of Asia Minor. By the time of Julius Caesar, some seven hundred years later, the myth had grown to include Aeneas's journey under Aphrodite's protection to the land of Italy in the west, where the descendants of the goddess transplanted themselves after the destruction of Troy. This story survives in Virgil's *Aeneid*, composed in Latin between 29 and 19 BCE—that is, after the death of Julius Caesar. Certainly Virgil is indebted to Caesar's family, and to the emperor himself, for the tradition that he brings to the written page.

## Aphrodite and Sovereignty

Apart from the Roman rulers how widespread was the belief in Aphrodite as a goddess of sovereignty? Evidence from the iconography and certain rituals associated with Aphrodite demonstrate that she was worshipped widely as a goddess who had a special relationship to political rule. Indeed, history links her to a complex of sacred kingship known already in the ancient civilizations of Mesopotamia—Sumer and Babylon.

As far as we know, Aphrodite's earliest temples were found on the island of Cyprus, especially in the harbor of Paphos, but also in Golgoi, Amathus, Tamassos, and Salamis. Because of its location in the eastern Mediterranean, close to both Asia Minor and Syria–Palestine, Cyprus served as a center of sea commerce. It was on this island that the Greeks first assimilated the Mesopotamian tradition of the Queen of Heaven.

The Cypriotes had long been in contact with the cultures of Mesopotamia, where certain goddesses identified as the Queen of Heaven—Inanna of the

Sumerians and Ishtar, worshipped by the Babylonians and Assyrians—held a prominent place. The Queen of Heaven was a patron of kingship, serving often as the divine consort of the living king and his source of sovereignty. Beginning around 1500, a new class of terra cotta figurines modeled on the Syrian Queen of Heaven appeared in Cyprus. In the form of a bird-woman, she wears a necklace and a triangular belt and appears nude with prominent hips and breasts and pierced ears.

Prior to 1200 BCE early Greeks known as Mycenaeans and comprising both the Achaeans and the Trojans lived in close contact with the Minoans of Crete. They had adopted many Minoan features into their own religion, including a goddess whose epiphany was in the form of a small white bird: Lady Dove. The downfall of the Mycenaean civilization occurred around 1200, when another Hellenic group, the Dorians, invaded Greece and settled in the Peloponnese and Crete. Many of the Achaean Greeks living in those areas fled eastward by sea, some of them resettling in Cyprus.

At Paphos, the Greek temple of Aphrodite, dating to around 1200, was constructed on the site of an earlier Cypriote temple. Excavations of the Cypriote temple demonstrate its close conformity to Mesopotamian models. Apparently the local sea goddess of Paphos had already been identified with the Queen of Heaven, probably by the local king. When the Greeks arrived, they may well have recognized a kinship between their own Lady Dove and this royal bird-woman, hellenizing her name as Aphrodite Ourania. As the Greek goddess imbued with the power of sovereignty, it is no surprise that the worship of Aphrodite spread throughout the Greek-speaking world, probably at the hands of local rulers wishing to legitimatize their divine right to rule.

Like the Mesopotamian Queen of Heaven, Aphrodite's role as goddess of sovereignty is represented by the throne, the crown, and the lion. Already at the beginning of the sixth century, the poet Sappho (ca. 610–580 BCE) identifies Aphrodite by her throne (Sappho, *Fr.* 2, 5, 1).

> Aphrodite of the brightly colored throne,
> wile-weaving daughter of Zeus, I entreat you:
> do not overpower my heart, Lady, with ache and anguish. . . .

Numerous statues, reliefs, and paintings of the goddess seated on her throne have survived,[9] including a relief from Locri (ca. 470 to 460 BCE) of Aphrodite sitting on a throne, holding in one hand a vessel and receiving with the other gifts of a ball and a rooster from a young girl (LIMC 1984, 81 [Taranto, Museo Nazionale I.G. 8327]).

Aphrodite often wears a crown, recalling the homage expressed in the Homeric Hymns. In the first Homeric Hymn dedicated to Aphrodite, she is addressed as "you who rule over Cyprus" (Boer 1979, 80) and fittingly as "the beautifully crowned Cytherean" (Boer 1979, 69, 76, 80). In the second hymn, she is "venerable, golden-crowned, beautiful Aphrodite" (Boer 1979, 81); in the third hymn, "sovereign of Salamis and of the seaplace, Cyprus" (Boer 1979, 83). "On her immortal head they placed a crown that was carefully made, beautiful and in gold" (Boer 1979, 81).

Sometimes the crown resembles the Anatolian *polos*, the simple cylindrical headdress worn also by Cybele, as in a statue of Aphrodite of Aphrodias now part of the collection of the Walters Art Gallery in Baltimore (figure 1.1).[10] The crown might be more complex, decorated for instance with rosettes, the eight-pointed flowers of the Mesopotamian Queen of Heaven. One head of Aphrodite from ca. 500 Argos, Greece, bears a crown on which rosettes and sphinxes alternate.[11] A coin from Salamis, Cyprus, dating between 361 and 351 BCE, shows Aphrodite wearing a crown that is constructed to represent the walls of a city; the lion and the eagle, symbols of sovereignty, appear on the reverse side.[12] Like Inanna, Aphrodite is depicted in art standing on a lion, seated on a lion throne, or accompanied by lions. In one statue from ca. 500 BCE the goddess stands barefoot on a platform flanked by two lions.[13]

Aphrodite shares in the astral symbolism of the Mesopotamian Queen of Heaven. Thus, in her iconography Aphrodite, like Inanna, is represented by the eight-pointed star. For example, a terra cotta vessel from around 660 BCE Naxos, Sicily, shows a goddess and Ares riding in a war chariot drawn by two winged horses. Above the heads of the horses hovers the eight-pointed star. The goddess is identified by name as Aphrodite.[14] The eight-pointed star appears on a Greek gemstone from the second century CE, identifying Aphrodite of Aphrodisias (figure 1.2).[15] The goddess may well appear twice on the stone: On the right she is engaged in some kind of ritual with a staff-bearing king; on the left she appears in her cosmic form accompanied by animals.

In the ancient world, meteorites, or "fallen stars," were commonly associated with divinity: For example, a meteorite sacred to Cybele was transported from Asia Minor to Rome in 204 BCE in order to establish her worship there. Likewise, the astral nature of Aphrodite could be represented by a fallen star. Roman coins show the goddess in her aniconic manifestation as an meteorite in her foremost temple at Paphos.[16]

From twelfth-century Cyprus until the christianization of the Roman empire in 381, nearly sixteen centuries, Aphrodite was experienced by her devotees as present and active in their lives. The popular rituals that surrounded her worship included sacrifices, the ritual bathing and clothing of her statues, festivals and games in her honor. The *Greek Magical Papyri* contain instructions for rituals to gain Aphrodite's help in matters of love, friendship, good luck, and success. For example, the Stele of Aphrodite[17] depicts a geometric image, with Greek letters and the eight-pointed star: "Take a strip of tin and engrave [this image] on it with a bronze stylus. Be sure you are pure while carrying it." These and other rituals involved the people as a whole in the worship of the goddess. For rites connected to her role as goddess of sovereignty, we must look to her relationship with kings, queens, and magistrates.

Visible to all as the brightest star in the sky, Aphrodite's movements were studied by court astrologists, seeking to divine her messages to the king. She also appeared in the dreams of the mighty, as in the dreams of Sulla, Caesar, and Pompey.

*Figure 1.1: Aphrodite of Aphrodisias. (Source: The Walters Art Gallery, Baltimore.)*

*Figure 1.2: The Star of Aphrodite.* (*Courtesy of the Staatliche Museen, Kassel.*)

During the Hellenistic period, Aphrodite might also have a special relationship with a queen,[18] who could be viewed as her living incarnation. Julia, the daughter of Caesar Augustus, was called Aphrodite Geneteira / Venus Genetrix in a bilingual reference at Eresus on the island of Lesbos. In Pergamum, an ancient Greek kingdom covering most of Asia Minor, queens were supposed to stay out of politics, and yet Teos, the wife of Attalos I, was honored as Aphrodite. In Smyrna, a city of Asia Minor, Stratonike, the daughter of Demetrios Polioketes (who was celebrated in Athens as the son of Aphrodite and Poseidon) served as wife and queen of Seleukos I, and later his son Antiochos I. After her death in 254 BCE, she was worshiped as Aphrodite Stratonikis. Coins depict her as Aphrodite Nikephoros (Bearer of Victory), standing erect and wearing a crown.

This custom of worshiping the deceased queen as a manifestation of Aphrodite was especially common in Hellenistic Egypt. Perhaps the most interesting example is the story of Arsinoe II, daughter of Ptolemaios I and Berenike I. At the age of thirty-nine she ruled jointly with her brother-husband, King Ptolemaios II, for eight years (178–170 BCE). She traveled widely and worked hard to solve the economic problems of their realm. Admired both by the Egyptian populace and the Greek ruling class, Arsinoe influenced greatly both the artistic and religious life of the period. She and her brother were honored while they lived as the Divine Siblings (Theoi Adelphoi), and after her death she was identified as a manifestation of Aphrodite. Belestiche, the mistress of Ptolemaios II, was likewise worshiped posthumously as an incarnation of the goddess.

Even in the democracies of classical Greece, where no kings and queens held sway, the goddess of sovereignty continued to govern. It was also common for civil servants to regard Aphrodite as their patron. Officials throughout Greece held ceremonies in Aphrodite's honor. For example, in 230 BCE the Athenian Council dedicated a votive inscription giving thanks to Aphrodite for her support and guidance. Inscriptions of this kind were made along with sacrifices to the goddess at the end of a term of service, similar to the celebration called Aphrodisia at the end of a war. The magistrates most likely to express their devotion to Aphrodite included the *agoranomoi* (clerks of the marketplace who regulated buying and selling), police officials, supervisors, and registrars. Similar inscriptions have been found on the Greek islands and in Asia Minor. In a dedication offered by the import officers on Samos, Aphrodite is praised for her power to create a sense of "team spirit."

One of Aphrodite's titles was Pandemos, Aphrodite of All the People. For example, in the marketplace of Athens there was a very old temple dedicated to Aphrodite Pandemos, which was supposed to have been established in mythical times by Theseus after the unification of the Attic communes into a single state. This ancient name of the goddess, Pandemos, refers to her role as a goddess of harmony and peace, providing the common bond and fellow feeling that is the basis for community (Burkert 1985, 155).

## Conclusion

The history of Aphrodite is long and complex, beginning with her origins as a sea-goddess in Cyprus who became assimilated to the Near Eastern Queen of Heaven and later adopted by the Greeks. Her myths, her iconography, and her role in history point to a central theme: Aphrodite as king maker. As warrior, she serves the king in battle; as ancestor, she provides him with his royal heritage. Julius Caesar exemplifies this relationship and helps us to appreciate the actual living religion that surrounded this ancient deity.

NOTES

1. From a tomb at Camirus, Rhodes (470 to 460 BCE). Location: no. D2, British Museum, London.
2. Letter to the Ephesians from Caesar Octavian.
3. For the history of Venus, see Robert Schilling's *La religion romaine de Vénus*. An interesting discussion of Schilling's theories and related views is found in Georges Dumézil (1970).

4. Following Sulla who founded Pompeii in 80 BCE as a colony of Venus.
5. Dio writes that Caesar claimed to have received the bloom of youth from Venus. A similar statement is found in Cicero.
6. The *Odyssey* does not include the myth of Aeneas and has only a few references to Aphrodite: Her beauty is mentioned, and the text also relates the myth of Aphrodite's adulterous affair with Ares.
7. According to Hesiod, Aphrodite is called Cytherea because after being born from the sea she passed by the island Cythera on her way to Cyprus.
8. "Aeneas was born to Cytherea, crowned with beauty, after she had united in sweet love with the hero Anchises on the peaks of Ida with its many wooded folds" (Brown 1953, 81).
9. *Lexicon Iconographicum Mythologiae Classicae* (LIMC) (1984) includes a section of enthroned Aphrodites that includes thirty-one examples (88–90).
10. Walters Art Gallery 54.969.
11. Nicosia, Cyprus Museum. (LIMC 1984, 15).
12. Luzern, Hess AG/Zurich, Bank Leu AG (LIMC 1984, 114).
13. London, British Museum BR 493 (LIMC 1984, 13).
14. Archive for Research in Archetypal Symbolism (ARAS), New York: 3Gd.009.
15. Kassel, *Staatliche Kunstsammlungen* A6 2087.
16. ARAS 2Eh.001.
17. PGM VII.215–218.
18. A detailed and fascinating account of the relationship between Aphrodite and the queens of the Hellenistic age is to be found in Neumer-Pfau (1982).

## REFERENCES

Boer, Charles, trans. 1979. *Homer: The Homeric Hymns* (2d rev ed.). Irving, Texas: Spring Publications.

Brown, Norman O., trans. 1953. *Theogony*, by Hesiod. Indianapolis: Bobbs-Merrill.

Burkert, Walter. 1985. *Greek Religion: Archaic and Classical*. Tr. John Raffan. Cambridge, MA: Harvard University Press.

Croissant, Francis, and François Salviat. 1966. "Aphrodite Gardienne des Magistrats: Gynéconomes de Thasos et Polémarques de Thèbes," *Bulletin de Correspondence Hellénique* 90: 460–471.

Dumézil, Georges. 1970. *Archaic Roman Religion* (2 vols.). Chicago: University of Chicago Press.

Erim, Kenan T. 1986. *Aphrodisias: City of Venus Aphrodite*. New York: Facts on File.

*Lexicon Iconographicum Mythologiae Classicae* (LIMC). 1984. (vol. 2). pt. 2. Zurich: Artemis.

Neumer-Pfau, Wiltrud. 1982. *Studien zur Ikonographie und gesellschaftlichen Funktion hellenistischer Aphrodite-Statuen*. Habelts Dissertationsdrucke: Reihe Klassische Archäologie, 18. Bonn: Rudolf Habelt.

Nilsson, Martin P. 1976. *Die Religion Griechenlands bis auf die griechische Weltherrschaft*. Vol. 1 of *Geschichte der griechischen Religion*. (2 vols.) Munich: Beck. [See "Religion im Dienst der Koenige," 132–184.]

Reynolds, Joyce M. 1982. *Aphrodisias and Rome*. (Journal of Roman Studies Monographs, 1). London: Society for the Promotion of Roman Studies.

———. 1980. "The Origins and Beginning of Imperial Cult at Aphrodisias," *Proceedings of the Cambridge Philological Society* 206 [n.s., 24]: 70–84.

Rose, H. J. 1924. "Anchises and Aphrodite," *The Classical Quarterly* 18:11 ff.
Schilling, Robert. 1954. *La religion romaine de Vénus*. Paris: E. de Boccard.
Sokolowski, F. 1964. "Aphrodite as Guardian of Greek Magistrates," *Harvard Theological Review* 57 (1): 1–8.
Weinstock, Stefan. 1971. *Divus Julius*. Oxford: Clarendon Press.

2

# How the Fearsome Fish-Eyed Queen Mīṉāṭci Became a Perfectly Ordinary Goddess

*William Harman*

Distinctions between humans and deities tend to be ambiguous in South Asia: Humans regularly achieve promotion to divine status for being gifted gurus, great poets, spiritually adept seekers, martyrs who die for a righteous cause, or able power brokers, such as royalty. People need not necessarily die to achieve divine status, but it often helps. In some cases, jealous or unkind deities do their best to thwart mortals whose virtue, penance, or sacrifices are about to transform their human status into that of a competing divinity.

While the Hindu belief in reincarnation suggests that most humans will achieve some sort of transcendental status eventually, tradition also specifies that deities may sometimes be demoted to human form for at least three reasons: (1) out of their own gracious compassion for human suffering, (2) as a punishment for conduct "unbecoming to a deity," or (3) as a stealthy disguise to accomplish some mundane task. Knowing this, Hindus have devised a system for distinguishing deities from humans. According to tradition, flower garlands placed on deities do not fade. Nor do deities blink, perspire, or leave footprints. A generic Tamil term for deities is *imaiyār*, "those who do not blink." And when they walk, they hover, it seems, imperceptible millimeters above the ground.

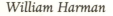

*Figure 2.1: The goddess Mīṉāṭci, holding a flower on which is perched a parrot.*

One of the more graphic representations of a world where rebirth recurs for deities as well as for humans is the Indian childrens' board game *Mokśa Patamu*, or Snakes and Ladders. Using dice, participants make their way alternately up and down the ladder of rebirths, and each rebirth is determined by acts committed as deities, animals, or humans. Rebirths in various animal, human, and divine forms are predicated on the notion that every action performed (in this case, determined by the block on which you land) has its absolute result. A generous act can send you directly to one of the highest heavens; a crime will cause rebirth as an animal or a low-caste human. In part due to the essential continuity of a world in which there are no radical disjunctures between the animal and the human or the human and the divine, scholars tend to describe the Indian cosmos as monistic (Marriott 1976a; Marriott 1976b). Here, there are no sharp divisions or dualities between heaven and earth or divine and human.

This notion of a graded continuum along which all souls move—whether divine, human, animal, or even spiritually sinister—is crucial in discussing Mīṉāṭci, the traditionally reputed, miraculously born (though apparently human) princess of the Pāṇṭiya dynasty of southern India. She must go through many changes eventually to become a goddess. Our discussion of Mīṉāṭci must, then, take into account a multileveled world in which human and divine realms overlap, and where this overlap most often occurs—in the contexts of royalty. In regal corridors, humans are exalted and deities deign to mingle with the best and brightest of mortals. Royalty and divinity are closely associated in South Asian political theory and ritual activity as well. Royalty presumably exercises civil power by virtue of divine permission, acquiescence, and assistance. If the rains fail, for example, royalty can be blamed for neglecting the proper relationships with divine powers that would normally promote fertility.

Indeed, royalty is said to be physically part-divine, constituted by "portions" of the gods (Harman 1995). So it is that acceptable and customary treatment for royal figures—indeed for most who lay credible claim to the exercise of civil powers—is the same treatment prescribed for deities in temples and includes, for example, ritual honors with special lamps and adornment with elaborate garlands and gifts.[1] This collapsing of royal-divine categories is also suggested by the use of identical words in several Indian languages for the terms *temple* and *palace*. The queen/goddess Mīṉāṭci exemplifies these dynamics in striking ways: Born into a human family to rule as a conquering queen, she eventually is recognized as a goddess. Stories portray her as a miraculously born queen-designate-become-goddess. Today, her reputation is so widespread that she has at least two major, separate temple/palaces, one on either side of the world. The earlier and larger one is the widely known, majestic fourteen-acre complex that remains the pride and spiritual focus of the famous Temple City of Madurai in southern India. In origin, this older shrine dates from at least the eighth century CE. It is still a popular place for pilgrimage and worship: depending on calendrical events, between 10,000 and 20,000 people visit this temple each day.

The second of Mīṉāṭci's major temples, a more recent five-acre complex, begun in the 1980s, continues to move gradually toward completion in Pearland,

Texas. Priests from the Madurai temple serve the Pearland temple on a regular basis, and the newer temple claims to address the religious needs of more than 1,400 immigrant Hindu families in the Houston area.

### The Queen/Goddess/Wife and Her King/God/Husband: Names, Relationships, and Other Preliminaries

The identities of Hindu deities can vacillate between specific, localized forms and more generalized, universal appearances. The queen/goddess Mīṉāṭci, for example, is also known more widely as a form of Parvatī, a goddess recognized throughout India. This is typical: The perception of divine power in any locale often comes to be associated with a more well-known and pan-Indian deity. This makes the specific appearance more recognizable, more comprehensible, and more available. Local deities are thus understood as forms or aspects of major ones, and major deities are rendered more accessible when portrayed as having specific, local forms. This process emphasizes once again the variable states deities and humans might occupy from one birth to another by assigning to them specific names indicating a specific state, birth, condition, or identity.

Queen Mīṉāṭci illustrates this well because she is known by a variety of local names. The best known is her title, the Goddess With the Eyes of a Fish—in Tamil, Mīṉāṭci. Among Westerners, the epithet Fish-Eyed Goddess may not sound particularly flattering, but it is complimentary in the Indian context: Large, unblinking eyes with dark pupils are considered a mark of human beauty. In addition, there are theological implications to the metaphor that focuses on the watchful care a mother fish gives her young (Brown 1947, 209ff.; TVP 1: 333; Hudson 1971, 214, n.30). The name is particularly apt because the fish was the totem, or symbol, of the Pāṇdya kingdom, where she was born as a princess. Frequently we find references to a Tamil variant, Aṅkayaṟkaṇṇammai (the Mother with Beautiful Fish Eyes).

But there are other names for this queen/goddess, particularly used in the literature to describe her before she was married. One is Taṭātakai, a name of ambiguous etymological roots. Some scholars have tried to trace it to the Tamil words *taṭu*, meaning "to hinder or prohibit," and *kai*, which means "hand." The term is taken to refer to the gracious hand of the queen/goddess, which does not hinder or ward off devotees, but rather welcomes them invitingly. She is also referred to in the texts simply as Pirāṭṭi (Lady), a term often added as a suffix to form Taṭātakaippirāṭṭiyār.

All these titles can be found in the varied literary corpus that describes and praises Mīṉāṭci. The popularity of the Queen Goddess of Madurai is such that several hagiographic texts have been written describing her youth.[2] The most common source we can trace to a thirteenth-century document entitled *Tiruviḷaiyāṭaṟpurāṇam*, or *The Story of the Sacred Games* (see also Harman 1987, 1987a).[3]

Mīṉāṭci is extolled and worshipped as a queen/goddess whose independence and power precede—indeed, are exercised despite—marriage to her husband.

The celebration of her wedding is the temple's largest annual festival. In fact, it is one of the largest festivals in southern India. Like Mīṉāṭci, her husband has several names. Locally, as the handsome bridegroom, he is called Cuntarēcuvarar, meaning the Beautiful Lord. The Sanskrit equivalent, *Cokkanātar*, is frequently found in texts. He is described as living and reigning with Mīṉāṭci in Madurai. Cuntarēcuvarar is not simply the husband of Mīṉāṭci; he is also a form of the pan-Indian deity Śiva. Thus, despite Mīṉāṭci's regional fame, she is sometimes understood by pilgrims as no more than another form of Śiva's well-known all-Indian wife, Parvatī.[4] Depending on a devotee's predisposition, preference, and frame of reference, either deity can be understood in general or specific terms: Parvatī is Mīṉāṭci; Śiva is Cuntarēcuvarar, and vice versa.

Several scholars have cogently proposed, though without conclusive proof, that the site of Mīṉāṭci's temple was once the shrine of a local, somewhat isolated Dravidian queen/goddess. The suggestion is that she was assimilated into the larger Hindu pantheon by her ritual and mythic marriage to Śiva, thus gaining more widespread acceptance and prestige under the identity of Parvatī. Today, we can see traces of specific ritual customs not normally found in shrines to Śiva, customs that suggest Mīṉāṭci's earlier origins. Mīṉāṭci, for example, is the focus of worship for certain groups of local people, but these people will not worship her husband or perform the more respectable Sanskritic worship styles the temple seems to have adopted.

A unique and abiding feature distinguishing this queen/goddess and king/god pairing is the pervasive perception among devotees that Mīṉāṭci is, by far, the more powerful and efficacious of the two figures. As the queen and goddess, it is she who rules. Indeed, the marriage of the Madurai divine couple is regarded as the classic instance in southern India of the female-dominated marriage, an arrangement referred to as "a Madurai marriage" (Daniel 1980, 71ff.). In casual discussions, the question "Is yours a Madurai or a Citamparam household?" is taken to mean "Who rules in your house, the wife or the husband?" (Perumā! 1860, 103). The male-dominated marriage is called the Citamparam marriage, referring to Śiva's uncontested dominance, ritual and mythic, in the famous Śaiva temple of Citamparam. More about Mīṉāṭci's perceived dominance follows a detailed description of her history.

## A Summary of Mīṉāṭci's Life

I move now to a synthetic account of the life of the queen/goddess, depending primarily on *The Story of the Sacred Games*. This sixty-four-chapter document in eloquent Tamil poetry narrates how she was born as the daughter of a Pāṇḍya king, became queen, and conquered all the world until she encountered in battle the Lord Śiva, whom she then married. He returned with her to Madurai, where the two reigned together as king and queen of the Pāṇḍya kingdom until their son assumed the throne. They then retired to the temple, where they remain as an eternal presence ready to appear at moments of crisis.

The story really begins with Malayattuvaca Pāṇṭiyaṉ, Mīṉāṭci's father, who was son of the founder of the city of Madurai. King Malayattuvaca Pāṇṭiyaṉ and his queen were childless, and because their religious devotion and good works did not seem sufficient to change this sad state of affairs, they began offering a series of horse sacrifices. These, they hoped, would please the deities and bring them a son. Unfortunately, horse sacrifices are not always conducive to the births of sons, and so the elaborate rituals were continued until they reached the point of bestowing on their sponsor extraordinary powers but still no children. At this juncture the jealous deity Indra, the king of the gods, felt threatened and intervened. He realized that if any human king successfully performed 100 horse sacrifices, that king could rightfully claim Indra's own throne. After the ninety-ninth horse sacrifice, Indra appeared and announced to the king that if he wanted a son, he should cease the horse sacrifices and perform instead "the sacrifice that brings forth a son," a reasonable suggestion, even from a deity who is not exactly disinterested (TVP I.4). The king agreed, but the results were not as expected: Instead of a son, the sacrifice produced a three-year-old daughter.[5] And to make matters worse, she was something of a freak, for she had three breasts (TVP I.4.19,20). The disappointed king complains:

> I was without a son, and I performed great sacrifices (*tavam*)
> for a long time.
> (And when that failed) I performed the sacrifice that was
> supposed to produce a son
> And from that sacrifice I got a daughter.
> But God! Even though this girl has come with a face that
> shines like the moon,
> She has three breasts! Such an appearance will make even enemies laugh.
> So he thought, plunged in depression and unhappiness. (TVP I.4.24)

The king's lament does not go unheeded, however. A celestial voice, that of Śiva's, responds:

> O King! Treat your daughter as though she were a son:
> Perform for her all the rites as specified in the Vedas.
> Giver her the name, Taṭātakai. Crown her queen.
> And when this woman, whose form is golden, meets her Lord,
> one of her breasts will disappear.
> Therefore, put your mind at ease.
> In this way, Śiva graciously appeared in the form
> of words spoken from the sky. (TVP I.4.25)

The king did as he was told, training his daughter as though she were the legitimate male heir to the throne. Once she is crowned (I.4.35), the king figures no more in the text: Shortly after the coronation he dies (I.4.41).

## The Queen: Her Conquests and Marriage

The fifth chapter opens with Mīṉāṭci as Pāṇḍya monarch: Her rule is just and beneficent, but she rules as an unmarried queen, a situation that, the commentator notes (TVP I.5.1 and 2), is not proper for an Indian monarch. Her mother laments her unmarried state (I.5.4), but Mīṉāṭci assures her that there are better things to do than to marry, for example, conquering the world (I.5.5).

The female monarch then prepares her impressive array of soldiers for their assault on the guardian deities of the eight directions (TVP I.5.6ff.). She leads the cavalry, followed by horse-drawn chariots, rutting elephants, and decidedly vicious hand-to-hand combatants. Significantly, the three southern kingdoms (Pāṇḍya, Cēra, and Cōḻa) are portrayed as united under her command as she sets out to conquer the rest of the universe (TVP I.5.18).

The attacking army is so impressive that its first scheduled combat with Indra never occurs: He flees at the sight of the troops (TVP I.5.23), and his white elephant and wishing tree are taken as booty. In fact, the same occurs with the seven other guardians of the directions: The troops march directly to the abode of Śiva, Mount Kailāsa, where they encounter their first real resistance.

Mount Kailāsa is besieged. Then a genuine battle between Mīṉāṭci's forces and the armies commanded by Nandin, Śiva's bull, ensues (TVP I.5.27–31). Blood and gore abound on the battlefield (I.5.32–38), and the Pāṇḍya queen appears particularly savage in the fray. Nandin's forces are completely routed: He has no choice but to appeal to Śiva for help. With appropriate fanfare, Śiva graciously appears to survey the carnage (I.5.42). Then the miracle occurs:

> The moment she saw him her (third) breast disappeared.
> She became bashful, passive, and fearful.
> She leaned unsteadily, like the flowering branch of a tree
> under the weight of its blossoms.
> Her heavy dark hair fell on her neck.
> She looked downward, toward her feet, with collyriumed eyes
> that were like *keṇṭai* fish.
> And there she stood, shining like lightning, scratching in the
> earth with her toes. (TVP I.5.43)

Mīṉāṭci's minister Sumati then points out that the ancient prophecy made at her birth has been fulfilled: Śiva as he stands before her now will be her husband. Śiva instructs her to return to Madurai where he will marry her.

Love-struck and loaded with plunder from her victories, Mīṉāṭci arrives in Madurai. The city is elaborately decorated and the townspeople are ecstatic over the news of her coming marriage. They drink, dance, sing, shout, and throw off their clothes in an orgy of celebrative abandon (TVP I.5.47–57). The extensive preparations for the wedding include assembling the bride's garments, preparing foods, and sending out wedding invitations (I.5.58–78). The list of wedding guests is impressive. The lengthy description of the wedding is unusually detailed.

Indeed, chapter 5, which begins with Mīṉāṭci's reign as unmarried queen and which ends with her marriage to Śiva, who then takes over the Pāṇḍya throne, is the longest of the sixty-four chapters. Eventually, Śiva and Mīṉāṭci retire into the temple precincts, leaving their son (and his sons) to rule. Sometimes their descendants call on them for assistance in a variety of tight spots.

## Marriage Changes . . . a Queen into a Goddess; a God into a King

In *The Story of the Sacred Games*, the marriage brings about significant transformations for the people of the city. Instead of losing a daughter and queen, the inhabitants of Madurai gain a son-in-law and a king, as well as a god who transforms Mīṉāṭci into a goddess. The Pāṇḍya dynasty is infused with divinity. Once again, we are reminded that the lines dividing the human from the divine, and especially those dividing royalty from divinity, are permeable given the "proper" conditions.

Mīṉāṭci's transformation is more dramatic. The miraculous conditions of her birth suggest that she is a special princess. Still, her assuming the identity of a goddess never explicitly occurs until she marries the great deity Śiva: Generally, the female spouse of a deity also becomes a deity.[6] Other changes transpire with the loss of her third breast when she first sees her husband-to-be. According to the instructions of the celestial voice that spoke to Mīṉāṭci's father on the day of her birth out of the sacrifice, this event allows her to recognize her lord and master. But there are several other possible interpretations worth considering: The learned commentator of our text, Vēṅkaṭacāmi Nāṭṭār (1:357), says that the disappearance of the third breast indicates the change from male to female. Until the moment she meets Śiva, Mīṉāṭci's father treats her as his male heir, training her in the necessary sciences and martial arts. As though she were a man, she rules powerfully over Madurai and conquers all the regions of the world. In short, she acts like a man. But when she sees Śiva, she changes radically. This fierce warrior, one moment disemboweling her victims and smearing her spear with their blood and fat, whom none of Śiva's demons can defeat, suddenly becomes "bashful, passive, and fearful." Like a shy adolescent, she scratches in the dust with her toes, unable to meet Śiva's eyes.

Philip Spratt (1966, 268) would probably agree with Vēṅkaṭacāmi Nāṭṭār's interpretation: He regards the third breast as a phallic symbol in Indian mythology. According to his interpretive structure Mīṉāṭci's transformation is the loss of her masculinity: With two breasts she is now a proper woman rather than one with a penis. Now she can marry Śiva. However, David Shulman (1980, 209–211) suggests that the change in Mīṉāṭci is not from male to female but from androgynous figure to female (see also O'Flaherty 1976, 342–343). Given the importance of divine androgyny in Śaiva thought, his suggestion makes good sense. Mīṉāṭci was, in some sense, the perfect ruler even before she met Śiva. Though not properly married, at least in her person she embodied the male/

female complementarity crucial to the administration of an ordered cosmos and kingdom.[7]

In her transformation from a violent, aggressive, unmarried queen to a passive, submissive, married queen/goddess, Mīṉāṭci recalls a widespread phenomenon among goddesses in much of India, one that Lawrence Babb (1970, 141) documents in his study of village religion in Madhya Pradesh. There the unmarried goddess (called Durgā, Mahāmāyā, or Kālī) is a bloodthirsty killer: vicious and dangerous. But when the goddess is featured as Śiva's bride, she is transformed into "a benevolent goddess . . . , an exemplar of passive devotion to her husband, and . . . dutifully subordinate."

Mīṉāṭci is not the only one who changes: Her transformations begin when marriage becomes inevitable, and Śiva's occur at the ceremony. There, he becomes the Pāṇḍya son-in-law and king. Normally, in pan-Indian iconography, Śiva is depicted together with his mount, the bull Nandin, snakes encircling his body, the crescent moon in his hair, bearing the tiger-skin clothing of the ascetic and the Indian laburnum plant. But all this changes at the wedding when Śiva becomes the locally incarnate Sundarēsvarar of Madurai. Specifically, Śaiva elements are replaced with Pāṇḍya royal symbols. The bull is replaced by a fish. The Pāṇḍya king was known as He of the Fish (*Mīnavaṉ*) and so Śiva assumes both the fish banner and that title. Similarly, Śiva is transformed from He Who is Crowned with Laburnum Flowers (*Koṉṟaicūṭi*), one of his pan-Indian titles, to He Who Wears the Garland of Margosa Flowers (*Vēmpaṉ*), an epithet of the Pāṇḍya kings. And the ascetic paraphernalia of the unmarried Śiva change to the royal garb of a married monarch: Snakes become golden ornaments, the crescent moon becomes a jeweled crown, and the tiger-skin becomes costly garments (cf. O'Flaherty 1973, 238–250).

The royal Mīṉāṭci thus rises to the level of goddess without losing her royal attributes; the deity Śiva condescends to assume a royal station without losing his divine attributes. Distinctions between royalty and divinity meld imperceptibly, deliberately.

The marriage constitutes a covenant whereby Mīṉāṭci and Cuntarēcuvarar become an eternal royal couple living in the palace/temple that stands even today in the center of the old city of Madurai. A queen who once operated in the realm of mortal royalty becomes immortal and always available, no longer subject to the vagaries of history or to the precarious variations in dynastic fortune. This is true even though the Pāṇḍya dynasty lost most of its power in the fourteenth century and ended by the beginning of the seventeenth century. Thus, if there are no longer Pāṇḍya monarchs, there is no longer the need for them. The covenant, which is the marriage alliance, is written on the hearts of the people of Madurai in two ways. First, it is celebrated, and therefore reaffirmed, every year in a remarkably large and festive ten-day occasion. The annual Cittirai Marriage Festival reenacts Mīṉāṭci's coronation and, more important, her marriage and queenly dominion over the city. Second, the covenant is renewed every time devotees read, hear, or remember the episodes that follow the marriage in *The Story of the Sacred Games*. In particular, those episodes that recount events taking place during later generations of Pāṇḍya rulers remind devotees of Śiva's and Mīṉāṭci's gracious vigilance over the kingdom.

## The Queen's Power and the King's Authority

An important matter for many devotees is Mīṉāṭci's relationship to her husband Śiva. He, too, is worshipped in the Madurai temple. Mīṉāṭci is clearly regarded as the more important of the pair among those who know the city firsthand, but it is not obvious to someone who reads *The Story of the Sacred Games*. Quite the contrary: In the text Mīṉāṭci is clearly subordinated to Śiva. It is he who defeats her, dominates her, and bestows his grace by marrying her. In fact, in the text twice he condescends to marry her (TVP I.5.87ff. and III.57.60–64).

After the grand marriage of chapter 5, Mīṉāṭci becomes a mere appendage to Śiva, little more than a foil for the comedy Śiva unfolds for us all. For example, after the marriage, Mīṉāṭci comes to Śiva playing the role of the dizzy housewife, distraught about the fact that there is just so much food left over from the wedding celebrations and she does not know what to do with it. In his infinite wisdom, power, and condescension, Śiva plays a trick on her by having one of his famous dwarf-servants with an incredible appetite devour everything in sight, much to the stunned amazement of the whole town. From chapter 6 through chapter 64, the pattern changes little. Śiva is always in control, always able to produce edifying miracles.

But in terms of the actual ritual life of the temple, and of the way most devotees talk about this royal-divine pair, Mīṉāṭci takes clear precedence. N. Subramanian calls attention to this striking contrast between the mythology and the ritual and concludes that Mīṉāṭci was a local Dravidian figure, originally unrelated to the northern, male, Sanskritic import, Śiva. He believes that the redactors of *The Story of the Sacred Games* tried, but unsuccessfully, to subordinate her to Śiva by means of ritually and mythically marrying her to him (Subramanian 1974, 215). Jan Gonda believes that Mīṉāṭci's marriage to Śiva was simply a way to incorporate a powerful, locally important Dravidian goddess into the Brahmin, Śaiva, Hindu pantheon (Gonda 1962, 29; see also Diehl 1956, 177 n.4).

Temple guidebooks are explicit about Mīṉāṭci's ritual precedence (Pañcanatam Pillai 1970, 55, 149; Paḻaniyappaṉ 1963, 147). She is always to be worshipped first. Although the imposing Eastern Gate stands directly before Śiva's shrine, pilgrims are instructed to, and almost always do, enter through the Hall of the Eight Goddesses, which leads into the goddess shrine. One branch of the tradition, embarrassed by Mīṉāṭci's dominance in a decidedly androcentric cultural context, strains to explain this by suggesting that pilgrims should enter by way of the Mīṉāṭci shrine because of Indra's initial experience (narrated in the first chapter of *The Story of the Sacred Games*) in first discovering the image of Śiva in Madurai. It was at the gate of Śiva's shrine that the sin that afflicted Indra left him. Thus, by this clever interpretation, the gate is termed "the leaving doorway" (*viṭṭa vācal*): One enters via the Mīṉāṭci shrine and leaves via the Śiva shrine (Centil Turavi 1970, 204). Another tradition says that entry through the main

Eastern Gateway is inauspicious ever since a temple servant committed suicide by jumping off it to protest "palace misdeeds" (Jeyechandran 1974, 374).

Even *The Story of the Sacred Games* is self-conscious about the apparent contradiction. In the earliest chapters, Śiva is clearly the preexistent, sacred presence at the spot that later becomes Madurai. But according to the fifth, Queen Mīṉāṭci does not encounter Śiva until she marches with her warriors to Mount Kailāsa to meet him in battle. As soon as she sees him, she becomes submissive and listens demurely to his instructions:

> "From the moment you started out
> intending to triumph over the eight directions,
> From that moment we and our forces also left Madurai,
> accompanying you all the way here.
> On the coming Monday I will marry you at the auspicious hour,
> and as prescribed in the Four Vedas.
> Go, then, back to your city!" he said. (TVP I.5.45)

Though these verses explain how Śiva can both be at Madurai before Mīṉāṭci's departure and yet meet her at Mount Kailāsa, textual ambiguity remains as to whose city it really is. But temple ritual practices are quite unambiguous. The temple is primarily the abode of the goddess/queen Mīṉāṭci and only secondarily that of Śiva.[8] This fact is underlined by the practice in the Mīṉāṭci temple/palace of offering each of the four daily worship (*pūjā*) ceremonies first to the goddess (Pañcanatam Pillai 1970, 18). Of the twelve major temple festivals, four are celebrated in exclusive honor of Mīṉāṭci but none is celebrated in exclusive honor of Śiva/Cuntarēcuvarar. The remaining eight are celebrated in honor of the divine couple together (Fuller 1980, 346).

Mīṉāṭci's ritual dominance over the city is dramatically represented in two of the Wedding Festival's ritual processions. The first, on the eighth day of the festival, immediately follows her coronation. The exclusive attention she receives as the city's newly crowned monarch is suggestive of, indeed a reenactment of, the traditional procession made by the Hindu monarch after the grand coronation. The processional path around the four concentric Māci streets is significant. These streets once formed the outer limits of the ancient city. Her procession marks off the outer boundaries of her domain. She is the newly crowned monarch of the territory her path circumscribes. On the following day the queen/goddess again is taken alone in procession around the four Māci streets in her ritual conquest of the deities of the eight directions. In so doing, she is securing the geographic space she has claimed as her own.

Although the marriage of Mīṉāṭci is the occasion for the celebration, much more than a marriage is being celebrated. Deities from temples in outlying areas are brought in procession to do homage to the newly married queen/goddess. Rural people arrive as pilgrims, more than doubling the population of the city, in order to pay respects to Mīṉāṭci.

It is indicative of Mīṉāṭci's primacy that Indian immigrants to the Houston, Texas, area have built a rather impressive five-acre temple complex, which they call the Mīṉāṭci Temple. Although the temple is dedicated to the triad of Śiva (addressed there as Cuntarēcuvarar), Mīṉāṭci, and Viṣṇu (in his form as Venkatēsvara), devotees have established an extended congregation in the Houston area that they call simply the Mīṉāṭci Temple Society.[9] In his book on the priests of the Madurai Temple, a book that, significantly, he entitled *Servants of the Goddess*, Fuller (1984, 8) explains the devotees' relationship with Śiva and Mīṉāṭci:

> [Śiva] is the supreme lord whose paramount concern is for the order of the world, not for the petty difficulties of individual human beings. Only a minority of devotees, usually theologically sophisticated, speak of their devotion for . . . Śiva. For the majority, that sentiment is mainly commanded by the goddess.

Perceived as "a local girl," this goddess/queen is closer to the people. Several works praising her concentrate on her childhood, emphasizing her role as a daughter of Madurai. Śiva came as an outsider, from a distant place, to take up his residence and to rule with her. In the temple as well as in *The Story of the Sacred Games*, she is addressed as goddess, mother, and queen, whereas Śiva is approached more formally as lord (*nāyakaṉ*). Vasudha Narayanan (1982, 225–226) points out that in the Indian family a mother is likely to be more accessible to her children, to mediate between them and their father, for she is less concerned with the demands of hierarchy, order, justice, and society. She represents qualities of nurturance, compassion, mercy, affection, and accessibility in a way that the father does not. Little wonder that Mīṉāṭci is seen as the mediator, as the one to whom devotees would more readily turn.[10]

## Reflections on Mīṉāṭci's Mythic History

What devotees know of Mīṉāṭci's unique history is primarily what they know of her as an unmarried queen. Before her marriage she is unique: a fierce, independent, triple-breasted, ambiguously gendered, world-conquering warrior-monarch. But the texts tells us that once she marries, she loses her distinctiveness and, in a sense, her history. Like any Hindu woman whose marriage is properly arranged, when she marries she becomes her husband's "half-body," subordinated to him, assimilated in many senses to his family "substance." He becomes her primary deity. In marrying Śiva, Mīṉāṭci becomes an anomalous monarch and a king's daughter. She becomes a wife of Śiva, a domesticated, unthreatening queen whose gender is no longer ambiguous, a sweet and gracious goddess, and therefore less subject to the contingent vagaries of the historical world: in short, no more distinctive and no more unique. Humans, royal or otherwise, function in a world of unpredictable and uncontrollable historically conditioned ambiguity, a world full of hazards. In the Hindu context, this is a world often described as "illusory" (*māyā*)[11] because it is liable to, and frequently does, depart from proper divine patterns, or *dharma*. Once the queen becomes a goddess, however, hers becomes an eternal, dharmic existence, properly ordered, without the intrusions of accident-prone history. She loses her distinctiveness, her identity, and her contingency, and that, strangely enough, is what constitutes her final triumph. True, her rule still has a topographically contingent, ritually geographic component. It includes Madurai and, more recently, Pearland, Texas. But the significant locus of her power is in the hopes and imaginations of her devotees and subjects, wherever they reside. In the stories the faithful tell about her and in the trust they give her, devotees understand themselves to be participating in a flawless divine perfection that is universal and eternal.

One remaining but unanswerable question is whether this female Pāṇḍya monarch was ever a reigning human queen. Was there ever such a person on whom these legends and stories have been based? Quite likely we shall never know, partly because the same fluidity that characterizes distinctions between humans and deities also characterizes distinctions we Westerners prefer to make between myth and history. Even accounts earlier understood to be historically descriptive thereby become suspect. For example, we do have reports from Megasthenes, a fourth-century BCE Greek envoy to northern India, who discusses a Pāṇḍya princess wedding a god (Dessigane, Pattabiramin, and Filliozat 1960, xii–xiii; Kārāvēlane 1956, 7).

That story, as told by Megasthenes, describes a deity venerated in "Methora." The deity's only female child was given a large army to rule the territory over which she governed, and from which she derived her name, Pandia. Unable to find an appropriate spouse for her, the god, though her father, finally married her himself. The argument presented by Dessigane, Pattabiramin, and Filliozat (1960) is intriguing:

> The Pāṇṭiya kingdom and its pearl fisheries were known in northern India, where Megasthenes collected his information, at the end of the fourth century B.C.E. A legend associated with the god of the Sūrasenas of Mathurā had, by then, been localized in the southern country of the Pāṇṭiyas among whom it has been preserved until today, along with much more recent legend, and among whom the capital is Madurai. (xiii, trans. Harman)[12]

If these conclusions are true, significant amounts of the basic plot of *The Story of the Sacred Games* were current in the oral traditions of northern India by the fourth-century BCE. Thus, certain elements of the document's plot appear to precede even the earliest known examples of Tamil literature.

But perhaps more relevant in understanding Mīṉāṭci's relationship to her devotees today is the fact that for them historically verifiable facts matter only secondarily. Karl Potter aptly notes in his analysis of the hagiographic tradition that consistently misrepresented historical facts about the famous Hindu Śaṃkarācārya:

> The actual philosopher is entirely lost in the myth. . . . In India persons are regularly subordinated in retrospect, perhaps out of a sense of the overwhelming and impersonal (or divine) ordering of cosmic history . . . and thus the details of a particular life are of no great importance, unless they serve some profound didactic function. (1982, 114)

In the Hindu tradition, enduring value accrues to what always is and always has been. Truth is divine and therefore eternal. It is never discovered for the first time; it is only rediscovered. If something is really true, it cannot be new; it has occurred or been said before. If it has not occurred before or has not been said before, it is obviously not of value. Uniqueness and originality are thus intrusive and illusory.

One of the better illustrations of the difference between the Hindu and Western attitudes toward history is reflected in the autobiography of Lesslie Newbigin, a Christian missionary to India in the early 1900s. He speaks of one experience in the Tamil city of Kanchipuram, where he studied Hinduism with a local group.

> I well remember how I astonished the Swami by saying that if it could be shown that Jesus had never lived and died and risen again I would have no alternative but to become a Hindu. He thought that only a lunatic would allow his ultimate destiny to hang upon a questionable fact of history which—even if it could be proved—belonged to the world of *maya* [illusion]. (1985, 157)

Similar problems appear when we ask the question about whether Mīṉāṭci was ever a human. The author of the text does not really worry about the issue. Mīṉāṭci is *both* the daughter of King Malayadhvaja Pāṇḍya *and* the incarnation of Parvatī, the divine consort of Śiva. The position is clear, for example, in the "Praise of Deities" section:

> See assumed a form identical to Śiva,
> a form even Brahmā cannot comprehend.
> She, who gives birth to all things
> in innumerable worlds here and afar,
> who has firm breasts,
> and black hair adorned with honey-like flowers
> is the queen with eyes like a fish,
> is the one who assumed the form of princess and
> daughter to the Pāṇḍya dynasty,
> is the one whose flower-like feet
> you must cherish forever in your heart.
> (I. Kaṭavuḷ Vāḻttu 8, "Aṅkayaṟkaṇṇamai")

The writer of our text, of course, has the advantage of viewing the issue retrospectively: The queen and goddess, who is Mīṉāṭci was also Taṭātakai, the royal and human daughter. And, if forced to take a position, he would have to insist on her divinity. She is, after all, praised in the "Praise of Deities" section of the work. But forcing the tradition into an "either/or" position would do it violence, at least on this issue.

Mīṉāṭci, as child-princess, victorious human queen, eternally reigning goddess, derives much of her power precisely because she can cross boundaries so easily and so naturally: male/female, human/goddess, princess and queen. Her immaculate birth from fire signals her special status at the very beginning, but her life story moves her from being an embarrassment to her father to becoming supreme queen and goddess.

Finally, in the portrayals of her as a young princess, a formidable queen, a shy and passive bride, a proper wife, and a reigning goddess—with none of these identities excluding any of the others; indeed, with each including all the others—the tradition makes her accessible to Madurai devotees. Because devotees can identify with her, they too are able to move beyond the temporary contingencies of time and place. The extent to which her sacred biography is historically accurate has little to do with mere and supposed fact. To work, it must fit the prevailing notions of what constitutes the sacred, and to work well, to make the divine truly accessible, it must reflect a sense of an "accessible" divine. Because there is much less a radical discontinuity between the human and the divine in Hinduism, and because doing one's inherent social duty (*dharma*) is a quintessential religious act, we find that most hagiographies in Hinduism are likely to present "imitate-able" models. By and large the subjects of Hindu hagiography fit the expectations tradition has precast for them.

## Conclusion: Will the Real, Historical Mīṉāṭci Please Sit Down?

As the life history of Mīṉāṭci demonstrates, Hindu tradition tends to devalue historical uniqueness in favor of perceived divine, eternal patterns. If events in human history are simply footnotes to an eternally repeated divine pattern, and if all humans are simply working their way toward that universal, transcendent, and inherent divinity in us all, known as *mokṣa*, there can be no hard-and-fast lines between the historical and the eternal, between the human and the divine. The hard-and-fast lines, rather, come in the realm of proper human behavior. Hindus must be more concerned with orthopraxy than with orthodoxy: What they believe may change, but what they do either is or is not in accord with the divine pattern mapped out for us all. What Hindus do matters, but it incurs censure only if it makes them stand out. To be a distinct, unique individual is to set oneself not simply apart but against the prevailing divine pattern. This is why this extraordinary figure of Mīṉāṭci relinquished her uniqueness as she became absorbed into—or perhaps we should say, "married into"—the larger Hindu pantheon.

NOTES

1. See this sustained argument imaginatively and graphically presented in Waghorne's (1994) provocative work.
2. See, for example, the texts *Maturai Mīṉāṭciyammaṉ* . . . ; *Mīṉāṭciyammai* . . . ; and *Maturai Aṅkayaṟkaṇṇammai*.
3. The best known devotional document dedicated exclusively to descriptions and praise of Mīṉāṭci is the *Mīṉāṭciammaṉpiḷḷaitamiḻ* and dates from the first part of the seventeenth century. It was written by the poet Kumarakuruparacuvāmikaḷ and seems to have been commissioned by the famous king Tirumalai Nāyakkar.

4. Approaching the identity of Mīṉāṭci from this perspective, one text describes how Parvatī once decided to be reborn in the city of Madurai in the form of Mīṉāṭci in order to satisfy a particular devotee's request. See Kirupā 1978, 1–6.
5. Note that the *Bhāgavata Purāṇa* (9.1.13–32, 36–39) recounts the story of King Vaisvata Manu, whose "son-producing sacrifice" also brought forth a daughter. The daughter, named Ilā, is later transformed into a son named Sudyumna.
6. This is not true when occasionally males are paired with goddesses, however. The general theory of what happens in Indian marriage is that women are transformed into the "substance" of their husbands. Men are not understood to be similarly "transformable."
7. On the role of marriage as a way of both reflecting and creating an ordered cosmos, see Harman (1987b). Other interpretations of Mīṉāṭci's third breast include three offered by J. Lindsay Opie (1974, 217–220). They are that (1) the presence of the third breast signifies spiritual virginity, which is lost "in mystical marriage with Śiva," (2) the third breast symbolizes a surplus of fertility and maternal character, and (3) the third breast provided Mīṉāṭci protection against threatening males, "like the miraculous growth of beards or other deformities in Christian legends to protect virgin saints from pagan suitors." Kumarakuruparacuvāmikal (*Mīṉāṭciyammai* . . . , 1902) claims that the third breast on Mīṉāṭci is simply intended as symmetry to match Śiva's third eye.
8. Shulman (1980, 139) notes the common repetition of this pattern in other Tamil place-history texts: The god is "drawn to the site by the goddess and . . . rooted there by marriage to her."
9. Paul Younger (1982, 253) notes a similar dynamic at the temple near Tirucirapaḷḷi, India: "While outsiders refer to Tiruvāṉaikkā as 'a Śiva temple,' most of the worshippers who come to the temple today come primarily to worship the Goddess, Akilāṇṭēsvāri."
10. Frédérique Marglin (1985, 46–89) supports this view in her description of the kinship dynamics in the city of Puri. She notes that it is through the male line that children inherit their rank and social identity. Women do not confer such rank, but are more concerned with nurturing the lineage: its unborn fetuses, its living children, and its deceased ancestors, who receive food offerings cooked by women. That women remain pure and chaste is important because they must be ritually fit to perform this nurturing function.
11. See, for example, Keyes' comment that, "The Indian tradition of sacred biography, a tradition that includes the biographies of Krishna and the Buddha, appears to have been . . . far less constrained by historical events in the lives of biographical subjects than has almost any other tradition of sacred biography known" (1982, 15).
12. Mathurā of northern India was the capital of the royal Sūrasena dynasty, and it has often been associated with Madurai of southern India. Indeed, the southern Madurai is sometimes called Ten Maturai (Southern Madurai) in order to distinguish it from the northern city associated with the deity Krishna.

## REFERENCES

### *European Language Materials*

Babb, Lawrence A. 1970. "Marriage and Malevolence: The Uses of Sexual Opposition in a Hindu Pantheon." *Ethnology* 9 (2): 137–148.

Brown, W. Norman. 1947. "The Name of the Goddess Mīnākṣi, 'Fish-Eye.'" *The Journal of the American Oriental Society* 67: 209–214.

Daniel, Sheryl B. 1980. "Marriage in Tamil Culture: The Problem of Conflicting 'Models.'" Pp. 61–92 in *The Powers of Tamil Women*, ed. Susan S. Wadley. [Foreign and Comparative Studies: South Asian Series, No. 6.] Syracuse: Syracuse University.

Dessigane, R., P. Z. Pattabiramin, and J. Filliozat. 1960. *La légende des jeux de Civa à Madurai d'après les textes et les peintures* (2 vols.). Pondicherry: Institut Francais d'Indologie.

Diehl, Carl Gustav. 1956. *Instrument and Purpose: Studies on Rites and Rituals in South India*. Lund: C. W. K. Gleerup.

Fuller, C. J. 1980. "The Divine Couple's Relationship in a South Indian Temple: Mīṇākṣī and Sundareśvara at Madurai." *History of Religions* 19 (May): 321–348.

———. 1984. *Servants of the Goddess: The Priests of a South Indian Temple*. Cambridge University Press.

Gonda, Jan. 1962. *Les Réligions de L'Inde* (3 vols.), trans. L. Jospin. Paris: Payot.

Harman, William. 1987a. "Two Versions of a Tamil Text and the Contexts in which They Were Written." *Journal of the Institute of Asian Studies* 5 (September): 1–18.

———. 1987. "The Authority of Sanskrit in Tamil Literature: A Case Study in Tracing a Text to its Sources." *Mankind Quarterly* 27 (Spring): 296–316.

———. 1987b. "The Hindu Marriage as Soteriological Event." *International Journal of Sociology of the Family* 17/2: 169–182.

———. 1989. *The Sacred Marriage of a Hindu Goddess*. Bloomington: Indiana University Press.

———. 1995. "Kingship." In *The Harper Dictionary of Religions*, ed. J. Z. Smith and W. S. Green. New York: Harper.

Hudson, Dennis. 1971. "Two Citrā Festivals in Madurai." Pp. 191–222 in *Asian Religions*, ed. Bardwell Smith. Chambersburg: The American Academy of Religion.

Jeyechandran, A. V. 1974. "The Madurai Temple Gopuras." Pp. 367–375 in *Maturait Tirukkōyil: Tirukkuṭa Nāṉṉīrāṭṭuppa Peruviḻā Malar*, ed. Jeyechandran. Maturai: Aruḷmiku Mīṉāṭci Cuntarēcuvarar Tirukkōyil.

Kārāvēlane, K., trans. and ed. 1956. *Kāreikkālammeiyār: Oeuvres Éditées et Traduites*. Pondicherry: Institut Francais d'Indologie.

Keyes, Charles F. 1982. "Charisma: From Social Life to Sacred Biography." Pp. 1–22 in *Charisma and Sacred Biography*, ed. Michael A. Williams. Chico: Scholars Press.

Marglin, Frédérique Apffel. 1985. *Wives of the God-King: The Rituals of the Devadasis of Puri*. Delhi: Oxford University Press.

Marriott, McKim. 1976a. "Hindu Transactions: Diversity Without Dualism." Pp. 109–142 in *Transaction and Meaning: Directions in the Anthropology of Exchange and Symbolic Behavior*, ed. Bruce Kapferer. Philadelphia: Institute for the Study of Human Issues.

———. 1976b. "Interpreting Indian Society: A Monistic Alternative to Dumont's Dualism." *Journal of Asian Studies* 36/1: 189–195.

McDaniel, June. 1987. *The Madness of the Saints: Ecstatic Religion in Bengal*. Chicago: University of Chicago Press.

Meena, V. n.d. *Madurai*. Cape Comorin: Harikumari Arts.

Narayanan, Vasudha. 1982. "The Goddess Śrī: The Blossoming Lotus and Breast Jewel of Viṣṇu." Pp. 224–237 in *The Divine Consort: Rādhā and the Goddesses of India*, ed. John Stratton Hawley and Donna Marie Wulff. Berkeley, CA: Graduate Theological Union.

Newbigin, Lesslie. 1985. *Unfinished Agenda: An Autobiography*. Grand Rapids: Wm. B. Eerdmans.

O'Flaherty, Wendy Doniger. 1973. *Asceticism and Eroticism in the Mythology of Śiva*. London: Oxford University Press.

———. 1976. *The Origins of Evil in Hindu Mythology*. Berkeley: University of California Press.

Opie, J. Lindsay. 1974. "Remember Taṭātagai." Pp. 217–220 in *Maturait Tirukkōyil: Tirukkuṭa Nāṉṉīrāṭṭuppa Peruviḻā Malar*, ed. A. V. Jeyechandran. Maturai: Aruḷmiku Mīṉāṭci Cuntarēcuvarar Tirukkōyil.

Potter, Karl H. 1982. Śaṃkarācārya: The Myth and the Man." Pp. 111–126 in *Charisma and Sacred Biography*, ed. Michael A. Williams. Chico: Scholars Press.

Rajagopalan, T. R. n.d. *Welcome to Madurai*. Madurai: Sri Karthikeiya Publication.

Ramanujan, A. K., trans. 1972. *Speaking of Siva*. Baltimore: Penguin Books.

Shulman, David Dean. 1980. *Tamil Temple Myths: Sacrifice and Divine Marriage in the South Indian Saiva Tradition*. Princeton: Princeton University Press.

———. 1976. "The Murderous Bride: Tamil Versions of the Myth of Dēvi and the Buffalo Demon." *History of Religions* 16/2: 120–147.

Spratt, Philip. 1966. *Hindu Culture and Personality: A Psychoanalytic Study*. Bombay: n. p.

Subramanian, N. 1974. "The Sports of Siva and the Lady of the City." Pp. 214–217 in *Maturait Tirukkōyil: Tirukkuṭa Nāṉṉīrāṭṭuppa Peruviḻā Malar*, ed. Jeyechandran. Maturai: Aruḷmiku Mīṉāṭci Cuntarēcuvarar Tirukkōyil.

Waghorne, Joanne Punzo. 1994. *The Raja's Magic Clothes: Re-Visioning Kingship and Divinity in England's India*. University Park, PA: Pennsylvania State University Press.

Younger, Paul. 1982. "The Family of Śiva in a South Indian Grove." *Sciences Religieuses/Studies in Religion* 11 (Summer): 245–263.

*Tamil and Sanskrit Language Materials*

*Bhāgavata Purāṇa*. Trans. J. M. Sanyal. 1930–1934. Calcutta: n. p.

Centil Turavi (pseud.). 1970. *Aimperu Viḻākkaḷ*. Ceṉṉai: Cāṣta Patippakam.

Kirupā (pseud.). 1978. *Maturai Mīṉāṭci Pāṇḍya Makaḷānatu ēṉ?* Maturai: Vivēkānantā Accakam.

Perumāḷ Ayyar, Caravaṇa, ed. 1860. *Maturai Aṅkayaṟkaṇṇammai, allatu Mīṉāṭciyammai Piḷḷaitamiḻ*, by Kumarakurupara Tampirāṉ. Rev. K. V. Aṟumaka Mutaliyār. n.p.

*Maturai Mīṉāṭciyammaṉ Tiruvaruḷpeṟṟa Poṉṉaḻakareṉṉum Kaḷḷaḻakar Ammāṉai*. 1974. n.a. Ceṉṉai: Ar. Ji. Pati Kampeṉi.

*Mīṉāṭciyammai Piḷḷait Tamiḻ of Kumarakuruparacuvāmikal* (2nd ed.). 1902. Ceṉṉai: Kalāratnākara Accuk Kūṭam.

Paḻaniyappaṉ, Ki. 1963. *Kōyil Māṉakar: Maturai Mīṉāṭci Cuntarar Tirukkōyil Varalāṟu*. Maturai: Tiruppaṇikkuḻu Mīṉāṭci Tirukkōyil.

Pañcanatam Pillai, R. 1970. *Srī Mīṉāṭci Cuntarēcuvarar Kōyil Varalāṟu* (2nd ed.). Maturai: Maturai Srī Mīṉāṭci Cuntarēcuvarar Alaya Veḷiyīṭu.

*Tiruviḷaiyāṭaṟpurāṇam of Parañcōtimuṉivar* (TVP). [1927] 1965. With commentary by Na. Mu. Vēṅkaṭacāmi Nāṭṭār (3 vols.). Ceṉṉai: Teṉṉintiya Caiva Cittāṇta Nūṟpatippu Kaḻakam.

# 3

# More Than Earth

## Cihuacoatl as Female Warrior, Male Matron, and Inside Ruler

*Kay A. Read*

The sixteenth-century Nahua (Aztec)[1] goddess Cihuacoatl (Snakewoman) presents the twentieth-century observer with a host of apparently contradictory and puzzling images. She was both a goddess of fields and crops and a woman warrior. Her powers were borne not only by childbearing women but also by the male governmental official second only to the king, often in a dual leadership. Just after the Conquest, the Spanish friar Bernardino de Sahagún called her a "savage beast" and "evil omen" because she brought "misery" (*Florentine Codex* [FC], 1.6: 11) while at the same time referring to her as the "highest of goddesses" because she aided women suffering in childbirth (FC 6.27–29, 31: 151–165, 179–182). Throughout these and other early resources, Snakewoman, depicted in both wildly negative and expansively positive terms, appears in both male and female roles.

A full survey of the pictorial and written texts describing Cihuacoatl's pre-Conquest world finds her painted in even more confusing imagery. As a Noble Woman (*cihuapilli*) and Eagle Woman (*quauhcihuatl*), she was a goddess of the sky (*jluicacioa*) (FC 6.29: 161–165). Yet as Quilaztli (Edible Heron Herbs),[2] she was patroness of Xochimilco, a region of rich farming land on Earth's Surface (Tlalticpac). At times she tied her hair up in proper matronly fashion (FC 1.6: 11); at other times, wore it loose and tangled

*Figure 3.1: Cihuacoatl in her guise as a goddess of the underworld.* (© *Kay A. Read.*)

as a sign of death and the underworld (FC 1.6: 11). One could enter her temple room only by crawling through a tiny opening into a pitch dark, windowless room resembling the Land of Death (Mictlan) beneath Earth's Surface.[3] This Place of Darkness (*tlillan*) housed all the gods, and a great sacrificial fire burned there on her feast day (Durán 1971). Cihuacoatl Tlacaellel, the male government official who claimed her name for his office, held Snakewoman's weapon-like weaving batten and eagle warrior's shield while also wearing her ocelot blouse in rituals requiring her participation (*Codex Borbonicus* 1974, 26). Cihuacoatl appears in many places and guises: as a woman warrior whose battlefield lies in the sky, as patroness of agriculture dwelling on Earth's Surface, and as an inhabitant of the underworld; as a female, familial matron; as a harbinger of death; and as a male-matron, warrior, and governor.

This present-day confusion may be due more to a twentieth-century distance combined with visions shaped, in part, by sixteenth-century Spanish interpreters[4] than to inherent inconsistencies in Snakewoman's imagery. Indeed, this goddess presents a quite coherent picture of a Nahua matron who advised those fighting in the battles of both birth and military conquest. And as creation depended on ongoing destruction, she brought prosperity to all regions of the cosmos. Many scholars claim that all Nahua goddesses, including Cihuacoatl, were simply different versions of a Great Earth Mother; in fact, Cihuacoatl is more interesting than this Euro-American stereotype suggests. Her primary powers extended beyond motherhood and earth. In this essay, I set Cihuacoatl in her historic and historiographic context. Then I explore her image as an old woman warrior and matronly advisor to male and female warriors. Finally, I describe the human Snakewoman's role as a male matron and inside ruler, who governed alongside a person called king by the Spanish and Chief Speaker (Tlatoani) by the Mexica.

## History and Historiography

In pre-Conquest times, the Nahua world and its history were both rich and complex. This complexity deepened even further when the Spanish added their own world and history to that of those they conquered. Both complexities—that before the Conquest and what came after—make the job of a twentieth-century researcher difficult, especially when examining topics concerning women. But before considering that issue, a brief look at the pre-Conquest world is needed.

### *Nahua History and Their Cosmos*

The goddess Cihuacoatl was honored in and around the Valley of Mexico. By the sixteenth century, many peoples inhabiting different urban centers densely populated this valley and its surrounding areas. Although all spoke Nahuatl, each center claimed its own patron deity and ancestral line, followed its own version of a common calendar, celebrated its own brand of the Nahua rituals, and produced its own particular goods. These urban centers had political and economic tensions with each other, sometimes allying and sometimes warring. The Mexica-Tenochca held hegemony throughout the area and much of Mesoamerica. Their city of Tenochtitlan is estimated to have had no less than 150,000–200,000 people. Cortés conquered them in 1521 with help from many of their neighbors, who disliked their suffocating imperialism. The remains of Tenochtitlan now lie beneath modern-day Mexico City.

Geographically, Tenochtitlan was built on an island in the southern basin of the Valley of Mexico. Connected by causeways to the surrounding shores, the city was ringed by rich agricultural fields. Although in a semi-arid zone, the whole southern basin was a wonderful source for the animals, birds, plants, aquatic life, and edible insects that constituted a large portion of the rich Nahua diet. By the sixteenth century, however, the area had become overpopulated, and these pressures along with an ever-present threat of drought forced the Mexica to expand their island domain to include other rich agricultural territories.

Socially, the Mexica constituted a complex society with numerous interconnected groups of governmental officials, judges, warriors, religious professionals, educators, merchants, vendors, craftspeople, agriculturalists, servants, and slaves. A ruler called the Chief Speaker (Tlatoani) was paired with a counselor called the Tlacaellel, or Cihuacoatl. The society's hierarchy is unclear, although it was more complex than a simple dualistic tension between elite and commoners

(F. Hicks, personal communication, November 1997). For example, one might assume that a noble title meant the possession of great wealth and political power, but in fact, this was not always the case. Economic and social classes were not always equated; nor did a title ensure political clout (Read 1995, 16–17).

Complex gender roles divided along both symbolic and pragmatic lines, apparently as complementarities. Male and female roles were different but absolutely necessary to each other, at times separate but sometimes overlapping. Symbolically, females represented coldness, moistness, the underworld, night, and death; males, hotness, dryness, the skies, day, and life (López Austin 1988, 53). Yet these were not strict divisions, for both male and female deities often were addressed with a polite "our mother, our father," and Snakewoman was associated with both the underworld and the skies. Moreover, although domesticity defined femaleness and warfare maleness, this division occasionally appears more symbolic than practical. During the first bath of a new female infant, weaving tools ceremonially appeared as did war tools for a male (FC 6.37: 201–204). Yet in practice, women warriors existed as did a few female Nahua rulers (Read 1995, 10–13; *Codex Chimalpahin* 1982, 85–87, 90, 180ff., 197). And, as we will see, one of the two highest Mexica offices—although executed by a man—was symbolically domestic.

Cihuacoatl moved through a dynamic cosmos. One can imagine Nahua cosmic topography as a great container in which water, a huge variety of beings (gods, people, animals), and numerous diverse powers continuously cycled, living and dying as they moved (López Austin 1988, 52–68; Read 1998, 123–155). Horizontally, the dry Earth's Surface was divided as a four-petaled flower, the cardinal and intercardinal directions marking its sides and corners. Particular gods governed each quarter, where also stood great trees, each with a bird perched upon its top. Standing at the edge of Tenochtitlan, mountains like great pots held the water that the rain gods periodically released in the form of springs, rivers, rain, and snow. The oceans surrounding Tlalticpac's edges stretched out until they met the watery skies. These sky waters (*ilhuicatl*) rose like great moist walls arching over the dry Earth's Surface, beneath which extended the dank, river-laced, cavern-pocked underworld.

A multitude of intimate connections among the watery upper and lower realms and dry Earth's Surface maintained an orderly flow of existence. Each morning, male warrior deities, who had died in battle, captured the sun from its nightly underground journey in order to carry it into the watery sky. Each noonday, female warrior deities (*cihuapipiltin*), who had died in either birth or war, battled the males for possession of the sun. Winning, they took it back to the Land of Death from whence the males would recapture it the next morning (FC 6.29: 161–165). Mictlan was the underworld place where things rotted away; seeds fed on this moist corruption to become full plants reaching up above Earth's Surface (López Austin 1994, 160–164). As rain, rivers, streams, and springs, water—the cosmic body's blood—did more than bring life to the parched landscape of Earth's Surface; it also caused the deathful corruption necessary to continuing life. For, as drought, floods, thunderstorms, frost, sleet, and hail, water also caused death, which led to decay and life-sustaining fertilizer (Read 1998, ch. 5). As Tenochtitlan's fields relied on the rich fertilizer dredged from the floors of its canals, life on dry Tlalticpac could not exist without Mictlan's deadly stuff. This was a world in which death and corruption gave rise to life and creation. Just as females were distinct from but inseparably intertwined with males, creation existed only in intimate conjunction with destruction.

### *Nahua Historiography*

Two enormous problems are faced in researching Nahua goddesses: the extreme fragmentation of virtually all the resources and the manner in which these sources were collected. Because no sustained primary texts describing Nahua life are extant,[5] all our information must be pieced together to present as coherent a picture as possible.

The latter problem, because of its subtlety, is even more problematic. First, most of our resources were originally collected in the sixteenth century by Roman Catholic celibate male clerics, whose life experiences colored their responses to the culture. This was, after all, the same epoch that gave the world *Maleus Maleficarum*, the infamous document detailing the Christian Church's view of women as particularly open to witchcraft, susceptible to malice, and embodying an insatiable sexual desire that caused them to lust after the Devil (Sprenger and Kramer 1948). In this era of the late Middle Ages and Reformation, writers often described women in a dichotomous manner: either good, as the gentle, asexual Mary, or bad, as the violent and promiscuous witches. Such highly restrictive, often negative attitudes frequently lie behind Spanish references to goddesses like Cihuacoatl.

Second, well attested by contemporary ethnographic studies, males often have difficulties collecting information from females, who may not want to talk to them about matters considered inappropriate for masculine ears.[6] How much more so when the collectors are also their severe conquerors? Thus, it is difficult to have any in-depth understanding of Nahua women that has not been shaped by particular sixteenth-century European masculine images. At the very least, midwives and birthing women, who called on Cihuacoatl's powers, probably responded cautiously to the Spanish investigators; topics concerning the physical aspects of birth may very well have been avoided (at least they are not there now). And we know that women warriors existed, but we have little knowledge about their nature or role. Much of their warfare techniques appear to have been closely associated with female sexuality (Read 2000), a topic women were not likely to discuss at length with their male, often celibate, interrogators. Both groups viewed bodily and sexual matters in such different ways that the conquered informants may very well have avoided those topics altogether, choosing instead to maintain their secrets. We do not really know if this was the case, but such a large void exists in the feminine side of the resources on Cihuacoatl that either the Spanish men did not look for it or the Nahua women did not choose to give it, or both.

The assumptions contemporary scholars sometimes bring to their work further exacerbate the problems. The more fragmented and piecemeal one's sources are, the more one's own cultural presumptions are likely to go unchallenged, and if they go unchallenged, we cannot learn new perspectives.[7] One must retain a healthy suspicion of the sources, the various voices they may embed, and one's own unexamined presumptions in order to recognize the points of conjunction and disjunction among sixteenth-century views of women, one's own, and the Nahua images. Those scholars who see all Nahua goddesses merely as versions of a single Great Mother Earth perhaps are allowing their own presumptions too much of a voice.[8] Cihuacoatl is unique: As a war strategist, she is not restricted to the earth; as a matronly dowager, she is more than a mother. Motherhood is, at best, a peripheral aspect.[9]

## More Than Earth

The early sources evoke a large variety of different images portraying Cihuacoatl and Tlacaellel, the male governmental official who bore her name. The sixteenth-century friars Bernardino de Sahagún and Diego Durán offer the most information. Sahagún accents her ritual aspects, especially those having to do with birth, while Durán, in volume one of his history (Durán 1992), focuses on her historical aspects, especially those having to do with her form as a human governor, and in volume two, on her ritual aspects (Durán 1971). The Spanish also commissioned native artists to create books mimicking their pre-Conquest style of pictographic writing. These pictorial collections offer information as well. The *Codex Borbonicus*, a book on the Nahua ritual calendar, accents the ritual role that Tlacaellel played as the Cihuacoatl, and the *Codex Magliabechiano*, a book describing Mexican "evil rites and superstitions," emphasizes aspects of death and sacrifice. A number of dispersed references exist in other sources as well (see, e.g., *Codex Mendoza* 1992; Tezozómoc 1992; Torquemada 1969; Serna 1953; and Garibay 1965).

It is not surprising that the most derogatory references appear in the texts that have the most Spanish feel to them. For example, Durán frequently accents negative aspects in those things related to sacrifice and religion. It appears that blood and violence held a great fascination for him, and the case of Cihuacoatl is no exception. Therefore, he elaborates in great detail on the gory aspects of sacrificial rituals associated with Cihuacoatl, while ignoring a host of other possible topics. Sahagún calls Cihuacoatl a "beast" who brings "misery" in the same book of the *Florentine* where he calls her a devil, exhorting the reader to avoid idolatry (FC 1.6: 11, 1.16: 63, 69–70). But in the passages from another book describing birth rituals and in a Nahuatl poem, he presents no negative references (FC 6.27–29, 6.31: 151–165, 179–182, 2.236). Perhaps it was not the Nahuas who saw Cihuacoatl as a terrible goddess but only the Spanish. This negative attitude, so typical of sixteenth-century thought, is hinted at elsewhere in passages such as one calling her the "fallen Eve" (Garibay 1965, 122).

Cihuacoatl, however, was much more than the early Spanish image of hell-bound monster or loving mother. Rather, she was primarily a matron and war strategist who lent her powers to a human ruler. Moreover, she counted the entire cosmos as her domain. Snakewoman attended to domestic affairs with the same strong control that a wise, confident, and imposing dowager might wield. She created the war strategy used by women and men on the battlefields of both childbirth and conquest. Through her name and vestments, she lent counseling powers to the inside ruler Cihuacoatl Tlacaellel, who, as would a matron, handled the domestic affairs of Tenochtitlan and created its political and military strategy.

### *Matron and Female Warrior*

As a matron, Cihuacoatl provided food for the Fifth Sun, the age of the Nahua peoples. One well-known myth describes how Cihuacoatl shaped people from the fertilized ground bones of a man and woman just as a woman forms tortillas from ground maize (*Codex Chimalpopoca* 1992, 145–146). Her dough was moistened by blood from the penis of the god Quetzalcoatl,[10] who had just stolen the bones from the Land of the Dead, bringing them to her in the Land of the Western Tree. The story's teller calls her Quilaztli (Edible Heron Herb),[11] perhaps because she was patron of the agricultural fields and their products, including maize. Therefore, as part of her matronly duties, Cihuacoatl also prepared tortillas for the gods, that is, human "tortillas."

The only direct references to Cihuacoatl as a mother come in texts specifically referring to birth; there she is addressed as Tonan, or Our Mother (FC 6.26–35: 149–196). But, in the same texts many more forms of address are used for Cihuacoatl, including Quilaztli, War Woman, Noble Woman, and Eagle Woman. Moreover, the sun likewise is addressed as Your Mother, Your Father (*in monan, in nota*) (FC 6.29: 164). Perhaps *tonan* was simply a form of polite address and should not be taken literally. Frances Karttunen (1986) notes a number of ancient Nahuatl kinship addresses that may have had little to do with signifying one's relatives but everything to do with expressing polite behavior. She reports that "the paired terms, *-nan -tah* 'mother, father'," were often used for aides and skilled assistants. In other words, Cihuacoatl's ability to assist women in childbirth was the important issue here, not her ability to bear children.

As a Nahua matron, Cihuacoatl expressed the intimate complementarity between creation and destruction. Creation resulted in destruction and vice versa, an interdependency that was viewed as a simple fact of reality (Read 1998, ch. 5). One story relates how Cihuacoatl cried out to all in the marketplace that she would be leaving the Mexica soon; she warned them that their destruction was imminent. A similar story takes place in the fabled Mexica homeland Aztlan. There Huitzilopochtli's mother Coatlicue warned the magicians of Chief Speaker Motecuhzoma I that their god Huitzilopochtli would soon abandon them, and their many conquests would turn against them in the same order they had been conquered. These stories suggest that whatever was created inevitably would be destroyed, what is born eventually must die.

One of Snakewoman's primary duties was to aide warriors and create effective strategies for warfare. As a strategist in the war for childbirth (FC 6.24–38: 135–208), she was considered a wise counselor, presenting a model of valor for women entering parturition's battlefield. Her image as a seasoned and knowledgeable female military general seems extremely appropriate. Even with modern medicine, birth is difficult, requiring great physical strength, concentration, and bravery—the same qualities one needs in war. How much more appropriate in an era when childbirth was one of the leading causes of death among women and their children?

A symbolic homology existed among the battles of birth, agriculture, and conquest in which a captive became simultaneously a member of the captor's family and corn to feed the Fifth Age.[12] If a birthing mother emerged victorious, she captured her new infant as a military warrior took a captive. Later, the small child was likened to young maize stalks captured in symbolic battle from new fields (Durán 1971, 423–424).[13] Extending the homology, male captive warriors were considered corn for the gods (Durán 1992, ch. 28). In the feast of Tlacaxipihualiztli, the male war captive became a member of his captor's family[14]; likewise in the female war of birth, the infant captive became a member of its mother's family. These were all likened to each other because they all constituted edible products such as corn.

As a woman of the sky (*jluicacioa*) and noble woman (*cihuapilli*), Cihuacoatl acted as the patroness of male warriors. Whenever a mother died in childbirth, she transformed into one of the celestial goddesses (*cihuapipilli*) who, each day at noon, captured the sun from dead male warriors. The dead mother's power to win in war was so strong, that young male warriors "truly made war" on her relatives in an effort to capture a middle finger and a bit of hair from the body of the deceased. The young warriors attached these body parts to their shields in order to tap into their powers for making a warrior valiant and for paralyzing the feet of his enemy.[15]

As Eagle Woman (*quauhcihuatl*) and dressed in the eagle plumes of the great warrior Mixcoatl, Cihuacoatl carried a shield made also of eagle plumes and she wielded a weapon-like weaving batten.[16] Perhaps because war resulted in death, Cihuacoatl sometimes also wore a jawbone and tangled hair associated with the Land of Death (*Codex Borbonicus* 1974, pls. 23, 26–28, 36f.; *Codex Magliabechiano* 1983a, 45r, 91r). The Nahua considered these powers both important and positive because the underworld required dead beings to eat in order to sustain the living on Earth's Surface and in the sky.

### *Male Matron and Inside Ruler*

Cihuacoatl's powers appear even more complex when we consider her human governmental counterpart the Tlacaellel. This office existed in several Nahua centers. High governmental officials in Texcoco and Azcapotzalco bore the title of Cihuacoatl (H. B. Nicholson, personal communication, 20 August 1996), and the goddess claimed attention in Xochimilco and Chalco (Durán 1971, 13: 210; Garibay 1965, 40; FC 2.app.: 236). She was probably the patron deity of

*Figure 3.2: Cihuacoatl in her guise as a noble woman.* (© *Kay A. Read.*)

Culhuacan.[17] Acamapichtli, Tenochtitlan's first Chief Speaker (ca. 1364–1404),[18] claimed lineage to Culhuacan through his mother and held the title of Cihuacoatl before becoming Chief Speaker (*Codex Mendoza* 1992, 8; 1980, 2v). Her importance in Tenochtitlan perhaps rose a bit when, in the epoch of Itzcoatl (1424–1440/45) and Motecuhzoma I (1440/45–1469), the Mexica conquered a region of great agricultural wealth that included Xochimilco and Chalco (Klein 1988, 238–239; *Codex Mendoza* 1992, 15; 1980, 5v, 6r, 7v, 8r). Cihuacoatl's temple, for example, was established in Tenochtitlan after the conquest of another regional city, Cuitlahuac.[19]

It is possible that, with the capture of Cihuacoatl and her centers, she assumed new forms more appropriate to a vanquished but honored warrior. Durán (1971, 13: 217) tells us that the Mexica called her the sister of their patron deity, Huitzilopochtli. This could indicate that Cihuacoatl had become his wife, for Karttunen (1986, 3) reports that "elder-sister-cousin" was a polite address used by a husband for his bride. As Durán writes in Spanish, not Nahuatl, it is difficult to know precisely, but such a relationship fits the pattern of wives offered as war tribute.[20] During Cihuacoatl's festival, Huey Tecuilhuitl, both she and a young Nahua goddess named Xilonen wore their hair down: Cihuacoatl in the manner of those associated with the Land of Death, Xilonen in the manner of a vegetation goddess.[21] Perhaps the agricultural regions' productive lands had become symbolic vanquished warrior women, who wore their hair down because they now produced fruits for Tenochtitlan and not for their own cities.

If so, with this conquest, the Mexica won both natural and supernatural tribute of goods and women.

Cihuacoatl's powers of war and her association with Mictlan may have helped control the wars of conquest. The *Codex Borbonicus* (1974, pls. 23, 26–28, 36–37) shows the Snakewoman Tlacaellel wearing an ocelot-skin blouse, Cihuacoatl's vestments of eagle feathers, and the jawbone and tangled hair of the underworld. Durán (1992, 362) tells his readers that, when the Tlacaellel died during the time of Ahuitzotl (1486–1503), the Mexica may have carried his embalmed body into the victorious war with the urban center of Tliliuhquitepec. Like the young warriors who wore the fingers and hair belonging to the powerful Cihuapipiltin, the Tlacaelleltin[22] wore powerful garments belonging to the vanquished warrior-woman Cihuacoatl and, when dead, their bodies helped warriors win battles.

Cihuacoatl's governmental office drew also on her matronly powers. As each woman had her work taking care of the home and training the children, much of the Tlacaellel's duties involved taking care of the city and training young Chief Speakers. Hence one can call the Snakewoman the inside ruler of Tenochtitlan. Like a midwife who, with Cihuacoatl's powers, would counsel her patient and carefully plan the strategy for parturition's war, the Tlacaellel used this goddess' powers to counsel the city on matters of war and political strategy.[23] Rarely leaving the city on official business, his most important tasks took place at home; even when a ruler was very young and inexperienced, the Tlacaellel did not accompany him into battle (Durán 1992, 299).

Before the reign of Motecuhzoma II (1503–1520) the Cihuacoatl Tlacaellel exercised tremendous power, different from but often as critical as the Tlatoani's. When offered the office of Tlatoani after Tizoc's death (1486), the Tlacaellel refused, noting that he already had the powers of a king and needed no more (Durán 1992, 311; Torquemada 1969, 1.2.54: 171.1, 2.2.25: 352.1–353.2; Tezozómoc 1992, 218: 121). The Tlatoani and the Cihuacoatl Tlacaellel usually operated in different areas. On the one hand, the Cihuacoatl's primary duties involved less overtly aggressive activities, although on very rare occasions he went to war when needed (see, e.g., Durán 1992, 82, 429). As the Snakewoman, he served primarily as a domestic counselor and military aide par excellence. Besides counseling, his duties included governing the city when the Tlatoani was at war (Durán 1992, 299, 423–424), receiving the prisoners of war and visiting dignitaries in the Tlatoani's absence (Durán 1992, 415), welcoming the ruler home from battle (Durán 1992, 169, 289, 328–336), ruling over one of Tenochtitlan's sectors, which included the temple of Cihuacoatl (Tezozómoc 1992, 273: 140–141; van Zantwijk 1966, 182), and judging elite crimes (see, e.g., Durán 1992, 311; Torquemada 1969, 2.2.25: 352.1–352.2). On the other hand, when acting as a farmer, the Tlatoani (Read 1994, 50–57, 1995, 8–12, 2000, 1–2) marshaled and controlled an efficient work force and sustained a bountiful environment. As a ferocious warrior, he expanded his territory, controlled and exploited his conquests, and harvested sacrificial offerings. Exercising his sexual power, he crossed normal Nahua social boundaries in order to safeguard a strong fecundity for the city's kinline. A city depended on the strength of its royal line; if the line failed, the city failed.

Therefore, even though a ruler had one primary wife, he also could have as many as a hundred or more other wives, and he was expected to procreate with as many as possible.[24] Finally, as the Chief Speaker, he cooperatively ensured people's appropriate behavior so that the social order could be maintained. Although not all these activities took place in foreign lands, the first three usually involved both outsiders and war. Agricultural productivity, for example, was increased through aggressive territorial expansion.

I suggest this dual leadership operated along the lines of what Michael Walzer (1983, 3–30) has called "complex equalities" (Read 1995). In this system (perhaps better thought of as one of complex differences than equalities), social goods are distributed via local, interlocked spheres of influence interacting with each other. Each distinctive sphere creates its own particular identity; harmony is maintained as long as the boundaries between spheres are maintained. But because spheres are necessarily different from one another, conflicts are endemic (Walzer 1983, 318). In other words, harmony exists as long as the boundaries are kept clear, but that necessity inevitably leads to conflict and often rapid shifts in boundary definition. If boundaries are not maintained, tyranny can replace harmony.

The Mexica system defined the Cihuacoatl's and Tlatoani's spheres of influence according to their specific duties. Although their duties occasionally overlapped (especially in ritual and when the Chief Speaker was unavailable), the Tlatoani concentrated largely on affairs outside the city, especially in matters of provisions and war, while the Cihuacoatl largely organized affairs inside the city, especially in matters of ritual and political and military strategy. Like his goddess, he was the aide that surpassed all aides, the honored matron of the city.[25] It is doubtful that these two spheres operated in a totally balanced harmony throughout Mexica history. Many references to the great powers of the Tlatoani and the differential distribution of tribute and favors suggest otherwise. But as was noted previously, statements to the contrary also exist that describe Tlacaellel as a kind of ruler with powers matching those of the Tlatoani. These apparent contradictions can be explained if one sees Mexica history as a case of shifting boundaries between Walzerian spheres, in which their neat balanced harmony broke apart under certain circumstances.

For example, Johanna Broda (1978, 221–270) noticed that, on the eve of the Conquest (1521), the Tlatoani's and Cihuacoatl's relations appeared to be unequal and their differences seemed to be growing. Although little discord between the two is recorded, it is interesting to note that except for one diplomatic appearance at the death of Texcoco's Tlatoani Nezahuapilli, the Cihuacoatl disappears from the scene in the latter period of Motecuhzoma II's reign. This disappearance occurs shortly after the deaths of the two previous Snakewomen, one in Axayacatl's reign (1440/45–1469), the other in that of the Ahuitzotl (1486–1503), who ruled just before Motecuhzoma II (1503–1520) (Tezozómoc 1992, 222: 122, 301: 146). This was not, I think, a loss of an earlier egalitarianism in favor of greater stratification, as Broda suggests. The stratification between these spheres existed from early on; indeed the Cihuacoatl had less power during the first Tlatoani

Acamapichtli's reign (1364–1404) than he did later on, which suggests that a return to an earlier form of stratification appears to be at work during Motecuhzoma II's reign.

Such a return may point to the discord that occurs between spheres of influence. Because three people had held the position of Cihuacoatl in short succession, it is likely that the office had become unstable, unable to maintain clear boundaries around its proper sphere of influence. This then would have given the Tlatoani a chance to take more power, redefining the boundaries between his and the Cihuacoatl's sphere while greatly expanding and elevating his own. Indeed, the more this ruler moved toward a kind of tyranny, his Snakewoman appears to act less as a strategist and more as one who carried out the Chief Speaker's often unpleasant orders. But such a singular attempt to attain both the inside and outside powers might have worked against the Mexica in the end. Because of the Tlatoani's tyranny, many enemies were willing to challenge him by allying with Cortés,[26] and when Cortés seized Motecuhzoma II, no one strong enough remained to take up the cause in his absence. Just as in her warning for all to hear in the marketplace, Cihuacoatl had left their home. She had abandoned the Mexica.

The varied, puzzling descriptions and apparently contradictory depictions of Cihuacoatl make sense in the end. Once sixteenth-century Spanish interpretations of her are understood as often shaped by their own visions of the world, her complexities become more comprehensible. As with all Nahua deities, she wielded a complex but related array of powers that varied according to particular circumstances. As a matron and war strategist, she counted the entire Mexica cosmos as her domain. As a matronly midwife, female warriors fighting on parturition's battlefield hoped to successfully capture their child with her wise and clever counsel. As the male matron of Tenochtitlan and the Mexica's inside ruler, Snakewoman contributed both to its success and, with her leaving, to its collapse. Cihuacoatl, inhabitant of both sky and underworld, certainly extended her wisdom and powers over more than Earth's Surface.

## NOTES

Earlier versions of this chapter were delivered on two occasions: (1) Tercer Simposio Internacional de Códices y Documentos (Puebla Mexico, August 1996) as *Madre Tierra y más: Cihuacoatl como madre, guerrera, y gobernante interior*; and (2) American Academy of Religion (New Orleans, November 1996) as *More than Earth: Cihuacoatl as Mother, Warrior, and Inside Ruler*. My thanks go to Ian Evison, for offering wonderful help on the issue of the Euro-American Earth Mother; Laura Grillo, for offering some very useful insights into Cihuacoatl's matronly character; and Carol Anderson, for commenting on portions of the drafts.

1. The term *Aztecs* is both somewhat historically inaccurate and quite imprecise. Therefore, many scholars now use *Mexica* for those people whom Cortés conquered in 1521 and *Nahua* for those who shared the language of Nahuatl.
2. This name may form an appropriate picture of the agricultural regions such as Chalco and Xochimilco from whence the title originated because its roots appear

to be *quilitl* (edible herbs) and *aztatl* (heron). However, translating Nahuatl names can be tricky, and this one is such a case. It appears to break down like so: <quil[itl]>-<az[tatl]>-tli or <edible herb>-<heron>-noun ending. But this does not account for the *ta* in *aztatl*. Because of this discrepancy, I will not automatically translate Quilaztli's name into English as its meaning is not completely clear.

3. One of the places to which the dead go is Mictlan, which is described as a dark place with no smoke holes (FC 3.app. 1: 42).
4. The Spanish who collected the resources we use today were a varied lot. A large number were clerics, but others included military personnel, governmental officials, and business men. Most of these men were informed by sixteenth- and seventeenth-century Roman Catholic sensibilities.
5. The many, diverse resources on the pre-Conquest Nahua include (a) histories and descriptions of religious beliefs and practices written in Spanish, such as those by Durán; (b) Sahagún's twelve-volume medieval-style encyclopedia in both Spanish and Nahuatl; (c) codices containing Nahua songs and poetry; (d) codices drawn in pictures, sometimes closely mimicking the indigenous glyphic style of writing, and always including Spanish commentaries; and (e) archaeological evidence. For the Mexica, only the last is truly primary, for all the others were either written or commissioned by the Spanish, or written by Spanish-tutored natives. Although these sources were often based on interviews, older but now lost texts (some probably pre-Conquest), or on an author's general knowledge, all are laden with the perceptions and immediate concerns of their authors and, therefore, must be used carefully. Although not strictly primary, those sources collected in Nahuatl and in glyphic or pictorial forms offer particularly important information in this difficult research situation because their use of original forms of expression sometimes allows their authors to subtly circumvent the Spanish collectors' voices.
6. For example, because she was a divorced woman with two children, the Australian Aborigines placed the ethnographer Diane Bell (1984) in their women's house. No one had ever been allowed in that area before, for no one had so clearly fit aborigine models of femininity. On the other hand, the ethnographer Nancy Munn, even though a woman, acted like a man and so they classified her as one (personal communication, Mary MacDonald, 28 October 1996).
7. See Read (1998, 29–43) for more on methodological issues concerning analogical interpretation, and for a few Euro-American analogies that need rethinking in light of Nahua culture.
8. Moreover, in order to postulate a single Great Mother behind all Nahua goddesses, often authors employ a selective interpretation that denies interpretive parity between male and female deities and counters the evidence. Such authors claim that, if one goddess bears another's marks, it shows their essential unity. But this is not the case. All gods bore transitory potencies manifested in such things as their body parts, deeds, names, clothing, and hairstyle (López Austin 1988, 1990; Townsend 1992, 115–116; Read 1998, chap. 5); thus the most one can say is that imprecise complexes of deities existed, which temporarily shared some similar qualities and powers (Caso 1996; Nicholson 1971, 395–445). That is, if a deity bears the insignia of another god, it does not mean that they are the same; it only means that the first god bears some of the second's powers at that particular moment. If the male god Xolotl wears Quetzalcoatl's pectoral, it does not mean that Xolotl is an avatar of Quetzalcoatl but that, among all his powers, Xolotl has some of Quetzalcoatl's powers at that moment. And, if Cihuacoatl wears the underworld's jaw bone and hairstyle, it does not mean that she is an avatar of some earth mother but that,

among all her powers, she has two of the underworld's powers at that moment. (See Caso 1996; Pasztory 1976; Heyden 1979; López Austin 1990; and Klein 1988).

9. In earlier versions of this essay, an historiographic exploration and an explicit comparison of five specific characteristics common to the Euro-American Great Earth Mother model pointed out the huge differences between her and Cihuacoatl.
10. Quetzalcoatl was an ancient creator and trickster god and a patron of rulers. As was also true of Cihuacoatl, he displayed a multifaceted personality and bore many complex potencies. Nahua deities never retained absolute control over a single aspect. Hence it is a mistake to assume that the deities can be arranged in some sort of logical pantheon, in which they remain in stable relationships to one another. Each Nahua god wielded transitory powers that could be shifted around and borrowed like so many pieces of clothing. Which set of powers a deity bore at any given moment depended on what the particular circumstances demanded (see note 8). This meant that a deity's personality and his or her consequent relations with other deities and beings constantly shifted.
11. See note 2.
12. War was a pervasive symbol structuring much of Nahua reality, from politics to the home, because war gained the things needed to survive. Indeed, it is sometimes useful to think of almost the entire cosmos in terms of war. This did not mean that constant feuding within the family or among neighbors occurred or that outside enemies were always attacking (although warfare among cities was common). Rather, certain actions were described in the imagery of war. For example, at harvest time, crops were symbolically "attacked," and first fruits must be captured as though they were enemy warriors. A successful childbirth was considered a battle in which the mother "captured" her child. If the mother died, she was likened to a male warrior who had died on the battlefield.
13. Both corn and children came from Tamoanchan, the cosmic tree in the west, where Cihuacoatl-Quilaztli ground the bones into dough to shape people (*Codex Chimalpopoca* 1992, 145–146; FC 6.30: 167). And at a child's birth a midwife asked if the child would become a "smutty ear of corn" by failing in its duties (FC 6.30: 168).
14. In the feast of Tlacaxipihualiztli, the captor could not eat the flesh of his captive because he had become his captive's father (FC 2.23: 54).
15. Again, the symbolic and concrete power of war is evident. The young warriors attacked the bodies of women who had died in childbirth's "battle" because they needed their body parts to protect them and give them strength in their own battles. These men were not necessarily enemies of the women's families, although the women's male relatives vigorously protected their bodies while they were in transit to burial or cremation. Instead, female valor in war endowed body parts with concrete powers that could help male warriors, making them especially valuable (FC 6.29: 161–162).
16. For Cihuacoatl's visual appearance, see *The Florentine Codex* (FC 2.app.: 236; 1.6: 11; illus. 6) and the *Codex Borbonicus* (1974, pls. 23, 26, 27, 28, 36, 37). The Nahuatl text in the *Florentine* referring to Mixcoatl reads literally "before my noble person no longer [of] Mixcoatl land" (*iehoa nopiltzin aia mjscoatlan*). Since the poem is about a female deity, it does not make sense to translate the ungendered root for noble person (*-pil<li>-*) in masculine terms as the authors have done. The phrase seems to imply that this noble woman once was from Mixcoatl's land, but now no longer is (FC 6.app.: 236). Torquemada also links her with Mixcoatl (1969, 2.8.12: 148.2–149.1). See Heyden (1979) for further iconographic references to Cihuacoatl.

17. She also may have been important in Chalma (FC 2.app.: 236–237; Garibay 1965, 52; van Zantwijk 1966, 182).
18. The exact dates of the reigns of Mexica rulers vary with the source; for the sake of consistency, I use the dates given by Durán in his *Historia* or, when those are lacking, the *Codex Chimalpopoca* and the *Florentine Codex*.
19. Torquemada (1969, 1.2.42: 150.1) also reports that the temple to Huitzilopochtli was built the year following the erection of Cihuacoatl's temple, perhaps in part as a result of the successful wars in the agricultural region.
20. It was common with each conquest to give women to the conquering ruler. This indicated an agreement to alliance helping to extend the royal kinship line (Durán 1992; van Zantwijk 1985, 179; Read 2000).
21. Unbound hair indicated that either one was associated with the underworld or with agricultural production. In the first, the hair was tangled and matted, indicating the dirtiness and rotting infestation of the Land of Death. Therefore, people in mourning let their hair loose, neither washing nor delousing it. In the second, the hair lay smooth and clean like corn silk. Cihuacoatl is described as fitting the first category, and Xilonen, clearly a vegetation goddess, the second (Durán 1971, 212; *Codex Magliabechiano* 1983a, 36r; Heyden 1979, 6). The two are symbolically compatible, for the cycle of destruction and creation easily links the underworld with fruits of the field.
22. There were more than one Tlacaeleltin, indicating that Tlacaellel was a title of office and not the name of a man (Tezozómoc 1992, 222: 122, 301: 146).
23. Durán (1992) gives innumerable examples of Tlacaellel's governmental counseling duties, which included telling the ruler when and how to wage war and deal with foreign diplomats.
24. A ruler's wives appear to have broken down into three categories: (a) the primary wife, whose children usually (though not always) provided the pool for electing the next ruler; (b) secondary wives, who came as tribute from allied cities; and (c) tertiary wives, who came as tribute from conquered cities. This ranking also seems to have coordinated with how the ruler doled out his sexual favors for both political and physical reasons. Marriage and heirs, even for the conquered, could bring certain privileges; but also, the creation of children altered the powers of the royal line itself, making it preferable to gain potential heirs from powerful lineages and not from those who were so weak as to be conquered. See Read (2000) for more information on rulers' sexuality.
25. This situation recalls the political systems of the Cherokees and Natchez in North America. In these relatively small societies, there were two high positions of power, one to attend to the concerns of the community (often described as peaceful) and one to attend to those of war, one leader who stayed home and one who went out. The parallels between these systems and those of the Mexica are not exact. The divisions among the Cherokees and Natchez appear to have been quite sharply defined, at least at the time of contact. Among the Mexica, however, the divisions between the Tlatoani and the Cihuacoatl are not as clearly defined, overlapping at times and changing at other times in a way reminiscent of Nahua gender roles. Nor is there ever a sharp contrast drawn between peace and war. Nevertheless, a consideration of a possible dual leadership among the Mexica might prove fruitful. After all, the two cooperative rulers in both Chalco and Xochimilco—the region in which the goddess Cihuacoatl appears to have been particularly important—indicate that dual leadership was already practiced in the Nahua area.

26. A number of cities in the area allied with Cortés to fight the unpopular Mexica, including both traditional enemies such as Tlaxcala and Cholula, and even very close allies such as Texcoco. Without these allies, Cortés surely would not have been as successful as he was.

REFERENCES

Bell, Diane. 1984. "Introduction: Women and Aboriginal Religion." Pp. 295–303 in *Religion in Aboriginal Australia*, ed. Max Charlesworth, H. Murphy et al. St. Lucia: University of Queenland Press.

———. 1984a. "Women's Business is Hard Work: Central Australian Aboriginal Women's Love Rituals." Pp. 345–369 in *Religion in Aboriginal Australia*, ed. Max Charlesworth, H. Murphy et al. St. Lucia: University of Queenland Press.

Broda, Johanna. 1978. "Relaciones políticas ritualizadas: El ritual como una expresión de una ideología." Pp. 221–270 in *Economía política e ideología en el México prehispánico*, ed. Pedro Carrasco and Johanna Broda. Mexico: Centro de Investigaciones Superiores del Instituto Nacional de Antropología e Historia.

Caso, Alfonso. 1996. *El pueblo del sol*. Mexico: Fondo de Cultura Económica. 1st edition, 1953.

*Codex Borbonicus*. 1974. With commentary by K. A. Nowotny. Facsimile ed. Graz, Austria: Akademische Druck, U. Verlagsanstalt.

*Codex Chimalpahin*. 1982. *Relaciones originales de Chalco Amaquemecan: Escritas por Don Francisco de San Antón Chimalpahin Cuauhtlehuanitzin*, trans. S. Rendón. Mexico: Fondo de Cultura Económica.

*Codex Chimalpopoca*. 1992. In *History and Mythology of the Aztecs: Codex Chimalpopoca*, trans. John Bierhorst. Tucson: University of Arizona Press.

*Codex Magliabechiano*. 1983a. As reproduced in *The Book of the Life of the Ancient Mexicans*. Part I. Facsimile by Zelia Nuttall, ed. Elizabeth Hill Boone. Berkeley, CA: University of California Press.

———. 1983b. *The Codex Magliabechiano and the Lost Prototype of the Magliabechiano Group*. Ed. and commentary by Elizabeth Hill Boone. Berkeley, CA: University of California Press.

*Codex Mendoza* (vol. 2). 1992. Commentary and ed. by Frances Berdan and Patricia Rieff Anawalt. Berkeley, CA: University of California Press.

———. 1980. Reproduced in *Colección de Mendoza o Códice Mendocino: Documento Mexicano del siglo XVI que se conserva en la Biblioteca Bodleiana de Oxford, Inglaterra*, ed. Don Francisco del Paso y Troncoso. Original edition, 1925. Mexico: Editorial Innovación, S.A.

Durán, Fray Diego. 1971. *Book of the Gods and Rites and the Ancient Calendar*, trans. Fernando Horcasitas and Doris Heyden. Norman: University of Oklahoma Press.

———. 1992. *The History of the Indies of New Spain*, trans. Doris Heyden. Norman: University of Oklahoma Press.

Garibay, Angel Maria K., ed. 1965. *Teogonía e historia de los Mexicanos: Tres opósculos de siglo XVI*. Mexico City: Editorial Porrúa.

Heyden, Doris. 1979. "The Many Faces of the Mother Goddess: Deities of Water and Sustenance." Presented at the International Congress of Americanists, Vancouver. Photocopied.

Kartunnen, Frances. 1986. "Indirection and Inversion." Paper presented at the eighty-fifth annual meeting of the American Anthropology Association, Philadelphia. Photocopied.

Klein, Cecelia. 1988. "Rethinking Cihuacoatl: Aztec Political Imagery of the Conquered Woman." Pp. 237–277 in *Smoke and Mist: Mesoamerican Studies in Memory of Thelma D. Sullivan*, ed. J. Katheryn Josserand and Karen Dakin. London: B. A. R.

López Austin, Alfredo. 1988. *The Human Body and Ideology: Concepts of the Ancient Nahua*, trans. Thelma Ortiz de Montellano and Bernard Ortiz de Montellano. Salt Lake City: University of Utah Press.

———. 1990. *Los Mitos del Tlacuache*. Mexico: Alianza.

———. 1994. *Tamoanchan y Tlalocan*. Mexico: Fondo de Cultura Económica.

Nicholson, H. B. 1971. "Religion in Pre-Hispanic Central Mexico." Pp. 395–446 in *Handbook of Middle American Indians* (vol. 10, pt. 1), ed. Gordon F. Ekholm and Ignacio Bernal. Austin: University of Texas Press.

Pasztory, Esther. 1976. *The Murals of Tepantitla, Teotihuacan*. New York: Garland Publishing.

Read, Kay A. 1994. "Sacred Commoners: The Motion of Cosmic Powers in Mexica Rulership." *History of Religions Journal* 34 (August): 39–69.

———. 1995. "Huitzilopochtli and Quetzalcoatl: Ethical Images of Rulership at Tenochtitlan and Teotihuacan." Presented at the International History of Religions Conference, Mexico City. Photocopied.

———. 1998. *Time and Sacrifice in the Aztec Cosmos*. Bloomington: Indiana University Press.

———. 2000. "Sex, War, and Rulers: Mexica Royal Images of Boundary Breaking and Making." In *In Chalchiutl, In Quetzalli*, ed. Eloise Quiñones Keber. Lancaster, PA: Labyrinthos Press.

Sahagún, Fray Bernardino de. 1953–1982. *The Florentine Codex: A General History of the Things of New Spain*, trans. Arthur J. O. Anderson and Charles E. Dibble. [Monographs of the School of American Research, no. 14.] (12 bks., 13 pts.). Santa Fe, NM: School of American Research; and Salt Lake City: University of Utah Press.

Serna, Jacinto de la. 1953. "Manual de ministros de indios para el conocimiento de sus idolatrías y extirpación de ellas." Pp. 47–368 in *Tratado de las idolatrías, supersticiones, dioses, ritos, hechicerías y otras costumbres gentílicas de las razas aborígenes de México* (vol 1). Commentary by Francisco del Paso y Troncoso. 2 vols. Mexico: Ediciones Fuente Cultural.

Sprenger, J., and H. Kramer. 1948. *Malleus Maleficarum*, trans. Montague Summers. London: Pushkin Press.

Tezozómoc, Fernando Alvarado. 1992. *Crónica Mexicáyotl*, trans. Adrián León. Mexico: Universidad Nacional Autónoma de México.

Torquemada, Juan de. 1969. *Monarquia Indiana*. Introduction by León Portilla. (3 vols.). Mexico City: Editorial Porrúa.

Townsend, Richard F. 1992. *The Aztecs*. London: Thames and Hudson.

van Zantwijk, Rudolf. 1966. "Los seis barrios sirvientes de Huitzilopochtli." Pp. 177–185 in *Estudios de cultura nahuatl* (vol. 6). Mexico: Universidad Autónoma de México.

———. 1985. *The Aztec Arrangement: The Social History of Pre-Spanish Mexico*. Norman: University of Oklahoma Press.

Walzer, Michael. 1983. *Spheres of Justice: A Defense of Pluralism and Equality*. New York: Basic Books.

# 4

# Inanna

## The Star Who Became Queen

*Beverly Moon*

The Sumerian goddess Inanna was worshipped in ancient Mesopotamia, the land between the rivers Euphrates and Tigris, for more than 4,000 years. Although the origins of her cult lie in prehistory, between the arrival of the Sumerians ca. 3500 BCE and the transformation of the Near East under Islam in 637 CE this goddess, known as the Queen of Heaven, played a central role in the religious life of the many peoples who came to make this land their home. The Akkadians and Babylonians, who came to dominate the area after the Sumerians (ca. 2300 BCE), continued to worship her but called her Ishtar. Even the Hebrews of Judaea, forced to live and work in Babylonia from 586 to 538 BCE during what is called the Babylonian Exile, knew her: They learned how to bake crescent cakes marked with her image and offered her libations (Jeremiah 44.19).

### The Star Goddess

The most central and enduring symbol of Inanna is the eight-pointed star. The star represents her astral form, the morning and evening star (the planet Venus). One Sumerian hymn addresses her as a torch in the sky:

The pure torch lit in the sky,
the heavenly light, lighting like day,
the great queen of heaven, Inanna,
I will hail! (Jacobsen 1987, 13)

As the evening and morning star, Inanna helps to create the rhythm of daily existence. When she appears in the evening sky, all the creatures of Sumer—animals and people alike—prepare for bed, for sleep and love making. With her arrival at dawn, the people are called forth to work and to the concerns of community, above all the workings of social justice:

When sweet sleep has ended in the bedchamber
You appear like bright daylight.
When all the lands and the people of Sumer assemble,
Those sleeping on the roofs and those sleeping by the walls,
When they sing your praises, bringing their concerns to you,
You study their words.
You render a cruel judgment against the evildoer;
You destroy the wicked.
You look with kindly eyes on the straightforward;
You give that one your blessing. (Wolkstein and Kramer 1983, 103)

The Sumerians believed that the land belonged to the gods, and that they were servants of the gods. The gods, insisting that human beings live righteously, intervened in times of injustice.

Not only did Inanna serve to mark the beginning and end of the day, but as a star she was the object of intense observation. Sumerians believed that the heaven itself was an unmoving vault, that the sun, moon, and stars—both fixed and moving stars (or planets)—were divine beings whose movements could be interpreted as messages to those living on earth. Their tall temples, or ziggurats, served also as observatories. Each included a room called the "house of observation" (*bīt tamarti*), where astrologists observed and recorded celestial activity, interpreting the significance of individual events. These records survive; the oldest one is known as "When Anu and Enlil" and includes, for example, this astrological omen: "If Inanna appears in the East in the month of Airu and the Great and Small Twins surround her, all four of them, and she is dark, then will the King of Elam fall sick and not remain alive" (van der Waerden 1974, 49).

The kings of Sumer—and later those of Akkad, Babylonia, and Assyria—turned to Inanna not only for guidance but also for the gift of kingship. For in ancient Mesopotamia kingship was not inherited but bestowed by the gods, often through ritual marriage to the goddess Inanna.

## Kingship in Ancient Sumer

Sumerian kingship developed gradually out of an ancient form of "primitive democracy." Immigrating into Mesopotamia during the middle of the fourth millennium from somewhere in south central Asia, the Sumerians lived in small city-states. These were governed by local assemblies consisting of free males and a group of elders, bound together by allegiance to the city's chief deity. During times of war or natural disaster, such as flood or famine, a temporary single military ruler, the *lugal* (or "big man"), could be appointed.

Over time, military invasions of Semitic nomads, moving out of the Syrian and Arabian desert lands to the west, together with increased competition among the Sumerian city-states for political sovereignty led to the establishment of the *lugal* as a permanent role. Furthermore, there was a tendency for the role of military leader to merge with another Sumerian position of leadership, the *en*, a more religious figure. He or she played the role of spouse to the city's patron deity in the annual New Year celebrations. "One might speak of a 'priest-king' or 'priest-queen'" (Jacobsen 1987a, 9.449). More generally, the *en* was an inner ruler, responsible for city affairs, while the *lugal* conducted the defense of the city.

Eventually the two roles were combined under one person who was called the *ensi*, or king: "It is in fact asserted in the royal hymns that the king unites in his office the positions of *en* and *lugal*" (Ringgren 1973, 37). In this way the earliest royal dynasties were formed, the king living initially in the north, in Kish, and later, in other cities, such as Uruk and Ur. Uruk (modern Warka) was the city of Inanna. Her main temple, the Eanna, or House of Heaven, was located there.

As an institution, Sumerian kingship continued well after the Sumerians themselves ceased to exist. Around 2330 BCE, Sargon, a Semitic ruler from Arabia, conquered the Sumerians. Sargon established his government in Agade (biblical Akkad), a city not far from Kish. From there he ruled over most of western Asia. Henceforth, Sumer was referred to as Sumer-Akad. In 1750 BCE the Babylonian king Hammurabi defeated Rin-Sin, King of Larsa, and emerged as the sole ruler of Sumer-Akkad. By this time, the kings were all Semitic; and the language of the kingdom, Akkadian. Yet "the culture as a whole . . . remained predominantly Sumerian in form and content, and the schools and academies of the land continued to use the Sumerian language and literature as the basis of their curriculum" (Wolkstein and Kramer 1983, 119).

## King and Goddess: The Sacred Marriage

Although the god Anu, and sometimes Enlil, was occasionally referred to as king of the gods, Sumerian texts suggest that this kingship was neither absolute nor autocratic. The Sumerian gods made group decisions in their divine assembly, the model for the early human government. The king acted more like a presider, or convener. "Neither among the gods nor among men did the title 'king' denote the summit of a rigid hierarchical pyramid which was acknowledged as the only possible structure of society—for the memory of a kingless period in the past was never lost" (Frankfort 1948, 232).

Sumerians often referred to a moment in mythical time when kingship was sent down from heaven as a gift from the gods for their protection. Each king was understood to be divinely elected—called to kingship. How this was done is not really clear from the texts, although "omens, dreams, and the pragmatic proof of success were accepted at different times as indications of [the gods'] choice" (Frankfort 1948, 238). A common metaphor for this call to kingship is the god's glance: Face to face a god makes his will known. For example, in late Assyrian times Assurnasirpal II relates how the goddess Inanna/Ishtar chose him to be king.

> But thou, O Ishtar, fearsome mistress of the gods,
> Thou didst single me out with the glance of thine eyes;
> Thou didst desire to see me rule.
> Thou didst take me from among the mountains.
> Thou didst call me to be a shepherd of *me*.[1]
> Thou didst grant me the scepter of justice. (Quoted in Frankfort 1948, 239)

The relationship between the divine patron and a king could vary: Either he becomes the husband of a goddess or the adopted son of a deity. In Uruk, the ancient rites of sacred marriage between the chief priest (*en*) and the goddess, was modified, and the king was considered to be the living consort of Inanna.

In Sumerian poetry depicting the courtship of Inanna and Dumuzi the notion of divine election takes on a special meaning: when the goddess selects a husband, she is simultaneously choosing a king. The god Dumuzi appears to serve as a model for the living king, especially in the *hieros gamos* (sacred marriage) rites of the New Year festival, which may depict the king impersonating the god.

Inanna's older brother the sun god Utu wants her to marry Dumuzi the shepherd who offers her gifts of milk, cream, cheese, and wool. "No, brother! The man of my heart works the hoe. The farmer! He is the man of my heart!" (Wolkstein and Kramer 1983, 32). She prefers the farmer for his barley, flax, bread, and beer. Finally, her mother, Ningal, steps in and persuades her to accept the shepherd, who will be like a father and mother to her, protecting and caring for her in a loving way.

Once chosen, the man to be king of Uruk would undergo two important ceremonies: coronation and the *hieros gamos* rite. The insignia of kingship were kept in Inanna's temple. These included the scepter and the crown, each resting on a separate altar. After processing to the temple, the new king would approach the throne, take up the scepter and place the golden crown on his head. Discarding his personal name, he assumed a new, royal name, a new identity.

There is evidence that the *hieros gamos* rite may have taken place both during the coronation and annually as part of the New Year festival. According to the Sumerian text called the "Blessing of Shulgi," the second king of the Third Dynasty of Ur journeyed to Inanna's temple in Uruk, bringing in his boat sacrificial animals: bulls, sheep, goats, and kids. Dressed in ritual garments, his head covered by a crown-like wig, he learns from the goddess Inanna that he will acquire the powers of kingship as a result of their love making. Inanna sings to the people before the new king:

When on the bed he shall have caressed me,
Then shall I caress my lord, a sweet fate I shall decree for him.
I shall caress Shulgi, the faithful shepherd,
  a sweet fate I shall decree for him.
I shall caress his loins,
The shepherdship of all the lands I shall decree as his fate. (Kramer 1969, 64)

More details about the *hieros gamos* ritual are given in a Sumerian text that depicts the New Year's sacred marriage and banquet (Jacobsen 1987, 121–124; see also Wolkstein and Kramer 1983, 107–110). The rite takes place in the king's palace on the eve of the annual New Year's festival, the night of the dark moon.

The New Year's festival, or Akitu, is known best from Babylonian sources of the first millennium. By this late period, the New Year enacted a renewal of both kingship and cosmos. The Akitu lasted twelve days, during which the king underwent ritual rejection by the gods, a reenactment of the myth of creation (the victory of the god Marduk, or sometimes Assur, over the monster Tiamat and the establishment of cosmic order), and final reinvestiture.

In the earlier text, the focus is simply on the *hieros gamos* as a union of the king Iddin-Dagan impersonating Dumuzi (called by another of his names, Ama-Ushumgal-anna, god of dates and date palm) and the goddess Inanna. First the people of Sumer assemble in the palace and the king builds a throne for Inanna. We are reminded of the myth of the huluppu tree, where Inanna rescues the world tree that has become caught up in a violent rushing river. She plants the tree and nurtures it. Later, Gilgamesh carves for her a throne out of the trunk of the tree.

The king and the goddess sit side by side on the throne. Unfortunately, we do not know whether Inanna was represented by the king's wife, by a priestess, or by a statue of Inanna.

The people prepare the bridal bed, while Inanna bathes. The goddess then adorns the bridal chamber by sprinkling sweet-smelling cedar oil on the floor. When all is ready, the king makes love to Inanna, who rejoices, saying: "you are verily my beloved!" (Jacobsen 1987, 123). Afterwards, the king invites the people into the great hall. They come bearing gifts of food and incense. Musicians provide entertainment while one and all feast. Then a toast is offered to the goddess:

"Inanna, oldest child of the Moon,
Queen, evening star, to praise you is sweet!" (Jacobsen 1987, 124)

As a result of the union with the goddess, the king receives his powers of sovereignty. In one account of the Babylonian *hieros gamos*, the goddess is called upon to fulfill her promises:

"May the lord whom you have called to your heart, the king, your beloved
    husband, enjoy long days at your holy lap, the sweet.
Give him a reign godly and glorious,

Give him the throne of kingship on enduring foundation,
Give him the people-directing scepter, the staff and the crook,
Give him an enduring crown, a radiant diadem on his head." (Kramer 1969, 83)

The speaker then voices the benefits of strong kingship: All living creatures in the kingdom shall prosper, while peace and justice prevail.

In ancient Sumer and in those civilizations that grew in the soil of Sumerian culture, the king's role was both secular and religious. Evidence from collections of laws and other official documents, together with the correspondence of kings, informs us that the administration of the realm was a demanding job for the chief executive. For example, the king settled lawsuits, consulting the relevant documents in the palace archives. He collected taxes, and when a payment was postponed until after harvest, he sent out reminders at the appropriate time. He supervised the care and shearing of the royal herds of sheep. He was involved in the trade and transport of wood and slaves. He was responsible for guarding the rights of different social classes, such as merchants. And the canals (the basis of the Sumerian economy) needed constant maintenance and extension (Frankfort 1948, 251).

In addition, the king was obligated to obey strict rules of a religious nature. It was his job to represent the people in the presence of their gods: Fasting, prayer, and sacrifice made up his daily agenda. Further, it was up to the king to interpret the will of the gods; as chief diviner, he learned to read the messages from the stars, from the livers of sacrificed animals, and from his own dreams.

## The Powers of Inanna

In Uruk, and later elsewhere, Inanna was regarded as the deity who was the source of the king's power. She herself was a sovereign goddess. In her images, she bears the crown of the steppes on her head, sits on the throne, or rests her foot on the back of a lion. (See figure 4.1.)

Inanna's sovereignty is the subject of a creation myth about the huluppu tree (Wolkstein and Kramer 1983, 4–9). In this tale the cosmic tree becomes the raw material for the royal throne. The cosmic tree, a symbol found in numerous cultures (see, e.g., Eliade 1963), serves to connect the different realms of the created order. These may comprise the home of the gods, the world of humans, and the land of the dead.

According to the Sumerian myth, the huluppu tree was planted beside the Euphrates "in the first days when everything needed was brought into being" (Wolkstein and Kramer 1983, 4). But the South Wind uprooted the tree, and the waters of the Euphrates carried it away. This suggests symbolically a state of chaos, where the people feel cut off from the gods and their ancestors. The myth introduces Inanna as one "who walked in fear of the word of the Sky God, An" (Wolkstein and Kramer 1983, 5). Not yet queen, she lacks the emblems of her divine status. But she sees in the tree the means to her own self-realization. She rescues the tree and plants it in her garden in Uruk. There she cares for the tree—

*Figure 4.1: The Queen of Heaven. (Courtesy of the Oriental Institute of the University of Chicago.)*

one year, five years, ten. Now the tree is strong and massive. Pests invade its healthy body: A snake makes its home in the roots of the tree, an anzu bird (part eagle and part lion) rears its young in its branches, and Lilith, the maid who is part woman and part owl, builds her home in its trunk.

Inanna is unable to free the tree of these parasites. She weeps and calls upon her brother the sun, Utu, for help, but he turns his back on her. Then she calls to Gilgamesh, "the hero of Uruk." Wearing sixty pounds of armor and wielding a four hundred fifty-pound bronze ax, he slays the serpent. In fear, the anzu bird and Lilith flee.

Gilgamesh then carves a throne and a bed for Inanna from the trunk of the tree, while she fashions for him the *pukku* and the *mikku* (possibly emblems of kingship) from its crown and roots. The tree lives on in the institution of sacred kingship, foundation of the sovereign, who will serve as a living medium connecting the gods and the kingdom.

Inanna's gifts are not limited to sovereignty. In time, she brings to Uruk all of the *me*, the arts of civilization. The temple of Inanna in ancient Uruk has been excavated, and the archaeological evidence suggests that it served as the center of economic, industrial, and intellectual life as well as a religious shrine. Cylinder seals, with images of Inanna and her symbols (the star, the eight-petaled rosette, and the gateposts), were rolled in the wet clay used to seal storage jars and to make clay tablets. Eventually, writing appears on the seals. "Writing probably developed as a means to keep track of the economic activities of the temple, providing documents of the number of sheep, the amount of barley, and the like that were brought to the temple by the farmers and shepherds, then redistributed to them and the remainder of the populace of Uruk by the temple managers" (Williams-Forte 1983).

As the oldest known civilization, Sumer was an astonishing achievement of literature, art, and architecture. In the myth about Inanna and Enki (Wolkstein and Kramer 1983, 12–27), civilization is seen as a gift of the gods. The *me* originally belonged to the god of wisdom, who lived apart in his watery home, the Abzu ("abyss"), in the southern Sumerian city of Eridu: Enki is the one who "knows the *me*, the holy laws of heaven and earth" (Wolkstein and Kramer 1983,

12). According to the myth, Enki gives the *me*, over eighty decrees, to Inanna, who in turn gives them to the people of Uruk.

In the beginning of this story, Inanna is already a goddess, a queen, and a mature woman. She wears her crown of the steppes, the *shugurra*, and rejoices in her feminine sexuality. She decides to visit Enki as a sort of pilgrimage: "I shall honor Enki, the God of Wisdom, in Eridu. I shall utter a prayer to Enki at the deep sweet waters" (Wolkstein and Kramer 1983, 12).

When Inanna arrives in Eridu, Enki tells his man-servant to offer her butter cake and beer and to treat her as an equal. Together Enki and Inanna drink and dine until he is quite intoxicated. He begins to offer her the *me*, and she accepts them all. These include, but are not limited to, the powers of kingship and divinity. One *me* governs love making; another, lamentations in times of death. There are numerous *me* that govern each of the human emotions, as well as the crafts of industry. Even psychological states are governed by *me* (for example, that of deceit, of kindness, and of straightforwardness). The entire life of the city of Uruk rests on the divine decrees.

After a good sleep, a sober Enki realizes what he has done. He sends forth various monsters to attack Inanna in her Boat of Heaven and to fetch back the *me*. But Inanna is protected by her friend and companion, the warrior goddess Ninshubur, formerly the Queen of the East. She fends off Enki's henchmen, and together they arrive in Uruk where Inanna calls the people to a day of holy festivities. Bringing the *me* to her temple, she meets the people of Uruk who line the canal rejoicing: The young men demonstrate their martial skills; the children laugh and play; the priests meet the Boat of Heaven with hymns; the king slaughters oxen and sheep for the sacrifice and offers libations of beer; music is everywhere—the drum and tambourine resound. Inanna offers the *me* to the people of Uruk; and Enki, too, joins in by blessing the city: "Let the city of Uruk be restored to its great place" (Wolkstein and Kramer 1983, 27).

Such a detailed description of the festivities that accompany the gift of the *me* suggests a regular holy day associated with Inanna. The myth itself, which recounts the transference of power from the realm of Enki to that of Inanna, may have had a political basis, corresponding perhaps to a time when the king of Uruk dominated the whole of Sumer. Clearly the goddess is assimilating to herself greater powers and greater importance in Sumerian culture. Therefore it is no surprise that she even seeks to gain a certain power over death itself.

In "The Descent of Inanna" the goddess undergoes death and humiliation in the underworld at the hands of the Queen of the Dead, Ereshkigal. But the loyalty of Ninshubur and the wisdom of Enki bring her back to the world of the living.

Among the gifts of power that Enki gives Inanna is "the descent into the underworld; the ascent from the underworld" (Wolkstein and Kramer 1983, 15). Inanna undertakes the journey in order to witness the funeral of Gugalanna, the Bull of Heaven, who is the husband of Ereshkigal.[2] As Inanna passes through each of the seven gates of the underworld, drawing ever nearer to its center and the throne room of the queen, she must remove one of the seven *me* of sovereignty and divinity that she is wearing: her crown, her royal robe, the measuring rod and line, and so on. Naked and powerless, she stands before the Queen of the Dead, who kills her without a minute's hesitation and hangs the corpse on a hook.

Ninshubur, who has been instructed beforehand, laments for the dead Inanna. This suggests that Inanna knew what to expect, that she courageously and willingly underwent her own death. Then Ninshubur goes for help. Enlil and Nanna, two important Sumerian gods, are indifferent to her plea, but Enki wants to help. He fashions two androgynous creatures, arms them with the food and water of life, and sends them to the underworld where they are to lament with Ereshkigal. This they do, crying out with her in her pain. She offers them a boon, and they ask for the corpse of Inanna, which they then restore to life.

They return to the world of the living, but the law of the underworld demands a substitute for Inanna. All who are sad and lament her death are allowed to live, but there is one who is indifferent. It is Dumuzi, her husband, who sits unmoved on his throne. So Inanna chooses him to take her place. Eventually she softens the sentence, because there is one who is willing to go in his stead, his sister Gestinanna.

> Inanna and Gestinanna went to the edges of the steppe.
> They found Dumuzi weeping.
> Inanna took Dumuzi by the hand and said:
> "You will go to the underworld
> Half the year.
> Your sister, since she has asked,
> Will go the other half." (Wolkstein and Kramer 1983, 89)

Inanna is primarily a celestial deity; the queen of the underworld remains Ereshkigal. Yet Inanna realizes to some extent the powers that she inherits from Enki, the God of Wisdom. Like the cosmic tree that binds together the gods, the humans, and the dead, Inanna's experience touches on each of these realms. As a goddess, she lives in the starry sky, brighter than all but the sun and the moon; among mortals, she experiences love and marriage with her chosen shepherd, the king; and she undergoes a death that is both terrifying and ugly.

## Inanna Beyond the Walls of Uruk

As a goddess of sovereignty, bestowing power and legitimizing kings, Inanna became a goddess of all Sumer. Her temples increased so that by the time of the Assyrians and Babylonians, numerous cities and not only Uruk claimed her patronage: Ashur, Babylon, Calah, Ur, Nineveh, and Arbela (Hooke 1963, 22).

The myth about Lord Enmerkar and the Lord of Aratta provides us with a legendary example of Inanna as city-patron in two separate places. The story is set in a time before the invention of trade and other arts of civilization. In Uruk rules Enmerkar, a priest-king (or *en*), who by virtue of his office unites each year in sacred marriage with the city's goddess, Inanna. In the fabled city of Aratta, situated in the mountains to the east of Uruk, Inanna likewise governs as city-patron. A conflict arises between the two cities: Aratta is afflicted with drought and famine. This is interpreted, both in Uruk and by the people of Aratta, as a sign that Inanna has withdrawn her protection from the Lord of Aratta. Therefore, Enmerkar seeks Aratta's submission; he desires stone and precious metals for his temple-building. The Lord of Aratta resists in every way that he can, and eventually the rains return to his land. This he interprets as a sign from Inanna:

> "Most magnificently
>     Inanna,
>     queen of all lands,
> has not abandoned her lapis lazuli house,
>     has not delivered it up
>     to Uruk
> . . . . . . . . . .
> the lord,
>     her one of the clean hands,
>     she has not abandoned,
>     has not delivered him up
>     to the lord of Uruk,
>     to the Lord of Kullab!
> Aratta, right and left,
> has Inanna,
>     queen of all lands,
> surrounded for him
>     as with the waters
>     of a mighty
>     burst of a dam." (Jacobsen 1987, 315ff.)

A peaceful relationship between the two cities develops. Lord Enmerkar arrives in Aratta with a female sage, who teaches the people of Uruk and Aratta how through mutual barter and trade all can benefit.

Eventually, Inanna serves as the archetype for goddesses of sovereignty throughout the ancient Near East and Mediterranean world. Other goddesses who were acknowledged as the source of the king's power and protector of the kingdom were identified with this model. They acquired many of her characteristics and, above all, her title Queen of Heaven. Like Inanna, each was believed to live in the sky as the morning and evening star. Wolfgang Heimpel (1982) has compiled a list of goddesses modeled on Inanna in his "Catalog of Near Eastern Venus Deities." Of these, the three best known are Ishtar, Astarte, and Aphrodite.

In the Sumer-Akkad founded by Sargon, the Akkadians identifed their goddess of war, Ishtar, with the Sumerian goddess of kingship, Inanna. One might argue that from this time on the Queen of Heaven appears more warlike than before. Later images of Innana/Ishtar often depict her fully decked out for battle.

Yet, the Sumerian goddess Inanna was always associated with military might to some extent. For example, one myth relates how Inanna subdued the personification of Mount Ebeh, which was threatening the land of Sumer:

> The spear will I swing against it (Ebeh),
> the boomerang, the weapon aim against it,
> the forests around it I will set on fire,
> against the evil (men) there
> I will swing the battle-axe . . . (Ringgren 1973, 10)

But Inanna was not always a warlike figure. When she carried the *me* home to Uruk, it was her companion, the warrior goddess Ninshubur, who fought off the monsters sent by Enki.

In contrast, Ishtar often appears in the literature as violent and willful. For example, the Akkadian version of the "Descent of Ishtar to the Nether World" differs from the Sumerian original in one important point: Whereas Inanna descends peacefully to witness a funeral, Ishtar seems to have no motive for her visit apart from pure aggression:

> When Ishtar reached the gate of the Land of No Return,
> She said (these) words to the gatekeeper:
> "O gatekeeper, open thy gate,
> Open they gate that I may enter!
> If thou openest not the gate so that I cannot enter,
> I will smash the door, I will shatter the bolt,
> I will smash the doorpost, I will move the doors,
> I will raise up the dead, eating the living,
> So that the dead will outnumber the living." (Pritchard 1958, 81)

Not only does Ishtar appear to be more aggressive, she seems to be a more powerful political figure. One hymn to Ishtar from the latter part of the First Dynasty of Babylon (ca. 1600 BCE) refers to her as supreme over all the gods, their queen, whose decrees the other gods must execute: "All of them bow before her" (Pritchard 1958, 233).

Another goddess who is identified with the Mesopotamian Queen of Heaven is the Canaanite war goddess Astarte (Phoenician Ashtart). We know little about her stories and rituals, but there is plenty of evidence that she was worshipped for thousands of years in Palestine and in various cities around the Mediterranean. For example, her name is found in the god-lists of Ebla (ca. 2500 BCE) and in the sacrificial and ritual lists of Ugarit (ca. 1500). She was adopted into the Egyptian pantheon (ca. 1500) and appears in Phoenician inscriptions as late as 500 CE. In the Hebrew Bible, her name is the generic term for any foreign goddess.

Apparently Astarte was originally a goddess of the animals of the steppe and hunting. Later she becomes more connected with the sea. But it is her warrior nature that dominates her role as goddess of sovereignty: "She was associated with training for battle and above all with horses and chariotry. A scene on the chariot of Thothmose IV that shows him going out to battle has the caption 'He is mighty in the chariot like Astarte'" (Fulco 1987a, 1:471).

Aphrodite is a third Queen of Heaven, modeled very much on the older figures of Inanna and Ishtar. The Greeks often referred to her as a foreign goddess, even after she became one of the most important deities of the Greek pantheon. Her early history lies, however, with the Greek settlers in Cyprus and Asia Minor. In Cyprus, the Queen of Heaven was already being worshipped in Paphos when the Greeks arrived there around 1200 BCE. They called her Aphrodite and saw in her a sea goddess, a goddess of love, and a war goddess. During the period of the Roman empire, she was called Venus and worshipped as the ancestor of the rulers of Rome, often appearing in their dreams as a battle goddess leading them forward to victory.

Even after the christianization of the Roman empire in 381 CE under Theodosius I, the Queen of Heaven did not disappear. Slowly but surely her title and her astral symbolism were assimilated to the figure of the Virgin Mary, mother of Jesus. Not a warrior, not a lover, Mary rules as mother of the king of peace.

## Conclusion

We see in the history of the Mesopotamian Queen of Heaven how the figure of a deity undergoes constant revision and transformation due to historical factors. Inanna of Uruk, star goddess and city-patron, becomes a goddess of sovereignty. Serving to legitimize the individual king, her cult moves beyond Uruk to pervade all of Sumer; later, as Ishtar, she becomes the supreme deity of the Assyrians and Babylonians. Eventually, the Queen of Heaven becomes the title for numerous sacred and divine queens in the West, including Astarte, Aphrodite, and the Virgin Mary.

At the heart of Inanna's story is the belief that the human community needs to have a living connection to the gods on whom all depend for both life and its meaning. In ancient Sumer, the king united the human community with that of the gods. Yet he was able to do so only as their chosen servant. His election was an expression of their will. The marriage of the king and the goddess was one way in which this election was manifest, and even more, through this union the king gained his powers for judgment and sovereignty.

### NOTES

1. The term *me* refers to the attributes of civilization.
2. There may be some astrological meaning to this funeral. The planet Taurus, the celestial bull, would have disappeared every year from the sky of Sumer for about six weeks, reappearing in the sky in March (Wolkstein and Kramer 1983, 157 n.24).

REFERENCES

Eliade, Mircea. 1963. *Patterns in Comparative Religion*. New York: World Publishing Company.

Frankfort, Henri. 1948. *Kingship and the Gods: A Study of Ancient Near Eastern Religion as the Integration of Society and Nature*. Chicago: University of Chicago Press.

Fulco, William J. 1987a. "Astarte." P. 471 in vol. 1 of *The Encyclopedia of Religion*, ed. Mircea Eliade. New York: Macmillan.

———. 1987b. "Inanna." Pp. 145f. in vol. 7 of *The Encyclopedia of Religion*, ed. Mircea Eliade. New York: Macmillan.

Heimpel, Wolfgang. 1982. "A Catalog of Near Eastern Venus Deities." *Syro-Mesopotamian Studies* 4 (December): 3–7, 9–22.

Hooke, S. H. 1963. *Babylonian and Assyrian Religion*. Norman: University of Oklahoma Press.

Jacobsen, Thorkild. 1976. *The Treasures of Darkness: A History of Mesopotamian Religion*. New Haven: Yale University Press.

———. 1987. *The Harps That Once . . . Sumerian Poetry in Translation*. New Haven: Yale University Press.

———. 1987a. "Mesopotamian Religions: An Overview." Pp. 447–466 in vol. 9 of *The Encyclopedia of Religion*, ed. Mircea Eliade. New York: Macmillan.

Kramer, Samuel Noah. 1969. *The Sacred Marriage Rite: Aspects of Faith, Myth, and Ritual in Ancient Sumer*. Bloomington: Indiana University Press.

———. 1961. *Sumerian Mythology: A Study of Spiritual and Literary Achievement in the Third Millennium B.C.* (rev ed.). New York: Harper & Row.

Pritchard, James B., ed. 1958. *An Anthology of Texts and Pictures*. Vol. 1 of *The Ancient Near East*. Princeton, NJ: Princeton University Press.

Ringgren, Helmer. 1973. *Religions of the Ancient Near East*. Philadelphia: Westminster Press.

van der Waerden, Bartel L., with Peter Huber. 1974. *The Birth of Astronomy*. Vol. 2 of *Science Awakening*. New York: Oxford University Press.

Williams-Forte, Elizabeth. 1983. "Annotations of the Art." Pp. 174–199 in *Inanna, Queen of Heaven and Earth* by Diane Wolkstein and Samuel Noah Kramer. New York: Harper & Row.

Wolkstein, Diane, and Samuel Noah Kramer. 1983. *Inanna, Queen of Heaven and Earth: Her Stories and Hymns from Sumer*. New York: Harper & Row.

# PART II

## Power Bestowed/Power Withdrawn

### The Goddess Who Gives and Takes Back Sovereign Power

Hearing her exceedingly kind words, Himalaya on
his part
Replied to the Great Sovereign Queen, his eyes and
throat congested with tears.
Himalaya spoke:
You greatly ennoble whomever you wish to favor,
For who am I, so dull and motionless, compared to
you who embody infinite being and consciousness?

—C. Mackenzie Brown, trans.
"The Devi Gita" (Song of the Goddess)

# 5

# Celtic Goddesses of Sovereignty

*Proinsias Mac Cana*

As with virtually all other aspects and constituents of Celtic religion and mythology, it is advisable to preface any discussion of Celtic goddesses with a significant caveat. The literary evidence of the insular Celtic vernaculars, particularly Irish and Welsh, is quite extensive, but it poses serious problems of evaluation and interpretation. Early Irish, for example, has a wide range of varied material bearing on myth and religion, but it is important to remember that the use of writing in the Irish language—in any substantive sense—dates only from the sixth century and is a Christian, monastic innovation. The bulk of the extant literature embodying pre-Christian tradition belongs to the eighth and succeeding centuries: In other words, it was composed in writing at least two or three centuries after the substantial christianization of the country. The extant material constitutes an invaluable source for native myth, ideology, and deities, yet in assessing its significance one must bear in mind that it has been filtered through the editorial activity of generations of monastic scholars and redactors who were remarkably sympathetic to vernacular tradition but whose purpose was, in large measure, to create a symbiotic relationship between it and the biblical, latinate learning of the monasteries.

That Ireland should have produced such an exceptionally rich corpus of traditional literature in manuscript may be attributed in no small measure to the fact that it was never colonized by the Roman Empire. Conversely, its location beyond the borders of the Empire explains why it has only a sparse iconography to complement its literature, whereas the territories of Roman government and mixed Romano-Celtic culture, in Britain as well as on the continent, have conserved an endless array of monuments and other artifacts including dedicatory inscriptions and images of deities. The problem is that most of them reflect in varying degrees the cultural synthesis that gradually came about during the centuries of Roman government and administration. Moreover, if we exclude western Britain, these are precisely the areas in which the Celtic vernaculars perished before the myths and hero tales could be recorded, which might have provided a context for the iconography. In other words, neither the "continental" iconographic and epigraphic repertoire nor the insular literary corpus provides an unalloyed reflex of an autonomous Celtic ideology. Taken in tandem, however, they constitute a rich, if often ambiguous, testimony to the nature of Celtic myth and religion and to the functional status of their gods and—our immediate concern—their goddesses.

One of the ambiguities—and one which even a more exhaustive dossier might not have remedied—is that of identity or disparity: For example, do different names and locations necessarily imply different deities? Of the numerous names or epithets in Gaulish inscriptions many occur only once and those that occur more frequently seem to be grouped within specific regions. For this reason some scholars have concluded that the Celtic gods were many and that they were local and tribal rather than national or universal. The polar opposite is represented by those scholars, fewer in number, who have argued that all the gods attested in epigraphy, iconography, and literature may be reduced to a single supreme deity, polyvalent and polymorphic; similarly, some have held that "Minerva" and all the other named goddesses are only so many particular manifestations of a single great mother goddess (Lambrechts 1942, 172). It is true that the resemblances between the several major goddesses are so pronounced that one can easily think of them, at least in some contexts, simply as variant realizations of a single archetypal figure, yet in practice the existing mythological material requires a greater measure of taxonomic distinction. Not only is it convenient to speak of goddesses of war, of fertility, or of sovereignty, without prejudice to the question of original unity or plurality, but one must also accept, if only in response to the evidence of the insular tradition, that popular belief and preference had already long since endowed many of the familiar named goddesses with sufficient distinctive attributes and local affiliations to lend them a convincing semblance of individuality. One suspects that the goddess Brigid would have been as much an individual in the eyes of the average man or woman in pre-Christian Ireland as her Christian avatar Saint Brigid still is for their modern counterparts.

When Caesar proposed a thumbnail sketch of the Gaulish gods, he simply selected the several principals among them, identified their functional repertoires and, in keeping with the customary practice of *interpretatio romana*, referred to them by the Latin names of their nearest functional equivalents in the Roman pantheon:

> Of the gods they worship Mercury most of all. He has the greatest number of images; they hold that he is the inventor of all the arts and a guide on the roads and on journeys, and they believe him the most influential for money-making and commerce. After him they honour Apollo, Mars, Jupiter, and Minerva. Of all these deities they have almost the same idea as other peoples: Apollo drives away diseases, Minerva teaches the first principles of the arts and crafts, Jupiter rules the heavens and Mars controls the issue of war. (*De Bello Gallico* VI, 17, 2)

Allowing for the synoptic nature of his comment and his preoccupation with the Roman archetype, I would suggest that Caesar's concise statement is closer to the facts than some of his modern critics would allow.

As with the male deities, the question immediately poses itself: What name, or names, has Caesar cloaked under the Roman *Minerva*? It may well be that he had in mind one or more widely known goddesses as well perhaps as the general class of more local goddesses they represented. One of the native deities explicitly equated with Minerva elsewhere was Sulis, otherwise Sulis Minerva, who gave her name to Aquae Sulis, Bath, the site of a prominent aquatic shrine. The related plural, Suleviae, is applied to triads of mother-goddesses at sites on the Continent and in Britain. In the Irish context, one of those who answer best to Caesar's "Minerva" by virtue of her functional repertoire and her wide-ranging cult is the goddess Brigid. According to Cormac mac Cuilennáin (ca. 900) she was the daughter of the father-god, the Dagda (literally "Good God"), and was worshipped by the *filid*, the exclusive fraternity of learned poets. In keeping with the Celtic *penchant* for triadic repetition, she had two sisters, also called Brigid, the one associated with healing, the other with the smith's craft, and their combined fame was such that "among all the Irish a goddess used to be called Brigid" (Meyer 1912, 15 §150). Thus Brigid was patroness of the artistic inspiration and learning of the poets as well as of healing and craftsmanship. "Minerva," for her part, is sometimes combined on reliefs with "Mercury" and "Vulcan," the one a master of all the arts, the other more specifically associated with the craftsmanship of the smith.

It is clear, moreover, that Brigid is merely the Irish reflex of a pan-Celtic goddess. Her name, which meant originally "the exalted one," has its close correspondent in **Brigantī*, latinized as *Brigantia*, the name of the tutelary deity of the Brigantes, who formed an important federation in northern Britain. She has also a remarkable Christian, or christianized, double in the person of her namesake Brigid, the great sixth-century abbess of the monastery of Kildare. The legend of the saint is inextricably fused with that of her pagan alter ego, and, as she is inevitably accorded a much fuller documentation by monastic scribes, there is the curious irony that our richest source for the mythology of the goddess is the hagiography of the saint together with the prolific folklore that commemorates her in popular tradition. Both the saint's *Lives* and her folklore indicate a close connection with livestock and the produce of the soil, and, appropriately, her feastday, February 1, coincides with *Imbolg*, the pagan festival of spring. In a passage that appears to draw on this conflate tradition, the twelfth-century Norman cleric Giraldus Cambrensis records that Brigid and nineteen of her nuns at Kildare took turns in maintaining a perpetual fire surrounded by a hedge within which no male might enter (*Topographia Hiberniae* II, 34, 48), and it is a curious, and perhaps significant coincidence that already in the third century Iulius Solinus, associating "Minerva" with the healing springs of Sulis, mentions that perpetual fires burned in her sanctuary also (*Collectanea Rerum Memorabilium* 22, 10). In secular texts Brigid is sometimes represented as aiding and giving courage to the men of Leinster, the province in which her monastery was situated, in their crucial battles with external forces. This is doubtless a reflection of her pristine role as territorial goddess, in the same mold, no doubt, as those Celtic deities reflected in such names as *dea Tricoria* of the Tricorii in the Narbonnaise, *dea Nemetona* of the Nemetes in the Rhine region, or indeed *dea Brigantia* of the Brigantes federation.

The notion of territory is not always clearly distinguishable from the more general one of the land, and, by the same token, territorial goddesses are not always clearly distinguishable from those others who represent more directly the material substance of the land. In keeping with their title—*Matres, Matrae, Matronae*, and so on—the mother-goddesses who are attested throughout the Romano-Celtic world frequently appear in groups of two and three and are shown with the various signs of their maternal and creative function: carrying and caring for infants or bearing such familiar symbols of prosperity as the cornucopia and the basket of fruits. They were also frequently thought of as nourishing and watching over specific peoples and regions and were named accordingly: the *Matres Glanicae* at *Glanum* (Saint-Rémy-de-Provence), for example, or the *Matres Treverae* among the Treveri. They would seem to have survived cultural and religious change in the guise of the *mamau* ("mothers") and the formidable *cailleacha* ("old women") of Welsh and Irish-Scottish popular tradition respectively (cf. Sjoestedt 1949, 37).

The mother-god specifically titled as such, Mātrona, gave her name to the river that is now the Marne in France. She was the mother of Maponos, "The Youthful (or Son) God," known in medieval Welsh as Mabon son of Modron. In Irish tradition the corresponding role belonged to Boann, eponym of the river Boann (anglicized Boyne): She was the mother of the Irish divine youth par excellence, Mac ind Óc, whose name is the semantic equivalent of the Welsh and Celtic Mabon/Maponos. As mother, the goddess is sometimes represented in Irish texts as ancestress of a distinguished line of descendants (Mac Cana 1955/1956, 88), and this is presumably what is intended by the author of the medieval Welsh tale "Branwen daughter of Llyr," when he describes Branwen as "one of the three great ancestresses" of the island of Britain (even though there is nothing in the story itself to confirm it). Moreover, in one of her *personae*, the mother-goddess could also be mother of the gods. The divine people of the Irish, the Tuatha Dé Danann, were, as their name indicates, held to be the progeny of the goddess Danu, as the gods of Wales were said to be the children of Dôn. In the medieval literature Danu is often confused with Anu, who is described by Cormac mac Cuilennáin (ca. 900) as the mother of the gods of the Irish (*mater deorum Hibernensium*) who "nourished them well." Her association with fruitfulness and her total identification with the land that produced it are neatly epitomized in the name of twin hills, the Paps, in County Kerry: *Dá Chích Anann* "the breasts of Anu," which, already over a thousand years ago, Cormac explicitly related to her nourishment of the gods (Meyer 1912, 3 §31).

This concept of the personification of the land and its fruitfulness is beautifully expressed in the opening section of a little tale about the goddess Macha, *Noínden Ulad* ("The Debility of the Ulstermen"), which dates from about the ninth century. In somewhat abbreviated form this segment of the narrative is as follows:

> There was a wealthy farmer of the Ulstermen, Crunnchu mac Agnomain, who lived on the deserted upland territories. His wife and the mother of his many sons died, and he was for a long time without a wife. One day while he was alone on his couch, he saw a beautiful young woman enter and come towards him. She sat by the fireplace and kindled the fire. They both remained there until the end of the day without speaking. Then she fetched a kneading trough and a sieve and set about preparing food and after that she went to milk the cows. When she came in again, she turned righthandwise (*for deisiul*) and went to the kitchen to do the chores. When everyone else went to bed, she remained behind, smoored the fire, and made a righthand turn, joined Crunnchu under his covering and put her hand on his body. They were together until she became pregnant by him, and in consequence of their union he became ever more rich. . . . (Hull 1968, *36*)

For all its easy laconic style, this short passage teems with mythic resonance: the initiatory role characteristic of the goddess, the connotation of action and movement highlighted by the absence of speech, the evocation of the symbolic values of the fire and the hearth, the ritual significance of going *for deisiul* (much like the Hindu *pradakṇiṣa*), and, finally, the succinct conjunction of pregnancy and material increase. Equally striking is her choice of partner. Generally when a divine woman pays a courtesy call on a mortal in Irish literature, he is either a prince or a hero. The fact that he is a farmer, however well endowed, in this instance underscores what the narrative already makes abundantly clear: that the goddess is here acting in her role as source and guarantor of the prosperity of land and people.

It was this intimate connection with the land in its several aspects that led Marie-Louise Sjoestedt to observe that the male deities dominate the historical and the female deities the topographical myths, their prominence being particularly notable in the "geographical" tales of the *Dinnshenchas*, the rich corpus of traditional placename lore in both prose and verse (Sjoestedt 1949, 24). It also helps to explain some of the variant, even contrasting, roles assigned individual goddesses depending on the motivational pull of the immediate setting. It is, for example, hardly surprising that in a society in which the ideology of war figured so pervasively, there should have been certain goddesses especially identified with the concomitants of conflict—blood, death, and destruction—though in the Irish context they are not normally represented as engaging directly in the fighting; their characteristic weapon is magic. The river Aeron in Cardiganshire in Wales takes its name from a Celtic **Agronā* ("goddess of slaughter"), while a close namesake *Aerfen* ("renowned in battle") is mentioned in medieval Welsh verse. The Gaulish *Cassibodua* belongs in this category: She is assimilated to the Roman *Victoria* and the second element of her name equates to Irish *Bodb*, one of the principal titles of the Irish war-goddess (cf. Vendryes 1948, 248, 259; Duval 1957, 31–58). Thus also the British *Andraste*, who was invoked by the formidable queen Boudica of the Iceni in 61 CE before going into battle against the Romans; after the battle, according to Dio Cassius, she slaughtered her Roman captives, particularly the noble women, with frightful cruelty while offering sacrifice to the goddess in her sacred grove" (*Hist. Rom.* LXII, 6–7). In keeping with the Celtic predilection for triplication, the Irish goddesses of war are often represented as a trio whose members show some variation but generally include the *Morrígan* and the aforementioned *Bodb / Badb*, that is, "The Phantom (or Great) Queen" and "The Scald-crow," respectively.[1]

Generally the goddess of war is represented as instigating conflict or intervening to influence its outcome, but there are occasional instances in which she might more aptly be described as a warrior goddess than a war-goddess. The most notable is that of Macha, whom we have already encountered in another guise, as wife to the farmer Crunnchu. She it was who gave her name to Emain Macha, the ancient capital of the Ulaid, or Ulstermen, the people who dominated the north of Ireland until the fifth century, as well as to the nearby Ard Macha (modern Armagh), which was later to become the ecclesiastical center of the whole country. According to an early tale, Macha's father Ruad shared the kingship of Ireland with two others, Cimbaeth mac Fintain and Díthorba mac Dimmáin, each holding it in turn. When Díthorba died he was succeeded by his five sons, but when Ruad died, his daughter Macha was excluded from the succession. She defeated Cimbaeth in battle and took the kingship to herself. When the turn of Díthorba's sons came again she expelled them and they took to a life of marauding. She then married Cimbaeth but did not allow matters to rest there. She disguised herself as a leprous old woman and set off into the wilderness of Connacht in search of the five sons of Díthorba. When she found them cooking a wild boar she joined them beside their fire. Before long they desired to lie with her, and one by one she accompanied them into the wood, where she overpowered and bound them. Thus she brought them back to Emain Macha, where the Ulstermen wished to kill them. But she held that this would be a violation of "the truth (or justice) of a ruler" and instead she compelled them to dig the great rampart of Emain Macha (Meyer 1907, 325–326 and Best et al. 1954, ll. 2514–2554; neither has an accompanying translation. Cf. Gwynn 1924, 308–311).

This tale illustrates why Macha is sometimes included in the familiar triad of prominent war-goddesses, but its somewhat disparate character is due to the fact that it offers an inverted form of a well-known sovereignty myth that we shall examine presently. In this, Macha is a useful example of the capacity of the goddess to assume markedly different aspects in different mythic settings. We have seen that she appears elsewhere as the source of material fruitfulness, and in the story in question her association with horses has led some scholars to accept a correspondence, on the one hand with the widely attested deity Epona ("Divine Horse" or perhaps "Horse Goddess"), whose cult found especial favor with the cavalry of the Roman army and who is frequently titled *Regina* in Romano-Celtic inscriptions, and on the other, with the lady Rhiannon who features in the Welsh *Mabinogion* and whose name, from an original **Rīgantona* ("Divine Queen"), links her explicitly to the mythology of sovereignty.[2] Even this small sample suffices to show how fruitless it is to seek to impose any rigid classification on the goddesses of the Celts on the simple basis of their functions.

It has been remarked that Celtic goddesses are more prone than their male counterparts to zoomorphic transformation, and this applies particularly to the war-goddesses. Bodb foretells slaughter and haunts the battlefield in the form of a crow, recalling the recurring image in early Welsh verse of the ravens (*brain*) feeding on the corpses of the slain. The name sometimes occurs as *Bodb Chatha*, literally "the crow of battle," which corresponds precisely to the *Cathubodua* attested in Haute-Savoie, underlining the currency of both term and concept throughout the Celtic world, and a lingering memory of her dread role survived to our own time in some areas of Ireland, where her name was used to frighten children. Both she and the Morrígan could influence the outcome of battle by exerting their magical powers. During the long drawn-out series of combats that constitute the major part of the great hero-tale of *Táin Bó Cuailnge* (The Cattle-raid of Cuailnge) the Morrígan transforms herself into bird and animal forms. Her relationship with the exemplary hero Cú Chulainn is ambivalent: She comes to him as a beautiful young woman and seeks to seduce him, and when this fails she threatens to hinder him in the thick of battle. In the event she comes against him in the form of an eel coiling around his legs, a she-wolf attacking him, and a red hornless heifer stampeding cattle around him. Having been repulsed and seriously wounded by him, she returns later in the guise of an old woman and tricks Cú Chulainn into healing her by the virtue of his blessing (O'Rahilly 1976, ll. 955, 1982–2026, 2039–2053; trans., 152, 180–182). Both she and Bodb figure in instances of the characterisically Celtic scenario of "The Washer at the Ford," where an otherworld woman prefigures the outcome of conflict when she is seen washing the bloodied clothing or the mangled bodies of those who are fated to be slain; one of those who witness this portent of their own death is Cú Chulainn himself when he sees Bodb in the shape of a beautiful fair-skinned girl sighing and lamenting as she washes his torn clothing and equipment (Meyer 1910, 16f.; O'Grady 1929, I. 104f., II. 93f.; Van Hamel 1933, 95f.). As we have seen, it was not normal for the goddesses to engage directly in the physical conflict, even if they could foretell and sometimes influence its outcome; yet some of them held the secret of how to achieve martial prowess and this knowledge they imparted to those young warriors who one way or another came under their tutelage. Thus *Buanann* (The Lasting One) was teacher to the bands of youthful warriors known as *fiana* (Meyer 1912, 11 §104) and Cú Chulainn survived perilous trials as he sought out the domain of *Scáthach* (The Shadowy One) and compelled her to instruct him in those special feats of valor that from that time on rendered him supreme over both friends and foes (cf. Meyer 1898, 71–82; Rees and Rees 1961, 253–255).

However, war is not an end in itself, or is rarely acknowledged as such, and in the kind of society reflected in Celtic mythology its primary purpose was to affirm tribal boundaries and to vindicate the integrity of the tribal kingdom and the efficacy of its ruler. In Ireland at the beginning of the historical period the basic unit of political organization was the petty kingdom known as a *tuath*, literally "a people," of which there were scores in the country. There was also the "over-king" who was recognized as suzerain by the kings of several *tuatha*, and finally there was the "king of over-kings" or "king of a province." But the essential fact is that in terms of religious ideology, each kingship, on whatever scale, was a sacral office with the same inherited body of privilege, duty, and ritual. The king was the protector of his people against the perils posed by both the secular and supernatural worlds, and as such, certain qualities were ideally required of him, which are referred to collectively as *fír flaitheman*, literally "the truth (one might almost say *dharma*) of the ruler." The presence of these virtues ensures peace, security, and prosperity for his subjects, and the land, in harmonious response, produces an abundance of its fruits. Where, however, the king is blemished in his person or conduct, the results are correspondingly disastrous and there is no lack of cautionary tales to illustrate this danger.

In such a ritual context—which was not of course peculiar to Ireland or the Celts—it was important to have a ritual mechanism by which to legitimize the accession of a new ruler and at the same time place before him the responsibilities of his office. This mechanism was provided by the goddess of the land or territory assuming the ritually more defined role of goddess of sovereignty. This conjunction of ruler and validating goddess was one of the dominant concepts, and certainly one of the most tenacious, in Irish tradition and would seem to have been originally a feature of Celtic society in general. It is at least implicit in much of Welsh or British literary tradition,[3] and it evokes comparison with the countless instances in Romano-Celtic inscriptions and images of the pairing of male and female deities—"Mercury" and Rosmerta, Sucellus and Nantosvelta, "Mars" Visucius and Visucia, and so on. While the male figures vary considerably in these representations, their female partners show relatively little change, their habitual attributes being the cornucopia or other symbols of the fertility of the land and of well-being. Joseph Vendryes's observation that this veneration of the divine couple ("le culte rendu à des divinités accouplées") was one of the most particular features of Celtic religion has been echoed by many other scholars: In the words of Émile Thevenot, "if one were to seek an epitome or a symbol of the gods of Gaul, is it not in this couple, tirelessly recalled, invoked and represented, that one would be most likely to find it?"(Vendryes 1948, 269; Thevenot 1968, 237). It is true that most of the extant monuments date from a period of Romano-Celtic synthesis when the traditional role of Celtic kingship had become all but obsolete in political practice—as is clear from Caesar's testimony—but there can be no doubt, as is generally accepted, that the pairing of the divine protector of his territory with the goddess who embodied its substance was an integral feature of traditional Gaulish ideology and one that is cognate with the Irish pairing of the sacral ruler and the personification of his kingdom.

The accession of each new ruler was represented as a union with the goddess and was conventionally referred to as the *banais rígi*, "wedding-feast of kingship." That it was originally conceived as a physical union is indicated by the term *banais/banfheis*, a compound of *ben* ("woman") and *feis* ("passing the night, feast") from the verb *foaid* ("to sleep"), as well as by various narrative reworkings of the underlying myth. What form this ceremony may have assumed in pre-Christian times—a surrogate bride or a simulated union?—is a matter of speculation: The Christian Church, conscious of the pivotal significance of the sacral kingship in native society, sought to arrogate to itself a central role in "ordaining" the ruler and at the same time to sanitize the most incompatible elements of the traditional ritual. However, the ideological roots of the sovereignty myth went too deep for it to be easily set aside, and it continued to figure in the literature, both casually and consciously, for the next thousand years and more. Tara, situated in the central province of *Mide* (literally "center, middle"), enjoyed a special prestige as the focus of sacral sovereignty, as did its rite of inauguration, *Feis Temra* (The Feast/Wedding-feast of Tara). In the story of the "Wooing of Édaín," Eochaid Airem requested his people to convene this gathering the year after he became king, but they "would not convene *Feis Temra* for a king that had no queen: for Eochaid had no queen when he took the kingship"—in other words, the celebration was one of validation and followed at some remove the king's assuming power (Bergin and Best 1938, 30–31). The goddess Medb, euhemerized in the tales of the Ulster Cycle as a redoubtable queen of Connacht, claimed that "never was she without one man in the shadow of another," which has been read as evidence of sexual promiscuity but is in fact a fair summation of the goddess's primary role: to mate with each worthy successor and thereby to confer on him the seal of legitimacy. In her variant role as Medb Lethderg of Leinster she partnered nine kings of Ireland and it was said of her: "Great indeed was the power and influence of that Medb over the men of Ireland, for she it was who would not permit a king in Tara unless he had her for his wife" (Ó Máille 1928, 138).

As the consort of numerous rulers the goddess, inevitably long-lived, was often envisaged as passing through serial phases of youth and age. The tradition of her longevity is well attested: Of Édaín, who passed through several life cycles within the trilogy of tales that bear her name, "The Wooing of Édaín," the text comments: "Now it was a thousand and twelve years from the first begetting of Édaín by Ailill until her last begetting by Édar" (Bergin and Best 1938, 156–7 §21). A more curious instance perhaps is the information that King Ailill of Connacht, partner to Queen Medb in the Ulster Cycle, was still a baby when she was married to her third husband and that Medb's sister Éle was his grandmother (O'Neill 1905, 182–183; Ó Máille 1928, 134). In the absence of a fitting spouse the goddess is sometimes pictured as old and wretched, just as the land she personifies lies empty and barren, and, like the land, she is restored to youthful vigor and beauty through union with her rightful king. This scenario occurs, for example, in one of the most familiar of the narrative forms of the underlying myth, that of the hunt and the magical quarry. In the version told of the legendary Niall Noígiallach, founder and eponym of the Uí Néill dynasty, he and his four brothers stop to cook some of their game during a hunting expedition. One by one they go to look for water and find a well guarded by a hideous old woman who will only allow them to take water in return for a kiss. Three of the brothers refuse; one, Fiachra, yields her a brief kiss, but, when Niall's turn comes not merely does he kiss her but he lies with her as well, and instantly she is transformed into a beautiful young woman more radiant than the sun. She is, she explains, the sovereignty of Ireland and Niall and his descendants will hold the kingship without interruption, apart from two kings of the line of Fiachra by virtue of his fleeting contact with the goddess. The elective authority of the goddess is brought out clearly here. It is she who sets the test that only the true *damnae ríg* ("material of a king") can measure up to, and, while all the brothers are repelled by the old woman's ugliness, none is tempted to violate her guardianship of the well by appropriating water from it without her consent: The libation, which, as we shall see, was an essential element of the ritual conferring of sovereignty, could only be bestowed, freely, by the goddess herself.

There is an obvious correspondence—and at the same time a striking disparity—between this text and the story already cited of the encounter of Macha with the sons of Díthorba. It is a matter that merits more comment than is possible in the present context, but it may be noted that in the Macha story, it is the goddess who seeks out her would-be suitors, not to woo them—or be wooed by them—but to vanquish them and reduce them to the level of slaves. Read for its exemplary sense, the Macha tale demonstrates among other things that the goddess's role was not merely to legitimize the accession of a righteous ruler, as is most often the case in the literature, but also to prevent the accession of an unrighteous one, if necessary by main force.

In its two extant versions, one in verse, the other in prose, the story of Niall and his brothers is no older than the beginning of the eleventh century (Joynt 1908; Stokes 1903). Its aim is blatantly political: Since the ninth century the Uí Néill dynasty aspired to transform the ideological prestige of the Tara kingship into an actual suzerainty over the whole of Ireland, and our narrative was in effect a contribution to their publicity campaign (Mac Cana 1980, 104). Theirs was not a unique exploitation of the sovereignty myth in the historical period—I have noted elsewhere for example that the story of Mór Muman (Mór of Munster), which focuses on a period in the seventh century, reflects the claim by the Eoganacht peoples to a monopoly of the kingship of the province of Munster (Mac Cana 1955/1956, 78–83; O'Nolan 1912/1913). There is also a version of the hunting theme told of Lugaid Loígde, an ancestor of the several important peoples known collectively as Érainn, who, unlike the Eoganachta, were pre-Goidelic (or pre-Gaelic). In this case the hunt has two phases. In the first Lugaid and his brothers pursue a magic fawn, he captures it, and together they feast on it. In the second phase the brothers resume their hunt and encounter a huge old woman. All of them except Lugaid Loígde refuse her invitation to lie with her; he, however, accepts and the hideous hag is immediately transformed and identifies herself as the sovereignty of Ireland (Stokes 1897; Gwynn 1924).

The two phases are complementary, and there can be little doubt that the fawn in the first and the woman in the second are equivalent and indeed, in mythic terms, identical.

At the same time it would be wrong to imagine that the adaptation of the sovereignty myth to particular political interests was confined to the historical or Christian period, though it may well have become more consciously sophisticated in the context of the new literate learning mediated by the monasteries: The kingship myth was, after all, political in its origin and in its very essence. Moreover, even when we find the myth applied to particular medieval circumstances, it does not follow that its morphology has been radically altered in the process. It has been shown, for example, that the version of the myth represented by the Niall Noígiallach tale must have been current in early Celtic Britain. Rachel Bromwich (1960/1961, 459) concluded that "the Transformed Hag combined with the chase of the White Stag is one of the oldest elements in the story of Peredur-Perceval" (Perceval being the adaptive form given to the British Peredur in continental romance).[4] The hunting theme recurs in a number of the Breton lays and Bromwich has argued convincingly that it has, or had originally, an explicit dynastic motivation: "Old French sources have therefore preserved what appears to be a genuine survival of the lost Celtic literature of Brittany: a Breton dynastic tale corresponding to the Irish story-pattern which is attached to the names of Niall and Lugaid Laigde. This was appropriated to the traditional founders in the sixth century of two of the early kingdoms—Cornouailles in the west, and Vannes in the east" (Bromwich 1960/1961, 466).

The comprehensive *mise-en-scène* of these various tales may be summed up roughly in R. A. Breatnach's brief résumé of the constituent elements of the Irish examples: "a hero, a hunt in which the hero is victorious over a wild animal, the cooking and eating of the flesh of the animal, a search for water (in a royal cup), the encounter with the *puella senilis*, the coition (or oscultation), the metamorphosis, and finally the bestowal (or promise) of sovereignty" (1953, 334). There is, however, no reason to suppose, as some have tended to do, that this was the only, or even the normal, form of the sovereignty myth (even if it is true that hunting loomed large in Celtic heroic tradition and led frequently to the hunters crossing the boundary between the secular and the supernatural worlds). What is clear is that the myth had a number of components, not all of which were essential to any particular version of it. Probably the most significant of them is the draught of liquor, which, being bestowed on the candidate, sets as it were the seal of legitimacy on his claim to the kingship; the very term for such a drink, combined with the name of a territory, is used not infrequently to denote a ruler's lordship over it. In a poem cited in the genealogies in praise of Aed Dub mac Colmáin (+ 638 CE), abbot and bishop of Kildare, the expression *cuirm Cualann* ("the ale of Cualu," a district south of Dublin) is used as a familiar reference to the royal headship of the Lagin, the people who gave their name to the province of Leinster (O'Brien 1976, 339; Meyer 1913, 459–460). We have seen that Eochaid Airem could not hold the feast and assembly of Tara to celebrate his accession to the kingship until such time as he was wedded to his proper spouse, in this instance the beautiful Édaín, and it is in this context that we must read the statement in the same tale to the effect that "Etaín was serving the lords on that night, for the serving of drink was a special gift of hers" (Bergin and Best 1938, 182–183 §14).

A still more focused example occurs in a seventh-century text, *Baile Chuinn* ("Conn's Ecstasy"), which purports to be a prophecy by Conn Cétchathach ("Conn of the Hundred Battles") previewing a series of kings of Tara beginning with his son Art and continuing down to the contemporary period. Of the brief notes on the accession of each future king many employ the Old Irish verbal form for "he shall drink it"—meaning, of course, the ritual draught of liquor—as a synonym for union with the goddess and acquisition of the kingship (Murphy 1952). In a later, probably eleventh-century, text embodying a similar list, the royal names are announced in a somewhat iconic setting. Conn found himself in the vicinity of an otherworld dwelling. When he entered he saw a girl seated on a chair of crystal, wearing a gold crown, and with a vessel of gold and a golden cup beside her; the text identifies her as the sovereignty of Ireland. Nearby, on his throne, sat the god Lug, the divine model of kingship and, as most scholars accept, the Irish cognate of the Gaulish deity labelled "Mercurius" by Caesar. The woman prepares to serve the drink, and each time she does so she asks to whom shall be given the red ale, or *dergfhlaith*, a term in which the phonetic ambiguity between *flaith* ("sovereignty") and *laith* ("liquor, ale") neatly points up the intimate bond between the two. In response, one by one Lug names the rulers from the time of Conn onwards.[5]

The text is relatively late and some of the elements of the stylized description may have been influenced by external sources, or indeed by shifts in authorial attitudes; for one thing, the goddess here adopts a more passive and subsidiary role than was normal in the early literature, though her juxtaposition with Lug is curiously reminiscent of the pairing of god and goddess in Gaulish iconography. The strong focus on the ritual drink is certainly traditional. As we have seen, it is the most frequent and significant of the symbols of sexual union, and most specifically the union of king and territorial goddess by which royal inauguration was consummated (see also O'Rahilly 1946, 14–17). In the case of Medb of Connacht, who, despite the process of literary euhemerization, still carries many of the unmistakeable attributes of divine origins, the conclusive mark of her characteristic role is in her very name: *Mebd*, "the Intoxicating One." An early testimony to the wide currency of the motif, and probably the myth, occurs in the story of the foundation of Massilia (modern Marseilles) as reported by Athenaeus:

> The Phocaeans, merchants of Ionia, were the founders of Massilia. Euxenus of Phocaea was a guest of the king Nannus (for that was his name). As Nannus was celebrating his daughter's marriage, Euxenus chanced to arrive and was invited to the feast.
>
> The marriage took place in this way: after the meal the girl was to come in and to give a bowl of drink which she had mixed to the man whom she preferred among the assembled suitors. He to whom she offered it was the bridegroom. When she came in, the girl gave the bowl—whether by chance or for some other reason—to Euxenus; her own name was Petta.

> When this happened, her father concluded that she had acted in accordance with divine will; Euxenus took her as his wife and lived with her, changing her name to Aristoxene. And even now there is a kindred descended from this woman in Massilia, called the Protiadae: for Euxenus and Aristoxene had a son named Protias. (Athenaeus, *Deipnosophistae* 13.576)[6]

Here the woman's proffering of the drink indicates not merely her acceptance but also her selection of a husband, in a way that is broadly paralleled in many occasional references in Irish literature. The Celtic connection is made explicit by two items of nomenclature: the girl's name, Petta (Welsh *peth*, Irish *cuit*), and that of her and her father's tribe, the Segobrigii, given in another version of the tale.

If, as seems evident, the myth of the union of king and goddess was a feature of traditional ideology throughout the Celtic world, it was in Ireland that it proved most enduring. In the pre-Norman period, that is, before the middle of the twelfth century, it ran like a leitmotiv throughout the secular literature, whether as passing reference, allusion, or comparison, or in the more extended form of tale and apologue. Later, in the aftermath of the Norman settlement, which was to lead eventually to the conquest of Ireland, the elitist fraternity of schooled poets responded by creating, between ca. 1200 and 1650, a vast corpus of highly crafted encomiastic verse that reaffirmed the inherited ideology of sacral kingship with its evocation of age-old ritual and relationships—including the hierogamos. How much of its original significance the concept of the marriage between ruler and goddess retained for these poets and their audience is difficult to assess, but it is certain that it remained a potent symbol of the survival of the native political and cultural order; as R. A. Breatnach (1953) remarks, "the installation ceremony of every princeling was a recurring reminder to a people, whose sense of the presence of the past was so acute, of the pristine belief, common to all races, in the divinity that hedged around the regal office" (327).

That this long uninterrupted currency of the sovereignty myth was in large measure due to the peculiar sociopolitical environment of medieval Ireland is hardly open to doubt, and it does not imply that the goddess of sovereignty may be treated as if functionally distinct from the other female deities. Even from this brief survey it should be evident that the different functional roles attributed to the several goddesses are for the most part interrelated, and that the same deity may fill disparate roles in response to the particular mythic contexts in which she is engaged.

Macha typifies this functional mobility. She is sometimes included in the triad of exemplary war-goddesses, as the wife of Crunnchu she is the source and agent of fertility, and as the adversary of the sons of Díthorba she is the goddess of sovereignty, who defends its integrity by main force against those who would claim it unworthily.

NOTES

1. The precise meaning of *Morrigan* depends on the length of its first vowel, which is uncertain in the early instances. Reading short *o*, it has been taken to mean "Phan-

tom Queen" (with *Mor* related to English *mare* in *nightmare*); *mór* with long vowel means simply "great."

2. Cf. Claude Sterckx (1986, 40–47) on Rhiannon and Epona. On Macha's relevance to such deities, see Ross (1967, 224–227); Green (1992, 187–188).
3. See note 4.
4. For a further discussion of the concept of sovereignty in Welsh literature, see Goetinck (1975, esp. ch. III), "Sovereignty themes in *Peredur, Owein*, and *Gereint*." As her chapter title indicates she focuses particularly on the three vernacular romances that correspond to Chrétien de Troyes's *Erec et Énide, Yvain* (or *Le Chevalier au Lion*), and *Le Conte del Graal* (or *Perceval*).
5. The text of *Baile in Scáil* ("The Phantom's Frenzy") has been published from different manuscripts, without translation, by Meyer (1901, 1921). It is summarized in Dillon (1946, 11–14).
6. For the translation, with comments, see Koch and Carey (1995, 32–33). They append a variant version of this episode from Justin's *Philippic Histories* 43.3, which on one or two points offers a little extra precision.

REFERENCES


Bergin, Osborn, and R. I. Best, eds. 1938. *Tochmarc Étaíne*. Dublin: Royal Irish Academy.

Best, R. I., et al. 1954. *The Book of Leinster* (vol. 1). Dublin: Dublin Institute for Advanced Studies.

Breatnach, R. A. 1953. "The Lady and the King." *Studies* 42: 321–336.

Bromwich, Rachel. 1960/1961. "Celtic Dynastic Themes and the Breton Lays." *Études Celtiques* 9: 439–471.

Dillon, Myles. 1946. *The Cycles of the Kings*. London and New York: Oxford University Press.

Duval, Paul-Marie. 1957. *Les Dieux de la Gaule*. Paris: Presses Universitaires de France. Revised ed., Payot 1993.

Goetinck, Glenys. 1975. *Peredur: A Study of Welsh Tradition in the Grail Legend*. Cardiff: University of Wales Press.

Green, Miranda. 1992. *Animals in Celtic Life and Myth*. London and New York: Routledge.

Gwynn, Edward. 1924. *The Metrical Dindshenchas* (vol. 4). Dublin: Royal Irish Academy. Reprinted ed., Dublin Institute for Advanced Studies 1991.

Hull, Vernam, ed. 1968. "*Noínden Ulad*: The Debility of the Ulidians." *Celtica* 8: 1–42.

Joynt, Maud, ed. 1908. "Echtra mac Echdach Mugmedóin." *Ériu* 4: 91–111.

Koch, John T., and John Carey. 1995. *The Celtic Heroic Age: Literary Sources for Ancient Celtic Europe*. Malden, MA: Celtic Studies Publications.

Lambrechts, Pierre. 1942. *Contributions à l'Étude des Divinités Celtiques*. Brugge: Uitgeverij "De Tempel."

Mac Cana, Proinsias. 1955/1956. "Aspects of the Theme of King and Goddess in Irish Literature." *Études Celtiques* 7: 76–114.

———. 1980. *The Learned Tales of Medieval Ireland*. Dublin: Dublin Institute for Advanced Studies.

Meyer, Kuno, trans. 1898. "The Wooing of Emer." Pp. 57–84 in *The Cuchullin Saga in Irish Literature*, ed. Eleanor Hull. London: D. Nutt.

———. 1901, 1921. "*Baile in Scáil* (The Phantom's Frenzy)." *Zeitschrift für Celtische Philologie* 3: 457–466; 13: 371–382.

———. 1907. "The Dindsenchas of Emain Macha." *Archiv für Celtische Lexikographie* (vol. 3). Halla a. S.

———, ed. 1910. *Fianaigecht*. Dublin: Royal Irish Academy. Reprinted, 1993.

———, ed. 1912. "*Sanas Cormaic*: An Old-Irish Glossary." Pp. 15 §150 in *Anecdota from Irish Manuscripts* (vol. 4), ed. O. J. Bergin et al. Dublin and Halle a. S.: Hodges, Figgis.

———. 1913. "Aed Dub mac Colmáin, Bishop-Abbot of Kildare." *Zeitschrift für Celtische Philologie* 9: 458–460.

Murphy, Gerard. 1952. "*Baile Chuinn* and the Date of *Cín Dromma Snechtai*." *Ériu* 16: 145–151.

O'Brien, M. A., ed. 1976. *Corpus Genealogiarum Hiberniae* (vol. 1). Dublin: Dublin Institute for Advanced Studies.

O'Grady, Standish Hayes. 1929. *Caithreim Thoirdhealbhaigh*. Dublin: Irish Texts Society.

Ó Máille, Tomás. 1928. "Medb Chruachna." *Zeitschrift für Celtische Philologie* 17: 129–146.

O'Neill, Joseph, ed. 1905. "*Cath Bóinne* (The Battle of the Boyne)." *Ériu* 2: 173–185.

O'Nolan, T. P. 1912/1913. "Mór of Munster and the Tragic Fate of Cuana Son of Cailchin." *Proceedings of the Royal Irish Academy* 30C: 261–282.

O'Rahilly, Cecile. 1976. *Táin Bó Cúailnge: Recension I*. Dublin: Dublin Institute for Advanced Studies.

O'Rahilly, T. F. 1946. "On the Origin of the Names *Érainn* and *Ériu*." *Ériu* 14: 7–28.

Rees, Alwyn, and Brinley Rees. 1961. *Celtic Heritage: Ancient Tradition in Ireland and Wales*. London: Thames & Hudson.

Ross, Anne. 1967. *Pagan Celtic Britain*. London: Routledge and Kegan Paul.

Sjoestedt, Marie-Louise. 1949. *Gods and Heroes of the Celts*. London: Methuen.

Sterckx, Claude, 1986. *Élements de Cosmologie Celtique* (vol. 2). Bruxelles: Éditions de l'Université de Bruxelles.

Stokes, Whitley, ed. 1897. "*Cóir Anmann* (The Fitness of Names)." Pp. 317–323 in *Irische Texte* (vol. 3, ii). Leipzig: Verlag von S. Hirzel.

———, ed. 1903. "Echtra mac Echach Mugmedóin: The Adventure of the Sons of Eochaid Mugmedóin." *Revue Celtique* 24: 190–303.

Thevenot, Émile. 1968. *Divinités et Sanctuaires de la Gaule*. Paris: Fayard.

Van Hamel, A. G., ed. 1933. *Compert Con Culainn and Other Stories*. Dublin: Dublin Institute for Advanced Studies. Reprinted, 1978.

Vendryes, Joseph. 1948. "La religion des Celtes." In *La religion de l'Europe Ancienne*. Paris: Presses Universitaires de France.

# 6

# Sovereignty and the Great Goddess of Japan

*Delmer M. Brown*

For more than 1,300 years Japanese sovereignty has been sanctified by the most powerful of Japanese deities, the Great Goddess Amaterasu (*Amaterasu Ōmikami* 天照大神). Sanctification comes in two special ways: first, by making certain that each emperor or empress of Japan is a person born in the "single and unbroken" line of descent from the Great Goddess; second, by making certain that each occupant of the throne celebrates a Great Enthronement Ceremony (*daijō-sai* 大嘗際) in which the spirit of the Great Goddess enters the occupant's body and makes him or her the sacred sovereign of Japan.

The relationship between the ruler of Japan and the Great Goddess has been sanctified further, several times each year down through the centuries, by rituals (*matsuri* 祭り) held at the Imperial Court, at the Ise Grand Shrine (frequently referred to as the Mecca of Japan), and at thousands of other shrines (*jinja* 神社) throughout the archipelago. Spiritual ties have also been affirmed and reaffirmed in historical chronicles, novels, poems, plays, and pictorial art, and in recent times by the mass media. Such affirmations flow from belief in the myths about Amaterasu recorded in Japan's oldest extant chronicle (the *Kojiki* 古事記), which was compiled in response to an edict handed down by Emperor Temmu (d. 686). Temmu proclaimed that the

*Figure 6.1: The Imperial Main Sanctuary of Ise's Inner Shrine.* (*Source: Ise Shrine Office, Ise-shi, Japan.*)

"ancient origins" (*honji* 本辞) of the imperial line must be preserved because they reveal "the framework of the state and the foundations of sovereignty" (*Kojiki* 1959, 10:3).[1]

I raise two questions about these foundations. Why have they been sanctified—for such a very long time and in one of the most paternalistic societies of the world—by the worship of one particular female deity? And why has belief in a spiritual connection between the emperor and the Great Goddess (the core of religious beliefs and practices referred to here as Imperial-Country Shinto[2]) become especially strong in two widely separated periods of Japanese history: the three centuries of the Great Reform period (roughly 600 to 900) and the seventy-seven years of Meiji modernization (1868 to 1945)?

## Female Shamans and the Great Goddess

Extensive archaeological, ethnological, and mythological research by Japanese scholars makes it increasingly clear that female shamans (*miko* 巫女) have been prominent throughout the long evolution of Imperial-Country Shinto. The dynastic history of Later Han (25 to 220 CE) reports what Chinese envoys encountered when they were in a small Japanese state[3] ruled by a shamanistic queen:

> For a number of years there was no ruler. Then a woman named Pimiko appeared. Remaining unmarried, she occupied herself with magic and sorcery and bewitched the populace. Thereupon they placed her on the throne. She kept one thousand female attendants, but few people saw her. There was only one man who was in charge of her wardrobe and meals and acted as the medium of communication. She resided in a palace surrounded by towers and stockade, with the protection of armed guards. (Tsunoda 1951, 2–3)

The dynastic history of Wei (221 to 265) carries a similar story with additional information obtained from Japanese envoys sent by Queen Pimiko to China in the years 238 and 243:

> When Pimiko passed away, a great mound was raised, more than a hundred paces in diameter. Over a hundred male and female attendants followed her to the grave. Then a king was placed on the throne, but the people would not obey him. Assassination and murder followed; more than one thousand were slain.
>
> A relative of Pimiko named Iyo, a girl of thirteen, was [then] made queen and order was restored. (Tsunoda 1951, 16)

Information obtained from Chinese sources and from archaeological and ethnological discoveries has led Japanese scholars to conclude that Pimiko—they now prefer to call her Himiko—and her niece Iyo were female shamans and that sovereignty had both a political and a religious character (Hori 1968, 181–215; Piggott 1997, 15–93). But we do not know whether other states—or even that particular state after the time of Iyo—were ruled by women who performed a shamanic role.

And yet Japan's earliest chronicles, the *Kojiki* 古事記 and the *Nihon shoki* 日本書記, compiled at the beginning of the eighth century,[4] have much to say about a legendary Queen Jingū who ruled the unified state of Yamato during the third or fourth century CE. The *Kojiki* reports a conversation between Amaterasu and Queen Jingū when the queen was giving birth to the future King Ōjin (*Kojiki* 1959, 95).[5] The *Nihon shoki* version focuses on the divine assistance Queen Jingū received while leading an army against the Korean state of Silla (*Nihon shoki* 1974, 1: 330–361). These legends suggest not only that female shamanism was strong when Japan was becoming a unified state but that one particular female shaman ruled that state and gave birth to a king who was later enshrined, and is still worshipped, as an ancestral *kami* 神.

Japan's two early chronicles tell us that all later rulers of the Yamato state were kings, not queens. But the chronicles state that when Soga no Umako (d. 626) seized control and a new administrative order came into existence, a woman called Empress Suiko (554–626) was enthroned. Why didn't Umako occupy the throne himself? He surely knew that a Chinese general who had destroyed a ruling dynasty usually made himself emperor and started a new dynasty. But in Japan hereditary succession had already become firmly established, and sovereignty had already been sanctified for centuries by the worship of ancestral *kami*.

Umako must have realized that his control would be accepted only if he ruled as a minister appointed by an empress born in Japan's sacred line of imperial descent.

But Prince Shōtoku (574–622), who was Crown Prince under Empress Suiko, was attracted to China's conception of sovereignty and maintained that any ruler of Japan, whether emperor or empress, should assume control of both secular and sacral affairs as indicated in Article 3 of his Seventeen Injunctions written in 604:

> When the emperor speaks be sure to obey. The emperor is Heaven and his ministers are Earth. Heaven envelops and Earth upholds. With the passing of the four seasons, everything happens as it should. When Earth invades, Heaven is violated. When the emperor speaks, his ministers listen; when the superior acts, the inferior complies. Consequently an imperial pronouncement should always be scrupulously respected. If not, the minister himself is violated. (*Nihon shoki* 1975, 2: 181–183)[6]

This was a view of sovereignty that Umako could not accept, for he was in control of the state's armies and material possessions and had no intention of relinquishing it. Thus Prince Shōtoku never reached the throne. Nor did his son. Indeed the struggle for power that erupted in 645 was between leaders of the Soga clan who were determined to retain control over secular affairs and clan chieftains who preferred the absolutist view of sovereignty advocated by Prince Shōtoku.

As soon as the Soga were removed from their seats of power in 645, victorious clans arranged to have Emperor Kōtoku (596–654) enthroned as both secular and sacral head of state. This is what Kōtoku himself said about his sovereignty in an edict issued a few days later:

> Heaven envelops and Earth upholds. There is only one way to rule. But because of degeneration during previous reigns, emperor-subject order collapsed. When I became emperor, rebels were punished. Nowadays blood is being spilt. But henceforth there will not be two ways to rule, and subjects will not be duplicitous. If anyone breaks this oath, he will be subjected to the curse of Heaven and Earth, and to punishment and death by demons and human beings. This is as clear as the sun and the moon are clear. (*Nihon shoki* 1975, 2: 270–271)

Eleven sovereigns—including five empresses, one of whom reigned twice—occupied the throne during the next 125 years. Each was responsible for both worldly and religious affairs as in China and as had been advocated by Prince Shōtoku.

What contemporary Japanese chronicles say about these eleven autocratic rulers suggests a common Japanese assumption that the sovereign should be a man and that the most sacred portions of an important ritual should be performed by a female relative of the emperor, preferably a healthy young virgin. This conclusion is based on the observation that the three most influential sovereigns (Tenchi, Jimmu, and Shōmu) were male rulers and that four of the empresses (Saimei, Jitō, Gemmei, and Gensei) occupied the throne only until it could be handed over to a son or brother. The last reigning empress of the period (Shōtoku, 718–770) fell in love with a Buddhist priest and dared to favor him as her successor. Not surprisingly, Japan did not have another empress until the seventeenth century.

Still, female shamanism continued to be intertwined with sovereignty. During that one hundred twenty-five-year period of autocratic rule, imperial daughters were regularly appointed as Consecrated Princess (*saiō* 斎王) and assigned to the Ise Shrine, where they participated, as the sovereign's representative, in rituals honoring Amaterasu. An entry in the *Nihon shoki* carries a mythical account of how this happened:

> Up until this time two kami, the Great Goddess Amaterasu and the Spirit of the state of Yamato (Yamato no Ōkuni-tama), were worshipped together in the king's palace. But being awed by their power, the king became uneasy about living with them. So he entrusted the worship of the Great Goddess Amaterasu to his daughter Princess Toyo-suki-iri-hime and had her worship this Goddess in the village of Kasanuhi of Yamato where a sacred stone structure called a *himorogi* was erected. Likewise the worship of the spirit of the state of Yamato was entrusted to Princess Nunaki-no-iri-hime. But since Princess Nunaki-no-iri-hime was skinny and bald, she was unfit to conduct services. (*Nihon shoki* 1974, 1: 238–239)

Although the dating is dubious, this entry discloses thought and action associated with the emergence of two centrally important and interrelated institutions of Imperial-Country Shinto: Ise's Inner Shrine (*naigū* 内宮) and the Palace of a Consecrated Princess (*saigū* 斎宮). Both were at different locations in Ise and emerged, probably toward the end of the seventh century, in an interdependent relationship with each other. A Consecrated Princess was an unmarried imperial relative selected by divination and then subjected to a year of ritual purification at the imperial palace before she occupied her palace at Ise. There she lived in a state of purity—not even hearing Buddhist words—and then was sent to the Inner Shrine to worship the Great Goddess on behalf of the emperor, playing an especially important role in the ritual complex known as the Great Enthronement Ceremony (*daijō-sai* 大嘗際). Archaeological investigations as well as literary evidence show that the Palace of the Consecrated Empress continued to be inhabited until late in the twelfth century, providing incontestable evidence that an imperial princess had functioned for centuries as a female shaman at the ritual and institutional heart of Imperial-Country Shinto. This strong female-shaman tradition helps one to understand why the emperor's ancestral *kami* has long been a goddess and why female shamans continue to figure prominently in rituals at the Ise Grand Shrine.

## The Great Goddess and Imperial-Country Shinto

Imperial-Country Shinto grew by two great surges of reform to become a strong emperor-centered religious movement: first, from 645 to 900; second, between 1868 and 1945. The two reform movements—the first more religious than political and the second more political than religious—arose from an urgent demand that a strong state headed by a strong sovereign be built as quickly as possible.

The first surge seems to have emerged from a deep and widespread concern, especially among the ruling elite, that state control was being threatened by both rebellion at home and invasion from abroad. Contemporary chronicles indicate that after 645 Japan's major clans (*uji* 氏) were involved in a particularly bitter struggle for control of the state, and that after the coup of 645 Soga leaders were either killed or ejected from their high offices and then replaced by men who had engineered the coup. In years following the civil war of 672, post-645 reformers were themselves driven out of office by a new clan coalition (Miller 1974, 135–146). Thus prominent officials in those turbulent years after 645 must have been fearful that they, like their predecessors, would soon be victimized by still another violent political upheaval. The situation undoubtedly made them ardent proponents of reforms to increase the power of the state and strengthen their hold on positions at the top of the political ladder.

Still, the reformers were probably even more concerned about invasion from abroad than rebellion at home. Surely they were alarmed to hear in 660 that an army of the T'ang empire in China, allied with the Korean state of Silla, had made a joint attack on the Korean state of Paekche, seized its capital, and forced its king to surrender. Just three years later the reformers were again shocked by the report that Japan's naval force of some 400 vessels, sent to help Paekche, had been annihilated. Then in 668 reports were suddenly received that the Korean state of Koguryö, like Paekche at an earlier date, had been subjugated by the combined forces of the T'ang and the Silla (Brown 1993a, 30–36). As a result of recent archaeological discoveries we now know that extensive defense works were then being built along the western shore of Kyushu where Chinese forces might strike, as well as along the shore of the Inland Sea and on the road to the capital where the Chinese might move to subjugate the whole of Japan. Feverish attention to national defense in the face of Chinese aggression suggests that members of Japan's ruling elite were then driven to press for reforms that would make Japan a powerful Chinese-like empire headed by an autocratic sovereign sufficiently strong to defend Japan against foreign enemies.

The reform program was focused on the creation of a strong military force backed by a substantial increase of revenue, more efficient administrative arrangements, and additional schools for training young men to function effectively as state officials. Vigorous implementation of this ambitious program resulted in fundamental change in all major areas of public life, change that is commonly equated with the establishment of a new administrative (*ritsuryö* 律令) order modeled after that of China. The form and functions of offices in the new order were spelled out in a code of civil procedures (the *Taihō ritsuryō* 大宝律令) that, after years of reinterpretation and revision, was promulgated in 702.

Evidence of truly remarkable cultural change can still be seen in the remains of Chinese-style capitals. Particularly impressive was the capital at Nara where five sovereigns reigned in a Chinese and autocratic style between 710 and 770. In addition, we can still see the remnants of a statewide Buddhist-temple system that, centered on the Great Eastern Temple (Tōdai-ji 東大寺) and its fifty-two-foot Great Buddha Statue (*daibutsu* 大仏), reached the zenith of its grandeur during the years when the state's capital was at Nara. We also know that the reforms produced a new Chinese-like system for collecting state revenue (*handen shūju* 班田収授), the minting of coins by the government, a statewide system of public roads, and a school of "great learning" (*daigaku* 大学) with branches in most provinces. All this was coupled with startling achievement in the arts and learning, making the Nara period a truly remarkable time in the cultural history of Japan (Naoki 1993, 221–267).

We have also come to understand that Japanese attempts to build a powerful state like that of China were intermingled with moves to develop two religious systems for sanctifying sovereignty: Imperial-Country Shinto and State Buddhism. The two sanctifying movements evolved from two quite different religious traditions: the worship of ancestral *kami*; and the building of impressive mounds for the burial of deceased predecessors. Although performing a common function, one was consistently separated from the other because shrines were for worshipping life-giving ancestral *kami* that abhorred anything associated with death, whereas mounds were for the burial of rulers whose bodies had become contaminated by death. Even today, a shrine is not built over a place where someone has been buried and a graveyard is never found on the grounds of a shrine. Thus Imperial-Country Shinto emerged on the ancestral-*kami* side of Japan's religious tradition, and temples of State Buddhism on the burial-mound side.[7] Down through the centuries, these two religious movements—the first indigenous and the second imported—have served to sanctify Japanese sovereignty in deep and diverse ways. Here, however, I consider only the emergence of Imperial-Country Shinto, for that has always been focused on the Great Goddess and her sacred ties with the emperor of Japan.

Imperial-Country Shinto first became an organized religious movement during the reigns of Emperor Temmu (672 to 686) and his spouse Empress Jitō (686 to 697). Archaeological discoveries are now making it increasingly clear that what these two rulers did to institutionalize Great-Goddess worship followed two earlier stages in the evolution of ancestral-*kami* worship. First came an early agricultural stage (from about 200 BCE to 250 CE) when clan heads (*uji no kami* 氏の上) ruled over small states and worshipped their ancestral clan *kami* (*ujigami* 氏神). Then came a centralized Yamato-state stage (from about 250 to 600) when Great Kings (*ōgimi* 大王) ruled over Yamato and worshipped a Great Kami (*ōgami* 大神) that stood above all other ancestral *kami* of the land (Murakami 1984, 19–28). Stage three might be called the imperial stage (from about 600 to 770) when emperors (*tennō* 天皇, or "Heaven's sovereigns") of the Sinified state of Japan worshipped Amaterasu ("Heaven's shining" Great Goddess[8]) as their ancestral *kami*.

Imperial-Country Shinto emerged, therefore, when an emperor and empress, and their courts, were doing their utmost—in the face of crises both at home and abroad—to tighten control over Japan's land and people. Clearly this development, centered on belief in the Great Goddess as the divine founder of Japan's "unbroken" line of sovereigns, was intertwined with a parallel endeavor to make Buddhism another instrument of state control. These parallel movements produced a bifurcated religious order, on one side of which was Imperial-Country Shinto and on the other State Buddhism. Interactive relationships between the two—one native and focused mainly on life concerns of the present, and the other foreign and concerned primarily with life after death—precluded any sense of rivalry or antipathy. Being patronized by the same rulers, and offering up prayers and holding services for the sanctification of imperial control, the two movements complemented each other in a centuries-long process of fusion. Consequently, historians are inclined to think of the two movements as organized ingredients of one broad and enduring Japanese religion. Every single stage in the spread of Imperial-Country Shinto has therefore been linked with, and affected by, parallel developments in the spread of Buddhism. But such relationships cannot be explored in this brief treatment of the Great Goddess and Japanese sovereignty.

The shinto side of Japan's seventh-century reforms was administered by a new Council of Kami Affairs (*Jingi-kan* 神祇宮) located along side the Council of State (*daijō-kan* 太政官), directly under the emperor. Actions taken by this Council of Kami Affairs were at three levels: (1) revising and reordering old *myths* in ways that would highlight and strengthen belief in Amaterasu as the *kami*-ancestor of Japan's "unbroken line" of sovereigns; (2) recasting *rituals* in ways that would make them more effective instruments for directing the creative power of Amaterasu to the sanctification of sovereignty; and (3) building a grand *shrine* where Amaterasu would reside and where imperial sovereignty would be enhanced by rituals held in the spiritual presence of Amaterasu.

Activity at the first level produced a revised and restructured cluster of myths about beginnings (*honji* 本辞) centered on the creative power of Amaterasu. This myth structure was made the core of "kami generations" (*kami no yo* 神の代) chapters in Japan's earliest chronicles (the *Kojiki* and the *Nihon shoki*) that were completed early in the eighth century. As noted previously, the compilation and preservation of these ancient myths were ordered by Emperor Temmu (672 to 686). Because his belief in the power of myth to sanctify sovereignty has persisted, both the ancient and modern surges of Imperial-Country Shinto have been associated with renewed interest in the *Kojiki* (Japan's ancient classic sometimes referred to as the Shinto Bible) in which these myths have been preserved. Even the present-day preoccupation with Japaneseness (*Nihon-ron* 日本論) is linked with a revival of the urge to discover what the *Kojiki* really says and means.

Second-level moves—making old agricultural rituals into instruments for the sanctification of sovereignty—emerged at about the same time. The *Nihon shoki* reports that in 690 (the fourth year of Empress Jitō's reign) an enthronement ritual was held at the imperial court. Although not called a Great Enthronement Ceremony (*daijö-sai* 大嘗際), it was a ritualization of Jitö's enthronement that included four principal parts of a *daijö-sai*: (1) the Minister of Kami Affairs offered up a prayer to Heaven's Kami (*amatsukami* 天神)[9]; (2) another court official presented the Three Imperial Regalia to the new empress; (3) nobles and court officials lined up according to rank to pay their respects to the *kami*; and (4) on the following day nobles and court officials paid their respects to the new empress at the imperial court (*Nihon shoki* 1975, 2: 500–501). The only part of a *daijö-sai* missing was the one in which the emperor-to-be proceeds, at the most liminal point of the ritual, to a "great enthronement palace" (*daijö-gü* 大嘗宮) in front of the imperial palace. In the middle of the night and alone he enters first one sacred hall and then another. Each of the halls has a "kami couch" (*shinza* 神座). What the new sovereign does at (or on) the two couches has been the subject of considerable study and speculation (Blacker 1990; Bock 1990). But it is assumed that in one way or another he is symbolically united with Amaterasu, making him the *kami*-sovereign of Japan.

By the end of the Great Reform period in about 900, the *daijö-sai* and numerous other rituals performed throughout the Imperial-Country Shinto system had been shaped into a complicated and impressive ritual-complex focused on Amaterasu. Five volumes in the religious section of the *Engi-shiki*'s 927 code of civil procedures are devoted to such rituals: two on seasonal rituals; a third on extraordinary rituals; a fourth on the *daijö-sai*; and the fifth on prayers (*norito* 祝詞) (Bock 1970, 1972).

Steps at the third level—the establishment of a central shrine for Imperial-Country Shinto—seem to have been interactively connected with the shaping of ancient myths and rituals centered on the Great Goddess. This pivotal Inner Shrine at Ise and the nearby Palace for the Consecrated Princess seem to have appeared at about the time of Empress Jitö's reign (686–697). As noted, it was her spouse who had handed down the edict that ancient myths should be preserved; she herself was enthroned by a ceremony similar to the *daijö-sai*. Religious historians therefore deduce that both the Inner Shrine and the Palace of the Consecrated Princess (subjects of the myth translated earlier) were erected at about the time of these two reigns. That was probably when Ise's Inner Shrine (*naigü* 内宮) was built near an older Ise shrine for the worship of the local clan's ancestral *kami*, a shrine that was later called Ise's Outer Shrine (*gegü* 下宮). In time the two shrines became integral parts of the Ise Grand Shrine that has functioned for 1,300 years as the institutional center of Imperial-Country Shinto (Matsumae 1992b, 9–30).

The most sacred place within Ise's Inner Shrine is the Kami Body (*shintai* 神体) where the spirit of the Great Goddess is believed to reside. This Kami Body is symbolized by a mirror that is one of Japan's Three Sacred Treasures (*sanshu no jinki* 三種の神器), which are retained by the living emperor as the most sacred symbols of his sovereignty. But the mirror is special. It is not only the Kami Body of Amaterasu but, according to the *Nihon shoki* myths, it appeared in heaven and was sent down to earth by the Great Goddess for presentation to successive

Japanese sovereigns (*Nihon shoki* 1974, 1: 112–124; Holtom 1972, 7–17). This sacred mirror, ritually transferred to Emperor Akihito during his recent enthronement, can therefore be thought of as the most central symbol of the Imperial-Country Shinto symbol system.

In trying to understand the power of Imperial-Country Shinto to sanctify sovereignty, we need—in addition to assessing the significance of myths, rituals, shrines, and symbols—to appreciate the importance of imperial patronage. Throughout the Great Reform period of 600 to 900, the imperial court assigned an increasingly large number of high-ranking officials to the Council of Kami Affairs, the Ise Grand Shrine, the Palace of the Sacred Princess, and various other shrines around the country. These officials administered and regulated rituals, offerings, ranks, and religiopolitical relationships within the expanding Imperial-Country Shinto system. The Ise Grand Shrine also received larger and more numerous tax-free estates (*shōen* 荘園). By the end of the Great Reform period in 900, and largely because of generous material patronage received from the imperial court, the Ise Grand Shrine was the only shrine important enough to be made the subject of a separate volume in the religious section of the *Engishiki*'s code of civil procedures (Bock 1970, 123–150).

## The Down-Up-Down of Imperial-Country Shinto

### *Down*

Imperial-Country Shinto had become highly institutionalized during the three centuries of Great Reform, but the next 900 years were a time of deterioration. The downward turn seems to have been due mainly to the seizure of secular control by aristocratic and feudal lords, leaving the imperial court a penurious patron.

But much of the patronage that Ise lost between the two surges of Imperial-Country Shinto seems to have been recovered, after 900, from contributions by other patrons: first, by the millions of commoners who went on pilgrimages to Ise (*Ise sangū* 伊勢参宮); second, by aristocratic and military lords who, while channeling most of their contributions to their own ancestral-*kami* shrines, also sanctified their sovereignty by recognizing and patronizing shrines where Amaterasu (the ancestral *kami* of the emperor they nominally served) resided. Both types of patronage were for the Ise Grand Shrine, but with a fundamental difference. For the pilgrims, Amaterasu was honored not so much as the ancestral *kami* of the Japanese emperor as a goddess who could mysteriously bestow blessings on human individuals.[10] From aristocratic and feudal lords, the Ise Grand Shrine received far less patronage than did the shrines where the ancestral-*kami* of these lords resided.[11] Nevertheless such secondary patronage for the institutional lynch pin of Imperial-Country Shinto was significant.

Even during the century of incessant civil war between 1467 and about 1568, when the *daijō-sai* as well as the practice of completely rebuilding the Ise Grand Shrine every twenty years (the *shikinen sengū* 式年遷宮) had been discontinued, both the imperial court and the Ise Grand Shrine survived. Rituals in which the spirit of the Great Goddess entered the sovereign's body and sanctified his sovereignty were apparently still performed. Moreover, shoguns continued to value—even to fight each other over—imperial appointments and recognition. Such secondary patronage was quite significant during the 400 years that followed the first surge of Imperial-Country Shinto (900 to 1400), and was surprisingly strong during the 268 years that preceded the second (1600 to 1868). In those two periods, belief in the sacred sovereignty of the emperor of Japan was reflected in contemporary poetry, novels, and historical writings.[12]

### *Up*

Then came the second great surge of Imperial-Country Shinto, commonly referred to as State Shinto (*kokka shintō* 国家神道), after the Meiji Restoration of 1868. Just as with the first upward surge, this one appears to have been generated by a concern among the ruling elite that the state was being threatened by both rebellion at home and invasion from abroad. And as was true during the earlier period of Great Reforms, the years before and after 1868 were marked by turmoil and civil war that plummeted a new set of leaders into positions of state control.

The Meiji leaders, like the earlier Reformers, were alarmed most however by the threat of foreign danger, especially because Western powers were then firing their guns at Japanese people on Japanese soil. Commodore Mathew C. Perry of the United States was backed by a fleet of armed vessels when he exerted pressure on the military government (*bakufu* 幕府) in 1853 and again in 1854. In the face of such military might, Japan drew back from its isolationist policy and agreed to permit limited trade. Then after two retaliatory attacks by foreign warships—first by those of the English in 1863 and then by the four allied powers (England, Holland, France, and the United States) in 1864—a joint letter was submitted to the military government by representatives of these same four powers. Delivered with nine armed ships in attendance, the letter was essentially an ultimatum. In return for waiving two-thirds of an indemnity, it demanded the opening of two more ports, a reduction of duties on foreign imports, the emperor's approval of all treaties, and a reply within seven days. Six days later the Japanese military government yielded on all points. W. G. Beasley writes that the resulting treaty settlement of 1866 made Japan as much "a client state of the West as China was" (Beasley 1989, 306). And during the next twenty-five years, while Japan was trying desperately to head off further advances by Western powers and to free itself from "unequal" treaties and extraterritoriality, Meiji leaders adopted drastic reforms for strengthening Japan—militarily, economically, and spiritually.

Results of their efforts in the material realm were quite impressive. Backed by a modernized army and navy, amazing industrial development, and a statewide system of education, Japan became strong enough by 1905 to defeat Russia in war. And in the spiritual realm Japan was experiencing, by the time of Pearl Harbor, one of the world's most virulent outbursts of nationalism.

How did this happen? A defining point in the upswing of the movement seems to have come in 1866 when Iwakura Tomomi (1825–1883), like Prince Shōtoku over 1,200 years before, put into writing just what he thought the role of a Japanese sovereign should be at that particular time of crisis. Iwakura claimed that if national prestige was to be restored, three changes had to be made: The country must be united, national policy and administration must derive from a single source, and the imperial court must become the "center of national government" (Jansen 1989, 353). Although both Prince Shōtoku and Iwakura Tomomi stressed reliance on Japan's sacred sovereign, their views of sovereignty were fundamentally different. For the prince, a sovereign's role was to be autocratic; but for Iwakura, symbolic. The "center of national government," to use Iwakura's words, was to be the "imperial court," not the emperor. The Meiji-era record shows that Iwakura himself, along with vigorous "young samurai" from Satsuma and Chōshu, made recommendations (decisions) that were then handed down as Imperial Edicts by Emperor Meiji, who at the time of his enthronement in 1867 was only fifteen years of age.

The symbolic power, or "sacred-centeredness,"[13] of the emperor, although immeasurable and difficult to articulate, was clearly a force of considerable importance throughout this second surge of Imperial-Country Shinto. Power of this type certainly flowed from the Charter Oath (*gikajō no seimon* 五か条の誓文) that, proclaimed by Emperor Meiji on 14 March 1868, enabled the nation to accept the revolutionary changes being announced: the abolition of *bakufu* control and the establishment of government by Meiji leaders serving a symbolic sovereign. Because the new leaders consciously or unconsciously valued the symbolic power of their sovereign, they continued to have the emperor proclaim other edicts at key points in the modernization of Japan, including the edict of 1889 by which the constitution was promulgated and the 1890 Imperial Rescript on Education.

From the very beginning of Japan's 1868 Meiji Restoration, the new leaders were obviously intent on restoring the ancient principle of sovereignty expressed as "the unity of ritual and administration" (*saisei ittchi* 祭政一致). We know that this is what they had in mind because just two weeks after proclaiming the restoration of imperial rule they announced, on 17 January 1868, the establishment of a new administrative order of "three ministries and seven departments" that included a Department of Kami Affairs (*jingi jimu-ka* 神祇事務科). Then, on 3 February 1868, an order was issued calling explicitly for the restoration of the ancient Council of Kami Affairs that had stood along side the Council of State in the ancient emperor-centered *ritsuryō* state. That order also announced the new government's three famous Imperial-Country Shinto objectives: the revival of the Council of Kami Affairs, the separation of Buddhism from Shinto, and the prohibition of Christianity. Finally, on 13 March 1868, the day before the Charter Oath was issued, "all *kami* shrines and all *kami* rituals" were placed under the control of the Council of Kami Affairs. Such measures—all taken within the Restoration's first three months—indicate that the new Meiji leaders aimed not only to reaffirm the "ritual" side of Japanese sovereignty but to restore ancient bureaucratic instrumentalities for the generation of a second great surge of Imperial-Country Shinto (Murakami 1988, 45–46).

In November 1868, the Meiji government ordered all Japanese people to participate in the Shinto Festival for Tasting the First Fruits (*niiname-sai* 新嘗祭). This was justified by declaring that the festival had been celebrated by Japanese emperors for nearly 3,000 (*sic*) years (Murakami 1988, 68). Clearly the purpose was to promote Imperial-Country Shinto at all social levels, not just among the ruling elite as during the Great Reforms of ancient times. That was also what the government obviously intended when it initiated the Proclaiming-the-Great-Teachings (*taikyō senpu* 大教宣布) movement in 1870 and announced that each Japanese individual—as a "clan child" (*ujiko* 氏子) of a particular shrine in the burgeoning state-shrine system—was to participate in state festivals honoring the divine relationships between the Japanese emperor and the Great Goddess Amaterasu.

The popular thrust of the Imperial-Country Shinto movement was awesome, especially between 1932 and the end of World War II in 1945. That was when all schoolchildren and their teachers were expected to participate in ceremonies during which the principal of every school stood before a well-guarded picture of the emperor to read His Majesty's Imperial Rescript on Education. All means of written and oral communication, beginning with books and newspapers and eventually including radios and motion pictures, became powerful instruments for deepening and broadening the belief that the Japanese sovereignty had been, and always would be, sanctified by Amaterasu (Hardacre 1989, 21–132).

A major institutional innovation came with the creation of a new shrine—now called the Yasukuni Shrine—where Japan's war dead are enshrined as *kami*. Because the Japanese have always regarded anything dead or dying as pollution (*kegare* 汚れ), funerals and memorial rites are not usually held at Shinto shrines where *kami* reside but at Buddhist temples. Thus a religious historian cannot but be amazed that the Yasukuni Shrine was ever built but understands why this occurred one year after the 1868 order that Shinto shrines be separated from anything Buddhist (*shinbutsu bunri* 神仏分離). The founding of Yasukuni indicated that the government was not simply attempting to strengthen Imperial-Country Shinto but also trying to sanctify Japanese sovereignty in an essentially Buddhist way. Although Yasukuni became the center of a statewide shrine complex that undoubtedly enhanced the emperor's symbolic power, it has never been deeply rooted in popular Shinto beliefs and practices.[14]

After 1936, Imperial-Country Shinto became a dynamic movement that seems to have deeply affected most Japanese individuals. That was when the country was being threatened by the "ABCD encirclement" of America, Britain, China, and the Dutch, Japanese generals and admirals were moving into positions of governmental control, and tension with China was developing into war. In 1937, the People's Spiritual Mobilization Campaign (*kokumin seishin sōdōin undō* 国民精神総動員運動) was launched, and the Ministry of Education published "Principles of Nation Body" (*kokutai no hongi* 国体の本義), copies of which were distributed to schools throughout the country (Gauntlett 1949). Aroused by what was heard on radio and read in newspapers and magazines, many Japanese were convinced that Japan was ruled by a divine emperor and was fighting for a righteous cause. Indeed many claimed that Japan was endowed with a sacred mission to save all Asians from the exploitation of greedy Western powers.

After Pearl Harbor, expressions of loyalty to the emperor became quite fanatical. That was when we in the United States began hearing stories of Japanese soldiers marching toward certain death or making suicidal attacks on U.S. aircraft carriers, yelling "Long Live the Emperor!" (*tennö heika banzai* 天皇陛下万歳). Such fanaticism has led Matsumae Takeshi, a Shinto scholar who was a Japanese soldier in Borneo at the end of the war, to write that the war was not caused by the army or the government but by Japan's "imperial-country way of thinking" (*kökoku shisö* 皇国思想). More precisely he writes that the war was due mainly to the Japanese belief that "changes in Heaven and on Earth" are the doings of *kami*, leading Japanese people to think that they were the only *kami*-chosen people on earth and to look down on others as outcasts or slaves (Matsumae 1992a, 69–71).

### *Down*

Following Japan's surrender in 1945, state support for Imperial-Country Shinto was constitutionally forbidden. State patronage and state control of religious institutions therefore have virtually disappeared. Schoolchildren, viewers of television, and readers of books and newspapers now seldom hear or read anything about the Great Goddess Amaterasu and her sacred ties with the Japanese emperor. Internationalism is in the air. And yet the emperor of Japan probably is one of the strongest "sacred centers" in the modern world, as was vividly demonstrated by the long and expensive Great Enthronement Ceremony held for the enthronement of Emperor Akihito. Rituals performed in the presence of Amaterasu at Ise, and at thousands of shrines all over Japan, no longer generate feelings and beliefs properly described as militarism or ultranationalism. But by nourishing pride in the uniqueness and antiquity of Japan's imperial line of descent from the Great Goddess, these rituals continue to sanctify Japanese sovereignty.

NOTES

1. Philippi (1968) translates this phrase differently: "the framework of the state, the great foundations of imperial influence" (41). The characters that I translate as "sovereignty" are *öka* 王化. The first is commonly rendered as "king" or "ruler" and the second denotes change in that which is represented by the first character.
2. This term comes from the Japanese word *kökoku* 皇国 (Imperial Country) used by Muraoka Tsunetsugu when stating that *kökoku shugi* 皇国主義 (Imperial-Country-ism) is the first of three basic characteristics of Shinto (Muraoka 1964, 11–21). I do not think that *kökoku shugi* has been basic to popular Shinto. However *kökoku shugi* has figured prominently in Imperial-House Shinto (*köshitsu shintö* 皇室神道) of ancient times, in State Shinto (*kokka shintö* 国家神道) since 1868, and in that part of post-1945 Shrine Shinto (*jinja shintö* 神社神道) focused on the worship of the Great Goddess as the founder of Japan's imperial line. I therefore use *Imperial-Country*

*Shinto* to denote all forms of Shinto in which the Great Goddess is worshipped as the founder of Japan's endless line of sacred emperors.

3. The Chinese character that I have translated as "small state" is 国, which has been translated by Tsunoda as "community" (Tsunoda 1951, 1–20). But I join those who prefer the term "small state" (*shōkoku* 小国).
4. Both have been translated into English by Philippi 1968 and Aston 1956.
5. Scholars are now inclined to think that the name Amaterasu Ōkami did not appear until the seventh century, when the Imperial-Country Shinto system was officially established.
6. This and other items from the *Nihon shoki* have been translated by me but I often use Aston's words and phrases (Aston 1956). For an excellent study of Japanese kingship in ancient Japan see Piggott 1997.
7. Around 250 CE large and impressive mounds (*kofun* 古墳) were built for the burial of Great Kings who ruled the state of Yamato, whereas smaller ones of the previous Yayoi period were for the burial of clan heads who ruled small states. After 645 Buddhist temples—also erected for the purpose of honoring deceased rulers—became more grand. Whereas those of the previous fifty years or so seem to have been built by heads of the Soga clan for consoling and honoring the souls of deceased predecessors, the more impressive later ones were erected by emperors and empresses for honoring their own predecessors (descendants of the Great Goddess) in a new and exotic way.
8. Note that the first character for both *emperor* and *Amaterasu* is Heaven, a character that Chinese Confucianists and Taoists had long used for ultimate power and authority.
9. This Heavenly Kami may well have been the Great Goddess since the characters for *amatsukami* are included in the name Amaterasu Omikami.
10. Pilgrimages enter the picture of state sovereignty only tangentially and will therefore be a separate study (see Davis 1992, 45–80).
11. A Fujiwara patronized the Kasuga Shrine in Nara, a Miinamoto the Tsurgaoka Hachiman Shrine in Kamakura, and a Tokugawa the Tōshō-gū Shrine in Nikko.
12. For the intellectual history of Ise after 900 see Teeuwen 1996; and for the "systematic sacralization" before the Meiji surge, see Ooms 1985.
13. This is the kind of power that Shils writes about in such sentences as this one: "One of the most striking changes in modern societies is the increase in the power and au- thority of the center over its own periphery and the simultaneous increase in the power of the periphery over the center of its own society" (quoted in Hardacre 1989, 3).
14. For a superb study of the "politics of death," see Ebersole 1989.

## REFERENCES

Aston, W. G. 1956. *Nihongi: Chronicles of Japan from the Earliest Times to A.D, 697*. London: George Allen & Unwin. Reprint.

Beasley, W. G. 1989. "The foreign threat and the opening of the ports." Pp. 259–308 in *The Cambridge History of Japan* (vol. 5). Cambridge: Cambridge University Press.

Blacker, Carmen. 1990. "The *Shinza* or God-seat in the *Daijosai*: Throne, Bed, or Incubation Couch." *Japanese Journal of Religious Studies* 17: 179–197.

Bock, Felicia. 1970. *Engi-Shiki: Procedures of the Engi Era* (Books I-V). Tokyo: Sophia University Press.

———. 1972. *Engi-Shiki: Procedures of the Engi Era* (Books VI-X). Tokyo: Sophia University Press.

———. 1990. "The Great Feast of the Enthronement." *Monumenta Nipponica* 45: 27–38.

Brown, Delmer M. 1993a. "Introduction." Pp. 1–47 in *The Cambridge History of Japan* (vol. 1). Cambridge: Cambridge University Press.

———. 1993b. "The Yamato Kingdom." Pp. 108–162 in *The Cambridge History of Japan* (vol. 1). Cambridge: Cambridge University Press.

Davis, Winston. 1992. *Japanese Religion and Society: Paradigms of Structure and Change.* Albany: State University of New York Press.

Ebersole, Gary L. 1989. *Ritual Poetry and the Politics of Death in Early Japan*. Princeton, NJ: Princeton University Press.

Gauntlett, John Owen. 1949. *Kokutai no Hongi: Cardinal Principles of the National Entity of Japan*. Cambridge: Harvard University Press.

Hardacre, Helen. 1989. *Shintō and the State, 1868–1988*. Princeton, NJ: Princeton University Press.

Holtom, D. C. 1972. *The Japanese Enthronement Ceremonies: With an Account of the Imperial Regalia*. Tokyo: Sophia University Press.

Hori Ichiro. 1968. *Folk Religion in Japan: Continuity and Change*. Chicago: Chicago University Press.

Jansen, Marius B. 1989. "The Meiji Restoration." Pp. 308–366 in *The Cambridge History of Japan* (vol. 5). Cambridge: Cambridge University Press.

Kojiki 古事記. 1959. Shintei zōho: Kokushi Taikei 新訂増補国史大系 [Great Collection of Historical Materials: new and revised edition], ed. Kuroita Katsumi (vol. 10). *Kojiki*. Tokyo: Yoshikawa Kōbunkan.

Matsumae Takeshi 松前健. 1992a. *Aru shinwa gakusha no hansei-ki: senjō no shisen to sengo no kutō wo koete.* ある神話学者の半生記一戦場の死線と戦後の苦闘を越えて [An account of the last half of the life of a certain scholar of myth: transcending the deathline of war and the troubles that followed]. Tokyo: Kindai Bungei Sha.

———.1992b. "Kōtai Jingū: Toyouke Daijingū" 皇大神宮。豊受大神宮 [Imperial Great Shrine and Great Toyouke Shrine]. Pp. 9–42 in *Jinja to seichi* 神社と聖地, [Shrines and Sacred Places]. Vol. 6 of *Nihon no kamigami* 日本の神 [The Kami of Japan]. Tokyo: Shiromizu Sha.

Miller, Richard J. 1974. *Ancient Japanese Nobility: The Kabane Ranking System*. Berkeley: University of California Press.

Murakami Shigeyoshi 村上重良. 1984. *Kokka shintō* 国家神道 [State Shinto]. Tokyo: Iwanami Shinsho. 14th printing.

———. 1988. *Tennō no saishi* 天皇の祭祀 [Kami-worship of the Emperor]. Tokyo: Iwanami Shinsho. 6th printing.

Muraoka, Tsunetsugu. 1964. *Studies in Shinto Thought*, trans. Delmer M. Brown and James T. Araki. New York: Greenwood Press.

Naoki Kōjirō. 1993. "The Nara state." Pp. 221–267 in *The Cambridge History of Japan* (vol. 1). Cambridge: Cambridge University Press.

Nihon shoki 日本書紀. 1974–1975. *Nihon koten bungaku taikei* 日本古典文学大系 [Great Collection of Japanese Classics], ed. Sakamoto Tarō et al. (vols. 67 and 68). *Nihon shoki* (vols. 1 and 2). Tokyo: Iwanami Shoten.

Ooms, Herman. 1985. *Tokugawa Ideology: Early Constructs, 1570–1680*. Princeton, NJ: Princeton University Press.

Philippi, Donald L. 1968. *Kojiki: Translated with an Introduction and Notes*. Tokyo: Tokyo University Press.

Piggott, Joan R. 1997. *The Emergence of Japanese Kingship*. Stanford, CA: Stanford University Press.

Teeuwen, Mark. 1996. *Watarai Shinto: An Intellectual History of the Outer Shrine in Ise*. Leiden: Research School CNWS.

Tsunoda Ryūsaku, trans. 1951. *Japan in the Chinese Dynastic Histories: Later Han through Ming Dynasties*. South Pasadena, CA: P.D. and Ione Perkins.

# 7

# Yorùbá Goddesses and Sovereignty in Southwestern Nigeria

*Jacob K. Olúpọ̀nà*

*Ọ̀ṣun Ọ̀ṣogbo, I greet you;*
*Hail the great mother—goddess Ọ̀ṣun Ọ̀ṣogbo.*
*The great spirits in the deep water*
*The Ọba's beloved water, do not forget me,*
*Aládékojú, my Olódùmarè (supreme god).*
*Ọ̀ṣun is the savior goddess who will save us all,*
*The savior goddess who saves the devotees of Òrìṣà.*
*You with the protective scarf, wrap me in your protective arms;*
*Mother, come quickly and give me gift of children.*
*Ọ̀ṣun is trustworthy enough to live with;*
*She stands by her devotees till the end.*
*Whenever we hear a joyful music from the river, it is Ọ̀ṣun who is dancing, Ọ̀ṣun who is honored with a banquet after her melodious music.*
*Ogbóǹmẹ̀lẹ́, the great healer who resides in the river,*
*From the deep river, come quickly and give us the gift of children.*
*Ogbóǹmẹ̀lẹ́, only Ọ̀ṣun can provide me with children—*
*Ogbóǹmẹ̀lẹ́, the one who bestows exquisite ornaments of brass to the Ọba of Ìgèdè.*
*As a sign of her intrinsic beauty, her long neck enables her to wear many rows of coral beads.*[1]

As the recitation by an Ọ̀ṣun priestesses clearly shows, the beautiful river goddess of the Yorùbá, Ọ̀ṣun, plays many roles; not only is she a savior and a healer, it is she who bestows gifts of kingship on the ruler, the Ọba. Further, she is one of many Yorùbá goddesses connected with the living rulers of several Yorùbá towns and cities where the river Ọ̀ṣun passes through.

In spite of the prominence of Yorùbá goddesses in scholarly works on African religions in Africa and the African Diaspora (Bádèjọ 1996; Gleason 1992), discourses on Yorùbá goddesses and Yorùbá goddess religion have not experienced the popularity that goddess scholarship has enjoyed in the history of religions and cultural studies in other regions of the world. Indeed, the ideological and scholarly impetus that propels goddess movements and goddess religiosity in Western academic cycles has hardly gained prominence in African studies of religions. Nevertheless, a cursory look at some of the available works on Yorùbá goddesses reveals that these goddesses play a significant role, not only among the Yorùbá pantheon of deities, but in the political and social setup of villages, towns, and city-states where such deities are revered and worshiped. This essay examines the role of a set of Yorùbá goddesses—Ọ̀ṣun, Yemòó, Òrósùn, Ọ̀rọ̀ṣẹ̀n, and the Oǹdó-Yorùbá culture heroine and goddess Púpùpú—in the political rituals and governance of the Yorùbá towns where they are most prominent. Although my analysis is based on the myths and rituals of these goddesses in relation to sovereignty and kingship ceremonies in general, the symbolic meanings and their representations in the yearly enactment ceremonies of sacred kingship form the core of the essay.

In most of the traditions of Yorùbá towns and cities the goddesses maintain a spiritual relationship with the male king, whom they may adopt as a son or choose as husband or cohort, and who assists in maintaining peace, order, and prosperity in the kingdom. At the core of Yorùbá religion is the sacred quest to obtain from the deities blessings of wealth, longevity, and children. More than the male deities in the Yorùbá pantheon, goddesses seem tuned to performing these functions and fulfilling these roles for their devotees, a factor that makes the male sovereign's close spiritual relationship to a goddess quite beneficial to the sovereign and his subjects. I also argue that a viable civil religion in several Yorùbá city-states emanates from the goddess traditions. The goddesses hold the moral fabric of their communities together, especially in the face of the new plurality and modernization.

## The Goddess in Creation Mythology

One way to approach the place of goddesses in the Yorùbá religion and thought system is to examine the entire religious worldview in the sources available to us and locate therein the names of the goddesses. In other words, one can write a whole treatise on Yorùbá religion from the perspective of the role and symbolism of Yorùbá goddesses. As this approach might take more space than is allotted to me, I devote my analysis to a consideration of some aspects of Yorùbá religion, which nevertheless is not exhaustive: the cosmology, ideology, and rituals of kingship in relationship to goddess traditions in specific Yorùbá towns and cities.

## Ọ̀ṣun Goddess and the Creation of the Universe

The Yorùbá people of Nigeria, who number more than thirty million, claim that the world was created in Ilé-Ifẹ̀, their sacred city. In spite of the descent of 201 deities into the created universe, life nevertheless was unpleasant because the world was not properly established. Chaos,[2] symbolized by sterility, death, famine, and epidemic, threatened to destroy the newly created world. The primordial gods, nearly all male, returned to inform Olódùmarè—the supreme being—about the situation of the world, urging him to set things aright. To their surprise, Olódùmarè noticed that Ọ̀ṣun, the only female deity who had accompanied the male deities to the earth and witnessed the creation of the universe, was absent, left behind by the gods. Olódùmarè then asked the male deities, "Where is Ọ̀ṣun?" (Bádèjẹ 1996). He knew that they had left Ọ̀ṣun behind because she was female. Olódùmarè ordered the male gods to return to the earth to meet with Ọ̀ṣun and negotiate a peaceful resolution to the crisis. To Ọ̀ṣun the gods then revealed all their secret deliberations, whereupon Ọ̀ṣun used her *àṣẹ*, the ultimate symbol of vital sacred power, to prevent the world from total collapse.

The significance of this myth becomes clearer when we compare it to a similar narrative in the biblical tradition of Wisdom, a personified primordial female power present when Yahweh created the universe (Niditch 1997, 56).[3] The difference in the two narratives is also striking. Unlike the biblical story where Yahweh himself directly resolves the problem of chaos (Niditch 1997, 56), in the Yorùbá narrative, Olódùmarè sends the male deities back to Ọ̀ṣun to find the root of the crisis and sort out a peaceful settlement. The Yorùbá narrative traces the efficacy of the gods' *àṣẹ*, the creative power in the universe, to Ọ̀ṣun. In a way, Ọ̀ṣun's àṣẹ is similar to the Hindu *Śakti,* the creative force and power "through which the male principle is able to express itself in creation" (Contursi 1996, 46–47).

## Goddess and Founder of a City-State: Púpùpú as Oǹdó Culture Hero

If the Ọ̀ṣun narrative illustrates the centrality of the goddess in the making of the Yorùbá universe, the next myth illustrates her role in the construction and maintenance of a royal city-state (Ìlú Aládé) and its sacred kingship, using the example of Púpùpú, cultural hero and founder of Oǹdó, a Yorùbá city-state. I show how a "goddess-focused religion" becomes the basis for women to establish and control a Yorùbá religiopolitical system (Gordon 1996, 251) in the Oǹdó community.

Long after the world was created in Ilé-Ifẹ̀, one of the wives of Odùduwà gave birth to twins. The birth of twins was considered an abomination there, but because the wife was Odùduwà's favorite, her life and that of the twins were spared. However, Odùduwà sent them out of the city, and under the guidance of a hunter, the party traveled eastward. Before leaving Ilé-Ifẹ̀, they were instructed by the palace diviner to take a yam stick (è*dó*) as their walking stick and to poke it into the ground as they went along. Wherever the stick would not go into the ground the group was to settle. As predicted, when the group got to the site of present-day Oǹdó the yam stick would not penetrate the ground. The party exclaimed in surprise *èdó du do* ("the yam stick will not go in"). The myth explains that Oǹdó is a contracted version of the sentence *èdó du do*. By the time the group arrived, one of the twins, Púpùpú, now already a grown-up woman, was installed as the paramount ruler and accorded the rights and privileges of an Ọba (sovereign). Púpùpú reigned until a very old age. When the Oǹdó people asked her to give them a substitute ruler because she was too old to govern, Púpùpú then named her first son, who later became known as Airo, "a replacement," as king, placed her crown on his head, and disappeared into the underworld.

The myth illustrates how sovereignty passed from the female to the male line; Púpùpú became apotheosized and recognized as the first ruler, culture hero, and goddess-founder of Oǹdó city-state. She is credited with the establishment of legitimate kingship in Oǹdó. Today the Oǹdó Ọba (king) derives his authority through his mythic descent from the primogenitrix Ọba Púpùpú. The Oǹdó themselves insist that the ultimate source of their sacred kingship is female, or a queen. In reality, political authority and power wielded by a male king are not absolute and are not seen in isolation from an equally significant ritual authority and power that women control. For example, during the annual Ọduń Ọba (the king's festival), the king's drummer, kneeling in front of the king, recites the entire king list, and it is a great taboo for the drummer to forget to name Ọba Púpùpú as the first ruler in Oǹdó kingdom. I further illustrate this by examining the impact of the Púpùpú narrative on the actual political structure and the kingship rituals.

Oǹdó political structure reflects the primordial myth just summarized. It is a dual-sex political system (Okonjo 1976; Eames 1988; Olúpọ̀nà 1991). On the one hand, there is the male hierarchy of high chiefs (Ẹ̀hàre) headed by the male Ọba, who is called Ọ̀ṣemàwé. A female hierarchy of chiefs, referred to as Òpójì and headed by a paramount female chief called Lọ́buǹ constitutes a "parallel authority structure" (Gordon 1996, 251) to the Ẹ̀hàrẹ. In principle the apotheosis of Púpùpú, the Lọ́buǹ is the most revered title in the Oǹdó kingdom. Like Púpùpú, the office of the Lọ́buǹ is surrounded with mysteries and many taboos.

It is in her ritual performances that the role of Lọ́buǹ, and by extension Púpùpú, in Oǹdó kingship becomes clearer. The drama of Púpùpú's transfer of kingship to the male line is reenacted in the ritual installation of a new king in Oǹdó. Lọ́buǹ's primary role is to install a new Ọba whenever one is made, a realization of the mythic origin in the narrative cited earlier. Whenever a Lọ́buǹ dies, a new one cannot be appointed until the reigning Ọba dies because there should not be two "reigning kings" at the same time. The new Lọ́buǹ is thus elected for the main purpose of installing a new Ọba.

Whereas the goddess legitimizes the king and his sovereignty, her name and symbol may equally be invoked to protest what is considered unkingly behaviors and abuse of authority. Oǹdó celebrates an annual ritual of protest called Òpèpèé, in which ritual songs and lyrics of protest are sung. Several of these songs, performed by women, are directed at the king, the high chiefs, and commoners. One song I recorded during my fieldwork in Oǹdó in 1990 invited the male king to die conveniently so that a new Lọ́buǹ (female king) might be appointed (*Ọba wa Ùtíadé, ṣe duo ku o, di Lọ́buǹ jẹ*). This song and several others led by women and children convey the constant tension between the political power of kingship and the ritual power possessed by Oǹdó women and symbolized by the goddess. However, although such rituals symbolically demonstrate protest, ultimately, as Max Gluckman would argue, they are "intended to preserve and strengthen the established order" (Gluckman 1965, 109).

## Ajé: Goddess of Wealth, Trade, and Fertility and Sacred Kingship

In Oǹdó and Ilé-Ifẹ̀ towns, kingship is closely linked to and encompasses the market economy of the city, and women have total control over it. The word *Lọ́buǹ* in Oǹdó (the female Ọba) literally means a "village market" and indicates her role as controller of the market economy. One of the roles of the Lọ́buǹ and other women-chiefs is to carry out the ritual purification of the new market and to pay homage to Ajé, the goddess of wealth, prosperity, and fertility. Ajé, therefore, symbolizes female power and authority over all the city's commerce, fertility, and reproduction. Ọduń Ajé, the festival of Ajé, is a one-day ceremony in Oǹdó during which each female chief prepares and dresses up her assemblage of Ajé for a public veneration in an open space in front of the palace. Ajé's movable shrine consists of the Igbá Ajé, a big clean bowl, usually of brass, in which several symbols of wealth and fertility are placed. On the evening of the festival, the chiefs carry the Ajé shrine in a procession to the open space in the city, women supporters and children following. One of their songs conveys the power of the goddess.

Ajé excreted on my head
Whoever Ajé touches is made human
Ajé elevates me like a king
I shall forever rejoice
Ajé is happy, so am I

In this song, Ajé gives wealth, fertility, and success in trade. All these are made possible by the deity. The status that Ajé bestows on her worshippers is comparable to that of a king. This song in praise of Ajé indicates the position of honor accorded her in the Oǹdó pantheon. The faithful worshipper and the one who finds favor with the deity become rich and are elevated to the status of a king. This suggests, once again, the Oǹdó women's attitude toward kingship and political authority. That is what they had and controlled before it was taken away from them by men.

The importance of Ajé in the royal rituals of Ilé-Ifẹ̀, the mythical place of Yorùbá origins and center of the world, is illustrated in the celebration known as Ọlọ́jọ́. Ọlọ́jọ́ is the annual ritual that renews the Ọọni's kingship. On this day Òguń (god of war and iron) and Ajé are renewed by the Ọọni, the Ifẹ̀ king. Wearing a magical crown called the Arè, which covers his face and makes him invisible, the Ọọni and his palace entourage progress first to Òkè-Móguń, Òguń's shrine, where he pays homage to the deity with a sacrifice. The Ọọni then proceeds to Ọjà Ifẹ̀, the Ifẹ̀ market where the shrine of Ajé stands. There, two flat stones representing Ajé's shrine are placed on top of each other. The king honors Ajé, the market goddess, as recognition of her importance in the economy of his kingdom. Without prosperity, good harvest, and a good market economy, the king's reign will be not be peaceful because the king embodies the social and economic welfare of the people. But beyond the role of Ajé in the political economy of Ilé-Ifẹ̀, and Yorùbá towns in general, is the ontological meaning she provides. The market, the domain of Ajé, exists as the divine force that upholds the Yorùbá world of Ayé. As a Yorùbá proverb says, *ayé lọjà ọjà layé*—the world is a market and the market is the world. Ọjà Ifẹ̀ is particularly significant as a sacred site in Ilé-Ifẹ̀ because the pilgrimage of the dead to the world beyond begins at Ọjà Ifẹ̀. The Ọọni faces the spirits that regulate the Ifẹ̀ universe for him. When the Ọọni puts on the Arè to visit Òguń in Òkè-Mòguń, he is spiritually and magically prepared to venture into Ọjà Ifẹ̀, where he may confront malevolent spirits and humans with evil minds who try to negate his offering or subvert the prayers and wishes of his people. But Ajé protects the Ọọni against the market's violent forces. As I witnessed in the performances of the Ọlọ́jọ́ festival in Ilé-Ifẹ̀ in 1990, as the Ọọni proceeds to Ajé's place in the market, the Ifẹ̀ people sing, "Whoever would like to prevent this sacrifice from accomplishing its purpose will perish with the offering. This sacrifice of the Ọọni will be accomplished" (*ẹni bá ní kí ẹbọ mọ́ gbà, á bá ẹbọ lọ àṣẹ fiń o, ẹbọ Ọ́ọ́ni*). It is after the Ọọni's visit to Ọjà Ifẹ̀ that the king's emissary proceeds to the first mausoleum in which early Ifẹ̀ kings have been buried, there to make a sacrifice to his royal ancestors. Ajé closes one door against the malevolent spirits and opens another for the king's sacrifice to the spirits of the royal ancestors.

## Goddesses, Wives, and Sacred Kingship

Traditions of goddesses in Yorùbá religion and mythology include numerous stories about powerful wives of the Ọba (kings) who, for one reason or another, become apotheosized as goddesses and culture heroines. The narratives relate how the mysterious disappearance of such figures may result in a blessing for the people and the basis of the king's annual festival and ritual celebration. Two classic examples are the traditions of Ọ̀rọṣẹ̀ǹ in Ọ̀wọ̀ and Òrósuǹ in Ìdaǹrè, both in eastern Yorùbá.

Ọ̀rọṣẹ̀ǹ, an affluent queen and an unusually beautiful woman, was the wife of Ọlọ́wọ̀ Rẹ̀rẹ̀ńgẹ̀jẹ̀ǹ (Abíọ́dún 1998: 101) in the ancient Ọ̀wọ̀ kingdom. Ọ̀rọṣẹ̀ǹ had actually married many kings before coming to Ọ̀wọ̀ to marry Rẹ̀rẹ̀ńgẹ̀jẹ̀ǹ. Ọ̀rọṣẹ̀ǹ possessed beads and extraordinary power, both of which enhanced the status and prestige of Ọlọ́wọ̀ Rẹ̀rẹ̀ńgẹ̀jẹ̀ǹ when he married her. As a result, she was elevated to a status above her co-wives, who were all jealous. Further, Ọ̀rọ̀ṣẹ̀n insisted on several taboos, things people should not do in her presence: For example, one must not grind okra (used for preparing stew); one must not throw water out into the open yard; anyone coming from the farm must not dump loads of firewood. The taboos negate domestic and physical activities ordinarily associated with the daily activities of women and housewives. This indicates that Ọ̀rọ̀ṣẹ̀n was not an ordinary woman. Naturally, her co-wives were jealous of the special attention and adoration given Ọ̀rọ̀ṣẹ̀n and her sudden rise in status in the Ọ̀wọ̀ palace. They conspired against her, waiting for a time when the king was out of the palace to act. When Ọ̀rọ̀ṣẹ̀n, the myth goes, had an altercation with her co-wives in the Ọ̀wọ̀ palace, the co-wives decided to break all her taboos. Angered by this confrontation, she hurriedly left the palace. The palace chiefs pursued her, putting up a hot chase. The search party sent after her located her at Ugbó 'Laja but unsuccessfully tried to persuade her to return to the palace. As the search party tried to capture her to bring her back to town, she disappeared into the ground, but not until the search party had grabbed the *ọ̀jà* (a piece of cloth) she wore as head tie. The place where this event took place, now a sacred grove, is called Ugbó 'Laja (the sacred place of *ọ̀jà*). Ọ̀rọ̀ṣẹ̀n's terra cotta sculptured image, excavated from the sacred forest by Ekpo Eyo, is connected with the mythology. Standing at a distance, she informed the Ọ̀wọ̀ people that she would not return but that every year they should sacrifice 200 items of various articles for sacrificial ritual goals: kola nut, alligator pepper, and so on. In return, she promised to protect the city and to bestow the blessing of wealth and children upon its inhabitants. She promised that the town of Ọ̀wọ̀ would not be subjected to any invasions and that there would be peace in the kingdom.

The drama of Ọ̀rọ̀ṣẹ̀n's departure from Ọ̀wọ̀ and the sacrifice at Ugbó 'Laja is the core of the annual Igogo festival in Ọ̀wọ̀, a colorful festival where the Ọlọ́wọ̀, the incumbent king, dresses like a woman in coral beads and brass ornaments, his head plaited like a woman's, and pays homage to Ọ̀rọ̀ṣẹ̀n. In exchange for Ọ̀rọ̀ṣẹ̀n's guidance and protection, the king offers significant sacrifice to her at Ugbó 'Laja, one each of the 200 items she has demanded. In honor of Ọ̀rọ̀ṣẹ̀n, no man or woman is allowed to wear a head tie or cap during the Igogo festival.[4] In the Igogo festival, the Ọlọ́wọ̀ goes to Ugbó 'Laja to pay homage to Ọ̀rọ̀ṣẹ̀n, where he then declares, "I, Ọlọ́wọ̀, your offspring have come to pay homage to you. Let no war invade Ọ̀wọ̀. Let no epidemics visit this kingdom." It is in recognition of his lower status to the goddess that the Ọlọ́wọ̀, who normally does not keep his head uncovered, does not wear any crown on this day. During this ceremony, the Ọlọ́wọ̀ assumes a feminine posture and his ceremonial dress reflects Ọ̀rọ̀ṣẹ̀n's wealth and power. The Ọlọ́wọ̀ wears a set of coral beads called *patako*, a beaded wear criss-crossed to cover his chest like a woman's blouse. He also wears a big skirt called *abolukun*, as part of the association with Ọ̀rọ̀ṣẹ̀n's feminine gender. In praise of the king, the Ọlọ́wọ̀ is addressed as *ọ̀gẹ̀dẹ̀ so tọ̀ tọ̀* ("the prolific banana tree that bears much fruit"), a reference to the motif of crop fertility and by extension human procreation, the blessings bestowed by the goddess and signified by the Ọlọ́wọ̀'s protruding belly. The Ọlọ́wọ̀ is showered with praises that reflect his association with Ọ̀rọ̀ṣẹ̀n. Indeed, he assumes Ọ̀rọ̀ṣẹ̀n's persona as a wealthy, fertile, and rich woman of enormous power. The Ọlọ́wọ̀'s acolytes say to their king, *Ọwá me di lani o* ("the king is pregnant today"). Ọlọ́wọ̀ is described as *Òkun Àràgbàrigbì* ("the mighty ocean") associated with his might and symbolized in the king's big white skirt. These praises are a direct reference to the honor and power of Ọ̀rọ̀ṣẹ̀n. Although Ọ̀rọ̀ṣẹ̀n's story is located in Ọ̀wọ̀'s mythic past, it is not unlikely that it has solid historical evidence. It may refer to the period of trade success in Ọ̀wọ̀ kingdom when a powerful woman who once ruled Ọ̀wọ̀ had lucrative trade contacts with distance kingdoms. She then became apotheosized as a goddess long after her reign.

The goddess Òrósùn in Ìdànrè has a mythic origin similar to that of Ọ̀rọ̀ṣẹ̀n in Ọ̀wọ̀. Òrósùn, a hill goddess, was said to be a beautiful stranger who visited Ìdànrè, a mountainplace in eastern Yorùbá territory. Òrósùn was married to Ọlọ́fin, the legendary powerful ruler of Ìdànrè, associated with the act of the magical spoken words. Òrósùn, often addressed as great mother by the Ìdànrè people, lived for a long time. When she died, her grave became a pilgrimage center and a place for the king's emissary to worship her on behalf of the city. During the annual Òrósùn festival in 1990, which I witnessed, the priests and priestesses divided into various priesthoods under the guardianship of chief priests that constitute Ìdànrè Òrósùn's priestly class and gathered in the house of their leaders on Ìdànrè hill. In the early morning, the priests began a procession to the Òrósùn's place at the grove to offer her sacrifices. At noon, the Ìdànrè people gathered at the Jọmọ's market to welcome the returning pilgrims. Then the priests distributed kola nuts as gifts from the goddess to members in the awaiting crowd. The shout of *yere mi o* ("do not forget me") filled the air as individuals in an orderly manner called the attention of the priests to him or herself. This is also an indirect reference to the great goddess not to forget their supplications. The Òrósùn festival day is also the occasion to shower praises upon the goddess. Her devotees describe her as *yèyé ajé lùsọ̀*, ("the great mother, who brings wealth and prosperity"). She is also described as Yelọ́mọ ("the goddess who provides plenty of children to her devotees"). I was told that her festival day must not be disrespected. Because Òrósùn also symbolizes purity, each priest must bathe three times on the day before the celebration. Their white ceremonial clothes must be properly washed and immaculately clean. I was told that a number of taboos surround Òrósùn's cult. Òrósùn's priests are forbidden to have intercourse with minors and must refrain from lying and thievery. Such moral constraints make the selection of her priests and priestesses very difficult. It also imposes a strict ethical standard on the community, especially since she commands a very large priesthood.

After this morning pilgrimage, the priests visit the Ọba's palace to give him feedback. They inform the Ọwá (king) of Ìdànrè that they have offered sacrifices to Òrósùn on his behalf and that Òrósùn has accepted his offerings. A climatic event in the entire ritual occurs late in the evening. A special party of priests quickly enter the inner chamber of the Ọba's palace to take from him a second offering of gifts along with the king's *àṣẹ*, the powerful magical object and symbol associated with the kingship, for renewal at Òrósùn's shrine. The king very swiftly brings out the *àṣẹ*, points it in the direction of the sun, offers prayers and praises to Òrósuǹ, and hands it over to the priests, who wrap it in a little white cloth and proceed very quickly to the sacred grove. When I asked the Ọwá, who was dressed in a ceremonial white cloth, his hair plaited like a woman's with a long hair attachment, what this meant, he informed me that the *àṣẹ* was the most sacred power of kingship. Whatever the king says when he holds it must come to pass. Òrósuǹ reinvigorates this sacred symbol for the king during her annual festival, and without this renewal the king's command and authority will come to naught.

Whereas Òrósuǹ is intricately linked to Ìdaǹrè sacred kingship, she is also linked to Ìdaǹrè's popular culture and social order. Revered as a deity with a strong moral stature in Ìdaǹrè's cosmology, Òrósuǹ is the regulator of the social order. She punishes evildoers and compensates those with good behavior. Several of the prayers I heard during her annual festival relate to requests for children, longevity, and a good life. Quite a number of the devotees urged her to punish their enemies. Indeed, belief in Òrósuǹ's ability to punish evildoers is reflected in some of the common names Ìdaǹrè people bear, such as Orósuǹguǹlekà ("Òrósuǹ overpowers the evildoer") and Orósuǹṣuyì ("Òrósuǹ provides honor and affluence").

## Goddess, Sacred Kingship, and Civil Religion

Another feature of Yorùbá polity in which the goddess tradition plays a significant role is what I have referred to in several places as civil religion (Olúpọ̀nà 1988, 1991), where a community's moral and political fabric is anchored in the mythology and ritual of a culture hero/heroine, deity, or ancestor. The community's religion, growth, and well-being are intricately connected with the narratives of this particular suprahuman entity. The latter forms the basis of the community's civil religion. I illustrate my thesis with the tradition of goddess Ọ̀ṣun in Òṣogbo, a Yorùbá city located 170 kilometers from Lagos. Ọ̀ṣun's tradition, her myth, rituals, and symbolism, is the source of Òṣogbo's political, spiritual, and moral fabric. The city's sacred kingship provides the glue that holds the community together.

Òṣogbo was founded by a prince called Làróyé (Ọláróyè) who left his place in Iléṣà, another major Yorùbá town, and settled first in a village called Ìpolé. When there was water shortage in Ìpolé, Làróyé sent a hunter called Tìmẹ̀hìn (Olútimẹ̀hìn) to go in search of water. Tìmẹ̀hìn discovered the Ọ̀ṣun River, and when he felled a tree to make a mark at the river bank before returning to Làróyé, a loud shout came from the river, *wọn ti wo gbogbo ikoko aro mi o, ẹyin ọṣo inu igbo, ẹ tun de* ("you have destroyed my pots of dyes; you wizard of the forest, you are here again"). Tìmẹ̀hìn was frightened and attempted to run away. But the river goddess appeared to him asking him not to panic. Tìmẹ̀hìn went back to Làróyé to narrate his experiences and encounter with Ọ̀ṣun. The group then left Ìpolé and moved to the site discovered by Tìmẹ̀hìn and made the bank of Ọ̀ṣun River their new home. Ọ̀ṣun frequently appeared to people in the new settlement. Once, there was heavy flooding and it was revealed through divination that Ọ̀ṣun wanted the settlement to be moved to another location not too far from the riverbank. In obedience, the people moved to a new site and henceforth began to honor the river goddess annually.

From the narrative, we gathered that the goddess was in the habit of sending her emissary, Ikọ̀, a goddess in the form of a fish, to the people of the new settlement. Ikọ̀ would emerge from the river and, like a diving dolphin, pour cool water into the hands of Làróyé. Ever since, because of his habit of stretching forth his arms to welcome the fish-goddess, Làróyé, the Ọba of Òṣogbo, came to be called Àtaọ́ja ("one who spreads forth hands to welcome fish"). Ọ̀ṣun's water is regarded as sacred, a potent medicinal substance that the Ọba and the Òṣogbo people may use for healing and other rituals. Because of these experiences, the Òṣogbo people adopted Ọ̀ṣun as the tutelary deity of their city and as protector of their king and the royal lineage. The annual festival of Ọ̀ṣun honors the goddess and serves as the festival of the king, reenacting the mythology in an essential renewal of the life of the Òṣogbo community. Evidence suggests that the Òṣogbos' knowledge of Ọ̀ṣun and their various encounters with her in no small way explain their love for the goddess. In the mythic narrative, Ọ̀ṣun is portrayed as a benevolent deity, a source of goodness and kindness. From her *oríkì* ("praise epithets") one learns that Ọ̀ṣun affirms "the legitimacy and beauty of female power" and governs "life, death, and rebirth" (King 1990, 207). The goddess champions the cause of her devotees, who seek her help in struggles against evil magic and medicine. Several of her devotees relish her strength and power and her ability to wage war against evildoers.

In the legends of Òṣogbo, Ọ̀ṣun is credited with a victory Òṣogbo claims over the powerful invading force of the Hawsa-Fulani soldiers. According to this story, during the Yorùbá civil war of the nineteenth century, an event took place that changed the course of Yorùbá and Nigerian political history. Having liquidated the former Ọ̀yọ́ empire, the Fulani Muslim Jihadists camped outside the gates of the city near the home of Ọ̀ṣun, ready to overrun the remaining Ọ̀yọ́ soldiers who took refuge in surrounding villages and towns. But the invaders were defeated when Ọ̀ṣun, who took the form of a food vendor, sold poisoned vegetables (*ẹ̀fọ́ yánrin*) to the Fulani Muslim soldiers. The Jihadists instantly developed uncontrollable diarrhea; in their weakened state they were routed out of Òṣogbo. The Òṣogbo battle had significant consequences for the Yorùbá people, especially as it stopped the rapid Jihadist's expansion into southwestern Nigeria. Ọ̀ṣun's victory over the Muslim forces continues to be recalled in Ọ̀ṣun's festival, where her songs castigate fanatical forms of religious and sacred tradition, especially those hostile and antagonistic toward Ọ̀ṣun's moral authority.

The tradition of Ọ̀ṣun links the goddess with Òṣogbo's prosperity and entrepreneurship. Centrally placed at the intersection of various Yorùbá cities, Òṣogbo has emerged as a growing political and economic center of the region. A major trading center and administrative headquarters during the colonial period, Òṣogbo served as the main railway terminal between Kano in the northern region and Lagos in the southwestern region. Linked with Ọ̀ṣun, Òṣogbo's traditional trade and commerce brought fame for indigo dye, kola nut trade, and arts and crafts. Several *oríki* Ọ̀ṣun (Ọ̀ṣun's praise poetry) refer to the goddess as a superwoman owning a wealth of coral beads (Ìlẹ̀kẹ̀) and brass ornaments (*ide*). Ọ̀ṣun is an archetypal female who embodies the core values and provides the impetus for Òṣogbo's economic success.

Next, I would like to examine the role of Ọ̀ṣun in the ideology and rituals of Òṣogbo kingship. As I observed earlier on, the goddess as such, embodies the religiopolitical structure of the city. As the tutelary deity of Òṣogbo, she forms the core of Òṣogbo's civil religion, a body of symbols, myths, and rituals that affirm the core values and unity of the community. Even though Òṣogbo people today espouse different and at times conflicting "ultimate meaning systems" (Woocher 1990, 156), nevertheless, the people acknowledge their descent from a common ancestral origin, Làróyé and Tìmẹ̀hìn. The Òṣogbo people affirm this unity under the canopy of the sacred kingship whose ideology, rituals, and symbols are derived from their religious experience of Ọ̀ṣun.

Ọ̀ṣun's tradition, especially her ritual process, illustrates not only that she is the embodiment of Òṣogbo's ideology and rituals of sacred kingship but that she is the very expression of royal protection (Frankfurter 1998, 3). Ọ̀ṣun is at the core of both royal kingship and the pantheon of deities in Òṣogbo's cosmology. The collective propitiation of Òṣogbo's deities and cultural heroes by the king takes place in conjunction with Ọ̀ṣun's festival, during which three major spiritual agents are particularly prominent: Ifá (divination god), Eegún (ancestor spirit), and Ògún (god of iron and war).

The festival begins with the ritual of *wíwá* Ọ̀ṣun (literally "in search of Ọ̀ṣun"). This is a quest for the divine presence and power of the goddess. The priests and priestesses of Ọ̀ṣun visit the home of key Ọ̀ṣun functionaries, including high chiefs, other civil chiefs, and the private home of the Ọba in Òṣogbo. They are announcing the commencement of Ọ̀ṣun's festival. Wíwá Ọ̀ṣun is also an entry into the communitas as stage of Òṣogbo's own rite of passage. It represents a time at which the Òṣogbo people set aside individual and communal squabbles to prepare for the propitiation of the goddess. In the next phase, Ìwọ́ Pópó, the Àtaọ́ja (the Ọba) accompanied by a great assemblage of his wives, the town and the palace chiefs, friends, and palace messengers proceed through the main street over the length and breadth of the old city. In this ritual, the king "represents himself to the people precisely as the sacred king, who, as premier ritual intermediary between the realm of [Ọ̀ṣun] and the human sphere, had sole power to assure peace, prosperity and fertility of the land" (Ebersole 1989, 40). The Ìwọ́ Pópó ceremony symbolically establishes Òṣogbo's ancient space, the territory over which the king exercises his power and dominance. Simultaneously, the king also pronounces blessings on his subjects and the territory on behalf of the goddess.

The second phase of Ọ̀ṣun's ceremony consists of a series of rituals renewing the king's authority and power. In the town rituals of Ìbọrí and Ìbọadé, four days before Ọ̀ṣun's day, the town's notables, the royal and priestly classes, assemble in a palace hall in which all the ancient crowns and other royal wares, such as the beaded shoes and staff of office, are kept. The king's ancestor and other royal ancestors are propitiated. The royal drummer recounts the long list of all their past kings. After each king is mentioned by the chanters, the audience responds *kábíyèsí* ("long live the king"). In this way they acknowledge the ongoing presence and power of the deceased royalty together with the conviction that the incumbent king needs their blessings and assistance to achieve a peaceful and prosperous reign. In the recitation, the royal chanters and drummers usher the community into an active participation in the reality of the sacred time of Òṣogbo's mythical history as charted by past rulers. A private ceremony of Ìbọrí follows, during which the king's spirit (*orí inú*, literally "the inner head") is propitiated. This spirit is the king's invisible and ontological self, which controls his earthly destiny.

Perhaps the main part of Ọ̀ṣun's festival is the ritual procession and pilgrimage of the king, the Arugbá (the young maiden who carries Ọ̀ṣun's gifts to the river bank), and the Òṣogbo people to the Ọ̀ṣun River to present their sacrificial offerings. The procession takes place amidst shouts of prayerful wishes to the goddess.

As the Arugbá moves along, she stops in auspicious places, for example, at shrines and temples of supporting deities to whom priests in various places offer prayers for a peaceful pilgrimage. At the river bank, all the various segments of the community proceed to pay homage to the king, acknowledging the authority and power bestowed upon him by the great goddess. The Ọba then wears the ancestral veiled crown, which he dons once a year before Ọ̀ṣun. The king proceeds to Ilé Ọ̀ṣun ("Ọ̀ṣun's house"), sits on the sacred stone where Tìmẹ̀hìn, the first king, sat to receive Ọ̀ṣun's blessings. There, the priests and priestesses of Ọ̀ṣun propitiate the goddess on his behalf, and the Àtaọ́ja himself "encounters" her. Sacrificial offerings to Ọ̀ṣun are made at the river during this ceremony. Here the priests and priestesses of Ọ̀ṣun, led by the Ìyá Ọ̀ṣun, Ọ̀ṣun's chief priestess, place gifts of food presented by the king to Ọ̀ṣun inside a bowl (*ọpọ́n ọ̀ṣun*), which a young man carries to the riverbank, where Ìyá Ọ̀ṣun will present it to the goddess. The solemnity of the ritual is indicated by the teeming crowd, members of which appropriately remove head scarves and caps as the offerings are conveyed to the river. This is both a sign of reverence to the goddess and at the same time an indication that this sacrificial moment is the most auspicious time.

Ọ̀ṣun's festival combines various elements: the invocation of a savior goddess and the two cultural heroes and founders of Òṣogbo—Tìmẹ̀hìn and Làròyé—for the purpose of bringing about human and agricultural well-being to the community. Through this ritual and these ceremonies, the community is guaranteed good health, vitality, prosperity, success in agriculture, and peace in the town. As the founding ritual of Òṣogbo, the burden of its performance lies with the king, who has adopted the festival as his own ritual and ceremony. Òṣogbo civil religion emanates from the institution of sacred kingship, which draws its energy from the Òrìṣà Ọ̀ṣun tradition. The connection between sacred kingship and Ọ̀ṣun can be illustrated by the way the crowd responds to the appearance of the Arugbá carrying the sacrificial offerings to the river. The drummers for the festival recite that it is the Arugbá who is the real king (*lwọ lọba, lwọ làgbà, lwọ lọba lọba lọba*) (Ogungbile 1998, 75). Further, the Arugbá's attendant, in sympathy with the Arugbá who carries a heavy load, utters the following chant of assistance, *Olúwa mi ọfẹ o* ("my Lord, may the load be lighter"); *mọ̀, rọra ṣe, ìyá Àtaọ́ja* ("walk gently, Àtaọ́ja's mother") (Olagunju 1972). The Arugbá, as the incarnation of Ọ̀ṣun, becomes the great goddess. She is honored as the surrogate "mother" of the king and she is bestowed with the sacred aura that befits the Ọ̀ṣun. Hence, she must accomplish for her community the elaborate taboos that surround the office of the Arugbá and the rituals. Throughout the ceremony, Ọ̀ṣun is praised as the lord of the city and her emblem carried by Arugbá is well guarded throughout the journey.

The Ọ̀ṣun festival is a theatrical and visual rendition of, and statement about, Ọ̀ṣun's personality, her essence, and her role in the salvation history of Òṣogbo. She is the one who first provided an abode for the drought-stricken people of Ìpolé. More important, Ọ̀ṣun plays a role in Òṣogbo's modernity as the force of an invisible religion that heals potential social and religious cleavages within Òṣogbo society and provides the foundation of Òṣogbo's political life and economic prosperity.

## NOTES

1. My translation of Ọ̀ṣun recording by the Institute of African Studies Research Team, University of Ìbàdàn, Ìbàdàn, Nigeria, carried out with an unnamed Ọ̀ṣun priestess in Òṣogbo, 1970.
2. Chaos, as Susan Niditch has suggested in the case of the Genesis cosmology, can be symbolized by such things as death, sterility, famine, etc. (Niditch 1997, 56).
3. I am struck by the similarity between Yorùbá cosmology and the biblical story in Proverbs 8 about Wisdom. Susan Niditch observes that the writer of Proverbs 8 "comes closer than any other biblical writer to describing the goddess, one who is thus not uncomfortable with the ideas of the male creator's consort being directly involved in the cosmogonic process and essential to it" (Niditch 1997, 56).
4. My summary of Ọ̀rọ̀ṣẹ̀n's story is taken from a personal conversation (March 1999) with Roland Abíọ́dún, author of "The Kingdom of Ọ̀wọ̀" (1998).

## REFERENCES


Abíọ́dún, Roland. 1998. "The Kingdom of Ọ̀wọ̀." Pp. 91–113 in *Yorùbá: Nine Centuries of African Art and Thought*, ed. Henry John Drewal, John Pemberton III, and Roland Abíọ́dún. New York: The Center for African Art and Harry N. Abrams.

Bádéjọ, Deidre. 1996. *Osun Ṣẹ̀ẹ̀gẹ̀sí: The Elegant Deity of Wealth, Power, and Femininity*. Trenton, NJ: African World Press.

Contursi, Janet. 1996. "Language and Power in Images of Indian Women." Pp. 43–63. *Images of Women in Maharashtrian Literature and Religion*, ed. Anne Feldhaus. New York: SUNY Press.

Eames, Elizabeth A. 1988. "Why the Women Went to War: Women and Wealth in Ondo Town, Southwestern Nigeria." Pp. 81–97 in *Traders Versus the State: Anthropological Approaches to Unofficial Economies*, ed. Gracia Clark. Boulder: Westerview Press.

Ebersole, Gary. 1989. *Rituals, Poetry, and the Politics of Death in Early Japan*. Princeton, NJ: Princeton University Press.

Eyo, Ekpo. 1976. "Igbo 'Laja, Owo, Nigeria." *West African Journal of Archeology* 6: 37–58.

Frankfurter, David. 1998. *Religion in Roman Egypt: Assimilation and Resistance*. Princeton, NJ: Princeton University Press.

Gleason, Judith. 1992. *Ọya: In Praise of the Goddess*. San Francisco: Harper San Francisco.

Gluckman, Max. 1965. *Custom and Conflict in Africa*. Oxford: Blackwell.

Gordon, April A. 1996. "Women and Development." Pp. 249–272 in *Understanding Contemporary Africa* (2nd ed.), ed. April A. Gordon and Donald L. Gordon. Boulder, CO: Lynne Rienner.

King, Ursula. 1990. *Women in World Religions*. New York: Paragon Press.

Niditch, Susan. 1997. *Ancient Israelite Religion*. New York: Oxford University Press.

Ogungbile, David. 1998. "Islam and Cultural Identity in Nigeria." *Orita: Journal of Religious Studies* 1(2): 125–137.

Okonjo, Kamene. 1976. "The Dual-Sex Political System in Operation: 1960 Women and Community Politics in Midwestern Nigeria." Pp. 45–58 in *Women in Africa*, ed. Nancy J. Hafikin and Edna G. Bay. Stanford: Stanford University Press.

Olagunju, J. O. 1972. *Osun Osogbo Festival* [B.A. Long Essay in Religious Studies]. University of Ìbàdaǹ.

Olúpọ̀nà, Jacob K. 1988 "Religious Pluralism and Civil Religion in Africa." *Dialogue and Alliance* 2(4): 41–48.

———. 1991. *Kingship, Religion, and Rituals in a Nigerian Community: A Phenomenological Study of Ondo-Yoruba-Festivals*. Stockholm: Almqvist and Wiksell, International.

Woocher, Jonathan. 1990. "Civil Religion and the Modern Jewish Challenge." Pp. 146–168 in *Social Foundations of Judaism*, ed. Calvin Goldscheider and Jacob Neusner. Englewoods Cliffs, NJ: Prentice Hall.

# 8

# Śrī-Lakṣmī

## Majesty of the Hindu King

*Constantina Rhodes Bailly*

I invoke that goddess Śrī,
Who takes on a golden form
With gentle smile.
She is the glistening of cool water.
She is the effulgence of fire.
Contented, she bestows contentment.
Seated on a lotus,
She radiates its luminescent hue.

(*Śrī Sūkta*, 4)[1]

Before the goddess Śrī appeared in Indic literature, the concept of majesty remained an abstract notion. Linked with auspiciousness, it was something highly sought after in the prayers and propitiations of the Vedas, the earliest texts of Indian civilization, and it was called *śrī*. *Śrī* can be translated as majesty, prosperity, fullness, auspiciousness, abundance, loveliness, illustriousness, and well-being. In the splendor that is *śrī* lies the power to eradicate debility, to illuminate darkness, to flood a hollow and meaningless void with light, fluidity, and consciousness. *Śrī* is radiance—the bright sparkling of the sun and the cool luminescence of the moon. *Śrī* is the "luxurious bounty of the earth."[2] *Śrī* is the force of creativity and the impetus behind a flourishing creation.

When we consider the role of kingship in Hindu society, it comes as no surprise that the institution has from its beginnings been closely associated with the concept of *śrī* and

*Figure 8.1: Śrī-Lakṣmī. (Source: Smith Poster Collection, Syracuse University Library.)*

with the blessings of the goddess Śrī-Lakṣmī. There could be no kingship and no sovereign without invoking the active presence of this goddess.

*Śrī* is a type of power, yet it is clearly distinct from that other power so prevalent in the Vedas, *brahman*. Indeed, in referring to kingship, *Taittirīya Brāhmaṇa* 3,9,12,2 states that "Śrī does not associate with brahman" (Gonda 1969, 188). The concept of *brahman*, or sacred power, may be thought of as essential life energy, whereas *śrī* is the quality of how that life force is manifested in the world. The concept of *brahman* transformed over time into the idea of the impersonal "oversoul" of the universe, but it did not become personified as an individual deity. *Śrī*, however, acquired a specific identity as a goddess, at the same time remaining an abstract concept.

At some point in late Vedic times, *śrī*, the concept of abundance and prosperity, also became Śrī, the goddess who embodies these qualities. This new identification did not entirely replace the original one, however, and as *devanāgarī* (the Sanskrit script) does not distinguish between capital and lower-case letters to distinguish proper names from common nouns, the ambiguity persists. Too strong an attempt to label and categorize one aspect to the exclusion of another not only proves frustrating but also cuts off the majestic quality of *śrī*, which defies such limiting characterizations in which a divine entity would be fitted into human-sized designations of time, space, or category. Whereas to a certain degree this is the case with Hindu deities in general, it is especially remarkable with this goddess, whose very nature is that of radiant movement. Therefore, it is perhaps best to think of *śrī*-the-concept and Śrī-the-goddess as interchangeable, and to consider the ambiguity of identities as a multivalent perspective from which to understand her relationship with the sovereignty of the king.

In much the same way the goddess Lakṣmī makes her first appearance in the Vedas as an impersonal concept. *Lakṣmī* indicates a marking, more specifically an auspicious sign or an indicator of auspiciousness. This term, too, later developed into a separate, or rather, an additional identity as the goddess called Lakṣmī. In her specific relationship with the king, she is known as Aiśvaryalakṣmī (Lakṣmī of Sovereignty) or Rājyalakṣmī (Lakṣmī of Royalty). Śrī and Lakṣmī seem originally to have been two independent goddesses, but as their personalities and mythologies developed, the two were conflated into one goddess with a singular identity (Gonda 1969, 212–225). Together they embody both the concept of auspiciousness as well as the marking, or physical manifestation, of that auspiciousness. The relationship between "abstract" auspiciousness and its embodied form is particular to Śrī and Lakṣmī. However, it is interesting, especially in light of what Gonda (1969) observes about abundant wealth and the *display* of that wealth, that it is not so much a matter of utility as display: "In so-called primitive or undeveloped societies the natural tendency to display is of a social and ceremonial character and has nothing to do with an economic use of goods and property. . . . A prosperous man is an honoured man, because he gives evidence of possessing uncommon abilities" (190).

In the broadest sense, then, we could say that Śrī-Lakṣmī manifests as prosperity and the abundance of all good things, most certainly appropriate associations for the image of the ruler. In the iconographic depictions of this goddess, the symbology of her accoutrements indicates specifically her close relationship with the king. The illustration accompanying this chapter is titled "Aiśvaryalakṣmī," that is, the Lakṣmī of Sovereignty. The vantage point seems to be from within the palace, facing outward past a decorative archway that also frames the graceful image of the goddess. She has approached the king's portal not only to accept the offerings of paper money, gold coins, and jewelry but to add to them in turn. Not only does Śrī-Lakṣmī bring abundant good things, she increases them when they are accepted, distributed, and honored appropriately. Her lower right hand is opened in *varadamudrā* (the gift-bestowing gesture), and from it pour forth gold coins in an endless stream. Her rich ornaments and crown are symbols of royalty, as is her attendant elephant, who not only symbolizes the thunderclouds that bring water to the dry earth but who, decorated with his own charming ornaments, also represents the king's retinue of elephants groomed for the royal processions.

## The Sovereign Is One Who Is "Possessed of Śrī"

Whoever or whatever is blessed by Śrī may be called *śrīmant*, *śreyas*, or *śreṣṭha*, that is, "possessed of Śrī" or "filled with Śrī"; by extension, *śreṣṭha* also means "the best," the "most blessed." These terms are used in the Vedas for the king when he displays power and an abundance of material goods, for these are indicators of the presence of Śrī. Evidence of healthy expansion, as opposed to dearth or to active deterioration, is a sign of Śrī's presence. These apply not only to the economic realm but to the natural world as well, which must necessarily support material wealth. Fattened cattle, favorable rains, sprouting green fields, fragrant blossoming flowers, the chanting of mantras by the brahman priests, and householders who abide by the laws of the land are visible signs that the kingdom is in the hands of a righteous king. It is the duty of the king to attract Śrī-Lakṣmī to his realm, to obtain her blessings, and to retain her continued presence.

The king is a powerful being not simply because of his status but because he is a vessel for *śrī*. He is responsible for living according to *rājyadharma* (the duties of being a king), not according to his personal whim. The more powerful and high-ranking the king, the stronger are the restraints on his personal "freedom" and the more stringent the ritual designations for his daily activities. Before we consider how this is done, let us further consider the specific qualities of the Hindu king. Although earliest references come from the Vedic period (ca. 1500 BCE–400 BCE), these discussions and designations continued in the epics (the *Rāmāyaṇa* and the *Mahābhārata*) and in the Dharmaśāstra texts of the classical period (ca. 400 BCE–600 CE). Subsequently, various other genres and collections of texts, especially the Purāṇas, contributed to the portrayal of kingship in the medieval period (ca. 600 CE–1800 CE).

Although a human being, the Hindu king has always been conferred with divine status. According to *Mārkaṇḍeya Purāṇa* 226.1–12, for example, the king is made up of "parts of the gods" (Kane 1946, 24). *Mānavadharmaśāstra* VII.8 states that "One should not disrespect a boy-king with the thought 'he is a human being (like others)' for it is a great deity that stands (before people) in human form as a king" (Kane 1946, 23). If the king embodies divine qualities, it is partly because his position entails superhuman responsibilities. Personally responsible for the prosperity of the kingdom, the king's primary duty, from earliest times, was to protect the kingdom and its subjects, a responsibility that extended to include the weather and the condition of the crops. A drought, a plague, or any other natural disaster was ultimately the fault of the king, for he had failed in maintaining the blessing of Śrī-Lakṣmī. Beyond the natural world, the king's duties entailed the establishment and maintainence of institutions that furthered the harmonious workings of society and religious expression: The king was the patron of the rituals to sustain the cosmic order, and once temples and image-worship became a feature of medieval Hindu piety, it was the king who had to foster their construction, consecration, and care of the priestly attendants.

It was not the king's prerogative to hoard the prosperity for himself but to understand that his was a sacred trust in which he was divinely charged to serve and protect the kingdom. Although the king is often cast in the light of a father figure, the *Śāntiparvan* 56.44–46 of the *Mahābhārata* also invokes maternal imagery: "A king like a pregnant woman should not do what is pleasing to him, but what would conduce to the good of the people, and the ancient dharma for a king is to keep the subjects contented" (Kane 1946, 37).

Under ideal circumstances, the king would enjoy the blessings of Śrī-Lakṣmī, for she is described as "residing in the sovereign" (Kālidāsa's *Raghuvaṃśa* 3, 36; 4, 14). If the good and righteous (dharmic) king was recognized as being made up of the parts of the gods, it is not surprising to find that "the king who oppresses the subjects and causes loss of dharma is made up of the parts of *rākṣasas* [demons]" (*Śukranītisāra* I.70).

A good king exhibited specific royal qualities. One of the sources that enumerates such qualities is also the first text to present Śrī in her form as a goddess. *Śatapatha Brāhmaṇa* 11,4,3 contains a story in which Śrī is produced by the creator Prajāpati through the heat of his fervent yogic austerities: When she "came forth," she "stood there resplendent, shining, and trembling." The gods then "set their minds upon her," and they said to Prajāpati, "Let us kill her and take (all) this from her." His response was that because she was a woman, they should not kill her, but that they could simply take everything from her! Thereafter, "Agni then took her food, Soma her royal power, Varuna her universal sovereignty, Mitra her noble rank, Indra her power, Brihaspati her holy lustre, Savitri her dominion, Pushan her wealth, Sarasvati her prosperity, and Tvashtri her beautiful forms."

When Śrī complains to Prajāpati, he advises her to ask for the return of all of her powers through sacrifice. By offering ten sacrificial dishes to each of these ten deities, Śrī is able to get back what properly belongs to her. It is significant that the first textual presentation of Śrī as a goddess characterizes her in terms of royal sovereignty, which the gods covet for themselves. The story therefore is significant. First, it establishes the relationship between Śrī and sovereignty. Second, it conveys the idea that her powers are "movable" and interchangeable;

they are not Śrī per se, but she is the one who owns them, enlivens them, and ultimately dispenses them. Third, we see the theme of sacrifice. Nothing comes for free; ritual exchange lies at the foundation of Vedic thought and continues in different forms throughout the development of Hinduism. The king must never take for granted the presence of *śrī*, for *śrī* is something that comes and goes, and there is always a delicate balance that is the king's responsibility to maintain.

It is not unusual to see references to Śrī-Lakṣmī as *cañcalā* or *lolā*, that is, flickering, wavering, even fickle. The scintillating quality of resplendence is an ethereal quality, but the notion of fickleness is certainly less attractive. Some texts state in exasperation that Śrī is so fickle that even in her pictures she moves. She is said to be attracted to Viṣṇu only because, with his many *avatāras* ("descents," or incarnations), he himself is restless and always changing form. Similarly, when one attempts to document and create a linear "history" of where Śrī has resided and with whom, a long list begins to develop: One can find reference to Śrī's alliance with Indra, Viṣṇu, Prahlāda, Kubera, Bali, and Dharma. Lest her appearance as the consort of so many lead to the impression that the "fickleness" of Śrī-Lakṣmī is somehow due to a kind of inattentiveness (flightiness) or even promiscuity on her part, another view may be considered. It is the very nature of this goddess of expansive blessing to permeate the three worlds and to show up where and when she is needed, to further the process of beneficent life on earth. In a specific way it may be "factually correct" to note that Indra, Viṣṇu, Prahlāda, and the others each had the same goddess for his wife. But in a wider sense, it may be perceived that only as long as each of these royal figures conducted his affairs in a dharmic manner, would he be blessed with the presence of *śrī*, divine splendor. Personified, that splendor is the goddess Śrī.

In an attempt to "trace the history" of Śrī-Lakṣmī and her relationship to royalty, further considerations are necessary. The king is often referred to as an earthly manifestation of Viṣṇu (Gonda 1966, 164–167). As Viṣṇu's wife or consort she becomes Mahālakṣmī and descends into the world at his side in each incarnation: When he is called Nārāyaṇa, she is called Lakṣmī; when he is Rāma, she is Sītā; when he is Kṛṣṇa, she is sometimes Rukmiṇī and at other times Rādhā. In yet other circumstances related to Viṣṇu, Śrī-Lakṣmī descends to earth in the form of Tulasī, the basil plant sacred to Viṣṇu.

Just as the king is recognized as an embodiment of Viṣṇu, he is also (more frequently in the earlier texts) revered as an incarnation of Indra. The *Nāradasmṛtī* (Prakīrṇaka section, verse 20), for example, states, "In the form of the king it is really Indra himself who moves about on the earth."

In the *Mahābhārata*, the five Pāṇḍava princes are each an incarnation of Indra, and Śrī has been born as Draupadī, their collective wife.[3] The Hindu tradition finds no problem with the seeming ambiguity of so many roles for the same "character," even when these roles overlap in the same epic or Purāṇic stories, as they sometimes do. As Hiltebeitel (1976) points out, "What one finds on the mythic or theological level need not be duplicated exactly on the epic level" (145). The full identity of Śrī-Lakṣmī pervades through and indeed beyond the individual (Draupadī, Sītā, Rādhā, etc.) and her circumstances to ensure the restoration of dharma in the kingdom. Hiltebeitel (1976) further cites a passage from the *Anuśāsanaparvan* of the *Mahābhārata* to illustrate this point. Here, Śrī addresses the goddess Rukmiṇī, who is the chief queen of Kṛṣṇa:

> In my embodied form [*śarīrabhutā*], single-heartedly [*ekamanā*], I dwell with my entire spirit [*sarveṇa bhāvena*] in Nārāyaṇa; surely in him is dharma penetrated to the fullest, piety [*brahmanyatā*], and also agreeableness [*priyatvam*]. Might I not explain here, O Lady [*devī*], that I do not dwell [elsewhere] in my embodied form [*nāham śarīreṇa vasāmi*]. But in that person [especially kings, for example, the Pāṇḍavas] in whom I dwell in spirit [*bhāvena*], he increases in dharma, fame [*yaśas*], *artha*, and *kāma*. [13:11,19–20] (146)

Wherever Śrī-Lakṣmī dwells "in spirit" (*bhāvena*), then, is where her influence takes hold, fostering the righteousness (*dharma*), fame (*yaśas*), wealth (*artha*), and enjoyment (*kāma*) that are the marks of a good king and his kingdom.

Another story illustrates the ways in which Śrī-Lakṣmī takes and leaves residence in the kingdom. Here, her movement is more particularized and specific than the above reference to her "spirit." On the other hand, in this example it is not the individual royal qualities that move back and forth, as was seen in the *Śatapatha Brāhmaṇa*, but rather the goddess herself who moves, taking the collection of qualities with her. The following is a passage from the *Mahābhārata* in which Prahlāda loses his sovereignty in the tangible form of Śrī. The goddess goes to reside in Indra (also called Śakra), thus taking the sovereignty and conferring it onto her new consort:

> A goddess made of effulgence [*prabhāmayī devī*] came out from his body. The chief [*indra*] of the Daityas asked her [who she was]. So she said, "Śrī. I dwelt happily, O hero, in you who are truly mighty [*tvayi satyaparākrame*]. Abandoned by you, I will leave. . . ."
>
> Then the fear of the high-souled Prahlāda became visible, and he asked her besides: "Where are you going, O Lotus Dweller? Surely you are a goddess devoted to truth, the supreme goddess of the world. Who is that best of brahmins? I wish to know the truth."
>
> Śrī said, "This *brahmacārin* who was instructed by you is Śakra. You are robbed by him, O splendid one, of that sovereignty [*aiśvaryam*] which was yours in the triple world. Surely it is by *śīla* that all the worlds were subdued by you, O virtuous one." [12:124,54ff.] (quoted, in Hiltebeitel 1976, 157)

When sovereignty (*aiśvaryam*) is conferred or taken away, it is always in the form of Śrī. It is important to note also that Śrī is the one who determines where or in whom the royal qualities will reside. This is not whimsical on her part; rather, as Śrī herself points out to Prahlāda, royal success is a result of his own *śīla*, or virtue. By cultivating the noble qualities in himself, a ruler attracts the attention and blessing of Śrī-Lakṣmī. Similarly he can behave in a way that can cause him to lose favor just as easily. It is noteworthy that when Śrī-Lakṣmī is embodied as the wife of a dharmic king, it is clear that she has selected her marriage partner after engaging in a *svayaṃvara*, the ceremony in which the bride selects the groom of her choice. Hiltebeitel (1976) refers to this pattern as the "Svayaṃvara mythologem," which "the epic poets found of the widest use in accounting for the relationship between the two concerns of the Brāhmaṇic Śrī: her interests in virtues and in kings" (155–156).

Prahlāda loses Śrī to Indra because he fails to nurture properly the boon of her blessing. In due time, Indra, too, will make a similar "mistake" and lose Śrī to Viṣṇu. In a myth known as "The Churning of the Milk Ocean," Indra allows his royal elephant, Airāvata, to trample a flower garland presented to him by the sage Durvāsas. In a characteristic fit of pique, Durvāsas curses Indra for the dishonor to himself as well as to Śrī-Lakṣmī, whose abodes include the fragrant flowers of the garland. Indra, then, is punished not only for his arrogance but for his failure to perceive Śrī-Lakṣmī in the aesthetically subtle manifestations of her form. She leaves him, and the world falls into chaos.

Later in the myth, when the gods and demons line up on opposite sides to churn the ocean, from its murky depths emerge the "fourteen gems," the most magnificent of which is Śrī-Lakṣmī, who sits resplendent on a lotus and floats to shore. Indra hopes to win her back, but the goddess chooses not to return to him. Instead, in her newest incarnation, she joins Viṣṇu and remains by his side in a fairly regular manner through each successive *avatāraṇa* ("descending") into this world.

Historically, as well, the times were shifting. The royal paradigm of the Vedic period that had placed high value on the physical prowess (*balam*) of Indra was giving way to a more multifaceted, perceptive, and nuanced royal persona, one that was exemplified by Viṣṇu in the epics and Purāṇas. For Viṣṇu is known as Dharmarāja—the king who embodies virtue. *Dharma* is derived from the root *dhṛ*, "to sustain," and it is only fitting that the one to fill that role would be Viṣṇu, whose name is derived from the root *viṣ*, "to pervade." That is, there is a sense of spreading out and blanketing the creation—with harmony and order. Thus, like Viṣṇu, the king draws his energy and potency directly from the goddess Śrī-Lakṣmī. As the *Śatapatha Brāhmaṇa* (2, 4, 4, 6) says, "The royal man is wedded to Śrī."

## Rājasūya: Establishing Śrī-Lakṣmī in the Sovereign

As we have seen, the king is understood to be a special human being who contains "parts," or aspects, of the gods, but as such he only has the potential for royal greatness. As Gonda (1969) explains: "Kingship and chieftainship are powers superior to their bearers themselves; power, prosperity, luck, admiration constitute a status or impersonal dignity which is imposed on a human being and, fusing with his own will and personality, makes him king or chief" (190). How does such fusion take place? This is accomplished by ritual. If the king is to be wedded to Śrī, a ceremony must first establish the union. Similarly, if divine powers are to be invoked and requested to reside in the special residence that is the king himself, and by extension, his kingdom, then it is only fitting that such invocation and establishment resemble other ritual paradigms, such as the Vedic wedding ceremony (*vivāha*), religious initiation (*dīkṣā*), and the ritual establishment of divine energy into a sacred image (*prāṇapratiṣṭhā*).

The powers necessary to the sovereignty of the king are established (*pratiṣṭhā*) in the royal person during the elaborate set of coronation ceremonies known as the Rājasūya. As with other types of ritual, this entails specific physical activities and ritualized movements, together with sacred implements, specific natural materials, and the recitation of specific mantras. The Rājasūya would require at least one full year to be completed, and sometimes as long as two (Kane 1941, 1214).

It is noteworthy that one of the preliminary rites, occurring on the fifth day of the Rājasūya, is a nighttime sacrifice to the goddess Nirṛti. Nirṛti, later called Alakṣmī (Inauspiciousness), Jyeṣṭhadevī, or Daridrā (Poverty), is a personification of Śrī-Lakṣmī's opposite. Nirṛti is poverty, disease, constriction, want, discord, and the like. In common parlance, one might say that Nirṛti is Śrī's "evil twin." The Brāhmaṇas, a body of texts somewhat later than the Vedas, frequently contrast the concept of *śrī* with that of *pāpman*, or misfortune, shrunkenness, misery, disease, ill-being, and even death (Gonda 1969, 186). In the Purāṇas, they are usually personified as two goddesses who are sisters. *Gautamī-māhātmya* 67, 2–3 (part IV of the *Brāhma Purāṇa*) describes a myth in which the sisters vie to inhabit the same place in the material realm: "Lakṣmī and Daridrā . . . approached the universe as mutual antagonists. There is nothing in all the three worlds that is not pervaded by them." The myth goes on to clarify that the two can never exist in the same place at the same time; whenever one is invoked, the other will leave.

In the Rājasūya ceremony, the personification of *pāpman* as Nirṛti serves as a counterpart to *śrī*'s embodiment as the goddess Śrī. By consciously calling on Nirṛti and distracting her from the sacred precinct and directing her toward a place more suitable to her own nature, the priests thus clear the area of negative influences and can proceed to invoke the beneficent powers of Śrī-Lakṣmī, unimpeded. Some texts prescribe the propitiation of Nirṛti with a clay image seated on a donkey and wearing dark clothing (Kane 1946, 79); others indicate how she may be identified in certain particles of grain that have fallen west of the sacred millstone in the consecrated preparation. This grain is then ritually offered to Nirṛti by casting it to the south of the sacrificial pavilion (*vihāra*) or onto some salty land (Kane 1941, 1215). Because Hindu cosmology designates the south as the direction of death, and because salty earth is hostile to the growth of food, the territory to which Nirṛti is banished is appropriately inauspicious.

Having protected the sacrificial area from inauspicious influences, the priests may now move to other aspects of the Rājasūya, although at times they return to this theme, consciously addressing these negativities and keeping them at bay. Like the ground site where his sovereignty is ritually established, the king must keep his "spiritual" house in order, for his own being is a microcosm of the kingdom. And situated at the center of that kingdom is Śrī (*Taittirīya Brāhmaṇa* 3, 9, 7, 2).

The invitation to Śrī-Lakṣmī to reside with the king begins with the priest's recitation of the *Śrī Sūkta*. In the hymn, the king addresses Agni (the fire god) and asks that Śrī be brought closer. The hymn is chanted during the Vedic fire sacrifice. Thus it is through Agni, the sacred fire, that the goddess may be drawn into the human realm. As the goddess draws near, she appears as a regent herself. Gorgeously decorated and wielding the royal scepter, Śrī-Lakṣmī sits resplendent in the royal chariot, moving along in a majestic procession attended by horses and trumpeting elephants. When Lakṣmī arrives at the king's side, she brings with her the signs of a prosperous and healthy kingdom: "gold, cattle, servants, horses, and good friends" (verse 15).

After chanting this hymn, the priests continue to recite mantras while washing the crown with cow's urine and dung, milk, yoghurt, clarified butter, and water mixed with the sacred *kuśa* grass. All are especially significant here, for India's "sacred cow" is sacred specifically because it is recognized as an embodiment of the goddess Lakṣmī (cf. *Mahābhārata*, the *Anuśāsana Parva*, section 82). Having purified the crown, the priest then ties an amulet on and sprinkles sacred water over the king and his horse (Kane 1946, 77). The refreshing and sanctifying lustrations of the sprinkling ceremony, called *abhiśekha*, recall the life-giving rains as they fall to the earth, a motif associated also with Śrī-Lakṣmī and reflected in her iconography.

Throughout the various sections of the coronation ceremony, the ritual is accompanied by prayers and mantras that articulate the establishment of *śrī* and the related royal qualities in the king. *Jaiminīya Brāhmaṇa* 1.272, for example, states: "In the construction of the sacred fire altar, by laying down a single brick in the fifth layer of the fire altar, *Śrī* and *kṣatra* [dominion] are attached to a single person." *Aitareya Brāhmaṇa* 8, 27, 2 instructs: "The priest coming to the king while consecrating the water meant for washing his feet, says—In this kingdom I am depositing *śrī*" (quoted in Dhal, 1995, 30). Once enthroned, the king literally sits in a position of glory; indeed, the very cushion of his throne is considered a repository of Śrī (Gonda 1969, 188).

The king's rituals do not end with the coronation ceremonies but, rather, continue on a regular basis. In the strictest sense, every moment of every day should be sanctified and lived in accordance with his exalted position and solemn responsibility. The ritual obligations of the king varied in different regions and during different time periods. In certain areas the propitiation of Śrī-Lakṣmī remained an essential daily activity at the royal court. In Orissa, for example, the sacred temple dancers known as *devadāsis* (literally, "servants of the gods") were regarded as living embodiments of Śrī-Lakṣmī, and they, like the king, lived in a state of perpetual ritual activity (Marglin 1985, 175). They were ritually dedicated to the royal temple, and their presence at the court was essential in fostering the prosperity of the kingdom.[4]

Because kingship is no longer officially recognized in India, the royal patronage that once supported religious festivals now is replaced partly through government funding and partly through commercial interests. The last vestiges of the sacred dance forms of the *devādasīs* remain in the teaching and performance of *bhāratanāṭyam* and other traditional dance genres, which are for the most part devoid of the original ritual significance and are promoted primarily for their aesthetic and cultural value.

## Mokṣalakṣmī and Sovereignty of the Self

We have considered how Śrī-Lakṣmī plays an essential role in sanctifying the king and instilling him with royal virtues. The king's sovereignty extends throughout the worldly domain of nature and society. The prosperous fulfillment of his existence rests on the appropriate attention to the first three *puruṣārthas*, or legitimate goals of Hindu life: *dharma* (sacred law and customs), *artha* (material wealth), and *kāma* (enjoyment). The province of each goal is richly delineated in the corresponding categories of literature that contain, for example, the *Mānavadharmaśāstra*, the *Arthaśāstra*, and the *Kāmaśāstra*, respectively. Directed primarily toward the householder, these texts provide the guidelines for living well in the world. Within the worldly realm of these three goals, the central figure is the king. When he attends to these three areas in a dharmic way, the kingdom, and by extension the entire world, flourishes. Śrī-Lakṣmī is propitiated so that her force of auspiciousness will pervade the entire creation, and so that earthly life may be experienced with abundant blessings.

The fourth *puruśārtha* is *mokṣa*, or liberation, specifically the liberation from the conditioned realm of cyclic existence (*saṃsāra*), or all that the first three goals entail. Whereas the king is the paradigmatic figure of sovereignty in the world, the *guru*, or spiritual preceptor, may be seen as a parallel represention of sovereignty in respect to the transcendent Self. The many parallels between these two figures are too extensive to discuss here in detail, but it is significant that both the Dharmaśāstra texts concerning kings as well as the Tantric texts concerning *gurus* indicate that kings and *gurus* together constitute a separate class, apart from others in their special relationship with the divine. Consider, for example, *Gautama Dharmasūtra* XI.32: ". . . a king and a spiritual teacher must not be reviled." Similarly, *Kulārṇava Tantra* 12.120 states: "One should not approach the king, the deity, or the guru empty-handed. He should offer fruit, a flower, cloth, or the like, according to his capacity."

As the king's throne is considered a sacred repository of *śrī*, the "seat" (*gaddī*) of the *guru* is revered. In occupying the sacred throne, or seat of authority, the king and the *guru* sit, literally, at the point where the realm of the subjects or devotees and that of the gods meet. The divine force supporting the successful relationship of the sovereign with his domain is *śrī*. Although Śrī-Lakṣmī is recognized more commonly in the augmentation of prosperity in the world, her presence and influence are also indicated in the successful pursuit of transcendence. As such, she is called Mokṣalakṣmī, the Lakṣmī of Liberation (Sivaramamurti 1982, 83).

In certain sectarian texts, such as the *Lakṣmī Tantra*, the goddess Śrī-Lakṣmī is identified as the Universal Absolute. As the highest divinity, she is the universal consciousness, encompassing all. Because the entire creation has emanated from her own essence alone, she embodies the whole universe. From this point of view, the divine auspiciousness of the goddess is seen to permeate the affairs of all, regardless of category.

We have considered how the *Śrī Sūkta* is a sacred text used specifically in the Rājasūya to invoke Śrī-Lakṣmī at the coronation of the king. The *Lakṣmī Tantra*, however, delineates a specifically esoteric application of the *Śrī Sūkta* whereby the focus of the ritual is turned inward and takes place within the subtle body of the practitioner. Here the tantric yogin instead of the king undergoes the ritual and invokes the blessings of Śrī-Lakṣmī for auspicious favor. Whereas the king seeks sovereignty of the royal kingdom, the goal of the yogin is to acquire sovereignty of the inner Self (Bailly 1997).

Whether in the harmonious applications of *kāma*, *artha*, and *dharma* or in the transcendent aspiration for *mokṣa*, the all-pervasive auspiciousness of Śrī-Lakṣmī is recognized as permeating through all boundaries. She lends her majesty to the sovereign, wherever his domain. When circumstances call for images, names, and forms, she presents herself with the name of Śrīdevī or Lakṣmīdevī. Behind these tangible appearances, however, remains the essence of majesty itself, that shimmering radiance that the Vedic sages declined to contain too closely in limited form but instead stood back to behold in its majesty and splendor, approaching it only closely enough to utter its name as a *bījamantra*, or essential seed syllable, the resplendent *śrī*.

## NOTES

1. Translations of the *Śrī Sūkta* are mine. See Constantina Rhodes Bailly, *Invoking Lakshmi* (forthcoming).
2. I am indebted to James Fitzgerald for this poetic turn of phrase. Personal conversation, March 1998.
3. See Hiltebeitel 1976, especially chap. 7, for a richly detailed discussion of Draupadī as an incarnation of Śrī.
4. Marglin (1985) provides an excellent discussion of the complex relationship between the *devadāsī*s and the king. See especially chapters 4, 5, and 6.

## REFERENCES

Bailly, Constantina Rhodes. 1997. "Discovering Lakṣmī in the Subtle Body of the Yogi: An Esoteric Reading of the *Śrī Sūkta* According to the *Lakṣmī Tantra*." Paper presented at the annual conference of the Society for Tantric Studies, Flagstaff, AZ.

*Brahma Purāṇa*. 1986. Part IV: Gautamī-Māhātmya. Trans. Board of Scholars. Delhi: Motilal Banarsidass.

Dhal, U. N. 1995. *Goddess Lakṣmī: Origin and Development* (2d rev. ed.). Delhi: Eastern Book Linkers.

Gonda, J. 1966. *Ancient Indian Kingship from the Religious Point of View*. Leiden: E. J. Brill. Reprinted from *NUMEN*, III (1956): 36–71; IV (1957): 24–58, 127–164.

———. 1969. *Aspects of Early Viṣṇuism* (2d ed.). Delhi: Motilal Banarsidass.

Hiltebeitel, A. 1976. *The Ritual of Battle: Krishna in the Mahābhārata*. Ithaca, NY: Cornell University Press.

Kane, P. V. 1941. *History of Dharmaśāstra (Ancient and Medieval Religious and Civil Law)* (vol. II, part II). Poona: Bhandarkar Oriental Research Institute.

———. 1946. *History of Dharmaśāstra (Ancient and Medieval Religious and Civil Law)* (vol. III). Poona: Bhandarkar Oriental Research Institute.

Kinsley, D. 1986. *Hindu Goddesses: Visions of the Divine Feminine in the Hindu Religious Tradition*. Berkeley: University of California Press.

*Kulārṇava Tantra*. 1983. Trans. R. K. Rai. Varanasi: Prachya Prakashan.

Kumar, P. 1997. *The Goddess Lakṣmī: The Divine Consort in South Indian Vaiṣṇava Tradition*. Atlanta: Scholars Press.

*Lakṣmī Tantra: A Pāñcarātra Text*. 1972. Trans. S. Gupta. Leiden: E. J. Brill.

*Mahābhārata*. 1981. Trans. K. M. Ganguli. Delhi: Munshiram Manoharlal.

Marglin, F. A. 1985. *Wives of the God-King: The Rituals of the Devadasis of Puri*. Delhi: Oxford University Press.

Rao, S. K. Ramachandra. 1985. *Śrī Sūkta: Text with Translation and Explanation*. Bangalore: Kalpatharu Research Academy.

*Śatapatha-Brāhmaṇa According to the Text of the Mādhyandina School* (part V, 2d ed.). 1966. Trans. J. Eggeling. Delhi: Motilal Banarsidass.

Sivaramamurti, C. 1982. *Śrī Lakshmī in Indian Art and Thought*. Delhi: Kanak Publications.

# PART III

# Traditions in Collision

## Political Change and Perspectives on Sovereignty

We will not listen to what you tell us in the name of the Lord. We intend to fulfill all the promises by which we have bound ourselves: we will burn sacrifices to the Queen of Heaven and pour libations to her as we used to do, we and our fathers, our kings and our princes, in the cities of Judah and in the streets of Jerusalem. We then had food in plenty and were content; no calamity touched us. But from the time we left off burning sacrifices to the Queen of Heaven and pouring libations to her, we have been in great want, and in the end we have fallen victims to sword and famine.

—Jeremiah 44:16–19.

9

# Transformations of Wen Cheng Kongjo

## The Tang Princess, Tibetan Queen, and Buddhist Goddess Tara

*Elisabeth Benard*

This essay examines one of the earliest phases of the political and spiritual relationship between the Tibetans and Chinese by reviewing the life of Wen Cheng Kongjo, the Tang imperial princess. As the second wife of the first Buddhist Tibetan king, Srong Tsen Gampo in the seventh century, she was a Tibetan queen from 641 to her death in 680. By the twelfth century Tibetans had deified her as an emanation of Tara, one of the most popular Tibetan Buddhist goddesses. The interpretations of Wen Cheng's life and deification remain central to the present-day politics between the Tibetans and Chinese.

Sun-Moon Mountain in northeast Tibet stands over 12,000 feet high amidst a brilliant azure sky with rapidly moving clouds. These clouds remind Tibetans of the summer migration of white cranes, which used to breed near Blue Lake (Kokonor) but now are rarely seen, the Chinese having disturbed their breeding place. Like the cranes, many Tibetans have abandoned their ancestral home, as more and more Chinese settle in Tibet upsetting the fragile balance between the Tibetans and their land. On two neighboring hills close to Blue Lake, the Chinese government has recently erected two pagodas, each with walls and roofs made of imperial yellow tiles outlined by sparkling sea green tiles. Only when the brilliant sun reflects their shiny surfaces do

*Figure 9.1: Srong Tsen Gampo, Wen Cheng Kongjo, and Thoni Sambhota* (*South Tibet*). (© *Elisabeth Benard.*)

they seem to have a presence; otherwise, the vast terrain of majestic mountains and howling wind eclipses all human structures. The pagodas commemorate the matrimonial alliance between the Tang princess Wen Cheng Kongjo and the Tibetan king Srong Tsen Gampo that took place in the seventh century. In this place of nature's extremes one wonders what Princess Wen Cheng might have thought when, having left behind the cosmopolitan Chinese capital of Changan, she arrived on the windswept Tibetan plateau dotted with sheep, yaks, and their herders.[1] When I visited the area in 1997, I asked some Chinese tourists visiting these new pagodas what they thought about this place. They replied that the scenery was breathtaking but they were glad that they did not live here. For them this is nothing more than one of several tourist sites to be visited in Qinghai Province. As I entered one of the pagodas, I expected to see a painting or image either of Wen Cheng or Srong Tsen Gampo, but the interior has only some modern painted tiles depicting dancing and singing Chinese women. Neither pagoda has an inscription or any historical information.

Below on the road between the two hills a newly inscribed stone plaque in Chinese discusses the marriage of Wen Cheng and Srong Tsen Gampo. Though many Tibetans live in this area, there is no Tibetan translation. The plaque's inscription interprets the Sino-Tibetan relationship as fraternal, China being the older brother who helps the younger brother, Tibet. A small pamphlet that I purchased reiterates this common theme:

> This story shows that Turfan (the ancient name for Tibet) and China have had a younger/elder brother relationship ever since this time (seventh century). Wen Cheng brought to Tibet the culture and technology of China. On this basis was established the flourishing relationship between the Han and Tibetans.[2] Therefore our country commemorates her with murals depicting singing and dancing women.

Ever since the seventh century, many rulers in China have tried to assert their cultural superiority and political hegemony over Tibetans. Since 1959, incorporated forcibly, Tibetans are regarded by the Chinese as one of its minorities; their land, as Chinese territory. The significance of the two pagodas and the curious language of the plaque can only be understood by revisiting a history that began during the period of the Tang dynasty over one thousand years ago.

From the Tang dynasty (618–906) to the present, the Tibetans and Chinese have engaged intermittently in a struggle of sovereignty and the establishment of distinct borders. Numerous scholars have discussed in detail the question of sovereignty between Tibet and China over the centuries, demonstrating that the two independent nations have experienced an intricate relationship with many changes (see Shakapa 1984; Smith 1996). Tibetan Buddhist history is divided frequently into two periods: the imperial age, or age of kings (seventh–ninth centuries) and the first diffusion of Buddhism, and later, a second diffusion of Buddhism, which includes both the decentralized rule of Tibet during the eleventh–fourteenth centuries and the establishment of the Dalai Lama as the spiritual and temporal ruler of Tibet (1642–1959). Since 1959, following the Communist Chinese invasion and establishment of their effective control and domination of Tibet, the Dalai Lama has ruled in exile in India. During these 1,300 years the political and spiritual relationships of Tibetans and Chinese have been complex. This complexity is complicated further because the rulers of some Chinese dynasties were not even Chinese: Ancestors of the early Tang emperors were a mixture of Chinese, nomadic Hsien-pei, and Turkish aristocracy (Twitchett 1979, 151). During the Yuan dynasty (1271–1368) the emperors were Mongolian; during the Qing Dynasty (1644–1911), Manchu.

Buddhism has played a crucial role in many of the relationships between Tibetans and Chinese emperors. Though Buddhism first came to Tibet from India in the fourth century, the Tibetan aristocracy and imperial court showed little interest in this foreign religion until the seventh century. Then, during the imperial period, Buddhism gradually became accepted as the main religion of Tibet; however, followers of the indigenous religion, Bon, resisted strongly the spread of this development. For example, the last imperial king, lGang Darma, nearly eradicated Buddhism in Tibet before a Buddhist monk assassinated him in 842. Within two centuries, however, Buddhism revived and became the dominant religion (see Richardson and Snellgrove 1968; Stein 1972). During the Tang dynasty, Tibetans received Buddhist teachings from India, Nepal, and China. However, in the twelfth century Buddhism was established so firmly in Tibet that Tibetans themselves became the spiritual preceptors of the Mongolian

Khans, beginning with Genghis Khan in 1206, and subsequently of the Mongolian emperors of the Yuan dynasty, the Chinese emperors of the Ming dynasty, and the Manchu emperors of the Qing dynasty.[3]

## The Role of Chinese Princesses

To understand the role of Princess Wen Cheng vis-à-vis other Chinese princesses married to foreign rulers, one needs to begin with the Han dynasty (206 BCE to 220 CE). During the Han dynasty the Chinese established an economic and political system together with the nomadic pastoral groups living on their western borders. Beginning with the nomadic pastoral Hsuing-nu state in 200 CE, the Chinese and the Hsuing-nu established the *ho-ch'in* policy, which had four major provisions (Barfield 1989, 45–46):

1. The Chinese made fixed annual payments of silk, wine, grain, and other foodstuffs to the Hsuing-nu.
2. The Chinese gave a princess in marriage to the leader, the Shan-yu.
3. The Hsuing-nu and the Chinese were ranked as coequal states.
4. The Great Wall was the official boundary between the two states.

Although over the centuries and succeeding dynasties this agreement became modified, the persistent features that survived until the early Tang dynasty were that the Chinese gave valuable commodities and princesses to the rulers of the neighboring countries in exchange for peace along its western borders. From the rulers' perspective, a princess was one of many valuable commodities to be exchanged bringing peace to the Chinese and prestige to the neighboring countries. It is clear that the Chinese rulers practiced intermarriage for political reasons, whereas the neighboring countries' rulers did so for primarily economic reasons. During the Han, Sui, and early Tang dynasties these matrimonial alliances were tacit agreements; no written treaties were exchanged.

In reading about the princesses, mostly from later Chinese historians or perhaps from some poems written by a princess, one wonders about them. Most princesses grew up in the main imperial Chinese city, which was urban and sophisticated, especially in contrast to the nomadic pastorals who lived in the steppes of inner Asia. Most became brides in their late teens or early twenties and spoke only Chinese. The historians do not discuss how these princesses adapted to their new homes in mobile tents, eating dairy-based food, living with people of a different culture and with a husband who might not know a word of Chinese. Because of the drastic uprooting, forced adaptation, and the precariousness of acceptance in the new society, the princesses faced one of the most traumatic years in their lives.

In the *Han History* Princess Hsi-chun, who against her will was compelled to marry the King of Wu-sun, wrote this song.

> My family married me to the other side of Heaven
> And entrusted me in a foreign country to be married to the King
> of Wu-sun.
> The yurt is my house and felt is my walls.
> Meat is my food and sour milk is my drink.
> Living here, I am always longing for native soil, wishing to turn
> into a yellow crane and fly back home.[4]

Much later, during the final years before the Sui asserted their supremacy over the Chi in 579, Princess Chien Chi (of Chi lineage) married Tabar Khan.[5] These tumultuous times created a tragic life for her because she had three husbands in succession and in 597 was killed by the third husband.[6] In 589 she wrote this poem.

> Originally I was a child of the Royal Household,
> now darting around the camp of the barbarians.
> Seeing both success and failure, the emotion in my heart is
> unrestrained.
> It's the same from ancient times.
> I am not alone in my complaint.
> The feeling of a far-married woman was described in the song of
> Ming-chun.[7]

As seen in these varied records, many Chinese princesses, who were compelled to marry leaders of neighboring countries, died young and frequently ignominiously.

Our knowledge about Princess Wen Cheng rests on three major kinds of sources. The earliest texts include the *Old Tibetan Annals and Chronicles* from Tun Huang (mostly fragmentary); the Chinese *Old Tang Annals* (*Chiu Tang-shu*), compiled between 940 and 945; the *New Tang Annals* (*Hsin Tang-shu*) compiled circa 1032–1060[8]; and Tibetan Buddhist histories written after the twelfth century. Some of the more popular Buddhist histories are *The Will Hidden Near the Pillar* (*bKa'chems Ka-khol-ma*), *The Precious Teachings* (*Mani bKa'-'bum*), and *The Clear Mirror of Royal Genealogies* (*rGyal-rabs gSal-ba'i Melong*).[9] From *The Precious Teachings* Tibetans developed a very popular folk opera known as the *Chinese Princess and Nepalese Princess* (*rGyasa Balsa*), which presents the story of how the wily Tibetan minister Gar performed impossible feats as he competed against the ministers of India, Iran, and Mongolia, each of whom was vying to win Wen Cheng Kongjo for his king. In Lhasa, the capital of Tibet, *Chinese Princess and Nepalese Princess* was included among nine operas performed annually. It continues to be performed by the Tibetan Institute of Performing Arts of India (Josayma 1993, 27–31). In the 1960s, the Chinese playwright T'ien Han created a version of the opera that emphasizes Wen Cheng's role as bestower of culture and omits the Nepalese princess's contribution. Furthermore it implies Chinese sovereignty over Tibet as early as the seventh century.

## Wen Cheng as a Tibetan Queen

*The Clear Mirror* contains a lament ascribed to Princess Wen Cheng. Arriving in Tibet she feels that the Tibetans, especially Minister Gar, are ill treating her (Sorensen 1994, 247–248). Wistfully she remembers her home. Although the Tibetans have benefited from her marriage to their king, she feels forlorn and suffers in her isolation.

> "Wen Cheng Kongjo's Lament"
>
> The daughter must go to Tibet. As dowry I took Jowo Shakya,[10] astrology books, precious gems, silk, and brocades. As I traveled (to Lhasa, the Tibetan capital), I made yogurt from milk and butter from cream. From buttermilk I made *thud* (a mixture of butter, cheese, and honey). I grinded rose seeds *(sewa)* into flour and from grass I made rope. From clay I made earthen pots. I made watermills and brought turnip seeds.[11]
>
> China lost prosperity but Tibet is prosperous. I miss the beauty of the daughter in her mother's kitchen and I always remember fondly being in the kitchen (with my mother). But I came to Tibet, now my home. You call the dog at home and beat it up. Tibetans have no shame and no appreciation. In the hand a little knife is sharp.[12] A little song is sweeter when you grind roasted barley. When in the mother's kitchen, a daughter is wise. The lord is influenced by his ministers. The man is influenced by a woman. Fields are filled with wild grass. I, the daughter, cannot live like this. Minister Gar is shameless.

The lament indicates clearly that Wen Cheng Kongjo is upset. The lament is followed by Minister Gar reminding her how poorly he was treated in China by her father and mother. She had never thought about Gar's treatment in China. Wen Cheng Kongjo's father, the Tang emperor Taizong (reign 626–649) compelled her to marry Srong Tsen Gampo, the king of Tibet. She did not want to leave her beloved China and her family to marry this Tibetan king, who lived in a desolate, cold, and almost uninhabitable environment. But she had no choice: She, too, like previous Chinese imperial princesses, was forced to marry a leader of another country in order to support peace between China and its neighbors. She was the first of two Chinese imperial princesses to marry Tibetan kings.[13]

Judging from the lament, Wen Cheng had difficulty adapting to her new home. Except for her retinue of twenty-five Chinese female attendants and the one hundred Chinese men who transported the Jowo Buddha statue and other valuables,[14] she was surrounded by Tibetans. Nevertheless according to Tibetan Buddhist histories, as a queen she made a tremendous impression on the Tibetans. Though many Chinese princesses married to neighboring rulers died young and often ignominiously, Wen Cheng lived in Tibet for forty years. In comparison to that of other princesses, Wen Cheng's life among the Tibetans was more favorable despite the feelings expressed in this lament. The *Tang Annals*, which are filled with battles and wars, record no wars between the Tibetans and the Chinese from the time of Wen Cheng's marriage in 641 to the death of Emperor Taizong in 649. Perhaps one may attribute this decade of peace to Wen Cheng's presence in Tibet.

## Marriage as a Political Strategy

It is important to note that China had different relationships with these neighboring countries: Some were allies; others were under Chinese protection and were considered by the Chinese to be both dependent and subordinate (Kaneko 1988, 75). One method to create a semblance of Chinese superiority was to offer an imperial princess in marriage to the ruler of another domain. Having married a Chinese princess, the foreign ruler was compelled to acknowledge the Chinese emperor as his father-in-law. An excellent example is the marriage between Princess Chien Chi and her second husband, She-t'u Khan, in 581. The Chinese court official Chang-sun Sheng presented the Turkish Khan an imperial decree, commanding him to stand and bow. He refused because he considered himself equal, or even superior, to the Sui Chinese emperor. The Sui envoy praised the Khan as an equal to the emperor because they were both Sons of Heaven; however, he asked, "How can the Khan refuse to honor his father-in-law?" This question put the Khan in an uncomfortable position. In the end, he felt that he had to show respect by bowing to his father-in-law, the Chinese emperor. For the Chinese, this act of bowing indicated the Khan's inferior position, but for the Khan, he acted only as a proper son-in-law by showing respect to his father-in-law. Further, accepting a Chinese princess, the Khan received many desired commodities, such as silk and other valuables as well as enhanced prestige (Jagchid and Van Symons 1989, 148).

Typically, rulers in neighboring countries were offered a Chinese princess if they were perceived as a threat to the security of China. The Tibetans under Srong Tsen Gampo had displayed major shows of force against China and threatening her border areas so that Emperor Taizong finally had to present the Tibetan king one of his imperial princesses. The *Old Tang Annals* record how the Tibetans first requested an imperial princess in 634 because the neighboring countries of the Tuyuhun and the Turks had received princesses. The leaders of Tuyuhun interfered and advised the emperor not to present a princess to the Tibetans. When Srong Tsen Gampo heard of this interference, he attacked the Tuyuhun, defeating many of their troops. Then he sent a threat to the Tang emperor: "If you refuse to give us a princess, we shall invade and plunder China as we did to the Tuyuhun." After several battles fought with the Chinese, some won by the Chinese and others won by the Tibetans, Princess Wen Cheng was married to the Tibetan king (Beckwith 1987, 23).

According to the *Old Tang Annals* the Tibetan king was very pleased: "Among our ancestors, no one has been married with (a princess) of the great empire. Now that I have been honored with the gift of a princess of the great Tang, my happiness is very great. In honor of the princess I will build her a walled city and proclaim my glory to future generations."[15] The Tibetan king and his warriors awaited Wen Cheng's arrival at Pohai; and he personally met her at Hoyuan near the Chinese border. Showing respect, he received Emperor Taizong with the rites of the son-in-law.[16]

The Tibetan Buddhist histories describe the events differently. In the Tibetan texts the princess does not meet the king until she is near Lhasa several months' journey from the border (Sorensen 1994, 242). This discrepancy reflects the different political perceptions of the Tibetans and Chinese. Unquestioningly, Tang China was a puissant empire, but as recorded in the *Tang Annals*, Tibet (referred to as Turfan) was also a country with a strong military, which needed to be placated through a matrimonial alliance. As mentioned earlier, the Chinese applied the term "father-in-law" to China and "son-in-law" to the king or leader who received an imperial princess in order to convey to the people of China and other countries that China held the superior position. However, the neighboring countries, such as Tuyuhun and various Turkish groups, did not see their position as inferior and considered themselves equals with China. Indeed, having received an imperial princess clearly showed the Tibetans and other countries that Tibet was a powerful country.

From the seventh through the ninth centuries, Tibet and China made numerous treaties (some of them as equals). Some were inscribed on steles and situated at the border of Tibet. One such stele stands in front of the Jokhang Temple in Lhasa: it records the treaty of 821/822, which is based on the equal relationship of the two independent countries.

> Both Tibet and China shall keep the country and frontiers of which they are now in possession. The whole region to the east of that being the country of Great China and the whole region of the west being assuredly the country of Great Tibet, from either side of that frontier shall be no warfare, no hostile invasion and no seizure of territory. (Richardson 1985, 121–123)

During Srong Tsen Gampo's reign, he succeeded in establishing Tibet as a military force in Central Asia that would last for over two centuries. The Chinese annals frequently report the bravery of the Tibetans and their own amazement at the almost impenetrable armor worn by Tibetan warriors and their horses (Pelliot 1961, 81; Bushell 1880, 442). Apart from Princess Wen Cheng's marriage, Chinese annals record only her date of death. In Tibet, on the other hand, Wen Cheng left a rich legacy: Buddhist images and Ramoche, a famous temple in Lhasa, plus the tradition that she was in fact an emanation of the goddess known as Green Tara.

## Wen Cheng's Buddhist Legacy

Chinese annals do not describe Wen Cheng's journey to Tibet or where she stopped and had Buddhist images erected. As Tibetan accounts also are vague and sparse, and some ancient names cannot be traced, her journey from the Chinese capital of Changan to the Tibetan capital of Lhasa is not known. But most Tibetan scholars agree that there are three places where she stopped and that continue to be associated with her. The one closest to China is Sun Moon Mountain, located in northeastern Tibet (Amdo province in Tibetan, or Qinghai province in Chinese). According to the nineteenth-century *Amdo History* (Brag-dgon dKon-mchog-brtan-pa-Rab-rgyas 1975, 1: 511), the mountain received its name due to an episode that occurred during Wen Cheng's journey. When Wen Cheng left home, she requested some items from her parents. Among them was supposed to be a precious crystal, the shape of which suggested the sun and the moon. As her travels took her farther away from China, Wen Cheng lingered on the road. She longed for family and home. Minister Gar, who was poorly treated by her parents, did not believe that they would give her this precious crystal. So he told her to see if the crystal was real, and if it was, it would prove that her parents really did care for her. The place where she examined the crystal became known as Sun Moon Mountain. The story continues that her parents had in fact deceived her and given her another crystal—one that displayed a gold sun and a silver moon, but not the most precious crystal. The *Amdo History* version ends here, but a popular Tibetan oral tradition continues the tale: Upset by her parents' deception, Wen Cheng hurled the crystal to the ground and it shattered. The two pagodas mentioned in the introduction were erected to commemorate this site.

Near the two pagodas is a Tibetan altar dedicated to the spirit of the mountain. The Tibetans know the mountain well and regard it as sacred. Because Tibetans have come to identify Wen Cheng as an emanation of Tara, when they visit Sun Moon Mountain, they give offerings to the local mountain spirit and to Tara.

The other two East Tibetan sites associated with Wen Cheng are Bidu (the modern name, Yushu) and lDan Ma Brag (the modern name, Rimda'), which have Buddhist temples and cliff carvings depicting Vairocana Buddha (the Sun Buddha). These are visited almost exclusively by Tibetans. Both are difficult to reach, and lDan Ma Brag can be reached only on horse or by foot. Tibetan Buddhist historical texts, such as *The Clear Mirror*, state that on her way to Lhasa, Wen Cheng stopped at different places and asked her accompanying artisans to erect cliff carvings of the buddhas (Sorensen 1994, 240). At both Bidu and lDan Ma Brag there are ten-foot relief statues of Vairocana Buddha flanked by four bodhisattvas on each side carved out of the sides of the cliff. Over time, Bidu and lDan Ma Brag became major pilgrimage sites frequented by Tibetans until the early 1960s, when the Chinese Communists outlawed any religious activity in Tibet.

lDan Ma Brag is one of the few sacred areas in Tibet that has escaped destruction by the Chinese Communists. The temple surrounding the cliff statues was destroyed in the early 1960s, but the statues were not. A Tibetan work force sent to destroy the statues refused, and they were willing to face torture rather than destroy their sacred images. The Chinese leader, infuriated by this disobedience, tried to destroy the statues himself out of anger. But he damaged only the knees and, partially, the nose of Vairocana Buddha. Embarrassed, he fled the area and never returned. The Tibetans felt that their deities continued to protect them.[17]

In 1985 the temple was restored and today Tibetan pilgrims are able to visit it once again.

According to Wen Cheng's "Lament," she brought with her to Tibet many precious items, such as gems, silks, and brocades. She also brought new forms of knowledge: divination texts and techniques for making yogurt, butter, and other dairy products. She taught the Tibetans how to make rope, pottery jars, and watermills as well as how to grind seed. However, for the Tibetans, the most precious gift was the statue of Jowo Shakyamuni, a depiction of the historical Buddha when he was twelve years old. Located today in Lhasa in the Jokhang Temple (literally, the house of Jowo), the most sacred temple in Tibet, the Jowo Shakya is the most venerated statue for perhaps all Tibetan Buddhists. For centuries, Tibetan pilgrims came to Lhasa to worship before Jowo Shakyamuni.[18] Though the Jowo Shakya is today in the Jokhang Temple, it was previously located in Ramoche Temple, Lhasa. Sometimes this temple is known as the Chinese temple because it is credited that Wen Cheng had Ramoche erected. The tradition states that Ramoche's main door faces east indicating that Wen Cheng came from the east.[19] Thus the northeastern site of Sun Moon Mountain, the eastern sites of Bidu and lDan Ma Brag, and the Ramoche Temple in Lhasa indicate the rich legacy of Wen Cheng Kongjo's contribution to Tibet.

Both Chinese and Tibetan traditions credit the princess with bringing Buddhism to Tibet: Buddhist statues, texts, and artisans versed in statue and temple building accompanied her from China. Chinese annals stress the civilizing influence of Chinese culture on Tibet.

> Since the princess disliked the fact that the Tibetans painted their faces red, Lungstan [Chinese name for King Srong Tsen Gampo] ordered his people to stop this practice. Discarding his own felt and furskin clothes, he wore brocade and silk. Gradually he copied Chinese customs. He also sent his chiefs' and nobles' children to request admittance into national schools [in China] to study the Chinese classics, and he requested learned scholars [to come to Tibet] from China to compose his official reports and memorials for the emperor. (Pelliot 1961, 5)

Tibetans acknowledge Chinese influences, but Tibetan Buddhist history also stresses the Indian and Nepalese contributions, which are not mentioned in Chinese histories. For example, before Srong Tsen Gampo's marriage to Wen Cheng, he already had married the Nepalese princess known as Khribtsun or Bhrikuti. She, too, brought important Buddhist statues, texts, and artisans to Tibet. Her most famous gift is the statue of Akṣobhaya, the Immovable Buddha, located presently in Ramoche Temple in Lhasa.[20] Furthermore, as Srong Tsen Gampo became acquainted with these major cultures and their strong textual traditions he realized that Tibetans needed a script for their own language. So he sent Tibetan youths to India to study the ancient Indian languages including Sanskrit and to find a script suitable for the Tibetan language. One youth, Thoni Sambhota, is credited with returning with a script that was adopted as official for the Tibetan language. Thus Tibet incorporated the diverse cultural influences of China, India, and Nepal during the imperial age.

## Apotheosis of Srong Tsen Gampo, Wen Cheng, and Bhrikuti

Wen Cheng's most extraordinary legacy is her transformation from a Chinese princess to the Buddhist goddess, Tara. Already by the twelfth century, many Tibetan historical texts refer to the deification of Wen Cheng. Between the seventh and the eleventh centuries, Buddhism was competing with the indigenous religion of Bon for royal favor and support. By the twelfth century Buddhism had become the dominant religion espoused by the majority of Tibetan rulers. Today, most extant Tibetan histories are predominantly Buddhist histories. For example, the popular text *The Clear Mirror of Royal Genealogies* begins with the teachings of the Buddha and the theme of the book is the introduction of Buddhism in Tibet, as well as its proliferation and influence there up to the fourteenth century. In *The Clear Mirror* and other Tibetan Buddhist histories, Srong Tsen Gampo and two of his wives, the Nepalese princess Bhrikuti and the Chinese princess Wen Cheng, are considered to be emanations of three famous bodhisattvas. Srong Tsen Gampo is identified with the most beloved bodhisattva of all Mahayana Buddhists, especially the Tibetans, the Bodhisattva of Compassion, Avalokiteśvara.[21] Likewise, the two princesses are regarded as emanations of the most popular female bodhisattva, Tara: The Nepalese princess is called Bhrikuti (sometimes known as Yellow Tara); Wen Cheng, Tara (or Green Tara).[22]

Because Tara is so popular, she has many different forms. She is considered by some to be a buddha; by others, a bodhisattva. According to the belief that Tara is a buddha and has the ability to save one from cyclic existence, it is understood that she was a princess before becoming enlightened. An abridged version states that when she awakened the supreme thought of enlightenment, a monk advised her to wish feverently to become a man.[23] Astutely she replied that there is no absolute distinction between a man or woman. Then she continued to inform the monk that many are enlightened with a man's body but few with a woman's body. So her personal vow was to help all sentient beings always with a woman's body. For the Tibetans one of these emanations is Wen Cheng Kongjo.

Second, among the Tibetans, Green Tara is considered the original form of the goddess.[24] Among the major twenty-one forms of Tara, the white and the green are most ubiquitous. White Tara is evoked in longevity rites, but Green Tara is evoked for situations that demand a swift response and rapid efficacy. She is known as the quick protector. Tibetans evoke Green Tara against both physical and mental enemies. According to Buddhist Tantra the three main means to accomplish things are by pacification, augmentation, and destruction. The great commentary by Buddhaguhya states:

> "Having a green appearance": this means that one gets the color green by mixing white, yellow, and blue, and these colors symbolize, respectively, the functions of pacifying, increasing, and destroying. Uniting all these means the performance of every function. (Beyer 1973, 279)

All these abilities are attributed to Green Tara.

The Avalokiteśvara section of *The Clear Mirror* (Sorensen 1994, 112ff.) teaches that Avalokiteśvara wants to help the Tibetans to be happy and to avoid suffering. When he arrives at the summit of Red Hill in Lhasa, he sees innumerable beings suffering. Saddened by this, a teardrop from his right eye falls to the ground and turns into Bhrikuti, who promises to help Avalokiteśvara alleviate the suffering of the Tibetans. The teardrop is reabsorbed and later reborn as the Nepalese princess Khribtsun. At the same time, a teardrop from Avalokiteśvara's left eye falls to the ground and turns into Tara. She, too, promises to help Avalokiteśvara and is reabsorbed. Later she is reborn as Wen Cheng Kongjo, the Chinese princess. Avalokiteśvara then tries to help as many Tibetans as possible, but it seems to be an impossible task. In despair, he gives up. However, previously he had made a vow that if he ever abandoned this task, his head and body should break into pieces, and so it happened. At this moment, Avalokiteśvara remembers the Buddha of Boundless Light, Amitābha, who had promised to help him. Amitābha reassembles the body, praying that from all the pieces Avalokiteśvara may have eleven heads and a thousand arms to help sentient beings. He then places himself at the pinnacle of Avalokiteśvara's ten heads. This form is known as the eleven-headed and thousand-armed (each hand has an eye) Avalokiteśvara.

Further relating to the life of Srong Tsen Gampo, we learn the following tradition (Sorensen 1994, 159); Avalokiteśvara realized that the time was ripe for the religious conversion of the sentient beings in the snowy land of Tibet, and four rays emanated from his body. The ray from his right eye went to Nepal and entered the womb of the King Amśuvarman's queen. After nine months Princess Bhrikuti was born. The ray from his left eye went to China and entered the womb of Emperor Taizong's consort empress. Nine months later Princess Wen Cheng was born. Another ray from the Avalokiteśvara's mouth went to Tibet, and his six-syllable mantra—*om mani padme hum* (Om, the jewel and the lotus, hum)—was placed there. The last ray came from Avalokiteśvara's heart and entered 'Briza Thod·dkar, queen of King gNamri Srongbtsan. Nine months later in 617 (the year of the fire-female-ox) a son was born. On his head was the image of the Buddha of Boundless Light, Amitābha. Later this son was known as Srong Tsen Gampo. These stories illustrate the Tibetan belief that Srong Tsen Gampo, Princess Khribtsun, and Princess Wen Cheng are emanations of Avalokiteśvara, Bhrikuti, and Tara, respectively; this triad is dedicated to help the Tibetans in all situations.

## Sovereignty

In the preceding pages, we examined the transformation of Wen Cheng from Tang princess to Tibetan queen and finally to an emanation of the goddess Tara. Why are these transformations important for our understanding of the political relationship between the Tibet and China? Initially in the seventh century, Srong Tsen Gampo sought to unify Tibet and establish himself as its sovereign. Likewise the Tang emperor Taizong (whom some consider to be the first Tang emperor rather than the second) also was trying to legitimize his rule as the emperor of all China. In both their countries, Srong Tsen Gampo and Taizong were admired foremost as great warriors and strategists. Each reinforced his rule by exhibiting great courage and demanding allegiance from his ministers, warriors, and people. In both domains, coercion and intimidation were necessary to maintain power. The display of force occurred within and between the two nations.

In this essay, we have examined how this conflict between Tibet and China occurred and how it was interpreted differently by the Tibetans and Chinese. When Taizong gave Wen Cheng Kongjo as an imperial princess to Srong Tsen Gampo, he further enhanced his position as a Chinese emperor because he was giving a woman related to his family who was accepted by the Tibetans as an imperial princess. By accepting Wen Cheng as an imperial princess, Srong Tsen Gampo was acknowledging Taizong as the Chinese sovereign. Furthermore, as Taizong was compelled to give an imperial princess because of Srong Tsen Gampo's show of force and threat to invade China, Taizong reinforced Srong Tsen Gampo's sovereignty in Tibet. Not only did the marriage alliance support Srong Tsen Gampo's sovereignty, but it enhanced his power and prestige vis-à-vis other neighboring nations, such as the Turks and Tuyuhuns. Thus Wen Cheng served as a symbol of sovereign power and prestige for both the Chinese ruler and the Tibetan ruler.

According to Amitai Etzioni (1975), who has examined power and the sources of control, there are three major sources of control that can be allocated or manipulated: coercion, economic assets, and normative values. Coercive power achieves compliance by alienative means, such as conquest, punishment, or deprivation. Remunerative power achieves compliance by controlling material resources and rewards, whereas normative power achieves control through the manipulation of esteem, prestige, and ritual symbols (xv). Srong Tsen Gampo and Taizong both used all three categories of power, but the dominant type during the formation of the marriage alliance was coercion.

By the twelfth century the imperial power in Tibet and Tang China had ceased to exist for over 200 years. For the Tibetans, Buddhism and its values were being incorporated in their general worldview. By the twelfth century most Tibetan histories were Buddhist histories. Buddhism was the cohesive component in providing a stable framework for Tibetan identity and its rulers. Whereas in the seventh century, the ideals were great strength, martial skills, and military strategy, by the twelfth century these ideals had been transformed into those of internal self-control, compassion, or skillful means, and liberative strategies to realize buddhahood. The warrior ideal still existed, but its importance was eclipsed by the ideal of becoming a buddha.

In these later Buddhist histories, Srong Tsen Gampo and Wen Cheng have been turned into the bodhisattvas of Avalokiteśvara and Tara, respectively. The dominant control has shifted from that of coercion to that of normative values. A Chinese princess as a symbol of power and prestige had lost its importance. By the late twelfth century the Mongols are perceived as a major force, not the

Chinese. Because Tibetan military prowess was no match against the mighty Mongols led by Genghis Khan, Tibetans did not demand recognition as an equal military power. Now, the Tibetans' main strength lay in Buddhism, especially its magic, influencing the Mongols to become the protectors, rather than enemies, of Tibet. Thus Wen Cheng as a Chinese was no longer highlighted, but her Buddhist legacy and her partnership with Avalokiteśvara, who was fast becoming the patron deity of Tibet, were emphasized (Kapstein 1992). Buddhist norms and values were reinforced; the construction of Buddhist temples and images flourished. Buddhism gradually pervaded the Tibetan culture, and this worldview persists to the present time. Thus for the Tibetans from the twelfth century to the present, Wen Cheng is foremost Tara and to a much lesser extent, a Chinese princess.

But in the 1950s and 1960s when the Chinese asserted their military strength against the Tibet, the primary source of control was again one of coercion. Systematically and thoroughly, the Communists tried to replace the Buddhist normative values with Communist ideology. Suddenly Wen Cheng resurfaced as a Chinese princess. Because the Chinese needed to legitimatize their conquest of Tibet, Wen Cheng again served as a useful symbol to demonstrate a long historical connection between the Chinese and Tibetans.

A revival of Wen Cheng occurred; posters displaying her sitting on a beautiful horse were sold in Lhasa during the 1960s and 1970s. The tree that Wen Cheng supposedly planted in front of the Jokhang was elevated to a special status and protected from destruction during the Cultural Revolution. The *Chinese Princess and Nepalese Princess* opera was rewritten in Chinese, omitting the Nepalese princess. The marriage of Wen Cheng and Srong Tsen Gampo continue to serve as a model for marriages between the Han and Tibetans. From the Chinese viewpoint, these were effective techniques and reminders to emphasize China's sovereignty over Tibet. Yet for the Tibetans, Wen Cheng as a Chinese princess had been nearly forgotten. For them, she is Tara, their protector and savior, not their oppressor or enemy. Furthermore reminded that Wen Cheng was initially a Chinese princess, the Tibetans long for the day to come when a ruler as strong and compassionate as Srong Tsen Gampo will rule them again.

NOTES

1. During the Tang dynasty, Changan was considered one of the most cosmopolitan cities of the world. Travelers and luxury goods came there from the Middle East and from all over Asia.
2. In the Chinese Foreign Broadcast Information Service (95–210) entitled "Tibet expanding Ties to Inland Provinces," on 31 October 1995 (57–58), the Chinese government continues to stress this relationship to strengthen ties between the Han and Tibetans. (See Smith 1996, 644.)
3. Two of these more famous relationships are Kublai Khan and 'Phags pa in the Yuan dynasty and Emperor Qianlong and Rolpa'i rDorje in the Qing dynasty.
4. Pan Ku and Pan Chao, "Account of the Wu-sun of the Western Region," *Han Shu* 96II, chuan 66.11, 2b–3b.
5. She has a tragic life because, being from the Chi family, the first Sui emperor kills

her father and brother to assert his supremacy in 581. Also this year her husband dies and the new Khan, She-t'u, demands that the Sui emperor give him an imperial princess. To save herself, she volunteers to become a daughter of the Sui emperor, the murderer of her family, and marries the nephew of her deceased husband.

6. She was married to Tabar Khan (r. 572–581), then to his nephew, She-t'u Khan (r. 581–587), and finally to his son, Yung yu lu (r. 588–599).
7. "Account of the Turks." *Sui Shu* 84, chuan 49, 9b–10a.
8. The Tibetan sections of the *Old and New Tang Annals* have been translated into English by S. W. Bushell 1880 and into French by Paul Pelliot 1961.
9. Written in the fourteenth century by Sonam Gyaltsen, *The Clear Mirror* has been translated in a popular way by McComas Taylor and Lama Choedak Yuthok 1996 and in annotated translation by P. K. Sorensen 1994.
10. This statue of the historical Buddha has become the most esteemed and holiest statue in Tibet; it is located in the Jokhang Temple in Lhasa.
11. This implies that she taught the Tibetans these things. I find these dairy techniques suspicious because Chinese have never been known to like milk products. This reflects knowledge a nomadic society would have, or perhaps even Indian influence.
12. This indicating once in Tibet, the Tibetans were mean to her.
13. The second imperial princess, Chin-cheng, came to Tibet in 710.
14. In Lhasa, in the Jokhang Temple and the winter palace of the Dalai Lama, the Potala, are miniature drawings illustrating the Buddha statue and the princess's retinue coming to Lhasa.
15. This is my translation from Pelliot's translation (1961, 5).
16. According to the Tang documents, the Tibetan kings were considered either nephews or sons-in-law, but never brothers as stated in the inscription at Sun Moon Mountain. (See Kaneko 1988.)
17. When I visited this site in 1983, some pilgrims related this episode.
18. At the present time, whenever the Jokhang Temple is open for worship, the chapel of Jowo is filled with pilgrims.
19. Srong Tsen Gampo's Nepalese queen is credited with constructing the Jokhang. Since she is from the west, the Jokhang's main door faces west.
20. According to tradition, originally the Jowo Buddha statue was in Ramoche but later it was hidden in the Jokhang for safekeeping. After the threat of theft was gone, the Jowo Buddha was placed in a chapel in the Jokhang.
21. The Dalai Lamas are also emanations of Avalokiteśvara.
22. Some earlier scholarship about these two princesses have reversed this and stated that Wen Cheng is White Tara and Bhrikuti is Green Tara, but this seems an attempt to adjust to ethnicity as generally the Nepalese have a darker complexion than the Chinese. Noteworthy is that the triad of Avalokiteśvara flanked by Green Tara and Bhrikuti are found in early Buddhist texts, such as *Mañjuśrīmūlakalpa* and *Mahāvairocana Sūtra,* which are well-known by Tibetans.
23. Some Mahayana *sūtras* state that in one's final life before enlightenment one must be a man because one mark of an enlightened being is a sheathed penis. Sometimes this means that one becomes a man in one's final birth, but in some cases, a female can magically transform herself immediately before she becomes a buddha in the same lifetime. But other *sūtras* see no ultimate distinction between being a man or woman. (See Paul 1979, 166–243.)
24. A popular Tibetan myth relates that the ancestors of Tibetans were the monkey

offspring from the mating of a monkey and an ogress. This monkey was Avalokiteśvara and the ogress, Tara (does not specify which Tara).

REFERENCES


Barfield, Thomas J. 1989. *The Perilous Frontier: Nomadic Empires and China*. Oxford: Blackwell.

Beckwith, C. I. 1987. *The Tibetan Empire in Central Asia*. Princeton, NJ: Princeton University Press.

Beyer, Stephen. 1973. *The Cult of Tārā: Magic and Ritual in Tibet*. Berkeley: University of California Press.

Brag-dgon dKon-mchog-brtan-pa-Rab-rgyas. 1975. *mDo sMad Chos 'Byung* (or *The Ocean of Annals of Amdo*) (3 vol.). New Delhi: n.p.

Bushell, S. W. 1880. "Early History of Tibet" [trans. of the *Old and New Tang Annals*]. *Journal of Royal Asiatic Society of Great Britain and Ireland* [New Series] 12: 435–541.

Etzioni, Amitai. 1975. *A Comparative Analysis of Complex Organizations: On Power, Involvement, and Their Correlates*. New York: Free Press.

Jagchid, Sechin, and Jay Van Symons. 1989. *Peace, War, and Trade Along the Great Wall*. Bloomington: Indiana University Press.

Josayma, Cynthia B. 1993. "*Gyasa Belsa:* An Introduction." *Tibet Journal* 18 (Spring): 27–31.

Kaneko, Shuichi. 1988. "T'ang International Relations and Diplomatic Correspondence." *Acta Asiatica* 55: 75–101.

Kapstein, Matthew. 1992. "Remarks on the *Mani bKa'-'bum* and the Cult of Avalokitesvara in Tibet." Pp. 79–93 in *Tibetan Buddhism: Reason and Revelation*, ed. Steve Goodman and Ronald Davidson. Albany: SUNY.

Paul, Diana. 1979. *Women in Buddhism*. Berkeley, CA: Asian Humanities Press.

Pelliot, Paul. 1961. *Histoire Ancienne du Tibet*. Paris: Adrian Maisonneuve.

Richardson, Hugh E., and David Snellgrove. 1968. *A Cultural History of Tibet*. London: George Weidenfeld and Nicolson.

Richardson, Hugh E. 1985. *A Corpus of Early Tibetan Inscriptions*. London: Royal Asiatic Society.

Shakapa, W. D. 1984. *Tibet: A Political History*. New York: Potala Publications.

Smith, Jr., Warren W. 1996. *Tibetan Nation: A History of Tibetan Nationalism and Sino-Tibetan Relations*. Boulder, CO: Westview Press.

Sorensen, P. K., trans. 1994. *Tibetan Buddhist Historiography: The Mirror Illuminating the Royal Genealogies*. Wiesbaden: Harrassowitz Verlag.

Stein, R. A. 1972. *Tibetan Civilization*, trans. J. E. Stapelton Driver. London: Faber and Faber.

Taylor, McComas, and Lama Choedak Yuthok, trans. 1996. *The Clear Mirror*. Ithaca: Snow Lion Press.

Twitchett, Denis, ed. 1979. *Cambridge History of China* [3:1 Sui and Tang China 589–906]. Cambridge: Cambridge University Press.

# 10

# Becoming the Empress of Heaven

## The Life and Bureaucratic Career of Mazu

*Vivian-Lee Nyitray*

Throughout cultural China, the goddess Tianhou (Empress of Heaven) ranks second only to the Buddhist bodhisattva Guanyin as a female object of popular devotion. Her cult originated in the southeastern coastal province of Fujian and it gradually spread outward, first to other Chinese coastal communities and then via migration and trade routes to Korea, Japan, Taiwan, Southeast Asia, Europe, and the Americas.[1] Owing to the vagaries of history and hagiography, the goddess is known in South China by her final enshrinement title of *Tianhou* (often romanized from Cantonese as *Tin Hau*), whereas Fujianese and Taiwanese devotees, believing themselves particularly close to the goddess, refer to her formally as *Tianshang shengmu* (Holy Mother in Heaven) but commonly call her *Mazu* or *Mazupo*, an affectionate kinship term meaning something like "Granny."

Mazu is not the highest-ranking deity in the vast and patriarchal Chinese folk pantheon. There are several emperors, among whom the most widely recognized are the Emperor Who Preserves Life (*Baosheng dadi*), the Emperor of the Dark Heavens (*Xuantian dadi*), and the generally accepted head of the celestial imperial bureaucracy, the Jade Emperor on High (*Yuhuang shangdi*). But there is only one Tianhou—only one Empress of Heaven—and the goddess's hagiographies and cultic

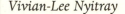

*Figure 10.1: Meizhou Mazu protecting the fleet.* (*Source: Vivian-Lee Nyitray.*)

history make clear the defining characteristics of her sacred rulership. From the days of her earthly existence to her continuing presence in Chinese sociocultural affairs, Mazu's qualities of celestial sovereignty are manifest and compelling[2]: Like other sovereigns she has always *mediated superhuman powers and society*. Her heavenly career has been propelled by claims of *active engagement in domestic defense and warfare*, and she has always been approached as *the righteous redistributor of wealth, benefits, and justice*. The present study of Mazu first illustrates her sovereign roles and then seeks to understand how it is that a thousand years after she first drew official notice during the Song dynasty (960–1279 CE), the goddess still plays considerable—if contested—roles as *pivot*, as *symbolic social center*, and even as *symbol of totality* in the People's Republic of China (PRC), in the Republic of China on Taiwan (ROC), and in the global Chinese diaspora.

## From Girl to Goddess

In Wolfram Eberhard's study of the aboriginal cultures of South China, he speculated that the sea-goddess's origins may have predated Han Chinese settlement in South China, that is, she may have emerged from the ethnic Han Chinese transformation of an aboriginal water deity, or from a conflation of female water deities (1968, 402–440). Beyond the problem of aboriginal origins, however, current scholarship has begun to question whether the *Tianhou* and *Mazu* necessarily have the same referent. Some Tianhou temples in South China offer no hagiography for their Tianhou at all. James Watson (1985) has suggested that such temples in Guangdong province and in Hong Kong's New Territories, now officially dedicated to Tianhou, originally may have housed a local female spirit who later became identified with the state-sanctioned goddess.[3] Other South China temples offer as their founding legend the miraculous discovery of a wooden image of the goddess found floating at sea or in the local river; still others recall a piece of wood that was miraculously formed into such an image and later credited with bringing good fortune to both the finder and the local populace.

In these legends, the individual who discovers the image or the piece of wood is sometimes surnamed Lin, but there may be no further reference to that clan. In striking contrast, contemporary Fujianese and Taiwanese devotees share a generally coherent popular hagiography of Mazu, which is firmly linked to the Lin family. Largely conforming to the broad outline of the life as recorded in the Ming dynasty (1368–1644) text of the *Tianfei xiansheng lu* (Record of the Celestial Consort's Divine Manifestation), the tale is of a young girl, Lin Moniang (Miss Lin, "the Silent One"), who was born on the twenty-third day of the third lunar month in 960 CE on the island of Meizhou, in the Minnanese Putian district of Fujian province. The hagiographical record is equivocal on the Lin family's occupation and social standing: Lin Moniang's father is identified frequently as a virtuous but low-ranking official, although the most famous incident in popular accounts of the goddess's life dictates that all the Lin males were active fishermen. From a young age, Miss Lin was credited with a range of traits and skills:

By the age of eight she was well-versed in the Confucian classics, and by eleven she was renowned for her knowledge of the principal Buddhist sutras; in early adolescence, she encountered a Daoist fairy or water sprite, who gave her a bronze talisman with which she later exorcised evil spirits, healed the sick, and performed other shamanic tasks.

At the mythic core of all accounts of her salvific power is an incident wherein, at the age of sixteen, Lin Moniang seemed to have fallen asleep or become entranced at her loom. Actually, her spirit was far out at sea, plucking the imperiled boats of her father and brother(s) from the waves during a great storm. In the midst of this rescue, her mother suddenly called the girl back to consciousness, thereby interrupting Moniang's rescue of either her father or one of her brothers, depending on the account. Lin Moniang was inconsolable. When the survivors subsequently returned to port with vivid recollections of having seen or heard Moniang in the storm, her reputation as a miracle worker spread to neighboring villages along the Fujian coast.

Reaching age eighteen, she refused to marry—an extraordinary declaration for a young woman who did not plan to enter an order of Buddhist nuns. Lin Moniang remained with her natal family, devoting herself to their care and to helping others. She once brought abundant rainfall during a drought, and she subdued two demons—Ears That Hear with the Wind (*Shunfeng er*) and Eyes That See a Thousand *Li* (*Qianli yen*)—whose lives she spared in exchange for their service as her "generals." She is said to have died at age twenty-seven or twenty-eight and has dedicated herself ever since to the protection of maritime and riverain communities.[4]

Numerous alternative accounts exist within the standard hagiography. Such discrepancies or ambiguities are evidence of the efforts of local populations to mold the life of the future goddess in their likeness, that is, to claim Mazu as one of their own. An official position for the Lins would make their daughter acceptable to local elites, whereas stories of a fisherman's daughter turned wonder-working shaman would enjoy broad popular appeal (Watson 1985, 296).

In addition to consideration of social station, official Confucian and lay or sectarian Buddhist and Taoist interpretations of the gods always vied for primacy in the popular imagination (Boltz 1986; Hymes 1996). This competition is observable in narratives of Mazu's death and apotheosis. The most frequent account presents Lin Moniang in good Daoist form as either disappearing into the hills or else ascending to heaven to join the immortals (on an auspicious double yang day); an anti-Buddhist version blames her death on the keeping of too strict a fast; yet another, owing much to traditional tales of filiality, has her disappearing into the hills after cutting flesh from her thigh to feed her parents in a time of famine. Finally, one oral tradition in Hong Kong's New Territories, related by Watson's informants, attributes her death to suicide, which she committed rather than agree to an arranged marriage with an older man—an extraordinary action that underscores Tianhou's special affinity for unmarried women and explains her occasional appearance in a red (wedding) dress (Watson 1985, 297).[5] Out of these and other alternatives and accommodations, a broad-based community of Tianhou/Mazu believers arose.[6]

## Becoming the Empress of Heaven

The process by which a local Fujian deity, Elder Aunt Lin (*Lin tagu*), ultimately became the pan-Chinese Tianhou is a seemingly straightforward one. In gratitude for the performance of actions deemed of service to the state, anyone—living or dead—was eligible for imperial citation and for the receipt of honorific titles and rank. For example, the first of the future Tianhou's numerous titles, *Linghui furen* (Divinely Favored Lady), was granted in 1155, when the Song court credited the goddess with preserving the boats of an imperial envoy during a storm at sea.[7] The honorific characters *Zhaoying* ([of] Glorious Response) were added in either 1157 or 1160 in response to the goddess's capture of a band of pirates (Boltz 1986, 217 n.38).

Continued examination of the goddess's historical progression in rank and title, however, exposes the subtle thrust and parry of local autonomy versus central government control. Beneath the formulaic bureaucratic surface was a calculated desire on the part of the imperial authorities to cultivate civic identity and order by expanding the sovereign reach of the goddess together with a corresponding desire by regional elites to acquiesce as means to their own ends. State officials wishing to "tame" a local deity (around whom rebellions might coalesce) could coopt her into the celestial bureaucracy and stress her orthodox Confucian virtues, chief among which would be filiality and, by extension, loyalty to the state. At the local level, any of a number of enshrined female worthies might become identified with the state-promoted goddess to increase temple assets and prestige or to allay imperial worries about local fealty (Chu 1996; Hymes 1996; Watson 1985). According to Watson, the promotion of Tianhou/Mazu's cult paralleled the gradual rise of state authority over China's southern coastal region and played a large role in the standardization of approved Chinese culture. Especially in times of political instability, then, the goddess was enlisted by a range of individuals to serve their disparate needs, whether through the creation of new myths or the appropriation of existing ones.[8]

There is at present no unambiguous record for the bestowal dates of Tianhou/Mazu's epithets and titles, although the overall progression can be discerned. In 1190, the Song emperor, finding it expedient to adopt her as a symbol of coastal pacification, promoted her from *Furen* (Lady) to the rank of *Linghui fei* (Divinely Favored Imperial Consort). In 1208, the goddess was granted the epithet *Huguo* (Protector of the State), in gratitude for her alleviation of a dual threat of bandits and drought. When the Mongols succeeded in establishing the Yuan dynasty, the potential value of promoting a Chinese symbol of stability and loyalty was clear to the new rulers: Kublai Khan rewarded the (Chinese) goddess for meritorious service to the (Mongol) state, elevating her to the highest ranks of the celestial bureaucracy with the title *Tianfei* (Celestial Consort) in 1278. The additional epithets *Mingzhu* (Illustrious Manifestation) and *Bimin* (Defender of the People) were granted in 1281 and 1299, respectively, the latter awarded for the goddess's protection of grain transports (Boltz 1986, 217 n.38). When Chinese rule was reestablished in 1368, the Ming emperors ordered the construction of a temple outside the capital city of Nanjing and reinstated formal sacrifices to the goddess. Then, in 1409, after the Celestial Consort had rescued three imperial envoys from stormy seas, the emperor granted her the impressive title of Celestial Consort of Universal Salvation, Magnanimous Benevolence, Glorious Response, Wondrous Efficacy, and Illustrious Manifestation Who Protects the State and Defends the People (*Huguo bimin mingzhu miaoling zhaoying hongren puji tianfei*).

Over the centuries, the goddess's purview had grown to encompass not only maritime affairs and domestic issues, such as conception and childbirth, typically associated with female deities, but also responsibilities that the state traditionally delegated to male earth gods and city gods, for example, the preservation of official and mercantile affairs, protection of the populace from banditry, and personal engagement in military and political endeavors. An early fifteenth-century Daoist canonical text, the *Taishang laozhun shuo tianfei jiuku lingyan jing* (Classic of Lord Lao, the Most High, Speaking on the Celestial Consort's Efficacy in Relieving Troubles), reflects the broad extent of the goddess's salvific reach by that time. Its opening lines explicitly demonstrate her sovereign status by proclaiming her "intense and equal relationship with all" her subjects, and by portraying the goddess's "righteous judgement" and cosmic omnipotence:

May her majestic countenance be made explicitly manifest upon the vast seas
And may all under heaven hold her in esteem, for her goodness extends to each and every one.
Her preservation of the state and deliverance of its people knows no obstacle;
She offers instant relief to those in distress and comes to the immediate rescue of those imperiled.
Whether she is to be found traversing the celestial or mortal realms,
Riding the waves and breakers, or likewise within terrestrial bounds,
All manner of demonic and spectral forces will bow in submission
And the water sprites and phantasmic apparitions will one by one take cover.
For, in the snap of a finger, she transforms the baleful into the auspicious,
Bestowing good fortune and eliminating misery as if it were a trifle. (Boltz 1986, 217)

Later, the goddess herself promises immediate and reliable response to anyone in need:

> whether a travelling merchant or resident shopkeeper seeking assets in doing business, whether farmers in their sowing or artisans in their professions, whether troops in transit engaged in battle arrays. . . . In my travels throughout the celestial realm, I will always keep watch over humankind, to the extent that whatever is sought on land, within spring waters, rivers, or at sea—in every location—all will be granted as wished. (Boltz 1986, 224)

Finally, having been canonized by Lord Lao (Laozi), the Celestial Consort pledges to uphold a lengthy series of vows, including the following:

> (1) I will rescue all boats, large and small, so that they may reach the other shore; (2) I will offer protection to visiting merchants so that they will all be content; (3) I will cast out all perverse and aberrant forces and make them vanish forevermore; (4) I will sweep away all sources of suffering and adversity, so that family homes will know pure quiescence; (5) I will seize all treacherous thieves so that there will be absolutely no trace of them left behind; (6) I will seize and behead all malevolent beings and chop off their heads with a hoe, while restraining them with thorns; I will relieve the people and preserve the state, so that humankind may proclaim great peace; . . . (9) I will offer my support to those with difficulties in childbirth so that mother and child will remain out of danger; (10) I will offer shelter and protection to people of good will so that they may have no encounters with oppression and tyranny; (11) I will stand guard over the sacred domain so that wind and rain will be timely; . . . (13) May those who engage earnestly in scholarly pursuits achieve full satisfaction in their meritorious work; (14) May those who seek office and promotion in their profession enjoy the prosperity of rank and reward. (Boltz 1986, 225)

The goddess's universal sovereign regard for her subjects was tested, however, in the mid-seventeenth-century Ming-Qing dynastic transition. As the Qing (Manchu) dynasty slowly consolidated its power over the country, Ming loyalists established a base on Taiwan, which was then under Dutch control. Loyalist leader Zheng Chenggong (known to the West as Koxinga) attributed his victory over the Dutch in 1662 to Mazu; at the same time, the first Qing emperor attributed two rescues to her, once from bandits and once from shipwreck. When the Qing forces eventually overtook Taiwan in 1683, the Celestial Consort appeared in the skies above the Straits, carrying banners and urging both sides to victory in exemplary bipartisan fashion.

The remaining details of the former Lin Moniang's imperial rise through the celestial ranks can be recounted quickly. In 1684, the Kang Xi emperor raised her status to Tianhou (Celestial Empress, or Empress of Heaven), a title confirmed by the Qianlong emperor in 1737. After the fall of the Qing dynasty, the Republican government mandated the upkeep of her temples and decreed that she be venerated for filiality (as opposed to being worshipped as an empress, celestial or otherwise); this has remained the official position of the Republican government-in-exile on Taiwan.

During World War II, Mazu intervened on behalf of her subjects by preserving temples and, occasionally, the homes of the faithful from Allied bombing raids. It is claimed that even American nonbelievers witnessed the goddess catching bombs in her apron.[9] After the Communist victory in 1949, the Mazu cult was suppressed on the mainland; later, during the Cultural Revolution (1965–1976), temples that had not already been put to residential use were badly damaged, if not entirely destroyed. In the 1980s, Tianhou temple reconstruction began, largely financed by Taiwanese and other devout overseas donors. The PRC government's intention was not to facilitate local religious practice, however, but to draw in foreign exchange through tourism, especially from overseas Chinese. Symbolic of this renewed interest in Tianhou/Mazu was the construction of a monumental image of the goddess high on a hill above the Meizhou mother temple. This imposing image, officially named the Straits Goddess of Peace (*Haixia heping nushen*), looks out over the ocean, across to Taiwan, where Tianhou/Mazu has been worshipped continuously since the first temples were founded there in the early seventeenth century. Over the past 300 years, the Taiwanese Mazu cult has weathered civil wars, colonial rule, industrialization, urbanization, and then modernization, becoming in the process a highly visible—though contested—symbol of local identity and cross-Straits interaction.

## Contested Sovereignty: Taiwanese "Mazu" or Chinese "Goddess of Peace"?

Historically, patronage and promotion of Tianhou/Mazu has reinforced a notion of a shared culture that supersedes the plethora of mutually unintelligible dialects and disparate local customs that have always characterized China. Appropriation of the goddess in recent years, however, has increasingly taken the form of undoing or reversing that historical trend toward Chinese unification. In a series of thoughtful studies of the Mazu cult on Taiwan, P. Steven Sangren (1987, 1988, 1993) has analyzed Mazu pilgrimage as linked to the construction and celebration of a distinctively Taiwanese identity. As the focal point of a pan-Taiwan pilgrimage community, the goddess has brought together many groups of the island's citizens, inclusively differentiating Hakka, Zhangzhou, Quanzhou, and other Fujianese "Taiwanese" from those "mainlanders" who fled to Taiwan in the wake of the Communist victory in 1949. Until the phased lifting of martial law began in 1987, the mainlanders' government-in-exile monopolized political power and determined cultural standards, often denigrating the practices and beliefs of the more than 70 percent majority Taiwanese population. Mazu cultic activity was characterized in the state-controlled press as "superstition" (*mixin*), unbecoming to an emergent economic power. Candidates for local office might kick off their election campaigns by worshipping at the village or town Mazu temple, but when high-level government leaders, such as President Chiang Ching-kuo, found it politically useful to visit temples or attend festivals, their activities were typically restricted to respectfully lighting incense or to promoting Confucian virtues by praising the filial acts of Mazu or her followers.[10] As a powerful focal symbol of Taiwanese local history and culture, Mazu had long carried tremendous potential for arousing native emotions; during the Japanese occupation of Taiwan (1895–1945), it was said that "to worship Mazu was to cherish the homeland" (*Bai mazu huai guguo*) (Boltz 1986, 213 n.16). For these reasons, the Mazu cult's activities were always closely monitored by the ROC authorities.

Events of the last fifteen years have shown that the goddess remains a central yet contested symbol of the struggle to define a "Taiwanese" sociocultural identity in light of competing visions of ethnic origin and nation-statehood. In May 1989, when Taiwanese devotees, in violation of national security laws prohibiting direct travel to the mainland, sailed their fishing vessels to Meizhou, the journey was tracked in the daily newspapers and the pilgrims returned to a cheering crowd of thousands (Nyitray 1996). Images of the goddess brought back from Meizhou were confiscated as contraband, and the fishermen were charged with sedition, a capital offense. On one side of the ensuing national debate was the mainlander government, and on the other side were legislators who cautiously defended "traditional" Taiwanese folk practices. As events unfolded, however, government officials resolved the potentially explosive situation by allowing the case to slip away in the wake of the mainland Tiananmen tragedy; charges against the pilgrims were dropped under the guise of championing freedom of expression—a public relations coup that contrasted the "democratic" freedoms enjoyed by Taiwan residents with the cruel suppression of such stirrings in the People's Republic. There were two immediate consequences of this interpretive reversal. First, religious pilgrimage was declared a legitimate reason for travel to the PRC, precipitating an explosion of religious tourism from Taiwan to the mainland. Second, the Mazu cult was elevated in official parlance from folk superstition to constitutionally protected religion, a shift in political discourse that went largely unnoticed at the time. A few years later, however, its force was felt when Mazu again crossed the Taiwan Straits.

With direct travel to and from the mainland still prohibited, the goddess arrived in Taiwan in late January 1997 via a flight from Macau. As before, her journey made front-page headlines in Taiwan—but for reasons quite different than those of 1989. A life-size "golden" image of a youthful Tianhou, which was said to have been hidden away and thus to have escaped the ravages of the Cultural Revolution, left the Meizhou mother temple to undertake a hundred-days' tour of Taiwan. The goddess and her entourage arrived at Chiang Kai Shek International Airport shortly after noon on January 24. One hundred and sixty representatives from Mazu temples islandwide were on hand to greet the goddess, as were a thousand of her followers.

But not everyone welcomed the "Meizhou Mazu." Following an initial flood of Taiwanese pilgrims to Meizhou, the numbers of Mazu faithful visiting the goddess's birthplace had been declining (Sangren 1993, 577). The trip's loss of novelty, its increasing expense, and its perceived danger—following the robbery and murder of Taiwanese tourists in China—contributed to this decline, compounded in no small measure by dissatisfaction with Meizhou locals, in whom Taiwanese pilgrims sensed more greed than devotion. Not surprisingly, then, there was open speculation that this visit of the goddess to Taiwan was just a "fishing expedition," in which the expected catch was cash for PRC officials' pockets—and plenty of it. During the tour, Taiwanese temples wanting to host the goddess had to ante up funds to support her entourage, and local temple members were also expected to express devotion in fitting style through donations of golden lotuses, golden plaques, and heavy "red envelopes" filled with cash.[11]

Speculation about the motives of the PRC government continued. For years, mainland officials had denied permission for Meizhou artifacts to travel to Taiwan; now, scant months after engaging in military exercises that showcased missiles hitting targets just miles offshore from Taipei, the PRC government's cooperation in arranging Mazu's tour was viewed with considerable suspicion. The ROC Mainland Affairs Commission commended the visit as fostering religious exchange, but a widely debated public contention was that the PRC was merely hiding behind the rhetoric of cultural exchange as part of their plan to bring the renegade island province back to the motherland. After all, as PRC officials noted, the Taiwanese and the Fujianese share the "same bones and flesh" (*gurou tongbao*). Suspicion of PRC intentions was expressed succinctly in colloquial references to Mazu's tour. Official temple literature was careful to describe the trip as the Meizhou Mazu's *qiannian toci yu* ("first trip in a thousand years"), whereas the term often used in conversation and in the popular press was *raojing*, meaning a deity's ritual emergence from her or his temple in order to inspect local precincts. To have the Meizhou Mazu "inspect" Taiwan, then, was to reconfigure territorial boundaries such that Taiwan now fell within her Meizhou/Fujian jurisdiction.

Perceptions of mainland avarice and of the Meizhou Mazu's participation in territorial/political expansionism led to repeated confrontations between the Meizhou entourage and members of the Taiwan Independence Party (*Jianguodang*), almost from the moment her palanquin crossed the threshold of the CKS Airport arrivals building. Even as cheering throngs welcomed her, approximately 200 Taiwan Independence Party members held a noisy protest outside the terminal. Some of the demonstrators wore Mazu costumes and held tinfoil bombs and missiles in their hands, demanding that "Meizhou Mazu go home!" Denouncing the tour as "a despicable example of waging a holy war of reunification and deceiving believers," they shouted, "Chinese people worship Chinese Mazu, Taiwanese people worship Taiwanese Mazu!"[12]

The force and significance of this particular rallying cry—that Taiwan neither needed nor wanted a mainland Mazu, even one from the "mother temple" in Meizhou—is striking when one considers the long-standing contention for primacy among Taiwan's major Mazu temples. For years, temples in Beikang, Dajia, Lugang, and Luermen (Tainan), among others, held out competing claims for the founding dates of their temples, the efficacy of their Mazu image, and the authority of their lineage—this last factor based on the identity of the mother temple in Fujian. In 1987, intertemple rivalry intensified when the Dajia Mazu temple sent a delegation to Meizhou to bring back an image of the goddess for enshrinement, intending thereby to solidify their claims of authority and spiritual efficacy (Huang 1994; Rubinstein n.d.; Sangren 1993). Taiwan's temples also carried their competitive one-upmanship to the mainland, pouring huge sums of money into the reconstruction of various mainland temples, with two in the Putian district of Meizhou receiving particular attention. Back on Taiwan, the Beikang temple then constructed its own sixteen-meter-tall Straits Goddess of Peace on a terrace behind the main shrine—a mirror image of the Meizhou statue.

Yet, in 1997, the relevance and validity of the Meizhou Mazu's image was openly contested. Although the Taiwan Independence Party represents only a fraction of Taiwan's population, its position on the "independence" of Taiwan's Mazu cult was provocative. Party spokesperson Li Yongzhi asserted that not all the Mazu temples in Taiwan had been founded by "incense division" (*fenxiang*), the formal process by which incense ash taken from one temple is used to establish a principal incense pot for a new "daughter" temple; rather, many of the oldest Mazu images on Taiwan had been privately held family images, making Mazu—like those who literally carried her to the island—an immigrant. Taiwan's Mazu was therefore "already independent" and the Meizhou Mazu was irrelevant.[13]

The entire hundred-days' tour was a study in contrasts. At the goddess's first stop in the southern city of Tainan, 3000 worshippers waited through the night to file past the image and pay homage. But as the goddess continued her tour of the island, the anti-Meizhou Mazu protests continued, sometimes turning violent, as when buses and trucks carrying the goddess's image were attacked by men and women wielding sticks, chains, and farm implements. What had happened in the span of a mere decade to generate such unforeseeable actions and unforgettable images?

By 1997, the political complexion of Taiwan had changed dramatically from that of the late 1980s, due principally to the lifting of martial law and the establishment of democratic elections. With proliferating political parties and multiple agendas, the earlier sociopolitical differentiation of "Taiwanese" from "mainlander" was further complicated. An expanded political spectrum now ranged from those favoring reunification with the mainland to "Taiwan independence" parties, all of whose constituencies cut across sociocultural lines; sensitivity toward Taiwan's indigenous tribal peoples had been growing; and, most important, second- and third-generation "mainlanders" had matured. Having been born and raised in Taiwan, they drew their sense of identity as much—if not more—from Taiwan as from a distant mainland province. Even among those "Taiwanese" who traced their ancestry to nearby Fujian, the passage of centuries had weakened family ties and, in many cases, PRC land redistribution policies had destroyed claims to ancestral turf. Out of all these permutations a new sense of Taiwanese identity was—and still is—emerging.

## Splintering States: Creating Community?

A world away in California, longtime witness to Chinese migration, new questions relative to Tianhou/Mazu's sovereign status and role are forming. In San Francisco's Chinatown, the goddess's independence appears to have yielded to city ordinance: No longer does she emerge from her Grant Avenue temple to inspect its precincts on her birthday, nor on a day selected for its auspiciousness on the traditional calendar; instead she participates in the annual Grant Avenue Chinese New Year's parade, on a tourist-friendly Sunday set by city council decree. Nevertheless, the San Francisco Mazu continues to exercise her sovereign rights when she attends the annual temple festival in the Sacramento Valley town of Marysville.

The Marysville temple is dedicated to another water deity, the god Bok Kai, but Tianhou/Mazu is enshrined along with three other "worthies" on the altar of a nineteenth-century temple abutting the Yuba River. In recent years, the long-established Chinese community in Marysville has dwindled to a few families, some of whose younger members have married non-Chinese. In contrast, the thriving San Francisco Mazu temple serves an ethnically Chinese but complex immigrant society from East and Southeast Asia. In the Marysville celebration, national and ethnic identity is downplayed, although it is not entirely absent; what matters more is a sense of shared affinity for the legacy of Chinese settlement in California, a criterion illustrated by the parade's announcer of recent years—an anthropologist and regional historian whose doctoral dissertation took as its subject the Marysville Bok Kai Temple Festival, but whose only tie to the Chinese-American community is a scholarly one (Chace 1992). In a manner reminiscent of the Meizhou Mazu "inspecting" Taiwan, the San Francisco Mazu appears to be inspecting her extended precincts in northern California, enlarging her visible sphere of influence beyond the traditional community of Chinese faithful. In her mediation of Chinese and non-Chinese culture, Mazu has expanded the parameters of her sovereignty: Not only have Marysville and Beikang in Taiwan become sister cities, but the goddess's distribution of wealth and goods now extends through the Bok Kai Festival to benefit a host of local merchants in this semirural American small town.

Mazu's mediation of distinct communities is observable elsewhere. As mentioned earlier, there is a long-standing tendency to associate or conflate the goddess with the Buddhist bodhisattva Guanyin, typical of the syncretic impulse common to Chinese religion. Further, there is a temple in the Philippines, where the goddess is worshipped as the Virgin of Casasay, a fusion of the goddess with the Virgin Mary, which suggests provocative new dimensions of sovereignty (See 1990). Another strikingly different but not insignificant dimension of the goddess's sovereign role as *righteous redistributor of wealth* may be taking shape in the form of Mazu credit cards, now available in Taiwan: Using the card generates funds for charity. Thus it may be said that the Mazu card creates of its holders a new economic community, even as it creates for them the opportunity to further the goddess's compassionate good works.[14]

The history of Mazu's celestial sovereignty is a long one. For centuries, the goddess has *held together the cosmos* of her believers, *acting as symbolic center for a society organized as a state*. But Mazu's symbolic role in Chinese culture and in Chinese societies is far from being a thing of the past.[15] Her cult today is vigorous, transforming, as it has always done, in response to demands of local and regional Chinese cultures, pan-Chinese states, and, owing to the Chinese diaspora, to the larger world beyond that of ethnic Chinese identity. In short, the multiple and powerful forces of modernization and shifting world populations have redrawn the boundaries of Tianhou's concern. What remains to be seen is the final map of the goddess's sovereignty: Will it be so localized that Chinese people worship Chinese Mazu, Taiwanese people worship Taiwanese Mazu, and North American devotees worship a Canadian or American or Mexican Mazu? Or will Tianhou's sovereignty shift from the identity politics of nation-states and ethnic origin to a conceptual realm of common culture? Perhaps in going out from her temples, Mazu is already inspecting the precincts of a new, global temple. In so doing, her cult may itself come to constitute a new "cosmos"—a faith community for which Tianhou/Mazu, the Empress of (all under) Heaven, will remain as symbolic center, a Goddess of Peace whose sovereignty transcends the geopolitical boundaries of local nation-states.

NOTES

1. The term *cultural China* refers to both the People's Republic of China and to the Republic of China on Taiwan; to states and territories where ethnic Chinese are either the majority population or a significant cultural force, for example, Macau and Singapore; and to global diasporic ethnic Chinese communities. Temples dedicated to the sea-goddess are prominent in southern and southeastern coastal areas of the Chinese mainland, number nearly 400 in Taiwan, and have been established as far afield as Paris, New York, San Francisco, and Sao Paulo, Brazil (Wu 1992, 203–221; Li 1995, 223–229).
2. At the suggestion of this volume's editors, my starting point for the present discussion of sovereignty was the cluster of articles concerning kingship in Eliade (1987). In particular, italicized definitional terms are drawn from Christiano Grottanelli's article "Kingship: An Overview" (1987).
3. For further discussion of Tianhou/Mazu's conflation with Guanyin and other female deities in the Chinese pantheon, see Nyitray (n.d.).
4. Artistic representations of the goddess reflect the variety of traditions related to Lin Moniang's physical death at an early age and to her continued life as Tianhou in the celestial realm. Taiwanese images often depict a well-fed, middle-aged female clad in the robes and beaded headdress appropriate to an empress; the goddess appears to have aged over the centuries. Moreover, sculpted images of the goddess found in Taiwan often show her with a dark or black face—a convention interpreted by contemporary believers as the result of Mazu's years of facing the incense smoke of the faithful. Mainland images are less consistent, ranging from a stately, mature portrayal to a slender and youthful goddess. The Straits Goddess of Peace statue, for example, shows a regal yet vigorous figure. Contemporary PRC paintings and posters can be quite fanciful, as in a poster that updates a traditional pose: Tianhou is shown floating protectively above a small fleet of boats, but rather than traditional fishing junks or warships, the sea-goddess serenely watches over powerboats and pleasure craft.
5. I have argued elsewhere that these alternative interpretations of Moniang's marriage resistance, death, and apotheosis work to alleviate tensions wrought by conflicting demands of filiality and social expectation on unmarried women (Nyitray, n.d.).
6. A number of innovative cultural, historical, and architectural studies on the goddess were presented at the conference on "The Tianhou/Mazu Temple," held at the Chinese University of Hong Kong, 3–4 January 1997; proceedings are now in preparation by editors Joseph Bosco and Ho Puay Peng. At this same conference, P. Steven Sangren succinctly described the Mazu cult as "unity within diversity," that is, its unity has been marked by the ways in which various levels of stories are able to articulate with one another.
7. The earliest record of imperial recognition of the goddess predates title bestowal: In 1123, the court presented a commemorative wooden tablet bearing the characters *xunji*, literally "smooth crossing," to the Putian Mazu temple in recognition of that same envoy's safe passage (Lin 1989; Soo 1990). Incomplete or contradic-

tory evidence abounds for many of the dates listed here, sometimes attributable to disparity in converting dynastic reign dates to conventional Western dates.

8. Watson (1985, 293f.) specifically discusses the appropriation of Tianhou/Mazu as symbol of the state pacification of coastal areas, but similar patterns of assimilation held for other deities (Baptandier 1996; Weller 1987, 1996).
9. This tale of miraculous protection from falling munitions is recounted in connection with a great many temples in Taiwan, often being reprinted in temple broadsheets and popular hagiographies. The same story is told for the bodhisattva Guanyin's protection of Taipei's Lungshan Temple.
10. On local officials' ties to Mazu temples, see Bosco (1992, n.d.) and Sangren (1988). During the early 1980s, in keeping with revisionist ROC policies, the Ministry of Education sought to reconfigure Mazu's legends in the service of Confucian values by depicting Lin Moniang in schoolbooks not as a goddess but as a legendary paradigm of filial behavior (Meyer 1987).
11. It should also be noted that local temples too stood to gain financially from greater-than-usual sales of incense, spirit money, amulets, and commemorative trinkets, as well as booth fees paid by independent vendors. Items offered "direct from the mainland"—ranging from "golden Mazu" photograph amulets to audiotapes of the Mazu sutra chanted to grainy videotapes of bloody shamanic performances at Mazu festivals—all sold at considerable profit in the carnivalesque atmosphere.
12. Quoted in *Zhongyang ribao* (Central Daily News), 25 January 1997 (*min.* 86), p. 5. Additional information regarding this incident has been drawn from the *Lianho bao* (United Daily News), *Lianho wanbao* (United Daily Evening News), *Zhongguo shibao* (China Times), and *Taiwan shibao* (Taiwan Times) from 23 January to 30 March 1997, as well as from broadcast news accounts and personal observation of events during this period.
13. Quoted in *Zhongyang Ribao* (Central Daily News), 25 January 1997 (*min* 86), p. 5.
14. Interestingly, both cards depict images of Mazu found at the Beigang temple: The VISA card shows the Beigang Mazu statue, which mirrors the Goddess of Peace image in Meizhou, and the MasterCard shows the more traditional, black-faced image of the goddess and bears the notation Beigang Mazu Peace Card.
15. The vision of Mazu's continuing vitality is not shared by some contemporary Taiwanese scholars. Yuan Hoping (1997), for example, notes the rise in educational levels and an increasingly secularized (i.e., "rational") worldview among younger Taiwanese; he thus predicts that Mazu will eventually become a mere symbol of traditional culture.

REFERENCES

Baptandier, Brigette. 1996. "The Lady Linshui: How a Woman Became a Goddess." Pp. 105–149 in *Unruly Gods: Divinity and Society in China*, ed. Meir Shahan and Robert P. Weller. Honolulu: University of Hawaii Press.

Boltz, Judith Magee. 1986. "In Homage to Tien-fei." *Journal of the American Oriental Society* 106(1): 211–232.

Bosco, Joseph. 1992. "Taiwan Factions: Guanxi, Patronage, and the State in Local Politics." *Ethnology* 31(2): 157–183.

———. n.d. "Mazu in Taiwan: Religion in Global and Local Identity." In *The Tianhou Temple: Religion and Culture in South China* [conference volume], ed. Joseph Bosco and Puay Peng Ho (forthcoming).

Chace, Paul G. 1992. "Returning Thanks: Chinese Rites in an American Community." Ph.D. diss., University of California, Riverside.

Chu, Ron Guey [Zhu Ronggui]. 1996. *"Taiwan minjian zongjiao zhong so chengjian de xiaodao—yi shanshu ji mazu xinyang wei li"* (Manifestations of filiality seen in Taiwanese popular religion: examples from morality books and Mazu beliefs). Pp. 67–98 in *Yishi, miaohui yu shequ—daojiao, minjian xinyang yu minjian wenhua* (Ceremony, temple organization, and community: Daoism, folk belief, and folk culture), ed. Li Fengmao and Chu. Taipei: Academia Sinica, Institute of Chinese Literature and Philosophy.

Eberhard, Wolfram. 1968. *The Local Cultures of South and East China*. Leiden: E. J. Brill.

Eliade, Mircea, ed. 1987. *The Encyclopedia of Religion*. New York: Macmillan.

Grottanelli, Christiano. 1987. "Kingship: An Overview." Pp. 313–317 in vol. 8 of *The Encyclopedia of Religion*, ed. Mircea Eliade. New York: Macmillan.

Huang Meiying. 1994. *Taiwan mazu de xianghuo yu yishi* (Mazu incense offerings and ceremonies in Taiwan). Taipei: Zili wanbao.

Hymes, Robert. 1996. "Personal Relations and Bureaucratic Hierarchy in Chinese Religion: Evidence from the Song Dynasty." Pp. 37–69 in *Unruly Gods: Divinity and Society in China*, ed. Meir Shahan and Robert P. Weller. Honolulu: University of Hawaii Press.

Li Xianzhang. 1979. *Boso shinko no kenkyu* (Research on Mazu belief). Tokyo: Taisan bunbutsu kai.

Li, Lulu. 1995. (*min.* 84). *Mazu xinyang* (The folk belief of Mazu). Taipei: Han yang.

Lin Meirong. 1989. "Zhanghua Mazu de xinyangquan" (Zhanghua Mazu belief circles). *Bulletin of the Institute of Ethnology, Academia Sinica* 68: 41–104.

Meyer, Jeffrey. 1987. "The Image of Religion in Taiwan Textbooks." *Journal of Chinese Religions* 15: 44–50.

Nyitray, Vivian-Lee. 1996. "The Sea Goddess and the Goddess of Democracy." Pp. 164–177 in *The Annual Review of Women and Religion IV*, ed. Arvind Sharma. Albany: State University of New York Press.

———. n.d. "Do My Eyes Clearly See? Questions of Gender in Tianhou / Mazu Scholarship." In *The Tianhou Temple: Religion and Culture in South China* [conference volume], ed. Joseph Bosco and Puay Peng Ho (forthcoming).

Rubinstein, Murray A. n.d. "Time, Space, and Word: Religious Rivalry, Ethnic Identity, and the Struggle for Spiritual Status and Socio-religious Power Among Matsu Temples on Taiwan." Unpublished paper.

Sangren, P. Steven. 1987. *History and Magical Power in a Chinese Community*. Stanford, CA: Stanford University Press.

———. 1988. "History and the Rhetoric of Legitimacy: The Ma Tsu Cult of Taiwan." *Comparative Studies of Society and History* 30: 674–697.

———. 1993. "Power and Transcendence in the Ma Tsu Pilgrimages of Taiwan." *American Ethnologist* 20: 564–582.

See, Teresita, and Go Bon Juan. 1990. "Religious Syncretism Among the Chinese in the Philippines." Pp. 53–65 in *The Preservation and Adaptation of Tradition: Studies of Chinese Religious Expression in Southeast Asia*, ed. Tan Chee-Beng. [Contributions to Southeast Asian Ethnography, no. 9]. Columbus: Ohio State University, Department of Anthropology.

Soo Khin Wah. 1990. "The Cult of Mazu in Peninsular Malaysia." Pp. 29–51 in *The Preservation and Adaptation of Tradition: Studies of Chinese Religious Expression in Southeast Asia*, ed. Tan Chee-Beng [Contributions to Southeast Asian Ethnography, no. 9]. Columbus: Ohio State University, Department of Anthropology.

Watson, James L. 1985. "Standardizing the Gods: The Promotion of T'ien Hou ("Empress of Heaven") Along the South China Coast, 960–1960." Pp. 292–324 in *Popular Culture in Late Imperial China*, ed. David Johnson, Andrew J. Nathan, and Evelyn S. Rawski. Berkeley: University of California Press.

Weller, Robert P. 1987. *Unities and Diversities in Chinese Religion*. Seattle: University of Washington Press.

———. 1996. "Matricidal Magistrates and Gambling Gods: Weak States and Strong Spirits in China." Pp. 250–268 in *Unruly Gods: Divinity and Society in China*, ed. Meir Shahan and Weller. Honolulu: University of Hawaii Press.

Wu Jinzao. 1992. (*min.* 81). *Jianghai nushen—mazu* (Goddess of rivers and the sea: Mazu). Taipei: Xinchao.

Yuan Hoping. 1997. (*min.* 86). *Xiandai yen kan mazu* (A contemporary look at Mazu). Taipei: Youshi wenhua.

# 11

# King Arthur and Morgan le Fay

*Serinity Young*

Morgan le Fay (meaning Morgan the Fairy) is known as the half sister of Arthur, the semilegendary sixth-century king of the Britons.[1] She is a complex character, one who has been woven from many ancient threads, and one who gives a fair picture of a deep Celtic belief in goddesses who can bless or curse as the mood takes them. In this essay I explore Morgan's association with divinity, especially her power to confer sovereignty, beginning with the earliest textual sources for her legend and concluding with contemporary literary and cinematic expropriations of her character. She is represented variously as a dangerous sorceress who enchants men with her magic and her beauty, a shape shifter, and a woman known for her wisdom, esoteric knowledge, and abilities as a healer.[2] She opposes Arthur and constantly seeks ways to harm him, yet in the end it is she who takes him to Avalon and immortality. These contradictions point to Morgan's composite character; she shares traits with the Irish trinity of goddesses Morrigan, Macha, and Matrona, as well as with the fairies. None of the sources on her ever fully explain how Morgan's human status as Arthur's sister cohabits with her supernatural fairy nature, though we find many stories of Celtic goddesses and fairies who become women in order to be with the hero they choose. One medieval tale offers the explanation that Morgan's interest in magic caused her to leave human society and to live in the forests. Eventually people began to think of her more as a fairy than a mortal and gave her that title (*Lancelot* II: lxix, cited by Paton 1960, 165 n.1).

Bits and pieces of Morgan's story can be found in the oral Arthurian legends that developed into medieval story cycles, such as those of Sir Thomas Malory (d. 1471), whose writings are the source of most modern interpretations of Morgan and Arthur (see Sklar 1992). Through 1,500 years of shifting gender ideologies that have kept pace with changing cultural and religious priorities, Morgan is seen descending from goddess to fairy to mortal woman.

## The Medieval Literature

The earliest literary sources for Morgan[3] were composed several centuries after the events they describe, if indeed Arthur's historicity is ever established.[4] In the meantime, Christianity had been established, an event that is often anticipated in the stories, and several invasions of the British Isles by foreign people had occurred.[5] The christianization of the Celtic people of the British Isles began in the third century CE, and they maintained their new faith even after the fifth-century invasion of pagan Anglo-Saxons who established permanent settlements. The Anglo-Saxons, in turn, began to be christianized during the last decade of the sixth century. This process took several centuries to complete and entailed a change in, among other things, the status of women, a change that is frequently understood to have been a reduction of status. The scribes who wrote down these stories were usually Christian converts who wanted to preserve the rich oral culture that was also their pre-Christian history.

The sources for Morgan are contained in the literatures of two peoples, the Celts, among whom the Arthurian legend began, and the Normans, who were first to write the legends down (discussed by Fries 1992, 5–6; see also Jackson 1960, 81–88). At the height of their power in the first millennium, the Celts ranged across Europe from the Caspian mountains to Ireland. They were an ethnically varied people who shared artistic and cultural traditions and spoke similar languages, some of which continue to be spoken today in parts of Ireland, Scotland, Wales, and Brittany. They were a fierce warrior culture who sacked Rome in 390 BCE and raided Delphi in 279 BCE. Eventually, they were crushed between the migrating Germanic tribes and the growing power of Rome. According to Julius Caesar (*The Conquest of Gaul*) the Celts had three social classes: the priests (Druids), whose center of learning was in Britain; the warriors; and the common people, or serfs. Though literate, the Druids refused to commit their religious teachings to writing, perhaps believing them to be too sacred for any but oral transmission. Consequently, much of their religious practice, especially their rituals, is lost to us. However, recent archaeological research shows they had an impressive understanding of astronomy and mathematics. References to this knowledge and related practices are found in the Arthurian legends in the figures of Merlin and Morgan, among others.

The Normans were actually the Norsemen (Scandinavians) of French Normandy. Their Norse heritage was similar to that of the earlier Anglo-Saxon invaders of England. A Norman presence was permanently established in England as a result of the Battle of Hastings in 1066, after which there was a continual flow of people and ideas back and forth across the English Channel.

The significant and active roles played by women in Arthurian literature suggest pre-Christian models for women, both Celtic and Norse.[6] Among both these peoples there is evidence for the high status of at least some women: They could own property, initiate divorce and choose whom they would next marry, rule countries, and command men. Some were powerful warriors or achieved status in the priesthood—among the Celts they were often *faiths*, or soothsayers. This is consistent with the role of many of the women in Celtic literature, which is to act as intermediaries between the natural and supernatural world or to be from the supernatural world.

On the other hand, the status of women varied among specific groups and probably underwent changes over time.[7] For instance, the frequent association of women with magic and the supernatural among both the Norse and Celtic peoples suggests suspicions about women and a fear of their power that contributed to negative assessments of womankind in general and the imposition of limitations on their rights and privileges. Some of the conflicts in the position of women are brought out in the Arthurian stories, which often undercut women's power and try to put limits on it.

Significantly, much of the literature composed during the medieval period was designed to educate courtiers in proper behavior; courtesy and hospitality are important virtues, while details about clothing emphasized stylish dressing and determined fashion for both women and men. These stories instruct rough warriors, female and male, in good manners. An important element in the medieval understanding of courtesy is the relations between women and men; in other words, they are reshaping gender roles (see e.g., Jackson 1960, 88–100).

An examination of the role of women in Arthurian literature shows how some of these issues were played out. Maureen Fries (1992) has persuasively argued for a distinction between heroinism, heroism, and the female "counter-hero":

> A heroine is recognizable by her performance of a traditionally identified, female sex-role. But any woman who, by choice, by circumstance, or even by accident, escapes definition exclusively in terms of such a traditional role is capable of heroism, as opposed to heroinism. [For instance, when they] assume the usual male role of exploring the unknown beyond their assigned place in society; and . . . reject to various degrees the usual female role of preserving order (principally by forgoing adventure to stay at home). The[ir] adventurous paths . . . require the males who surround them to fill subordinate, non-protagonist roles in their stories. . . . [T]he counter-hero possesses the hero's superior power of action without possessing his or her adherence to the dominant culture or capability of renewing its values. While the hero proper transcends and yet respects the norms of the patriarchy, the counter-hero violates them in some way.

> For the male Arthurian counter-hero, such violation usually entails wrongful force; for the female, usually powers of magic. . . . Always she is preternaturally alluring or preternaturally repelling, or sometimes both . . . but her putative beauty does not as a rule complete the hero's valor, as does the heroine's. Rather, it often threatens to destroy him, because of her refusal of the usual female role."(5–6)[8]

The female counter-hero, so well personified by Morgan, is indifferent to patriarchal values; she harkens back to an earlier time and earlier sources of knowledge. In an age not known for its love of learning, she is a woman of knowledge. At the beginning of the period associated with unconsummated courtly love she exhibits a sexual freedom unknown to other female characters. Morgan le Fey goes her own way.

### *Le Morte d'Arthur*

Malory presents Morgan as a decadent, adulterous, and murderous woman who uses magic to achieve her ends. Her ability to cast spells defines her, in the terms of Arthurian romance, as a female counter-hero, but for the rest she is acting in the male heroic mode, choosing her lovers and fighting her enemies (Vinaver 1947, 137–152).[9] At the same time, the easy sexual relations she pursues echo the earlier, self-motivated behavior of pre-Christian Celtic women and goddesses, who also frequently chose their own mates. One of Morgan's functions in this text is to be a counterpoint to the new, idealized Christian women of the period, and Malory accomplishes this in large part by simply preserving earlier images of women, both human and divine.

While Arthur is out hunting with her husband, King Uryens, and her lover, Sir Accolon, Morgan uses magic to cause the three men to fall into an enchanted sleep from which each one awakens in a different place. King Uryens wakes up in Camelot with Morgan. Sir Accolon wakes up in the company of a dwarf, who brings him a message from Morgan together with Excalibur, Arthur's magical sword,[10] which makes its wielder invincible. She wants Accolon to use it in combat against Arthur. King Arthur awakens in a dungeon, where he is coerced into fighting the disguised Accolon. Ultimately Morgan is thwarted in her efforts by the countermagic of the Lady of the Lake, who protects Arthur and helps him defeat and kill Accolon. Meanwhile Morgan attempts to kill her husband but is prevented from doing so by a female servant who warns him. She then rides off to steal once again Arthur's sword, but she succeeds only in capturing its magic scabbard (which prevents its owner from bleeding to death). Pursued by Arthur she flings it into a lake saying, "Whatsoever com of me, my brothir shall nat have this scawberde!" (Vinaver 1947, 151). She and her followers then ride into a valley "where many grete stonys were," and she transforms herself, her followers, and their horses into similar great stones.

Morgan's persistent efforts to capture Arthur's sword and to destroy him can be read as a struggle against various forces that were undermining the power of royal women, and/or goddesses, to grant the kingship to a male hero of their own choosing. Indeed, Excalibur had been forged on Avalon, the island of the fairies, Morgan's true home. Although there are no explicit connections between the sword and kingship, Excalibur empowers Arthur, even though the source of its power lies with the fairies. Significantly, as Arthur lies mortally wounded, Morgan displays her divine connections. In the company of two other queens (thus forming a divine trinity, similar to that of Macha, Martrona, and Morrigan, and echoing the trio she formed with her two sisters), Morgan takes him to the mythical island of Avalon, where time stands still, to be healed (1242). It is from Avalon, a land where no one ages, that Arthur will someday return to rule again as a wiser king, one worthy of sovereignty. Even in Malory's tale Arthur returns to the pre-Christian roots that drive his legend: divine kings who receive their sovereignty from exacting goddesses. (We will look at some examples from Celtic stories later.) The clearest surviving Celtic element in Arthur's, and thus Morgan's, story is that of the king who will renew himself on the magical island of Avalon from which he will return in order to rule again.

For Malory, Morgan represents a subversive force within Arthurian society. She opposes and sabotages the political and social structure of her brother's realm through her beauty, sexuality, magical powers, and occult knowledge. Malory's text says that Arthur is "the man in the worlde that she hatyth moste, because he is moste of worship and of prouesse of ony of hir blood" (Vinaver 1947, 146). She goes after Arthur most explicitly in the Accolon story, symbolically robbing Arthur of his kingship by stealing Excalibur. Elizabeth Sklar (1992) appropriately defines the concerns of this story as "regnal succession and aristocratic inheritance rights" (30). It is this, but further, by returning Arthur's body to Avalon, Morgan is returning him to a pre-Christian realm, the realm in which her power and her nature flourish, and where he will be renewed in pre-Christian understandings of the beneficial powers of goddesses.

Another aspect of Morgan's hatred for Arthur can be surmised from her earlier history in Malory's tale, when King Uther kills her father in battle, claims her mother for his wife, begets Arthur, and then marries off Morgan's two sisters. Morgan is one of the conquered royal women that are part of Uther's booty to dispose of as he wishes. Perhaps Morgan was too young to marry, because instead she is sent away from her mother to school (10) and replaced by Arthur, the son and heir. Some of the antipathy for Arthur is shared by Morgan's sisters, especially Morgause, whose seduction of Arthur and conception of a child (Mordred) can only have an evil outcome in Malory's view: This act of incest generates Arthur's destruction (Vinaver 1947, 44). Scraping away Malory's impressions and removing the Christian overlays leaves us with a story of royal sister/brother union, and beyond that the king's marriage with the goddess. Such a union was believed to lead to prosperity for the kingdom, not destruction.

Marriage between brother and sister among royalty is an ancient custom in many lands and whether an actual or a symbolical union, it points to the importance of the female royal line. J. G. Frazer (1920, 238–247) lists several examples from ancient northern Europe of kingship passed through the royal female line, not the male. In such traditions, mortal women conferred sovereignty most often through marriage (see, e.g., Dumézil 1973, 83–129). Morgan and Morgause, as Arthur's sisters, echo these ancient ideas. Traces of this status can be found even in Malory's text, when the men guarding Arthur let Morgan into the sickroom and she steals his scabbard. In self-defense they say, "'we durst nat disobey your sistyrs commaundemente'" (Vinaver 1947, 151). In other words, Morgan's power as the king's sister goes unchallenged. She also represents the goddess of sovereignty whose favor Arthur must win in order to be king.

### *Sacred Kingship*

The Arthurian legend is tied to the sacred nature of kingship in ancient Ireland, such as the belief that kings were responsible for the fertility of the land, the weather, and the general well-being of the realm (Draak 1959, 653; see also Mac Cana, in this volume). Royal inauguration ceremonies were called *banais rígi*, meaning the wedding feast of the king, where the land itself was personified as a woman the king married (Draak 1959, 657).[11] In many Irish texts the land is initially represented as an old woman whose marriage with the king retores her youth. In other words, the land is revitalized in the ceremonial marriage (Draak 1959, 657). Several tales reveal this female figure's connection to sovereignty,[12] as when an old woman challenges the young men of a hunting party by saying that one of them must sleep with her or they all will die. Only the true future king dares to approach her, and when he does, she becomes young and beautiful, announcing that she is "Sovereignty" and assisting him in winning the kingship. In a similar tale, *Baile in Sćail*, a woman called Flaith Erenn, Sovereignty of Ireland, gives Conn a drink that symbolizes her bestowing the kingship on him (Draak 1959, 659).[13]

There is some connection between Morgan and these early stories in that several sources show her frequently appearing as an ugly, old woman. This leads Lucy Allen Paton (1960, 151) to believe that a story, now lost, existed that focused on this aspect of Morgan's shape shifting. In the medieval Arthurian stories, on the other hand, Morgan is a reversal of Sovereignty. She is the subversive thread that runs through the tales, which depict her struggle to undo Arthur's kingship, most notably in her attempts to retrieve Excalibur, a symbol of his kingship, and return it to pagan Avalon. While Arthur, the legendary pagan king, has been transformed into a righteous Christian king, his semidivine half-sister, the divine woman who confers Sovereignty, is demonized.

### *Goddess and Fairy*

Morgan's supernatural nature is shown, in part, by her title "le fay," and by her behavior, which is in accordance with that of several related Celtic goddesses, such as Morrigan, Macha, and Matrona (Paton 1960, 148–166). She displays supernatural powers, as, for example, when she casts spells on Arthur, Accolon, and her husband, magically transporting them to distant places, and when she shape shifts. Of particular interest is her ability to turn herself into a stone, as when she enters a valley of great stones, possibly monoliths, similar to those at the ancient site of Stonehenge. It is well-known that Stonehenge was used as a site to measure the solstices and other important astronomical phenomena, a science Morgan is said to have mastered. In addition, the magical qualities of stones were commonly accepted in Celtic lands. Finally, Morgan's choosing and disposing of lovers, even going so far as to attempt to kill her husband, identifies her both with the fairies and with the more autonomous Celtic women, especially royal women, of the past (see, e.g., Queen Medb in Kinsella 1969).

In Arthurian romances, a great hero often wins the love of a fairy, a woman of exceptional beauty, indeed supernatural beauty. In and of herself she may be his greatest prize, the seal of his heroism, or she helps him to display his courage and strength by assigning him an almost impossible task. Thus fairies are prized, beautiful, and challenging. They also show a marked streak of independence, coming and going as they please.

Two of the earliest stories about fairies underline the quality of immortality, or timelessness, associated with fairies, an element that is essential to the ongoing popularity of Arthur's legend as the king who will return. One story comes from Irish literature, the *Imram Brain maic Febail* (The Voyage of Bran, Son of Febal), a tale told perhaps as early as the seventh century (Paton 1960, 2). In it a fairy queen appears to the hero and takes him back with her to a "land of women." Eventually the hero grows homesick and decides to return home, only to find out that centuries have passed during what he thought were years. He crumbles to dust as he steps off the ship onto land. Another early Irish story, the *Echtra Condla* (The Adventures of Connla), has another hero called to this land of women, lured by a fairy and the apple she has brought with her. He is never heard of again.

Despite their own comings and goings between the land of humans and fairyland, fairies do not themselves age; they remain eternally young, and eternally beautiful. They are as unaffected by time as they are by other human limitations; hence they are perceived to have magical powers to achieve their ends. It is love that draws them to the human world—after all, these are romances—yet their love for a mortal man has a misogynist edge, suggesting as it does that a great hero would never find his equal among mortal women. It is a view that does not embrace the idea of heroic roles for women unless they are supernatural; human women must be obedient, patient, kind, and faithful. Fairy women can be the opposite of all this: They command, are impatient, and can be cruel, and fidelity is not one of their virtues, all of which is understandable because they are immortal and prone to taking mortal lovers. In fact, they act just like the heroes, only they are even more powerful because of their magical powers.

Roger Loomis argues that the derivation of the fays in medieval romance and modern folklore from the goddesses of pre-Christian Europe explains Morgan le Fay's multiple personality: "She has acquired not only the attributes and activities of Macha, the Morrigan, and Matrona, but also the mythic heritage of other Celtic deities. She is a female pantheon in miniature" (cited in Paton 1960, 127).

Striking are the characteristics Morgan's shares with Morrigan, the Irish warrior goddess: Morrigan is known to incite heroes to brave deeds and help them plan battles. She accomplishes these ends by encouraging the warriors and by her prophecies. She is a goddess of strife and discord, all elements of Morgan's nature. When heroes fall in battle she carries them to eternal life among the gods, as Morgan does when she takes Arthur to Avalon (Paton 1960, 33–34; see also Mac Cana, in this volume). Morrigan is also a shape shifter and has the ability to change nature, in other words, to create illusions (Paton 1960, 11–12), both prominent features in Morgan's repertoire. In fact, the episode in which Morgan steals Arthur's scabbard and then shape-shifts is reminiscent of a similar story told about Morrigan, who steals a cow from the Irish hero Cuchulinn and then hides by shape shifting. Paton (1960) sees parallels between these two stories and suggests that Morgan and Arthur's relationship is modeled on that between Morrigan and Cuchulinn (148–166). This later story is contained in the Irish epic, the *Tain Bo Cuailgne* (The Cattle Raid of Cuailnge) (Kinsella 1969, 6–8),[14] set in the pre-Christian aristocratic warrior society of Ulster where women like Queen Medb exercised power and conferred sovereignty (see Dumézil 1973, 83–129).

The etymology of Morrigan's name, while problematic, is illuminating. *Rígan* means queen and *mor*, great. According to Paton (1960), *morrígan* could be used as a title to refer to the goddess Macha as "the third *morrígan* or great queen" (159). It seems clear, as Loomis also suggests,[15] that goddesses become fays in the later literature. Through variations in pronunciation and other factors, Morgan took on the queenly attributes of Morrigan as well as her divine powers and became the queen of the fairies.[16]

A second story from the *Tain* about another Irish war goddess, the horse goddess Macha, also shows some connections to the fairies and to Morgan. Appropriately for a society that had women rulers and warriors, Macha is associated with both war and fertility of all kinds, that of the land, of people, and of animals. Somewhat like Morgan's involvement with Arthur, or like a fairy, she lives with a human man, to whom she brings prosperity until he breaks her injunction not to brag about her (Kinsella 1969, 6–8). While noting her martial aspects and her shape-shifting abilities, Proinsias Mac Cana (in this volume) reads the beginning of this story as an example of the goddess as grantor of prosperity to land and people.

Morgan, too, has associations with prosperity, as in Geoffrey of Monmouth's *Vita Merlini* (twelfth century) where she is one of nine divine sisters who have custody of a magic cauldron that provides an inexhaustible supply of food (Evans-Wentz 1911, 353). Overall, though, in these early stories, Morgan's positive aspects and her divine nature are in conflict with changing social and religious ideologies about the proper behavior of women and new ideologies about royalty that are reducing the power of queens. As we now turn to modern representations of Morgan we will see exaggerations of these two aspects.

## Modern Literary and Cinematic Representations

Two distinctly different modern novels having Morgan as a character appeared almost simultaneously in England, Dion Fortune's *The Sea Priestess* (published in 1938) and T. H. White's *The Once and Future King* (published in 1939). Fortune was an influential English occultist, a member of the Theosophical Society, and an early student of psychoanalysis. She wrote numerous and highly regarded books on the occult and magic, including popular novels that contained fictionalized descriptions of magical practices and theory. Although she accepted prevailing ideas about men as active and women as passive in the ordinary world, Fortune emphasized women's occult powers on the "astral" plane, where the magician does her or his work and where gender roles are reversed. In her worldview, the astral plane is the more important realm. In *The Sea Priestess*, Fortune expressed these ideas through her heroine, Vivien Le Fay Morgan, an incarnation of Morgan le Fey and a woman possessing extraordinary knowledge. Throughout the novel Morgan struggles to bring a lost occult knowledge from the ancient past into modern life. In this sense Fortune has interpreted Morgan's legendary struggle with Arthur as a spiritual one, an idea she projects onto the twentieth century. For Fortune Arthur is not important; Morgan's knowledge and her powers are what must be preserved and passed on.

In contrast, White's novel is all about Arthur, and it builds up the character of the male magician and wizard, Merlin. Morgan is presented as a secondary, shadowy and terrifying character who can change shape and cast spells. He calls her variously a fairy and a witch; he takes away her beauty and describes her reclining on a bed of lard as "a fat, dowdy, middle-aged woman with black hair and a slight moustache" (White 1939, 111). White's novel also focuses on Morgan's hostility toward Arthur and her ultimate powerlessness, making her a somewhat comic and pathetic figure. As the ancestor of the popular "sword and sorcerer" novels, films, comics, and games that are marketed for male adolescents, *The Once and Future King* has had a lasting influence on the popular image of Morgan. Fortune's novel, on the other hand, attempted to rehabilitate Morgan, to spiritualize her struggle, and to make her a richer, more heroic character than she ever was in Malory's work. It is a foremother to more recent reclamations of Morgan in feminist fantasy literature.

## *Boorman's* Excalibur

John Boorman's *Excalibur* (released in 1981)[17] is one of the best of the sword and sorcerer films, and while it credits Malory, it adds new elements,[18] especially in the character of Morgan (so ably portrayed by Helen Mirren). It is clearly influenced by White's novel in the prominent role given to Merlin. Boorman uses music from Carl Orff's *Carmina Burana* and Wagner's *Götterdämmerung* to signify the passing of the ancient Norse gods and to support the theme of Arthur's kingdom being at the center of a religious conflict between paganism and the new religion of Christianity. Morgan's hatred of Arthur and attraction to the ancient religion are the guiding passions of her life. In Boorman's film it is she, not her sister Morgause, who seduces Arthur and conceives Mordred, the agent of Arthur's destruction. Morgan, in turn, is undone by Merlin, from whom she steals "the spell of making," the ability to conjure whatever she wants. Boorman acknowledges Morgan's occult powers yet subordinates them to Merlin's by making her his student. In the end Merlin tricks Morgan into reciting the spell of making that creates a fog, destroying Mordred's army even as Arthur's is destroyed. As she recites this spell, Morgan loses her strength and turns into a withered old woman whom Mordred soon strangles. At the end, the supernatural women from the Isle of Avalon come for Arthur's body, but Boorman abandons Morgan for dead and she is not present in their company. Thus, in Boorman's film Morgan loses her immortality along with everything else.

### *The Mists of Avalon*[19]

Marion Zimmer Bradley's enormously popular book *The Mists of Avalon*[20] was published first in 1982. It begins with a quotation from Malory, but her acknowledgements also list Dion Fortune, Starhawk, local neo-pagan groups, and books on Gardnerian Wicca. With Bradley we are on very different ground. She has a seductive opening, which makes it clear that it is Morgan's (or Morgaine's, as she spells it) book, not Arthur's; it will be the story of Camelot from her point of view. *The Mists of Avalon* is a genre of woman's fantasy in which the female characters are filled with a power they almost always restrain, make plans that run afoul, and occasionally have great sex. Their thoughts are usually directed inward—whatever else Morgan does, she does not speak her mind very often. All through the novel she is usually controlled or checked in some way by men, but she still manages to sleep around, spin yarn, have a premonition or two, work a little magic, and use herbs to abort an unwanted pregnancy.

Her relationship with Arthur begins as sibling rivalry (she is still the older sister). Their relationship is complicated by the fact that unknowingly they had ritual sex together: the enactment of Arthur's marriage with the land, in which Morgan is the priestess from Avalon chosen to represent the land. Morgan becomes pregnant with Mordred and alienated from Avalon and its priestesses, but she has already made the magical scabbard for Arthur's sword Excalibur, which is given to him by the head priestess in exchange for his vow to preserve Avalon against the encroaching Christian faith. Arthur, of course, betrays this vow and Morgan sets about, unsuccessfully, to get the sword back. The last third of the book follows the Accolon story in Malory, although it is excessively expanded. Indeed, her lover Accolon has become her husband's son by a previous wife. Morgan plans to have Accolon kill Arthur then put Accolon on the throne until her son Mordred, who is fully grown and with ambitions to match, can take over and restore goddess worship. Despite trickery, Arthur kills Accolon and Morgan is forced to steal the scabbard again. As Arthur pursues her she throws it into the lake. In the end Arthur dies and Morgan gets Lancelot to throw Excalibur into the lake as well.

Bradley humanizes Morgan, removing her supernatural connections, attempting instead to make her an autonomous woman who possesses spiritual wisdom and sexual freedom. Such a character is balm to the wounds of many modern women who have been scarred by patriarchal social and religious values.

In Bradley's novel, Morgan surrenders her divinity, but she holds onto her power to confer sovereignty. Only now she bestows it on a generation of women, who, like her, want to subvert a patriarchal civilization that limits the sphere of women and threatens the land with ultimate destruction through pollution and warfare.

## Conclusion

Congruent with the declining status of Celtic women, Morgan began to lose her divine characteristics during the Middle Ages, eventually becoming a mortal woman who possessed some occult knowledge. Today womanhood has been revalorized, and Morgan reappears not as a goddess but as a mortal possessing the innate powers of womanhood.[21] Her incarnation in feminist fantasy literature seeks to establish a harmonious balance between the earth and its people, one based on power from within, rather than power over (see Starhawk 1982, 1–14). Many modern women interpret her opposition to Arthur as an understandable, indeed noble resistance to a Christianity associated with the subjugation of women and the exploitation of the land. Such exploitation explicitly divorces Arthur from Sovereignty, and Morgan's attempts to capture his sword is seen as an attempt to take back sovereignty, to reclaim the kingship. Feminist Morgan confers sovereignty on modern women; she gives them dominion over themselves.

### NOTES

1. See the discussion of Morgan as Arthur's sister in Paton (1960, 136–144, and *passim*).
2. Malory alludes to some of these abilities, albeit with a heavy Christian overlay, when he says that only Morgan was sent to school in a nunnery while her two sisters were married off. (See discussion later.) It is interesting to try to get behind Malory's text here and to speculate about how the oral tradition described Morgan's education in an all female environment, especially one in which Malory says she became skilled in necromancy, an ability not usually associated with nuns. (See Vinaver 1947, 10.)

   In Geoffrey of Monmouth's *Vita Merlini*, Morgan first appears as a lovely, learned, and potent woman: She is a shape shifter, knowledgeable in healing and astrology. She is one of nine sisters from the island of Avalon where Arthur's sword Excalibur was forged, where he is taken after his final battle to be healed, and from which he will return to the world in the future. In slightly later literature, such as the *Lancelot* and *Sir Gawain and the Green Knight*, she appears more malevolent, predatory, ugly, and lecherous.
3. Paton (1960) conveniently lists passages in the major sources and their dates (7–8, n.1, 255–258).
4. This has most recently been attempted by Norma Lorre Goodrich (1986). Unfortunately, she is not very interested in Morgan and only mentions her in passing. C. Scott Littleton (1973) sees Arthur as an historical person who was a descendant of Scythian soldiers posted to Britain by the Romans (263–264). A summary of the early evidence for Arthur is to be found in Jackson (1960).
5. A good introduction to the social and religious background of this literature is Robert W. Ackerman (1966). The opening of Proinsias Mac Cana's essay in this volume succinctly presents this process.

6. Of course, one should not overlook the influence of later, aristocratic women on this literature, both as audience and as patrons (e.g., Eleanor of Aquitaine). Such women may not have been satisfied with a literature characterized by passive women.
7. For more information on the status of premedieval northern European women, see Chance (1986); Damico and Olsen (1990); and Davies (1983). For a colorful and early story about a powerful Celtic woman who ruled in her own right and chose her own lovers, see Queen Medb in *The Tain*, translated by Thomas Kinsella (1969). For a broad sampling of the literature on Celtic and Norse women, see Young (1993, 180–215).
8. Carolyn Heilbrun (1988) makes a similar point in her study of narratives about women, which she finds do not follow male models but have an integrity of their own.
9. An analysis of this edition as well as a discussion of modern scholarship on Malory can be found in Brewer (1970, 83–97).
10. The cult of the named, magical sword is found among the Celts, Germans, and North Iranian-speaking steppe peoples (Littleton 1987, 347). In Arthurian legend it is probably based on *Caladbolg*, the famous sword of Fergus in the *Tain bo Cuailgne*, forged in fairyland. Geoffrey of Monmouth says that it was made in Avalon; Malory, that the sword was given to Arthur by Vivian of the land of the fairy. (Leach 1949, 359).
11. Similarly, in Norse society the king was considered the husband of the fertility goddess (Ström 1959, 702). Ideas about both this sacred marriage and the king's responsibility for fertility survive in May Day and in other agricultural celebrations in which a king and queen of vegetation ensure the fertility of the land. For a discussion of these rites, see Frazer (1920, 161–168). Though much of his work has been rightly challenged, when he sticks to the ancient sources he is on more certain ground.
12. For instance, the *Echtra macn Echach*, *Cóir Anmann*, and *Dindshenchas*, all cited by Draak (1959, 658 n.17). These eleventh-century texts contain earlier material about princes from the third and fourth centuries.
13. See also the stories in Mac Cana in this volume. George Dumézil (1973, 88–98) briefly discusses these particular stories. For a fascinating analysis of the role of women in Celtic sovereignty, see 83–129.
14. The earliest manuscript version of this text dates from the twelfth century, but its origins lie in the oral traditions that predate the advent of Christianity into Ireland.
15. See his review of scholarly responses to Paton in Paton (1960, 280–291).
16. Morgan is also deeply connected with the sea. In addition to her home on the sea island of Avalon, in Brittany and Wales mermaids are called Morgans. See entries under "Morgan" and "Morgan le Fay" in Briggs (1976, 303–304). For a brief discussion of mermaids see *Funk and Wagnall's Standard Dictionary of Folklore, Mythology, and Legend* (Leach 1949, 710).
17. This film is available on video. Richard C. Bartone contrasts Boorman's *Excalibur* with Robert Bresson's *Lancelot du Lac* (1992, 144–155), and Liam O. Purdon and Robert Blanch (1992) compare *Excalibur* to Malory's *Morte d'Arthur*. Purdon and Blanch also refer to other cinematic versions of the Arthurian legend. (See also de Weever 1991, 145–156).
18. Purdon and Blanch (1992, 156) point out its emphasis on the miraculous also shows

the influence of Tennyson's *Idylls of the King* and T. H. White's *The Once and Future King*.

19. For a succinct summary of other recent novels in which Morgan is a character see Spivack 1992, 18–23. She discusses Ruth Nichol's *Marrow of the World*, Penelope Lively's *The Whispering Knights*, Paul Anderson's *Three Hearts and Three Lions*, Phyllis Karr's *Idylls of the Queen*, Parke Godwin's *Firelord*, and Bradley's *The Mists of Avalon*. See also Elizabeth S. Sklar's discussion of additional literary sources in which Morgan appears as a character as well as in modern films, board games and comic books (1992, 24–35). Sklar (1992) sees the feminist agenda of such works as having engendered a "gynophobic response of those mass-cultural texts whose primary target audience is adolescent and post-adolescent males" (33).
20. The cover to one paperback edition says it was three months on *The New York Times* best-seller list.
21. This is at least true for her modern literary and cinematic rebirth, though note her appearance in Hrana Janto's "The Goddess Calendar" of 1992 (St. Paul: Llewellyn).

REFERENCES

Ackerman, Robert W. 1966. *Background in Medieval English Literature*. New York: Random House.

Bartone, Richard C. 1992. "Variations on Arthurian Legend in *Lancelot du Lac* and *Excalibur*." Pp. 144–155 in *Popular Arthurian Traditions*, ed. Sally K. Slocum. Bowling Green, OH: Bowling Green State University Popular Press.

Bradley, Marion Zimmer. 1982. *The Mists of Avalon*. New York: Ballantine Books.

Brewer, D. S. 1970. "The Present Study of Malory." Pp. 83–97 in *Arthurian Romance: Seven Essays*, ed. D. D. R. Owen. New York: Barnes and Noble Books.

Briggs, Katharine. 1976. *A Dictionary of Fairies*. New York: Penguin Books.

Chance, Jane. 1986. *Woman as Hero in Old English Literature*. Syracuse, NY: Syracuse University Press.

Damico, Helen, and Alexandra Hennessey Olsen, eds. 1990. *New Readings on Women in Old English Literature*. Bloomington: Indiana University Press.

Davies, Wendy. 1983. "Celtic Women in the Early Middle Ages." Pp. 145–166 in *Images of Women in Antiquity*, ed. Averil Cameron and Amelie Kuhrt. London and Canberra: Croom Helm.

de Weever, Jacqueline. 1991. "Morgan and the Problem of Incest." Pp. 145–156 in *Cinema Arthuriana: Essays on Arthurian Film*, ed. Kevin J. Harty. New York: Garland Publishing.

Draak, Maartje. 1959. "Some Apects of Kingship in Pagan Ireland." Pp. 651–663 in *The Sacral Kingship: Contributions to the Central Theme of the VIIIth International Congress for the History of Religions (Rome, April 1955)*. Leiden: E. J. Brill.

Dumézil, Georges. 1959. *Gods of the Ancient Northmen*. Berkeley: University of California Press.

———. 1973. *The Destiny of a King*. Trans. Alf Hiltebeitel. Chicago: University of Chicago Press.

Evans-Wentz, W. Y. 1911. *The Fairy-Faith in Celtic Countries*. London: Oxford University Press.

*Excalibur*. 1981. Directed by John Boorman; screenplay by Boorman and Rospo Palenberg. Orion.

Fortune, Dion. 1938. *The Sea Priestess*. Reprint, York Beach, ME: Samuel Weiser.
Frazer, James George. 1920. *The Magical Origin of Kings*. London: Dawsons of Pall Mall.
Fries, Maureen. 1992. "Female Heroes, Heroines, and Counter-Heroes: Images of Women in Arthurian Tradition." Pp. 5–17 in *Popular Arthurian Traditions*, ed. Sally K. Slocum. Bowling Green, OH: Bowling Green State University Popular Press.
Goodrich, Norma Lorre. 1986. *King Arthur*. New York: Harper and Row.
Heilbrun, Carolyn G. 1988. *Writing a Woman's Life*. New York: Ballantine Books.
Jackson, W. T. H. 1960. *The Literature of the Middle Ages*. New York: Columbia University Press.
Kinsella, Thomas, trans. 1969. *The Tain*. Oxford: Oxford University Press.
Lacy, Norris J., ed. 1986. *The Arthurian Encyclopedia*. New York and London: Garland Publishing.
Leach, Maria, ed. 1949. *Funk and Wagnall's Standard Dictionary of Folklore, Mythology, and Legend*. San Francisco: Harper and Row.
Leahy, A. H., ed. 1905. *Heroic Romances of Old Ireland*. London: David Nutt.
Littleton, C. Scott. 1973. *The New Comparative Mythology: An Anthropological Assessment of the Theories of Georges Dumézil*. Berkeley: University of California Press.
———. 1987. "War and Warriors: Indo-European Beliefs and Practices." Pp. 344–348 in *The Encyclopedia of Religion* (vol. 15), ed. Mircea Eliade. New York: Macmillan.
Loomis, Roger Sherman. 1949. *Arthurian Traditions and Chretien de Troyes*. New York: Columbia University Press.
Paton, Lucy Allen. 1960. *Studies in the Fairy Mythology of Arthurian Romance*. New York: Burt Franklin. [Reprint of 1903 edition.]
Purdon, Liam O., and Robert Blanch. 1992. "Hollywood's Myopic Medievalism: *Excalibur* and Malory's *Morte d'Arthur*." Pp. 156–161 in *Popular Arthurian Traditions*, ed. Sally K. Slocum. Bowling Green, OH: Bowling Green State University Popular Press.
Sklar, Elizabeth S. 1992. "Thoroughly Modern Morgan: Morgan le Fey in Twentieth-Century Popular Arthuriana." Pp. 24–35 in *Popular Arthurian Traditions*, ed. Sally K. Slocum. Bowling Green, OH: Bowling Green State University Popular Press.
Slocum, Sally K., ed. 1992. *Popular Arthurian Traditions*. Bowling Green, OH: Bowling Green State University Popular Press.
Spivack, Charlotte. 1992. "Morgan Le Fay: Goddess or Witch?" Pp. 18–23 in *Popular Athurian Traditions*, ed. Sally K. Slocum. Bowling Green, OH: Bowling Green State University Popular Press.
Starhawk. 1982. *Dreaming the Dark: Magic, Sex, and Politics*. Boston: Beacon Press.
Ström, Ake V. 1959. "The King God and his Connection with Sacrifice in Old Norse Religion." Pp. 702–715 in *The Sacral Kingship*. Leiden: E. J. Brill.
Vinaver, Eugène, ed. 1947. *The Works of Sir Thomas Malory*. Oxford: Clarendon Press.
White, T. H. 1939. *The Once and Future King*. New York: G. P. Putnam's Sons.
Young, Serinity. 1993. *An Anthology of Sacred Texts By and About Women*. New York: Crossroad.

# PART IV

# Transcendence for All

## The Democratization of Sovereignty

That Empress doth all Heaven embrace
And Earth and Hell in her empery.
No heritage will she ever efface,
For she is the Queen of Courtesy.
The Court of the Kingdom of God alive
Holds to this law of its very being:
Each one that may therein arrive
Of all the realm is queen or king.
No one shall ever another deprive,
But each one joys in the other's having.

—*Pearl*

12

# The Goddess, the Emperor, and the Adept

## The Queen Mother of the West as Bestower of Legitimacy and Immortality

*Suzanne E. Cahill*

This essay examines the Chinese Daoist deity known as the Queen Mother of the West (*Xiwangmu*) and her relations with Chinese rulers. I investigate texts and pictorial images from China's middle ages, when the cult of the Queen Mother was highly developed, her worship was widespread, and sources are plentiful. I argue that she was associated with imperial legitimacy. Stories tell how she granted ancient Chinese emperors the powers and symbols that enabled them to rule. I further argue that according to Daoist religious texts, the adept (expert practitioner) takes over the powers and regalia of the emperor. The Queen Mother gives the adept her teaching and her symbolic presents. The Daoist adept then becomes a conqueror of death and ruler of paradise.

### The Queen Mother of the West

The Queen Mother of the West (*Xiwangmu*) is an ancient Chinese goddess of obscure origin. Her name reveals some of her most important characteristics: She is royal, female, and associated with the west. The *West* in her name refers to the western direction, associated in ancient China with death, the spirit world, and tigers, among many other things. She may have the longest unbroken history of any deity in China, with origins perhaps going back to oracle bone inscriptions of the fifteenth century BCE that record blood sacrifices to a "western mother," and continuing up to the present day in Taiwan, where under the name of the Golden Mother of the Turquoise Pond she guides the hands of spirit writers to deliver instructions to her adherents.

During this long period from the fifteenth century BCE through medieval times, the goddess's transformations were many. Perhaps originally an imperial ancestress, she came to be considered the ultimate embodiment of yin: the dark, female force. The first certain textual reference to the Queen Mother appears in an early classic of natural mysticism and self-cultivation known as the *Zhuangzi*, after its purported author. This text, dating to the third century BCE, was later incorporated into their canon by the Daoists, who regard it as a major source of their beliefs and practices. The author of the *Zhuangzi* lists the Queen Mother of the West, in a chapter entitled "Great Instructors," as one who has attained the Dao, or the Way. (The list also includes the sun, the moon, and the Yellow Emperor.) The Dao he characterizes as invisible and imminent, preceding and outlasting heaven and earth, underlying yet extending beyond the cosmos. The passage in question reads: "The Queen Mother of the West obtained it [the Dao] and took up her seat at Mount Shaoguang. No one knows her beginning; no one knows her end." The *Zhuangzi* already associates her with teaching, possessing the Way, and immortality.

By the second century of the common era, the Queen Mother of the West had become an important figure in both Daoism, China's native higher religion, and the lore of imperial legitimacy. By the Tang dynasty (618–907 CE), her image and her roles in religion were fully developed. References to her abound in early Chinese literary and religious texts. She is regularly depicted in Chinese pictorial art and mentioned in inscriptions. Ancient and medieval texts and pictorial representations show a goddess with the power to support or destroy a king. She controlled access to immortality and communication with the spirit realm, and she regularly visited Chinese emperors. This essay examines the goddess and Chinese rulers as Tang people understood their relationships.

## *The Tang Dynasty (618–907)*

The Tang dynasty was a 300-year period to which the Chinese people today still look back with pride. China ruled over vast geographical regions, controlling enormous wealth and a huge and diverse population. The capital city of Chang'an, with over a million inhabitants, was the largest city in the world. The silk route connected China with Western countries, allowing an unprecedented exchange of goods and ideas. Science and technology experienced enormous growth, including the invention of printing. The Tang is considered the golden age of Chinese poetry, when everyone composed poems, and many composed superbly. Chinese culture, at the beginning of this era, was expansive and self-confident. Foreign influences abounded in the capital. The main religions were Buddhism, which originated in India, and Daoism, China's native higher religion. The Queen Mother became the most important goddess of Daoism.

*Textual Descriptions of the Goddess*

Let us begin by examining two passages that describe her, one earlier and one later, both preserved in the *Daozang*, or Taoist Canon. An early passage from the *Shanhai jing* (Classic of Mountains and Seas), a geographical encyclopedia well-known in the Tang dynasty although it was compiled a few centuries earlier, stresses her shamanic attributes. A shaman was a person accepted by a community as chosen by the gods to be spokesperson for that community with their deities. In ancient China, shamans conversed with deities through both celestial travel and spirit possession. The *Shanhai jing* text (Yuan Ho 1979) is arranged like a ritual travelogue and ethnography, describing in order the landscapes and beings a traveler will encounter in a circuit of the world:

> Another 350 *li* (Chinese miles) to the west is a mountain called Jade Mountain. This is the place where the Queen Mother of the West dwells. As for the Queen Mother of the West, her appearance is like that of a human, with a leopard's tail and tiger's teeth. Moreover she is good at whistling. In her disheveled hair she wears a *sheng* headdress. She is controller of the Grindstone and the Five Shards constellations of the heavens. (Yuan Ho 1979, 2.19a)

This spare description, dating to perhaps the fourth century CE, associates the Queen Mother with holy mountains, a western paradise, and jade (a symbol of immortality). Her strange and frightening form, part human and part ferocious predator, recalls the ancient Chinese shaman's costume. Skill at whistling suggests breath control and the ability to summon spirits, also shamanic attributes. Disheveled hair is characteristic of ascetics and shamans. The *sheng* headdress, probably a copy of the brake wheel of a loom, attests to her power to weave the world into being. The Queen Mother's control over stars reminds us of the shaman's ability to ascend to heaven and visit high gods on behalf of her community.

About a thousand years later, an account of the goddess by the Daoist Master Du Guangting (850–933) in his "Records of the Assembled Transcendents of the Fortified Walled City" (*Yongcheng jixian lu*) presents her as a stately and elegant woman, riding a chariot drawn by auspicious mythical beasts:

> The Queen Mother rides an imperial carriage of purple clouds, harnessing nine-colored, dappled *qilin*. Tied around her waist, she wears the whip of the Celestial Realized Ones; as a belt pendant, she has a diamond numinous seal. In her clothing of multi-colored tabby-weave silk with a yellow background, the patterns and variegated colors are bright and fresh. The radiance of metal makes a shimmering gleam. At her waist is a double-bladed sword for dividing phosphors. Knotted flying clouds make a great cord. On top of her head is a great floriate topknot. She wears the crown of the Grand Realized Ones, with hanging beaded strings of daybreak. She steps forth on shoes with squared, phoenix-patterned soles of rosegem. Her age might be about twenty. Her celestial appearance eclipses and puts in the shade all others. She is a realized numinous being. (Du Guangting, 24161)

These descriptions of a tiger-woman and a regal matron could hardly be more different, yet both present the Queen Mother of the West as possessing divine powers she can use on behalf of Chinese rulers.

### *Pictorial Representations of the Goddess*

The Queen Mother of the West appears in Chinese pictorial art from the second century BCE up to the present. Her image is most frequently represented in the Han dynasty (206 BCE–220 CE), when she appears on the nonreflective surface of bronze mirrors, as well as on clay and stone reliefs found in tombs. One famous image of Xiwangmu occurs on several funerary tiles from Szechwan Province in the southeast of China (see figure 12.1). The pottery tiles show the goddess wearing Chinese robes and seated on a dragon and tiger throne symbolizing yin and yang, with her hair arranged in a high chignon pierced by the *sheng* headdress that stands for her creative powers. She sits formally, facing

*Figure 12.1: Rubbing of a clay funerary tile from Szechwan Province, dating to the latter Han dynasty (first century CE). The relief shows the Queen Mother wearing a* sheng *headdress, seated on a dragon-tiger throne, and surrounded by supernatural attendants including a nine-tailed fox, the three-legged sun crow, and the rabbit and toad in the moon. (Source: Suzanne E. Cahill.)*

forward. Her attendants embody her other powers: The rabbit holds the elixir of immortality in the form of a divine mushroom, suggesting her ability to bestow immortality, while the three-legged crow who lives in the sun and the toad who resides in the moon reflect her control of celestial bodies and cosmic transformations. Her attendants in human form may be minor deities or worshipers. The goddess's appearance has shed the wild ferocity of the "Classic of Mountains and Seas" while retaining the potency of that description. In the Szechwan tile, she already possesses the stately bearing and grandeur that Du Guangting tries to capture a few centuries later. The image of the Queen Mother in the Han dynasty is both potent and regal. Her powers originate in Daoism and notions of imperial legitimacy.

### *Medieval Chinese Daoism*

The Tang royal family were ardent Daoists and patrons of the faith. Daoism was already centuries old by the Tang dynasty and had undergone much evolution. The basic goal of the Daoist believer is individual immortality. This was achieved through ethical behavior, personal cultivation, and religious practice. Schools of Daoism divided according to the techniques they believed most effective for attaining transcendence. During the Tang there were two main schools, both of which go back to traditions of the preceding Six Dynasties Period (222–589 CE), and both of which contributed important texts to the Daoist canon. Daoists of the *Shangqing* (Supreme Clear Realm) lineage, the school favored by the imperial family and the literati, emphasized individual practices such as meditation and visualization, asceticism, and elixir alchemy. The *Lingbao* (Numinous Treasure) lineage emphasized collective worship and community ritual. The Queen Mother appears more frequently in texts of the *Shangqing* school. By the middle of the Tang period, under the leadership of several great *Shangqing* masters including Du Guangting, a synthesis of the two schools was created, recognizing the unity apparent in practice for decades.

### *Techniques of Imperial Legitimation*

Since the earliest textual records, Chinese rulers have been obsessed with legitimacy. The *Shujing* (Classic of History) contains the first statements of the theory known as the Mandate of Heaven (*tianming*). According to this notion, Heaven, the high god of the Zhou dynasty (1122–256 BCE), selects a person to govern China on the basis of his talent and virtue. His lineage establishes a dynasty, which rules as long as its virtue lasts. When the virtue runs out, Heaven withdraws its mandate and the dynasty falls. The idea of the Mandate of Heaven is often associated with the teachings of Confucius (ca. 551–479 BCE) and his followers. However, the concept predates Confucius and is widely found in early writings; it must be considered part of the general world of thought of ancient China rather than the property of one school.

The concept of the Mandate of Heaven is clear enough; what is difficult sometimes is to determine precisely when and upon whom the mandate has been bestowed and when it is withdrawn. Over centuries, different techniques of determining legitimacy developed. The ruler who possessed the Mandate of Heaven might be recognized by deeds, by omens in the natural world, or by the possession of symbolic objects such as seals, vessels, or maps. His charisma might attract benevolent deities, who might descend to help him in battle, teach him special arts, or grant him magical gifts. The Queen Mother was such a king-making divinity, whose visits verified the legitimacy of a ruler.

## The Queen Mother and Chinese Rulers

Here we look at Xiwangmu's relations with rulers of successive eras in chronological order, starting with the origin of the imperial institution in the reign of the legendary Yellow Emperor. As we examine her encounters with a series of rulers, we will note the details and development of her legitimizing role. Our historical standpoint is the Tang dynasty. Our main sources are Du Guangting's biography of the goddess, dynastic histories, Daoist canonical texts, and poetry by Tang dynasty authors.

### *The Yellow Emperor*

The Queen Mother's encounters with Chinese emperors begin in the realm of legend, with the deity known as the Yellow Emperor (*huangdi*), the first Chinese emperor and the first human to become an immortal. His traditional dates are 2697–2597 BCE. Du Guangting places her meeting with the Yellow Emperor at the head of the Queen Mother's biography, emphasizing its importance. She saves him in battle, then instructs him in civilizing the world:

> Formerly the Yellow Emperor punished Chiyu's violence and aggression. Before he was checked, Chiyu performed illusionistic transformations using many methods. He raised the wind and summoned the rain; he blew smoke and spat mist. The leaders and masses of the Yellow Emperor's army became greatly confused. The emperor returned home to rest in a fold of Mount Tai. Bewildered, he went to bed depressed. The Queen Mother sent an envoy wearing a dark fox cloak to bestow upon the emperor a talisman that said: "Grand Unity is located on the front; Heavenly Unity is located on the back. He who obtains this will excel; when he attacks he will overcome." The talisman was three inches wide and a foot long, with a blue lustre like that of jade. Cinnabar-colored drops of blood formed a pattern on it. The Yellow Emperor hung it at his waist.
>
> Once he had done this, the Queen Mother commanded a woman with a human head and the body of a bird to come. She addressed the Emperor: "I am the Mysterious Woman of the Nine Heavens." She bestowed upon the Emperor [Daoist plans, arts, techniques, and talismans]. . . . Consequently he subdued Chiyu at Zhongji. After he had exterminated this descendent of Shen Nong and

executed the rebel Yuwang at Banquan, the empire was greatly settled. Then he built his capital at Zhuolu in the upper valley.

Again after a number of years, the Queen Mother sent her envoy, the white tiger spirit. Then, riding a white tiger, she perched in the emperor's courtyard and bestowed some territorial maps upon him. (Du Guangting, 24159)

This is a Daoist version of the universal myth of a battle between order and chaos at the beginning of the world. The place names are all located in the cradle of Chinese civilization, the great plain of the Yellow River. Chiyu, who after this fight becomes a god of war, struggles with the Yellow Emperor for universal dominion. Daoist deities help him with skills and talismans. The Mysterious Woman of the Nine Heavens, an ancient goddess of warfare and sexuality, becomes the ruler's teacher. The Mysterious Woman's instructions come from her teacher, the Queen Mother, who stands at the head of a divine lineage. She is the ultimate source of his power to win victories and to rule civilization. The talismans represent heaven's support of his rule, granted through her, and the maps she gives him later represent control over the territory of China. His status as a universal Chinese culture hero and founder of the imperial institution rests squarely on the Queen Mother's gifts.

Tang poets emphasize the Yellow Emperor's successful practice of Daoist arts, such as alchemy, that allowed him to become the first immortal. According to the "Song of the Flying Dragon" by the Tang dynasty Daoist poet Li Bo (701–762):

> The Yellow Emperor cast tripods at Mount Jing,
> To refine powdered cinnabar.

The flying dragon of the title is a sign of heavenly selection. The tripod was a bronze ceremonial vessel used for offering food in ancestral sacrifices. The set of vessels the thearch cast at Mount Jing in present-day Henan Province becomes a symbol of dynastic legitimacy sought by subsequent rulers. Those, such as Qin Shihuangdi, who do not obtain the Mandate of Heaven also fail to find the vessels. By means of his cinnabar elixir, the Yellow Emperor was able to ascend to heaven on the dragon's back, taking many of his harem along, as Li Bo's poem concludes:

> Rambling and roaming within the blue heavens,
> Their delight cannot be put into words. (*Quan Tangshi* 924)

A second poem by Li Bo with the same title mentions a bow and double-edged sword the emperor leaves behind as tokens of his divinely assisted military prowess. He and his harem salute the Queen Mother in a ritual of reverence as they enter the Daoist heavens. According to Daoist biography and Tang poetry, the goddess provides the power and immortality that make the Yellow Emperor a primary culture hero. She also gives him the tokens that signify his mandate to rule.

*Shun*

Still in the realm of legendary prehistory, we come to the emperor Shun, whose traditional dates are 2255–2205 BCE. One of the great paragons of virtue honored by Confucian thinkers, Shun received tokens from the Queen Mother allowing him to control both time and space. The tokens, including maps, jade tubes, and a calendar, were traditional symbols of the legitimacy of the Chinese emperor. According to Du Guangting, the goddess's envoy bestowed upon Shun a white jade bracelet and territorial maps. Upon receiving these gifts, he expanded the Yellow Emperor's territory. Later she gave him an illustrious tube, which allowed him to harmonize the eight winds (Du Guangting, 24159). The tube signifies his control over the seasons and the calendar. Publishing the calendar was an exclusive prerogative of the Chinese emperor that manifested his cosmic power. Where Confucians stress Shun's virtue, which brought him the Mandate of Heaven, Daoist texts emphasize the Queen Mother's gifts, which allowed Shun to govern time and space. Daoists claim that their deity is responsible for responding to Shun's virtue and providing him with the opportunity to become an exemplary ruler.

Tang poets write of the goddess's ceremonial visit to the worthy Shun, her gifts, and her departure as an example of communication between the human and divine realms, and of the bestowal of legitimating tokens by the deity upon the worthy ruler. According to Bao Rong (fl. 820), leaving her paradise on Mount Kunlun,

> The Queen Mother grasps territorial charts;
> Coming east, she submits them to Yu Shun. (*Quan Tangshi* 2929)

Ding Zi (fl. 775) mentions her gifts of a jade bracelet and phoenix calendar (*Quan Tangshi* 1698). The poets hint at a love affair between goddess and king, whose contact involves both teaching and sensuality. After a brief meeting, the two must part. This theme will become more central in her relations with later kings.

*Yu the Great*

Yu the Great was the legendary founder of the Xia dynasty, according to tradition the first Chinese dynasty. Scholars used to doubt the historicity of the Xia, but recent archaeological excavations have provided possible evidence of its existence. Yu's reign is traditionally dated from 2205–2197. Yu was the ruler who saved the world from universal chaos in China's version of the flood myth that appears in many cultures. He drains the flood by following water's own nature and guiding it downhill off the arable land, so that agriculture and order may prevail. A folk saying attributed to Confucius states: "If it weren't for Yu, we'd all be fishes." The *Xunzi*, a third-century BCE classic of statecraft written by a follower of Confucius, was still read and admired for its thought and style of argumentation during the Tang. According to chapter 27 of that text, "Yu studied with the Queen Mother of the West." The statement about Yu appears in a list of masters of the great sage emperors of antiquity. Thinkers of the Warring States period (403–221 BCE), such as Xunzi, referred to ancient emperors like Yu as examples of virtuous and effective rule, possessors of the Mandate of Heaven, models for the rulers of their own time. Describing the Queen Mother of the West as Yu's teacher grants her enormous power, because according to Chinese thinking the teacher automatically surpassed the disciple in seniority and wisdom. She confers upon Yu both legitimacy, or the right to rule, and the techniques necessary for ruling.

### *King Mu of the Zhou Dynasty*

King Mu (reigned 1001–946 BCE) is the subject of one of the best known and most tragic stories of contact between a goddess and a mortal ruler. The Zhou dynasty (1122–256 BCE) held enormous prestige for people of later periods. This long and powerful dynasty included the composition of the Five Classics, the beginnings of Confucianism and Daoism, and the origins of central institutions later cherished as the framework of Chinese society. Later people look back to the Zhou as the source of the imperial state and the patriarchal family system. The Zhou state, governed by an emperor who possessed the Mandate of Heaven, assisted by a rational and hierarchical bureaucracy, was regarded as ideal by thinkers of later eras, including the Tang.

King Mu was one of the greatest rulers of the Zhou. Several accounts of his meeting with Xiwangmu exist. The important issues are his demonstration that he possesses the Mandate of Heaven and his search for divine communication and for eternal life. Several authors describe King Mu setting out with his charioteer and eight famous steeds on a trip to the far western regions of his empire. He encounters the goddess on the mythical Mt. Kunlun. Here is Du Guangting's version of the meeting:

> He was a guest of the Queen Mother of the West. As they toasted each other with drinks beside the Turquoise Pond, the Queen Mother of the West composed poems for the king. The king matched them. Their lyrics were sad. Then he observed where the sun set. In a single day, he had gone ten thousand *li*. The king sighed, saying: "I, the Unique Person, am not overabounding with virtue. Later generations will certainly trace back and count up my excesses!" It is also said that the king grasped a white jade tablet and heavy multi-colored tabby-weave silk, offering them in order to obtain the secrets of the Queen Mother's longevity. She sang the "Poem of the White Clouds" [in which she expresses her affection for him and her sorrow that human and deity cannot unite]. On top of Cover Mountain, he carved a stone to record his traces, then returned home. (24159–24160)

The story has five parts: a royal questing journey followed by a meeting in paradise, communion feast, exchange of poems, and finally a permanent separation. The great warrior King Mu sets off on a circuit of his empire, demonstrating his control over faraway territories and searching for adventure. Driving all the way to paradise, he has a love affair with the Queen Mother of the West. Hoping to obtain arts of immortality, he gives her important national treasures. But all is in vain; he must return to the human realm.

Tang poets loved this tale. It has all the elements of a great tragedy: A human king, unable to give up the pleasures and duties of his world, leaves a willing goddess in paradise and abandons all hope of immortality. Poets emphasized the tragic flaws in King Mu's character. A ruler seeks immortality and divine passion, but his own violence, lust, and ambition prevent him from attaining his goal. Li Junyu (fl. 847), for example, calls him "addicted to unrestrained ambition" (*Quan Tangshi* 3448). The poets write about the eight noble chargers, the Turquoise Pond, the toasts, but mostly they write about King Mu and the Queen Mother and the close encounter that nearly led to a divine union.

The Queen Mother summons the ruler in response to his charisma; she recognizes him as legitimate holder of the Mandate of Heaven. But she wants more: She wants to cross the boundary between the divine and human realms and make him her mate. Their eventual separation, echoing the shaman's parting after an encounter with a goddess in ancient hymns, leaves both drained and desolate. In a quatrain by Li Shangyin (813?–858), she stands at her open window, wondering:

> His eight chargers can proceed thirty thousand *li* a day,
> So why does King Mu not return again? (*Quan Tangshi* 3252)

This story presents both parties as vulnerable, and only one as divine. Gifts of tokens of dynastic legitimacy have given way to an oral exchange of poetry. The eight chargers and the circuit of his realm reveal that King Mu already has the Mandate of Heaven; possession of the right to rule is a precondition for his meeting with Xiwangmu. He wants something more from her: the secrets of immortality. The relationship between goddess and king resembles that between Daoist master and disciple. He salutes her with a metal memorial tablet like an acolyte or courtier in a poem by Cao Tang (fl. 860–874). He requests important secret teachings, which she passes on. In King Mu's case, the disciple fails to benefit and dies like any other mortal.

### *The First Emperor of the Qin Dynasty*

The first emperor of the Qin dynasty, Qin Shihuangdi (reigned 221–210 BCE), united the Warring States through brilliant military strategy and diplomacy to control the greatest territory ever yet seen in China. He is famous for two spectacular public works projects that remain to this day. Under his command, workers joined preexisting sections of wall to create the Great Wall along 3000 miles of China's northern frontier. And he ordered the magnificent underground army of life-size terra cotta soldiers, excavated in the 1970s, placed in long pits guarding his tomb near Xian. Still, history and folklore agree in condemning him as a failure, both as a king and as a seeker of immortality. Because of his cruelty and excess, he wasted his energy and skill for nothing. His rule died with him: He did not obtain the Mandate of Heaven and establish a dynasty. He had a chance to meet the Queen Mother and attain greatness but squandered it. For later men, his story serves as a warning. Despite huge and costly efforts to pursue immortality, he died and speaks no more. The ninth century poet Zhuang Nanjie writes:

> His flourishing breath once departed, he never more will speak;
> His white bones buried deep, the evening mountains turn cyan.
> (*Quan Tangshi* 2836)

*Emperor Wu of the Han Dynasty*

Only one story matches that of King Mu of the Zhou dynasty for passion and tragedy: that of Han Wudi, the "Martial Emperor of the Han" (140–87 BCE). The Han dynasty (206 BCE–220 CE), like the Zhou, was an era that later people looked back to with pride and nostalgia. China was united and wealthy, with its emperor controlling a large and diverse population living in vast territories. Trade, travel, and military expansion were active along the silk route, bringing the Chinese into contact with other peoples. Material cultures, technology, and ideas were exchanged, bringing about cultural change throughout the region. Han Wudi, arguably the greatest Han emperor, was a conqueror, institutional innovator, and religious leader. Legend tells us that in 110 BCE, at the height of his reign, he was visited by the Queen Mother of the West during the night of Double Seven, the festival of the Herd Boy and Weaver Girl stars and the night of all nights for encounters between mortal men and divine women. The story of the meeting of Xiwangmu and Han Wudi was popular in subsequent periods; several lengthy and detailed accounts remain. Du Guangting relies on them in constructing his own version of the events of that night. Here is an abridged translation of Du Guangting's account:

> The Filial and Martial Illustrious Emperor of the Han, Li Che, was fond of the Way of extending life. During the original year of the Primordial Enfoeffment reign period (110 BCE), he climbed the heights of Marchmount Song and there built a terrace for seeking realized ones. He fasted, observed abstinence, and made his thoughts seminal. . . . [The Queen Mother sends a messenger to tell him she will come.] Then he purified himself and fasted for one hundred days, burning incense in the palace.
>
> On the night in question, after the second watch (9–11 PM), a white cloud arose in the southwest. Dense and thick, it arrived and crossed over the courtyard of the palace. It gradually drew near; then came clouds and evening mists of nine colors. [Music from] pipes and drums shook empty space. There were semblances of dragons, phoenixes, men, and horses, with a guard mounted on *qilin* and harnessing deer. There were ranks of chariots and heavenly horses. With rainbow banners and feathered streamers, the radiance from a thousand vehicles and myriad outriders illuminated the palace watchtowers. Celestial

transcendents, both followers and officials, arranged in ranks, numbered one hundred thousand multitudes. All were ten feet or more tall. Once they had arrived, the followers and officials disappeared. . . . [The description translated above, page 4, follows here.]

[The Queen Mother] ascended the dais and sat down facing east. The emperor saluted her, kneeled, and inquired how she fared. Then he stood in attendance. After a good long while, she called the emperor and allowed him to be seated. She laid out a celestial feast consisting of fragrant flowers, a hundred fruits, purple mushrooms, as variegated as prismatic shellfish. Their seminal essences were rare and odd; they were not what regularly exists in this world. The emperor could not even name them. She also ordered a serving girl to fetch peaches. A jade basin was filled with several of the fruits. They were as large as bustard's eggs. She took four and gave them to the emperor. Mother herself ate three of them. . . .

Thereupon the Queen Mother commanding the serving girl Wang Zidong to play the eight-orbed chimes, Dong Shuangcheng to blow the Cloud Harmony Mouth Organ, Shi Gongzi to strike the jade sounding stone from the courtyard of Kunlun, Xu Feichiong to sound the Thunder Numen Flute, Wang Linghua to hit the musical stone of Wuling, Fan Chengjun to strike the lithophone of grotto yin, Duan Anxiang to make the "Harmony of the Nine Heavens," and An Faying to sing the "Tune of the Mysterious Numen." The whole ensemble of sounds was exciting and distinct; their nunimous timbres startled empty space.

When the song was finished, the emperor got down from his mat, kowtowed, and asked about the Way of extending life. . . . [The Queen Mother here delivers a long admonition denouncing lust, violence, and excess as elements that damage your health, spiritual progress, and longevity. She encourages the emperor to practice compassion, asceticism, and devotion to the Dao. The emperor receives her instruction on his knees and requests more. She then provides, at great length, further oral teachings on internal visualization, elixir drugs, and self cultivation. She promises to bestow it upon him in written form, then prepares to depart. When the emperor begs her to stay, she summons another goddess—the Lady of the Supreme Primordial—and orders her to join them.]

After a long time, the Queen Mother ordered the lady to bring out the Writ of the Eight Unions, the Veritable Shape of the Five Thearchs, the Talismans of the Six Cyclicals of the Five Emperors, and the Numinous Flying Beings: altogether twelve items. She said: "The texts may be transmitted from the heavens only once in four myriad kalpas. Once they are among humans, every forty years they may be bestowed upon a gentleman who possesses the Way."

The Queen Mother then commanded the serving girl Song Lingbin to open the cloud-patterned, multi-colored tabby-weave silk bag and take out a fascicle to bestow on the emperor. The Queen Mother stood up holding the text. With her own hands she granted it to the emperor. As she did so, the Queen Mother recited an incantation. . . . When the incantation was finished, the emperor saluted and bowed to receive the Queen Mother's words: "Now that you are beginning to study the Way and have received talismans, it would be appropriate for you to perform special sacrifices to various veritable numina of the rivers and marchmounts in order to pacify the state and the households. Cast tallies to the veritable numina in order to pray for the black-haired masses."

Her words finished, together with the Lady of the Supreme Primordial, she commanded the chariots, giving the words to depart. Her followers and officials collected in the dark. . . .

After that, the Martial Emperor could not make use of the Queen Mother's admonitions. He abandoned himself to strong drink and sex. He killed and attacked without respite. . . . From this time on, he lost the Way. . . . The Queen Mother did not come again. The texts he received, he arranged on the Cedar Beam Terrace, where they were burned by a celestial fire. The emperor grew more and more regretful and resentful. In the second year of the Primordial Commencement reign period (87 BCE), he died at Five Oaks Palace and was buried at the Fertile Tumulus. (24160–24163)

Xiwangmu visits the emperor in his palace after he demonstrates his worthiness, shares a banquet with him, grants him special teachings, and then departs. But he fails to put her teachings into practice, and so inevitably dies. According to Daoist master Du Guangting, Han Wudi was the Queen Mother's most spectacular failure. A great hero in Chinese history and the model of a successful monarch, he failed as a Daoist adept because he could not achieve the proper balance between religious and political concerns. The very acts that in traditional terms demonstrate his possession of the Mandate of Heaven—victory in war, potency in the harem, lavish expenditure at court—are seen by Daoist ascetics as tragic character flaws that ruin his chances for immortality.

The story of the goddess and the Han emperor, with its romance and tragedy, appealed deeply to medieval Chinese people. In more than a hundred Tang poems, writers tell this tale over and over, stressing now one aspect, now another. The Daoist poet Cao Tang (fl. 860–874) condenses the events of that night into two short pieces, highlighting the emotionally loaded moments before and after their meeting. The first captures Han Wudi's tense wait for her arrival:

Kunlun—he fixes his imagination on its loftiest peak;
The Queen Mother is coming, riding a five-colored dragon!" (*Quan Tangshi* 3827)

In a second poem, Cao Tang describes the emperor's loneliness in the deserted palace after her departure:

Autumn winds curl around like smoke; the moon is clear and distinct;
With the jade girls' pure song, the whole night comes to an end." (*Quan Tangshi* 3827)

Cao Tang echoes the Daoist hagiographer in his emphasis on the holy mountain, on iconographic details such as the five-colored dragon, and on ritual music that accompanied religious rituals and here marks the forlorn end of the encounter.

Li Qi (fl. 725) narrates the whole story in his long work "Song of the Queen Mother." His account parallels Du Guangting's quite closely, except that he substitutes intertwined pears for her peaches of immortality:

The Martial Illustrious One fasted and observed abstinence in his
  Basilica for Receiving Florescence;
As he stood upright with folded hands, instantly the Queen Mother came to
  grant him an audience.
Rainbow standards numinously flashing: her *qilin*-drawn chariots,
With feathered parasols streaming and pheasant fans.
Her fingers holding intertwined pears, she sent them along for the emperor to
  eat;
By means of them one can prolong life and preside over the cosmos.
On top of her head she wore the nine-starred crown;
She led a flock of jade lads, then sat facing south.
"Do you want to hear my essential words? Now I'll report them to you."
The emperor thereupon burned incense and requested such a discussion.
"If you can rarefy your earth soul and dispatch the three corpses,
Afterwards you will certainly have an audience with me at the Celestial
  Illustrious One's palace."
Turning her head back, she told the servant girl, Dong Shuangcheng,
"The wind is finished; you may perform on the Cloud Harmony Mouth Organ."
Red auroral clouds and the white sun, in strict attendance, did not move;
Seven dragons and five phoenixes in variegated disarray greeted them.
How regrettable! He was too ambitious and arrogant; the divinities were not
  satisfied,
But sighed and lamented over his horses' hooves and chariots' wheel tracks.
In his covered walkways, song bells became hard to discern in the
  approaching evening;
In the deep palace, peach and plum flowers turned snowy.
Now I just look at my blue jade five-branched lamp;
Its coiled dragon spits fire as the light is about to be severed. (*Quan Tangshi* 750)

Here the Queen Mother, wearing the crown of a Daoist priestess, bestows pears of immortality upon Han Wudi and offers to teach him transcendent arts. Because the emperor adheres to his royal tasks of increasing his kingdom and waging war, the Daoist gods are not pleased and abandon him. The Queen Mother who enabled the Yellow Emperor to fight off the forces of chaos, now wants her imperial student to be a self-cultivating pacifist. Her approval, withdrawn from the emperor in his earthly role as heroic leader of his people, will next be given to the exemplary Daoist adept, a model of another kind.

### *Mao Ying*

One last human encounter with the goddess was known to people of the Tang. This tale concerns Mao Ying, or Lord Mao, founder of the *Shangqing* school of

Daoism. Lord Mao is not a ruler but an ideal Daoist adept. The eldest of three brothers who lived in the south during the Han dynasty, Mao Ying received a visit from the Xiwangmu in 1 BCE. The goddess bestowed upon him the texts and entitlements of a high transcendent official. She also gave him Lady Wei Huacun as his divine spouse and teacher, beginning a pattern of intersex transmission of esoterica that *Shangqing* Daoists in subsequent periods longed to emulate. In Du Guangting's version of the tale, which is closely patterned on stories of Han Wudi and the Queen Mother, she descends to his chambers with an illustrious retinue in response to his ascetic practices. The opening scene presents one bestowal after another:

> The Celestial Illustrious Great Emperor sent his messenger in embroidered clothing, Ling Guangji Qi, to present Ying with a divine seal and jade emblem. The Lord Emperor of Grand Tenuity sent the Autocrat's Notary of the Left Palace of the Three Heavens, Guan Xiutiao, to present Ying with an eight-dragon multicolored tabby-weave silken carriage and purple-feathered floriate clothing. The Grand Supreme Lord of the Way sent the Dawn-Assisting Grandee, Shi Shumen, to present Ying with the Veritable Talisman of the Metal Tiger and a folly bell of flowing metal. The Incomparable Lord of the Golden Watchtower commanded the Realized Person of the Grand Bourne to send the Jade Squires of the Rectified Unity and Supreme Mystery, Wang Zhong, Bao Qiu, and others to present Ying with swallow wombs of the four junctions and divine mushrooms of flowing brightness.
>
> When the messengers from the four had finished the bestowals, they had Ying eat the fungi, hang the seal at his belt, don the clothing, straighten his crown, tie the talismans at his waist, grip the folly bell, and stand up. The messengers from the four told Ying: "He who eats concealed mushrooms of the four junctures takes up the position of a Steward of Realized Ones. He who eats jade mushrooms of the Golden Watchtowers takes up the position of Director of Destiny. He who eats metal blossoms of flowing brightness takes up the position of Director of Transcendent Registers. And he who eats the flying plants of extended luminosity takes up the position of a Realized Sire. . . . You have eaten all of these. Your longevity will be coequal with heaven and earth. Your place will be situated as the Supreme Realized Person who is Director of Destiny of Supreme Steward of the Eastern Marchmount. You will control all divine transcendents of the former [southern] kingdoms of Wu and Yue, and all the water sources left of the Yangtze River."
>
> Their words finished, all the messengers departed together. The Five Imperial Lords, each in a square-faced chariot, descended in submission to his courtyard. They carried out the commands of the Grand Emperor, presenting to Ying a purple jade plaque, writs carved in yellow gold, and patterns of nine pewters. They saluted Ying as Supreme Steward of the Eastern Marchmount, Realized Lord Who is Director of Destiny, and Realized Person of the Grand Primordial. The affair finished, they all departed. . . .
>
> [Next the Queen Mother of the West and Mao Ying's teacher serve a banquet, grant titles and texts to his younger brothers, and depart. Later the Queen Mother

returns escorting Mao Ying's divine bride, the goddess Wei Huacun. After supervising a divine marriage ceremony, including a feast and songs, the goddess's procession departs again to return to the heavens.] (24163–24164)

A poem by the Tang writer Bao Rong (fl. 820), who often wrote on Daoist matters, depicts a scene from this story. He describes Mao Ying's investiture from the point of view of an immortal observer in his "Song of the Transcendents' Meeting." Like Du Guangting, Bao stresses the ritual aspect of the occasion and the transmission of talismans and texts. One couplet reads:

Their ceremonious comportment completely appropriate for an affair between
ruler and vassals,
They request word on lesser transcendent arts." (*Quan Tangshi* 2918)

Lord Mao's meeting with the Queen Mother of the West is the final story in Du Guangting's biography of the goddess and his culminating statement. Mao Ying's case sums up the lessons taught by the Queen Mother to mortals. At the same time, his story transfers the regalia and charisma of the emperor to the Daoist adept. There is even an inflation and multiplication of titles and auspicious objects. Daoist Master Du Guangting implies that religious practice leads to spiritual attainments that surpass imperial majesty in permanence and glory. Writing for the emperor at his court in exile at the end of the Tang dynasty, just as the Mandate of Heaven was being withdrawn from the royal family, Du Guangting set forth a new Mandate of Heaven for the Daoist adept who can achieve immortality and celestial office through cultivation of the Way.

## Conclusion

Daoist scriptures and Tang literature tell us that the Queen Mother grants the earliest legendary monarchs, such as the Yellow Emperor and Shun, powers enabling them to rule along with symbolic objects demonstrating their possession of the Mandate of Heaven. Canonical scriptures appropriate notions of the relationship between divinity and kingship that go back to most ancient Chinese practices of ancestor worship and shamanism when they emphasize the goddess's role as creator, teacher, mediator, and bestower of immortality. Divine protection in the form of magical talismans, together with martial skills symbolized by her heavenly armies, descends upon the Queen Mother's command to assist the worthy and capable rulers of antiquity who began the patterns of Chinese culture. The world is hers to grant, perhaps in the form of a map or a jade tube, to a virtuous ruler. She connects rulers to the gods and to the heritage of their ancestors. She gives the gifts of civilization and immortality, the very things that make us human, to these first rulers and culture heroes, who in turn pass benefits on to their subjects.

According to medieval Daoist texts and Tang poetry, historical emperors such as Zhou Muwang and Han Wudi encounter the Queen Mother of the West, profess devotion to her, and receive symbolic tokens and esoteric teachings. The goddess recognizes their reigns as legitimate: They receive the Mandate of Heaven and continue the worthy accomplishments of their ancestors. But something is missing. Despite wealth, charisma, and fabulous accomplishments, Daoist texts and Tang poets tell us, these emperors have tragic flaws, which prevent them from obtaining the most valued prize of all: immortality. Their failure to perform their religious duties properly results in death. Daoist scriptures reinterpret the divine signs of royal legitimacy in their own terms.

Daoist canonical texts and works of the Tang poets reveal that during the Six Dynasties period, which saw the formation and spread among the literati of the beliefs of *Shangqing* Daoism, a transformation has taken place in the meaning of divine encounters and of royal regalia. The Daoists have coopted the traditional symbols of kingship. Poets accept and repeat the cooptation. As a result of this change, the Daoist adept, who in contrast to King Mu and Emperor Wu may have no wealth or royal lineage but pursues religious discipline singlemindedly, assumes the paraphernalia of kingship. The adept becomes the one who receives divine gifts and becomes the real victor. The rich and powerful king is the loser. The Queen Mother of the West changes from a maker of kings to a maker of transcendents. She bestows her blessings on the successful adept rather than on the next emperor of China.

The medieval Daoist reassignment of royal prerequisites and reallocation of divine resources is as revolutionary as Confucius's redefinition centuries earlier of the term *junzi* to mean no longer literally "the son of a ruler" but "the worthy person qualified to rule." The shocking message of the Daoist transformation is that royal powers are available to anyone who observes Daoist religious practices with total devotion. In turn, the goddess known as the Queen Mother of the West passes out of the lore actively used to legitimize the actual Chinese ruler.

## REFERENCES


*Daocang* (Treasure House of the Way). 1976. Zhengtong ed. First printed 1444. (60 vols.) Reprinted Taibei: Yiwen.

Du Guangting. *Yongcheng jixian lu* (Records of the Assembled Transcendents of the Fortified Walled City). HY 782, HY 1026, ch. 114.

*Quan Tangshi* (Complete Tang Poetry Anthology). 1967. Taibei: Fuxing.

Weng Tu-chien. 1935. *Daocang zimu yinde* (Combined Indexes to the Authors and Titles of Books in Two Collections of Taoist Literature). Beijing: Harvard-Yenching Institute. [Taoist canonical texts are cited by number in this index, preceded by HY.]

*Xunzi yinde* (Index to Xunzi). 1950. Beijing: Harvard-Yenching Institute.

Yuan Ho, ed. 1979. *Shanhai jing jiaozhu* (The Classic of Mountains and Seas with Comparative Commentaries). Shanghai: Guji.

*Zhuangzi yinde* (Index to Zhuangzi). 1947. Beijing: Harvard-Yenching Institute.


## SUGGESTIONS FOR FURTHER READING


Birrell, Anne. 1993. *Chinese Mythology: An Introduction*. Baltimore: Johns Hopkins University Press.

Cahill, Suzanne E. 1993. *Transcendence and Divine Passion: The Queen Mother of the West in Medieval China*. Stanford, CA: Stanford University Press.

Jordan, David K., and Daniel L. Overmyer. 1986. *The Flying Phoenix: Aspects of Chinese Sectarianism in Taiwan*. Princeton, NJ: Princeton University Press.

Knobleck, John. 1988–1994. *Xunzi: A Translation and Study of the Complete Works* (3 vols.). Stanford, CA: Stanford University Press.

Kohn, Liva. 1993. *The Taoist Experience: An Anthology*. Albany, NY: SUNY Press.

Loewe, Michael. 1979. *Ways to Paradise: The Chinese Quest for Immortality*. London: Allen & Unwin.

Robinet, Isabelle. 1993. *Taoist Meditation: The Maoshan Tradition of Purity*. Albany, NY: SUNY Press.

Watson, Burton, trans. 1968. *The Complete Works of Chuang-tzu*. New York: Columbia University Press.

Wong, Eva. 1997. *The Shambhala Guide to Taoism*. Boston: Shambhala.

13

# Goddesses and Sovereignty in Ancient Egypt

*Susan Tower Hollis*

Egyptologists have concerned themselves for over a century about just what constitutes kingship or sovereignty in ancient Egypt. The task is not made the easier by either the long time span—just under 3,000 years—or the available evidence, which is severely constrained by a number of factors: the chanciness of finds, the locations of modern towns, climate and ground water changes, and so on. The most recent scholarship on the topic makes all these issues clear (Baines 1995; Leprohon 1995; Silverman 1995). These same materials also make abundantly evident that the ancient Egyptians' own concepts surrounding kingship and sovereignty changed through the millennia and that the divinity of the ruler constitutes a significant feature from the earliest times. What is much less discussed is the place the goddesses held in relation to sovereignty, even in the most recent significant book on the topic, *Ancient Egyptian Kingship* (O'Connor and Silverman 1995). Both my own work (Hollis 1997) and that of a very few others, particularly Lana Troy (1986), suggest that kingship and sovereignty incorporated the feminine in many ways little noticed or addressed in the different studies on kingship.

## Kingship

In earliest times, the Egyptian king was the Horus king. Visually this concept appeared in the writing of the king's name in a serekh, a figure that depicts a falcon standing on top of a rectangle, the bottom part of which shows the façade of a building, commonly understood to be the royal palace (O'Brien 1996) (figure 13.1). The actual name was written in the space over the façade, as is King Djet's here. This name, and thus the person, served as a kind of bridge between the heavenly sphere or sky, where the falcon, viewed as a god, flew, and the earthly sphere, represented by the façade. Thus the iconography demonstrates that the king linked the two realms, the heavenly and the earthly.

Similarly, the royal titulary, consisting of five titles with accompanying names individual to each king, incorporated both the divine and earthly worlds into the king's being. The second of the five titles, the so-called Two Ladies or Two Mistresses name, is clearly feminine and refers to the vulture goddess Nekhbet of southern or Upper Egypt and the cobra goddess Wadjet of northern or Lower Egypt. Nekhbet was associated with the ancient town of El-Kab near Hierakonpolis and was often called the "white one of Hierakonpolis," due to her relation to the White Crown of Upper Egypt worn by the king. Throughout history Nekhbet filled a protective role, and it is not uncommon to see the vulture flying protectively over the king's head in many graphic contexts. The vulture also appeared as a headdress in which the bird's head rises from the forehead, while the bird's body stretches along the top of her head with its wings folded down the sides of her head behind her ears (figure 13.2). Initially worn only by goddesses, by the fifth dynasty (ca. 2510–2460 BCE), the queen occasionally appeared wearing the vulture headdress, and by early in the sixth dynasty (ca. 2460–2200 BCE), it had become a regular part of the queen's iconography. One may view this development as a demonstration of the complementary role the queen played in relation to the king, the vulture Nekhbet to the falcon Horus (Troy 1986, 117).

Given that the vulture hieroglyph itself represents the word for mother, one is not surprised to find Nekhbet appearing in a maternal role, particularly in relation to the king. Some of her earliest appearances in anthropomorphic form depict her nursing the king. She also acts as midwife, assisting in births in this world and in rebirths in the otherworld (Troy 1986, 118–119).

The second deity of the Two Ladies name is Wadjet, the cobra deity who was associated with the Delta town of Buto. Like Nekhbet, she was a protector deity and associated with a royal crown, in this case the Red Crown of Lower Egypt. As the hooded cobra, she was the Rising One, found on the king's brow as the uraeus, and by the sixth dynasty, on the queen's headdress as well (Troy 1986, 120).

Together the two goddesses, Wadjet and Nekhbet, the Two Ladies, represent the joining of northern and southern Egypt in the office of the king, and certainly this joining, clearly feminine, also stood for the joining of the divine world and the sovereign over both north and south. Occasionally they appeared together on the front of the king's diadem, a headband or fillet, as protectors and

*Figure 13.1: King's serekh.*

defenders, and in later periods even on that of queens. The Red and White Crowns associated with the two goddesses were combined as the Double Crown, emphasizing again the joining of Lower and Upper Egypt. The persistent presence of the uraeus on the ruling king, and eventually on the queen (even when she is not formally acknowledged as ruler), along with the vulture, flying above the king or as a headdress on the queen, attests to a very strong female presence in the kingship.

## Early Artifacts

Other early evidence found on different artifacts similarly show the king in relation to the divine feminine. For example, the Narmer palette (figure 13.3), a late fourth-millennium BCE ceremonial piece,[1] depicts four human-faced cows' heads that represent the goddess Bat, an ancient cow-deity who was assimilated in time to the cow-goddess Hathor, who was dominant in Bat's neighboring territory (Fischer 1962, 1963). The positions of the four human-faced cows' heads at the top of this ceremonial palette, two each on the recto and verso, flanking the royal

*Figure 13.2: Vulture headdress.*

serekh, suggest the protective and supportive role of the goddess. Both the prominent position and the multiple representations indicate the deity's importance. Similarly, the presence of the same form on the king's skirt, again in fours—the four compass directions—signifies protection and support, perhaps even empowerment.

Similar depictions of a human-faced cow's head appear on several other early artifacts, in each case accompanied by a star or stars within and around the horns, implying a celestial aspect to the goddess, and these heads certainly should be considered to be Bat, as should the heads that adorned the king's skirt. Indeed the skirt itself may have been called Bat in earliest times, following the verbal imagery of Hathor in one of the sixth-dynasty Pyramid Texts, mortuary texts appearing in the royal pyramids to assist the king on his trip to the next world: "My kilt that is on me is Hathor" (Pyr. § 546b).[2] With this understanding—eight cows' heads representing the goddess Bat on a palette signifying a celebratory act by the king—one finds another major feminine divinity within the earliest royal symbolism of ancient Egypt (Hollis 1997).

On the verso of this palette, one finds a depiction of Narmer's queen, Tjet, striding before the king, wearing a leopard garment not unlike that worn by the king when he acts in a priestly role. The queen on the palette also has two papyrus plants hanging upside down from her left shoulder, a symbol of flourishing life associated with several goddesses including Neith and Hathor (Wilkinson 1992, 123).

The Narmer macehead (figure 13.4), like his palette a ceremonial object rather than a weapon, shows similar divine feminine symbolism. Most notable is the vulture, likely Nekhbet, flying protectively above the king, who is seated under a canopy at the center. In addition, one sees a female figure representing the royal female children (Millet 1990, 56–57, 1991) in a carrying chair or palanquin coming toward the king, identifiable as female through the body-encompassing garb. This carrying chair itself represents the goddess Repit, a little known deity, who is a goddess in her own right but whose name may be used to designate other, better-known goddesses, for example, Bat and Nut (Rössler-Köhler 1983; Troy 1986, 82, 84). Behind the king strides the small figure of Queen Tjet, so

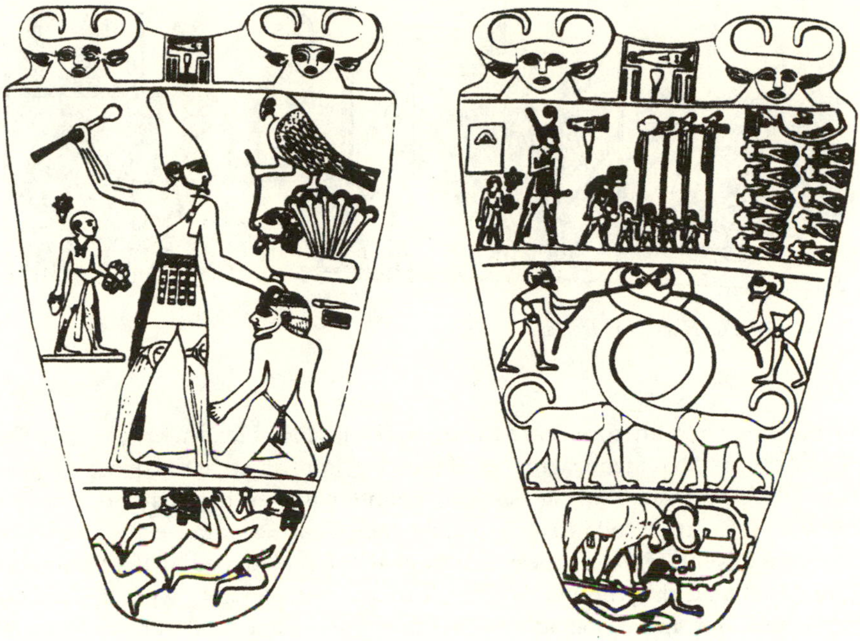

*Figure 13.3: The Narmer palette (recto and verso).*

identified by the hieroglyph above her head, again wearing a leopard-like dress, complete with tail. As on the palette, a plant hangs down from her shoulder, emphasizing the divine feminine through its associations with various goddesses (Lurker 1980, 94; Troy 1986; Wilkinson 1992, 123).

## Neith

A fourth early goddess is Neith, a very significant deity for royalty and nonroyalty alike in earliest historical Egypt. Her name appears as a component in about 40 percent of the known early theophoric names, personal names that incorporate divine names into them. These names are found in many contexts, though most commonly on cylinder seals used to seal containers and jugs. The number of Neith-related names in the early dynasties far surpasses that of any other deity, with her name even appearing as a component in the names of several early queens. Indeed, two of these queens, Neith-Hetep and Meret-Neith, both of the first dynasty, seem to have served as Queen Regnant, Meret-Neith possibly ruling in her own right, and serekhs exist containing each one's name (figure 13.5). In each case, Neith's cult-sign, a bilobate object with crossed arrows, surmounts the serekh in place of the falcon god Horus found on the king's serekh. Recent discussions of this cult-sign have suggested that the bilobate object, generally considered to be a shield, is rather a combination of two click beetles, an insect

*Figure 13.4: The Narmer macehead.*

identified with Neith from very early times (Hollis 1991; Hendrickx 1996, 40). The rest of the serekh is identical to that of the king, implying that the queen in question fulfilled the same role as her male counterpart, serving as a bridge or link between the earthly and heavenly realms. Indeed, one example exists where the Horus and Neith serekhs appear side by side, the one topped by the falcon, the other by the Neith symbol. It is difficult to say with certainty what this pairing represents, but the combination seems to suggest some kind of coexistence of male and female power or rule.[3]

Another example of Neith's relation to the king appears on an engraved diorite vase that belonged to Ni-Netjer, an early second-dynasty king. Here Neith appears in anthropomorphic form, the earliest of such representations. Coifed with the double bow, she holds an ankh, the sign of life, in her left hand and the *was*-scepter, a sign of rule and power, in her right. As she faces the royal serekh, she is ready to give the divine gifts of life and ruling power to the king, a common motif depicted in the relation of Egyptian kings to deities. A variant representation of the same motif may be seen on a sherd from a yellow alabaster vase dating to the time of Djet, the third king of the first dynasty. In this example, the serekh is tête-à-tête with Neith, represented here simply by the double bow over which is placed the pair of crossed arrows. Both artifacts attest to an interaction between the palace (i.e., the king) and the goddess.

Neith served also as protector of the Red Crown and commonly appears wearing this crown during the second and first millennia BCE.[4] The crown, associated with Lower Egypt and the goddess Wadjet, relates Neith to Lower Egypt as well. In fact, from very early times, the city of Saïs in the western delta in Lower Egypt was considered Neith's city, and the name of the crown, *n.t*, is homophonic with the goddess's name. Furthermore the relationship is clearly affirmed by a number of people who bore the title Director of the Mansions of the Red Crown, along with titles relating to Neith and her town of Saïs. Because there was no certain structure that went by this name, Ramadan el-Sayed has suggested that the phrase "Mansions of the Red Crown" symbolized a religious domain related to the western delta of Egypt, Neith's territory (el-Sayed 1976, 98). With this clear connection to Lower Egypt, it is surprising to find that a predynastic sherd bearing the Red Crown in raised relief was excavated at Naqada in Upper

*Figure 13.5: Neith serekh.*

Egypt (Wainwright 1923, 26). With great caution, I suggest this anomaly might be explained in light of the increasing evidence that the so-called conquering of Lower Egypt by Upper Egypt was instead a slow spread of Upper Egyptian powers northward during the fourth and early third millennia BCE combined with the fairly clear differentiation of the northern delta region of the land from the southern river valley. This explanation could allow Naqada to be the "northern area" that was incorporated into an Upper Egyptian sphere of influence. In such a scenario, the local Red Crown would have been assumed as symbolizing the success of the incorporation. Much more work must be done before making a more certain statement on the subject, but briefly it could help explain the strange fact that Neith-Hetep, often considered a northern queen, was buried at Naqada rather than at Abydos where King Hor-Aha, possibly her husband, was interred.

As Egyptian kingship developed during the early years of the Old Kingdom and the sun god Re became more and more prominent, the goddess Hathor, often viewed as his wife or his daughter, moved into ascendancy (Helck 1954, 976). At the same time, though questionably as an effect, evidence of Neith and her symbols diminishes greatly. From a dominant position in the corpus of theophoric names on the Early Dynastic seals (Kaplony 1963), vases, and palettes (el-Sayed 1982, 209–238) in the Old Kingdom, Neith seems to appear most commonly in the context of individuals serving as priestesses of Neith and Hathor, rarely of just Neith, particularly in Giza area (Galvin 1981).

Historically, one sees attestations of Neith throughout Egyptian history, but after the Old Kingdom, her visibility is quite limited until the twenty-sixth dynasty, the so-called Saïte period, when she reappears in a dominant role.[5] In addition, she appears prominently in the Roman temple at Esna in Upper Egypt, where she acts as primordial creator, a unique role for an Egyptian goddess. A suggestion of this role may be found in the twentieth-dynasty Papyrus Chester Beatty I telling of the struggles between Horus and Seth in which Neith is appealed to in order to help settle the two gods' dispute. She reacts emphatically, decreeing that unless Horus, the son of Osiris, be granted the throne, she will "get angry and the sky will crash to the ground" (P. Chester Beatty I, recto, 3,3).

It would appear that she maintained the world as it is known, and thus she was also capable of allowing it to cease to exist.

## Hathor

As noted previously, the goddess Hathor, who assimilated to herself the ancient human-faced cow goddess Bat with her celestial connotation, rose to prominence beginning in the second dynasty as the sun god Re gained in importance. Among the many guises in which she appeared was that of the cobra goddess, or the Fiery One (Roberts 1997). She was also the Distant One, the solar eye who had to be brought back from the foreign land, reflecting perhaps the natural annual solar cycle in the southern hemisphere. On her return, the sun god placed her on his brow as the uraeus. One thus sees her in relation to Wadjet, who similarly appears as the uraeus.

Her name, often understood to mean "house of Horus," referring to the falcon deity Horus,[6] places her in the sky as a sky goddess and relates her to the Horus king, who was also the son of her husband, the sun god Re. Certainly a great number of Old Kingdom seals show a pairing of the king and Hathor (Kaplony 1977, §78) or a triad with the king between Re and Hathor (Kaplony 1977, §79). In this latter form, the king is their son, as the establishment of the king's fifth title, the Son of Re, suggests. Notably, at least two kings, Pepi II of the sixth dynasty and Mentuhotep II of the eleventh dynasty, were known as Son of Hathor, a reference to Hathor as Mistress of Dendera, the Upper Egyptian town where she had a major temple, as well as Son of Re (Allam 1963, 12; Fischer 1968, 37 and n.152; Beckrath 1984, 57, 184).

Perhaps the most renowned depictions of the king together with Hathor appear in the famous triads of Menkaure (the fourth-dynasty king known to many as Mycerinus), the builder and owner of the smallest of the three great pyramids at Giza. Each of these triads (figure 13.6) depicts the king in the company of Hathor and a nome deity, that is, a deity identified with a specific region (Reisner 1931, 109–110, pl. 38–46). In each, either Hathor has her arm around the king or she is standing in very close proximity to him. Assuming that Hathor is minimally the divine mother of the king, as suggested by the triadic presentation on Old Kingdom seals where the king is between the goddess and his father Re (Kaplony 1977, 304), the goddess appears to be protecting the king in these sculptures, recalling this theme in the king's relation to other goddesses.

As Hathor rose to dominance, it is not surprising to see the queen beginning to identify herself with the goddess—particularly if the queen had a role parallel to that of the king, as suggested by the serekhs of the first dynasty. An excellent illustration appears in the slate pair statute of Menkaure and his queen, Khamerernebty II, which shows a parity of size, and thus perhaps power, between the king and his chief wife (figure 13.7). The two stand shoulder to shoulder, both simply garbed and coifed, lacking even an allowance for the expected size differential of male and female. The position of the bodies of the pair provides particular interest, for they are not just standing side by side but rather she

*Figure 13.6: Triad of King Mycerinus and two goddesses. (Courtesy, Museum Expedition, Museum of Fine Arts, Boston.)*

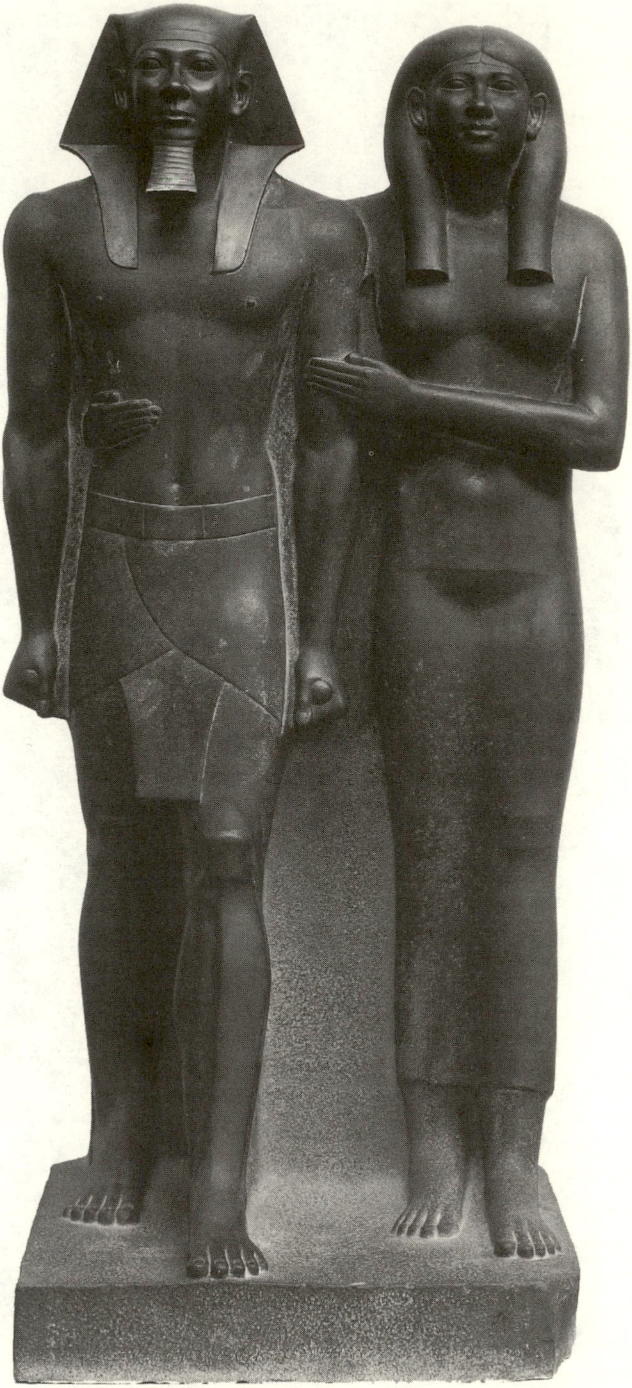

*Figure 13.7: Pair statue of Menkaure and Queen Khamerernebty II. (Courtesy, Harvard-Museum Expedition, Museum of Fire Arts Boston.)*

is embracing him, even protecting him, with her right hand around his back and her left hand on his left arm, recalling the embrace of the king by Hathor in some of the triads.[7]

Hathor's relation to the king appears very explicitly in the well-known Middle Kingdom narrative of Sinuhe, the tale of a courtier who, upon hearing of the death of King Amenemhet I, fled the land, fearing, it seems, some retaliation from a presumed harem conspiracy or palace uprising engineered by the queen. Sinuhe ended up in Syria and made a great success of his life in exile. In due time, however, the king, now Sesostris I, with whose army Sinuhe had been on maneuvers when Amenemhet I died, invited the exile to return to Egypt. Part of the letter the king sent to Sinuhe read:

> This your heaven in the palace (= the queen) lives
> and prospers to this day.
> Her head is adorned with the kingship of the land;
> her children are in the palace. (Sinuhe B 185–186)[8]

These phrases imply strongly that the queen shared the power of the king in ruling the land, participating, as he did, in the divinity that legitimized the ruling power of ancient Egypt.

Upon his return, following his greeting by the king, Sinuhe was presented to the queen and the royal daughters, at which time a hymn was sung, complete with the playing of the sistra and rattle, instruments sacred to Hathor:

> Your hands upon the radiance, eternal king,
> Jewels of heaven's mistress!
> The Gold (= Hathor) gives life to your nostrils,
> The Lady of Stars (Hathor) enfolds you! (Sinuhe B 270)[9]

Such verbal imagery provides support for the idea of Hathor as the mistress of heaven, that is, the sky or house of Horus the sky god (not the son of Isis and Osiris). The Gold, or the Golden One, is a common epithet for her, perhaps because of her relationship with Re, but more likely because of her identity as the sun's eye, as, for example, in the narrative about the Destruction of Humanity, found in some of the royal tombs of the New Kingdom. Probably the most interesting epithet here is the Lady of the Stars, which provides confirmation that the stars and the cow seen together on the early dynastic artifacts related to Bat were later assumed by Hathor as she assumed Bat's characteristics (Pinch 1993), especially as a sky deity.

Hathor continues to be an important deity throughout Egyptian history, with roles such as goddess of foreign lands, goddess of sexuality, and the goddess of love and drunkenness. From the beginning, her role relative to the living king and queen makes her very much a "this world" deity, whose appearance in the early mortuary texts is rare. However, in time, like most Egyptian goddesses, she becomes associated with the mortuary world as a goddess who assists in rebirth in the West (the place of immortality), but she never relinquishes her power and hold on this world, and her presence continues throughout Egyptian history, even into the Greco-Roman period.

### Nut

With Nut, another sky deity, one moves fully into the cosmic and otherworldly realm, away from active sovereignty in this world. Nut, the mother of the gods Osiris, Horus, Seth, Isis, and Nephthys, represents the otherworld, that of night and death, and it is to her that the Pyramid Texts most frequently refer. If one considers that the Pyramid Texts provide instructions to guide the deceased king successfully to the otherworld—envisioned variously as solar, stellar, or chthonic—Nut's role in these texts makes sense. For one thing, the king, both as the living Horus and as deceased Osiris, is her son. Much of the poetic imagery of the mortuary texts presents her in this role. The Old Kingdom Pyramid Texts, the Middle Kingdom Coffin Texts, the Underworld Books, and the Book of the Dead from the New Kingdom, as well as the mythological papyri from the Third Intermediate Period all emphasize her close relation to Osiris. For example, the Pyramid Texts frequently allude to her as his coffin, as in the following example:

> "O Nut, spread yourself over your son Osiris the King
>     that you may conceal him from Seth:
> Protect him, O Nut.
> Have you come that you may conceal your son?"
> "I have indeed come that I may protect this great one." (Pyr. §777)

In fact, her image is painted or carved on the interiors of the lids and bodies of numerous coffins and sarcophagi, especially during the later periods, where, as the actual coffin bed or lid she embraces and protects the deceased, a carryover from texts like the one cited here. In the Underworld Books, most notably the Book of Night and Day, she is the night sky through which the sun and the sunboat with the deceased king journey. The imagery is potent and persistent: Nut fills a role significant for the deceased sovereign, albeit for his afterlife.

Beginning in the Middle Kingdom, the texts and imagery originally restricted to the king began to be utilized by nonroyal individuals, reflecting the slow democratization of Egyptian afterlife. Thus the Coffin Texts, the immediate descendants of the royal Pyramid Texts (with new materials added), appear on the coffins of nobles of the Middle Kingdom, and later the Underworld Books, originally limited to royal tombs, appear, at least partially, in the mythological papyri that could be had by anyone with the means to pay. Similarly the imagery of being born of Nut each day, initially a royal prerogative, appears on the interior of later coffin lids of nonroyal individuals, suggesting the same rights and privileges of rebirth earlier limited to the king alone.

Nut, however, played no part in the king's ruling life. She had no known temples in Egypt, though there is one known from Syria. She received no cult, and her name appears in three theophoric names at most (Kurth 1981). She also appears relatively late, known first from the fifth dynasty.

## Isis

Isis is the ancient Egyptian goddess best known to those outside the field due to her visible presence in the Greek and Roman empires. For example, R. E. Witt (1997) reports how Isis was known to her Hellenistic devotees:

> There, in the beginning was Isis. Oldest of the old, she was the goddess from whom all Becoming arose. She was the great Lady—Mistress of the Two Lands of Egypt, Mistress of Shelter, Mistress of Heaven, Mistress of the House of Life, Mistress of the Word of God. She was the Unique. In all her great and wonderful works she was a wiser magician and more excellent than any other god. (14)

Eventually she indeed assumed all of these roles and epithets, but they did not belong to her in her earliest appearances and activities; rather they accrued to her over time. In fact the Great One (Pyr. §§1140c, 1214b) is the only epithet from before the Middle Kingdom that comes close to any of those cited by Witt (Münster 1968, 203).

Perhaps the most startling fact about Isis is the lack of any definitive mention of her before the end of the fifth dynasty at the time of the Pyramid Texts, and within this corpus, the majority of her eighty-two appearances occur in tandem with her sister Nephthys. Like Nut and Nephthys, there is no certain attestation of Isis in early theophoric names. Furthermore, no temples are dedicated to her alone before the late period, and the first evidence of her cult occurs no earlier than the latter part of the sixth dynasty.

In the Pyramid Texts, serving royalty only, Isis and Nephthys appear as two kites, Osiris's two sisters who seek and find him, and elsewhere as the two mothers who conceive, bear, and nurture the king—all this, of course, in the otherworld. They greet him, proclaim him to the gods, and extend to him goodwill as he comes announcing himself. The most prominent of their activities involves assisting him to life in the otherworld, that is, effecting his rebirth. For instance, in Pyramid Utterance 477, the king is told:

> Raise yourself, O Osiris,
> . . .
> Isis has your arm, O Osiris,
> Nephthys has your hand;
> So go between them. (Pyr. §§960a,c)

and in Utterance 366, he is informed:

Your two sisters, Isis and Nephthys, come to you
That they make you hale. (Pyr. §628a; cf. Utt. 364, §610c).

In yet another text, Utterance 511, the king announces:

Isis conceives me, Nephthys begets me. (§1154a)

The sisters also provide the king with milk, suckle him, and restore him, and they each hold him to give him a heart so that he may live. He climbs into their laps in numerous texts, presumably for nurturing, nursing, and protection. They lament his death, often as the mourning woman and the mooring post. The mooring post—sometimes identified with Isis and sometimes with Nephthys—places the scene on a funerary boat, which recalls the iconographic representation of the standing and kneeling women on such boats in the reliefs and paintings in private tombs (Settgast 1963, pl. 6, 7, 11–14) and on boat models of the Middle Kingdom (Fischer 1976). In fact, numerous references and images throughout Egyptian history place Isis and Nephthys at, respectively, the foot and the head of the coffin or the bow and stern of the funerary boat. It is quite likely that the two goddesses originally represented the royal version of the two female mourners who appear ubiquitously in ancient Egypt as well as in many other cultures, ancient and modern.

Of the twenty-five Pyramid Texts citing Isis alone, eight of them refer to her in the company of Horus, whereas just two of them connect her with Osiris, and these two texts, found only in the pyramids of the sixth-dynasty kings and depicting the stellar realm, are virtually identical with each other:

Your sister Isis comes to you, rejoicing for love of you.
She placed your phallus on her vulva
and your seed issues into her, she being alert as Sothis,
and Har-Sopd has come forth from you as Horus who is in
Sothis. |
It is well with you through him
in his name of "Spirit who is in the Djendrew-bark,"
and he protects you in his name of Horus, the son who
protects his father. (Pyr. §§632a–633b)

This episode, which appears in later mortuary texts as well as in hymns and other literary forms, relates the essential parts of the narrative that eventually resulted in Isis's rise to prominence: She enlivens the deceased Osiris king in order to conceive Horus, Osiris's heir, who will then avenge his father's death at the hands of Seth. In a late third- or early second-century BCE text, she describes her action as follows:

I have acted as a man although I was a woman,
In order to make [Osiris's] name survive on earth. (P. Louvre 3079 I, col. 110,
ll. 20–22)

This remarkable act contributed to her reputation as universal mother and goddess of magic, roles that began to be fairly prominent during the New Kingdom, as attested by various tales and magical spells or incantations. Thus, Isis, originally an otherworld deity, expanded her sphere of influence into "this world" activity. During this time, too, the goddess, previously identified by the throne sign on her head, began to appropriate the insignia of other goddesses, most notably the cow horns and sun disk of Hathor. Similarly, her cult, virtually nonexistent before the Middle Kingdom, only started to gain prominence in the New Kingdom. At this time, too, Isis began to appear actively in other narratives, such as that about Re's secret name, and to collect the series of epithets to which Witt refers, epithets often more commonly associated with other goddesses: "Oldest of the old, . . . goddess from whom all Becoming arose, . . . the great Lady—Mistress of the Two Lands of Egypt, Mistress of Shelter, Mistress of Heaven, Mistress of the House of Life, Mistress of the Word of God, . . . (and) the Unique" (Witt 1997, 14).

The Isis of the Hellenistic and Roman worlds, when Egypt was governed first by the Greeks and later by the Romans, while bearing these and related epithets, was not exactly identical with the Isis of the earlier Egyptian world, despite having the same name. The imagery of Isis in Greek and Latin texts derived largely from the need for a universal type of deity in a very complex world of conquest and empire, and she took many attributes from other goddesses to reach this universality, even to becoming part of the Greek mysteries (Egan 1990). At the same time, however, in Egypt itself she remained the Isis of older times, mourning Osiris in tandem with her sister Nephthys, as, for example in the "Lamentations of Isis and Nephthys," dating from the Ptolemaic period. Here she maintains her relation to the Osiris king.

In sum, ancient Egyptian goddesses played an important role in sovereignty, so great, in fact, that kingship in ancient Egypt would not have been what it was without them, affecting the king, both in ruling and otherworldly contexts. Furthermore, the queen, although not always involved in ruling the kingdom, nevertheless played a significant role by representing the royal goddess, just as the king represented the royal god. Embodying the feminine aspects of sovereignty, so much a part of Egyptian kingship from earliest times, she even shared the rule in some periods. At the same time, no one goddess can be said to be the primary goddess of Egyptian sovereignty, despite the modern knowledge of Isis, but rather many goddesses, borrowing often from each other, filled different aspects of this role.

NOTES

1. Palettes were commonly used to hold cosmetics, particularly kohl, an eye protection in this land of sun and sand.
2. All translations are the author's.
3. Neith serekhs do not appear after the first dynasty, however, despite the evidence that in several subsequent periods, women ruled Egypt, assuming the full royal titulary that developed during the Early Dynastic and Old Kingdom periods (Beckerath 1984; Troy 1986). Among these women are, of course, Nitocris

at the end of the sixth dynasty, Neferusobek at the end of the twelfth dynasty, Hatshepsut of the eighteenth dynasty, Tauwesret at the end of the following dynasty, and Cleopatra VII near the end of the Ptolemaic period.

4. There is no certain representation of her wearing the Red Crown earlier than a pyramidion of Amenemhet III in the early second millennium BCE (Maspero 1902; Otto 1938).
5. Lyla Pinch Brock reports in the July 1998 *Newsletter of the Society for the Study of Egyptian Antiquities* (Toronto) the discovery of a late eighteenth-dynasty tomb by the Japanese at Dahshur in which the tomb's owner is shown on a stele offering to the parents of Ptahemwia, high priest of the goddess Neith (3).
6. There were numerous falcon gods in ancient Egypt, many of which took on the Horus name over time. This Horus, probably among the earliest falcons by that name, commonly carries the epithet, "the elder."
7. In a presentation on 14 September 1999, in New York City, Dorothea Arnold suggested the female of this pair might be the king's mother, thus accounting for the embrace resembling that of the goddesses in other sculptures.
8. Translated by the author from the hieroglyphic text in Blackman (1972, 32).
9. Translated by the author from the hieroglyphic text in Blackman (1972, 38).

REFERENCES


Allam, S. 1963. *Beiträge zum Hathorkult (bis zum Ende des Mittleren Reiches)*. Berlin: Verlag Bruno Hessling.

Baines, J. 1995. "Kingship, Definition of Culture and Legitimation." Pp. 3–47 in *Ancient Egyptian Kingship*, ed. D. O'Connor and D. P. Silverman. Leiden: E. J. Brill.

Beckerath, J. V. 1984. *Handbuch der ägyptischen Königsnamen*. München-Berlin: Deutscher Kunstverlag.

Blackman, A. M. 1972. *Middle-Egyptian Stories*. [Bibliotheca Aegyptiaca II.] Bruxelles: Édition de la Fondation Égyptologique Reine Élisabeth.

Brock, L. P. 1998. "News from Egypt: A Year of Discovery." *JSSEA Newsletter* (July): 2–3.

Egan, R. B. 1990. "Isis: Goddess of the Oikoumene." Pp. 123–142 in *Goddesses in Religions and Modern Debate*, ed. L. Hurtado. Atlanta: Scholars Press.

el-Sayed, R. 1976. "A propos du titre *ḫrp- ḥwwt*." *Revue d'Égyptologie* 28: 97–110.

———. 1982. *La Déesse Neith de Saïs II Documentation*. Caire: Institut Français d'Archéologie Orientale du Caire.

Fischer, H. G. 1962. "The Cult and Nome of the Goddess Bat." *Journal of the American Research Center in Egypt* 1: 7–23.

———. 1963. "*Ba.t* in the New Kingdom." *Journal of the American Research Center in Egypt* 2: 50–51.

———. 1968. *Dendera in the Third Millennium B.C.* New York: J. J. Augustin.

———. 1976. "Representations of *Ḏryt*-mourners in the Old Kingdom." Pp. 39–50 in *Egyptian Studies I: Varia*, ed. H. G. Fischer. New York: The Metropolitan Museum of Art.

Galvin, M. 1981. "The Prietesses of Hathor in the Old Kingdom and the First Intermediate Period." Ph.D. diss., Brandeis University.

Grimal, N. 1992. *A History of Ancient Egypt*, trans. Ian Shaw. Oxford, England, and Cambridge, MA: Blackwell.

Helck, W. 1954. "Herkunft und Deutung einiger Züge des frühägyptischen Königsbildes." *Anthropos* 49: 961–991.

Hendrickx, S. 1996. "Two Protodynastic Objects in Brussels and the Origin of the Bilobate Cult-Sign of Neith." *Journal of Egyptian Archaeology* 82: 23–41.

Hollis, S. T. 1991. "Is the Figure on Neith's Standard a Shield?" A. R. C. E. annual meeting, Boston, MA.

———. 1997. "Queens and Goddesses in Ancient Egypt." Pp. 210–238 in *Women and Goddess Traditions in Antiquity and Today*, ed. K. L. King. Minneapolis, MN: Fortress Press.

Kaplony, P. 1963. *Die Inschriften der ägyptischen Frühzeit*. Wiesbaden: Otto Harrassowitz.

———. 1977. *Die Rollsiegel des Alten Reichs I: Allgemeiner Teil mit Studien zum Königtum des Alten Reichs*. Bruxelles: Foundation Égyptologique Reine Élisabeth.

Kurth, D. 1981. "Nut." Pp. 535–541 in *Lexikon der Ägyptologie* (vol. 4), ed. W. Helck and W. Westendorf. Wiesbaden: Otto Harrassowitz.

Leprohon, R. J. 1995. "Royal Ideology and State Administration in Pharaonic Egypt." Pp. 273–287 in *Civilizations of the Ancient Near East* (vol. 1), ed. J. Sasson. New York: Charles Scribners' Sons.

Lurker, M. 1980. *The Gods and Symbols of Ancient Egypt*. New York: Thames and Hudson.

Maspero, G. 1902. "Sur le Pyramidion d'Amenemhaît III à Dahchour." *Annales du Service des Antiquités de l'Égypte* 3: 206–208.

Millet, N. B. 1990. "The Narmer Macehead and Related Objects." *Journal of the American Research Center in Egypt* 27: 53–59.

———. 1991. "Figures for 'The Narmer Macehead and Related Objects' (from JARCE XXVII)." *Journal of the American Research Center in Egypt* 28: 223–225.

Münster, M. 1968. *Untersuchungen zur Göttin Isis vom Alten Reich bis zum Ende des Neuen Reiches*. Berlin: Verlag Bruno Hessling.

O'Brien, A. A. 1996. "The Serekh as an Aspect of the Iconography of Early Kingship." *Journal of the American Research Center in Egypt* 33: 123–138.

O'Connor, D., and D. P. Silverman, eds. 1995. *Ancient Egyptian Kingship*. Leiden: E. J. Brill.

Otto, E. 1938. "Die Lehre von den beiden Ländern Ägyptens in der ägyptischen Religionsgeschichte." *Studia Aegyptiaca* 1: 10–35.

Pinch, G. 1993. *Votive Offerings to Hathor*. Oxford: Griffith Institute, Ashmolean Museum.

Reisner, G. 1931. *Mycerinus: The Temples of the Third Pyramid at Giza*. Cambridge, MA: Harvard University Press.

Roberts, A. 1997. *Hathor Rising: The Power of the Goddess in Ancient Egypt*. Rochester, VT: Inner Traditions International.

Rössler-Köhler, U. 1983. "Repit." Pp. 236–242 in *Lexikon der Ägyptologie* (vol. 5), ed. W. Helck and W. Westendorf. Wiesbaden: Otto Harrassowitz.

Sethe, K. 1969. *Die altägyptischen Pyramidentexte nach Papierabdrücken und Photographien des Berliner Museums* (vols. 1 and 2). Hildesheim: Georg Olms Verlagsbuchhandlung. [Reprint of 1908 edition.]

Settgast, J. 1963. *Untersuchungen zu altägyptischen Bestattungsdarstellungen*. Glückstadt-Hamburg-New York: Verlag J. J. Augustin.

Silverman, D. P. 1995. "The Nature of Egyptian Kingship." Pp. 49–92 in *Ancient Egyptian Kingship*, ed. D. O'Connor and D. P. Silverman. Leiden: E. J. Brill.

Troy, L. 1986. *Patterns of Queenship in Ancient Egyptian Myth and History*. [Acta Universitatis Upsaliensis BOREAS/Uppsala Studies in Ancient Mediterranean and Near Eastern Civilizations, 14.] Uppsala: Uppsala University.

Wainwright, G. A. 1923. "The Red Crown in Early Prehistoric Times." *Journal of Egyptian Archaeology* 9: 26–33 and pl. XX,3.

Wilkinson, R. H. 1992. *Reading Egyptian Art: A Hieroglyphic Guide to Ancient Egyptian Painting and Sculpture*. London: Thames and Hudson.
Witt, R. E. 1997. *Isis in the Ancient World*. Baltimore & London: Johns Hopkins University Press. Reprint of 1971 *Isis in the Graeco-Roman World* (Ithaca, Cornell).

*Brief Chronology* (*after N. Grimal*, History of Ancient Egypt)

Predynastic: before 3150 BCE
Early Dynastic, Dynasties One and Two: 3150–2700 BCE
Old Kingdom, Dynasties Three–Six: 2700–2200 BCE
First Intermediate Period, Dynasties Seven–Eleven: 2200–2160 BCE
Middle Kingdom, Dynasties Eleven–Fourteen: 2040–1674 BCE
Second Intermediate Period, Dynasties Fifteen–Seventeen: 1674–1553 BCE
New Kingdom, Dynasties Eighteen–Twenty: 1552–1069 BCE
Third Intermediate Period, Dynasties Twenty-one–Twenty-three: 1069–702 BCE
Late Period, Dynasties Twenty-four–Twenty-six: 747–525 BCE
First Persian Period, Dynasty Twenty-seven: 525–404 BCE
Dynasties Twenty-eight–Thirty: 404–343 BCE
Second Persian Period: 434–332 BCE
Greco-Roman Period: 332 BCE–395 CE
Macedonian: 332–304 BCE
Ptolemaic: 304–30 BCE
Roman: 30 BCE–395 CE

14

# Queen Mary and Medieval Christendom

*Laurel G. Broughton*

On June 9, 1311, the people of Siena closed their shops and made holiday. Moving from the workshop of Duccio di Buoninsegna through the streets of the city to the Cathedral of the Assumption, they celebrated the completion of the great altarpiece the Maestà, or Virgin in Majesty. Layered with gold and rich pigments, Duccio's masterpiece portrayed Mary in regal splendor, enthroned with the infant Jesus on her lap and surrounded by saints and angels. The panels placed above the large central image depicted scenes from Mary's last days, her death, assumption, and coronation. The entire community joined the procession, as one unnamed observer reports:

> All the people and in order all the most distinguished were close behind the picture with lighted candles in their hands; and the women and children were following with great devotion; and they all accompanied the picture as far as the Cathedral, going round the Campo in procession, and according to custom, the bells rang in glory and in veneration of such a noble picture as this. . . . And all that day was spent in worship and alms-giving to the poor, praying to the Mother of God, our protectress, to defend us by her infinite mercy from all adversity, and to guard us against the hand of traitors and enemies of Siena. (quoted in Janella 1991, 21)

*Figure 14.1:* Mary, Queen of Heaven *by the Master of the Saint Lucy Legend.* (© *1999 Board of Trustees, National Gallery of Art, Washington.*)

Duccio's masterpiece, which now resides in the Cathedral Museum in Siena, celebrates Mary's regal nature and the episodes in her story that establish this royal state. The front of the altarpiece shows Mary, robed in deep, rich blue, seated on a marble, colorfully inlaid gothic throne. She inclines her head toward the child Jesus who sits in the curve of her left arm. The figure of the Virgin defines the central axis of the painting and dwarfs the images of numerous saints, angels, and Sienese civil officials that flank her throne. The painting clearly indicates that not only is Mary Queen of Heaven she is Queen of Siena. If the viewer had any doubt about Mary's sovereignty, this would have been dispelled by the Coronation of the Virgin that formed the highest pinnacle of the altarpiece.

Sienese devotion to this image did not slacken when the painting came to rest on the cathedral's high altar. Mary had been elected the city's supreme protector in 1260; the cathedral was dedicated to her bodily assumption into heaven at which time Christ crowns her queen, and it provided her with a setting worthy of her regal stature. The Maestà became a cult object: Citizens showed their devotion by nailing rosaries and other devotional items to the faces of Mary and the infant Jesus, causing damage revealed when the painting was restored in the 1950s (Janella 1991, 26).

Siena was not alone in its intense veneration of Mary, the mother of Jesus. Across medieval Europe, cities and towns, secular and monastic foundations, and private individuals displayed their devotion to Mary by dedicating places of worship to her, preserving her relics, and creating liturgies, music, visual images, poems, and stories to celebrate her unique nature. Chartres, in France, claimed to have the very shift Mary wore when she gave birth to Jesus, a relic miraculously saved from fire in 1194 (von Simpson 1962, 160). Marian piety so pervaded medieval English society that the island earned the epithet Our Lady's Dower. In Rome, over forty churches still bear their dedication to the Virgin, including the ancient churches Santa Maria sopra Minerva, Santa Maria in Trastevere, Santa Maria Maggiore, Santa Maria Antiqua, and Santa Maria in Aracoeli. Medieval Christians felt her abiding presence in their daily lives: They found her carved in stone or wood, painted on canvas or fresco walls, enjeweled in stained glass, and illuminated on manuscript pages. Theologians debated her role, choirs sang her praises, and the faithful prayed for her intercession and intervention in their lives. She remains to this day a powerful enigma, unlike any goddess in the Western pantheon: Mary, Queen of Heaven, virgin and mother, mediatrix and miracle worker.

## Mary's Story

For all the fanfare surrounding her, Mary plays a small role in Christian scripture. In the first two chapters of the Gospel of Luke we find several scenes that include the mother of Jesus: the Annunciation (1:26–38), Mary's visit to Elizabeth (1:39–56), the Nativity (2:1–20), as well as the purification of the mother and the presention of the infant at the Temple (2:22–39). Luke also tells of Mary's search for her adolescent son after the Passover celebration in Jerusalem, when he stays behind to dispute with the elders at the Temple (2:41–52). The author of the Gospel of Matthew tells the nativity story in more general terms. This narrative focuses on Joseph, affirming his descent from the Jewish King David and presenting his intention to break off his engagement with Mary when he finds her to be pregnant (1:16–25). The second chapter of Matthew presents episodes in which Mary remains in the background: the adoration of the magi (2:1–12), the flight into Egypt (2:13–15), and the slaughter of the innocents (2:16–18). Mary figures in the miracle at the wedding at Cana in John's Gospel (2:1–12) and he describes Mary standing at the foot of the cross, where Jesus asks her and the beloved disciple to care for each other (19:25–27). In the Acts of the Apostles, Mary is present during Pentecost when the apostles receive the gift of the Holy Spirit (Acts 1:13–2:43). The author of the Gospel of Mark makes a passing reference to Mary (6:3) as does Paul in the Epistle to the Galatians (4:4), but otherwise both writers ignore her.

Because the New Testament does not provide us with Mary's biography, or make any reference to her death, assumption, or coronation, we need to look elsewhere for these aspects of her story. Early Christians clearly felt a need to fill in the gaps left in what now comprise the canonical gospels. Sometime after 150 CE, the *Gospel of James* appeared, detailing the early life of the Virgin, including her conception and birth. This Greek text and a later Latin version, the *Gospel of the Pseudo-Matthew* (ca. ninth century), provide Mary with a life history demonstrating her unique nature, as chosen by God. Although these apocryphal works were not included in the canonical Bible, they became deeply embedded in Marian texts and popular lore.

The *Gospel of James* portrays Mary as special from the moment of her conception. Like Isaac and John the Baptist, she is born to aged, barren parents, Anna and Joachim, who receive the news of her conception from an angel. At the age of six months, Mary walks seven steps, a sacred number associated with the seven heavenly spheres. This prompts her mother to protect her from all common and unclean things. When Mary reaches age three, her parents take her to be raised in the Temple. Her father places her on the third step of the altar and "she danced for joy with her feet and the whole house of Israel loved her" (7.7). In addition to providing new information about Mary's life, the *Gospel of James* takes events known from scripture and tradition and fleshes them out. One such instance is the account of Mary's betrothal: When she turns twelve an angel appears to the high priest as he prays in the temple, telling him to summon all the widowers, each with a rod. A dove flies out of the reluctant Joseph's rod and rests on his head, designating him to be Mary's husband (9.1). The birth of Jesus takes on added detail as well. Salome, a midwife fetched by Joseph, does not believe that Mary could remain a virgin after giving birth. She examines her physically and her hand comes away withered as if from fire, only to be healed when she touches the infant Jesus (20.1–4).

The *Gospel of James* establishes Mary as holy and chosen but does not specifically define her place in the heavenly hierarchy. Another influential apocryphal text, the *Transitus Mariae*, provides details for Mary's death and assumption. This text dates from the fifth century and was ascribed to John the Evangelist. Like the *Gospel of James*, the *Transitus*, which has several variants in languages ranging from Greek to Ethiopian, heavily influenced later characterizations of Mary and her life (Graef 1985, 134). The Eastern church held that Mary in dying fell asleep (hence the tradition called the Dormition of the Virgin), and at that moment the resurrected Christ appeared and carried her soul into heaven. Graef summarizes the more complex interpretation of the Assumption that took hold in the West:

> An angel appears to Mary bringing her a palm and announcing her death. She calls together her friends and tells them about it; then arrives John, later all the other Apostles, including also St. Paul. On the third day before she is to die Mary goes out to pray. On the day of her death, at the third hour, Jesus comes to her; she thanks him and dies, and he give orders to Peter concerning her burial. When the funeral procession is on its way to the tomb the Jews attack it; the priest who tries to touch the bier has his hands cut off and all his companions are blinded. This miracle converts them and all are healed. The Apostles place Mary's body in the tomb; after three days Jesus returns, the angels take up the body and place it under the tree of life in paradise, where it is reunited with her soul. (Graef 1985, 134)

The influence of this narrative can be seen in Duccio's Maestà, which contains several panels devoted to the death of the Virgin. This series begins with the annunciation of Mary's death, a scene similar to the annunciation of Mary's miraculous conception of Christ. Rather than a lily, the angel in this scene carries the palm branch referred to in the *Transitus*. Subsequent panels show the last interview with the apostles and St. John, the death of Mary, and her funeral procession. In the depiction of Mary's death, Christ appears and takes her soul, looking much like a swaddled infant, to heaven. In its original form, the series would have culminated with an assumption panel topped by the coronation of the Virgin, both now missing.[1] Thus Mary's unique nature and her unique relationship to Jesus create for her a unique position in heaven. Not only does her soul attain paradise, but her body as well, because her body is the precious vessel where the incarnation took place. Throughout the scenes depicted on the Maestà Mary's prominence graphically demonstrates her royal position in the minds of medieval Christians.

Like Duccio's altarpiece, the fifteenth-century Assumption Play from the *N-Town Cycle*[2] shows the influence of the *Transitus Mariae* and records a version of the coronation scene now missing from Duccio's painting. In uniting Mary's soul to her body, Jesus says,

> Go then, blessed soul, to that body again.
> Arise now, my dove, my neighbor, and my sweet friend,
> Tabernacle of joy, vessel of life, heavenly temple, to reign.
> You shall have the bliss with me, mother, that has no end.
> For as you were clean in earth of all sin's stain,
> So you shall reign in heaven cleanest of mind. (Spector 1991, 408, ll. 509–514)

As the angels sing "Mary is assumed into heaven," Jesus pronounces:

> You to worship, mother, likes the whole (holy) Trinity.
> Wherefore I crown you here in this kingdom of glory.
> Of all my chosen, thus you shall named be:
> Queen of Heaven and Mother of Mercy. (ll. 523–26)

Elisabeth of Schönau, a twelfth-century Benedictine nun whose brother Ekbert recorded her visionary diary, describes numerous visions of Mary as queen, wearing royal robes and crowns (Clark n.d.). She also recounts a vision of the resurrection of the Virgin's body, which gave added credence to the idea of Mary's body miraculously translated into heaven. This account found its way into many legendaries, including Jacobus de Voragine's *Golden Legend*, the *Speculum Historiale* of Vincent of Beauvais, and the *Speculum Sacerdotale*, where it is wrongly attributed to Elizabeth, mother of John the Baptist. The *Golden Legend* describes Elisabeth's vision:

> She saw, at a great distance, a sepulcher upon which a brilliant light fell. In the sepulcher lay a form that looked like a woman, surrounded by a multitude of angels. Shortly the woman was taken out of the tomb and lifted on high together with her many attendants; and a splendid, glorious man, carrying the banner of the cross in his right hand and accompanied by countless thousands of angels, came from heaven to meet her. Quickly taking her they led her off to heaven amidst a great chorus of song. Not long afterwards Elizabeth asked the angel with whom she frequently talked what the vision had meant. The angel answered: "You were shown how our Lady was assumed into heaven in the flesh as well as in the spirit." (Voragine 1993, 82–83)

In Elisabeth's visions, as well as in other verbal and visual depictions, the Assumption and Mary's regal state are inextricably linked, constructing the belief that Mary corporeally exists in heaven where she reigns as queen.

## Mary, Queen of Heaven

As Queen of Heaven, Mary resembles a number of Near Eastern goddesses who bore that title, including Innana, Ishtar, Astarte, and Aphrodite. Thus Mary's queenship grows out of a pagan influence on early Christianity. But whereas Mary comes to embody characteristics shared with a number of ancient goddesses, she remains human. Indeed, for medieval theologians, this very humanity paradoxically forms the basis for her "divinity," for Mary's status derives from her relationship with Jesus. She gives him his humanity, that unique quality that distinguishes him from other gods, thus enabling the sacrifice that climaxes this incarnational process. As Bernard of Clairvaux points out in his sermons on the Annunciation, she contained God within her body and he was subject to her: "God, I repeat, to whom the angels are subject, he whom the principalities and the powers obey, he was obedient to Mary. . . . God does what a woman says—unheard of humility. A woman outranks God—unparalleled sublimity" (1: 7). The loving bond between mother and son positions her as mediatrix. Some medieval theologians viewed praying to Mary for her intercession as more efficacious than praying directly to Christ. Beyond this, by her willing participation in the incarnation, Mary becomes the prototypical Christian, open to God's presence in the world.

Visual images of regal Mary in Western Christendom antedate texts that refer to her royal stature. The first extant image of the crowned Virgin appears in Santa Maria Antiqua in Rome in the sixth century (Clayton 1990, 146). Clayton, in her study of the Virgin venerated in Anglo-Saxon England, describes an image of her coronation in the tenth-century *Benedictional of St. Aethelwold* (162). By the High Middle Ages, visual depictions of Mary's coronation decorated cathedrals and parish churches as well as illuminated manuscripts. York, a city that retains much of its medieval character, exemplifies the popularity of this image. York Minster, the cathedral church, has preserved in its stained glass five coronations of the Virgin. Around the corner from the Minster, in the Church of Holy Trinity, three separate windows of Mary wearing a crown have been preserved, and over the altar a rare image shows Mary being crowned by members of the Trinity.

In Western Europe, surviving written testimony to Mary as queen lags behind the visual evidence by about 200 years. Ambrose of Autpert (d. 784) writes that "She is raised above the angels and reigns with Christ. It should suffice that she is truly called Queen of Heaven, because she has given birth to the King of Angels." (quoted in Graef 1985, 168). Ambrose's statement is new in Latin Christianity, but long commonplace in the Eastern church. Mary as queen had other early champions as well, including Paul the Deacon, Walafrid Strabo, Pasachius Radbert, Hroswitha of Gandersheim, Fulbert of Chartres, Peter Damian, and Anselm of Canterbury (Graef 1985, 142–143).

However, Queen Mary really comes into her own during the twelfth century largely through the writings of Bernard of Clairvaux, as we have already seen, and Bonaventure, who states:

> Therefore the Creator of all things reposed in the tabernacle of the virginal womb, for there he made himself a nuptial chamber, so that he might become our brother; he prepared a royal throne so that he should become our Ruler; he assumed priestly vestments so that he should be our High Priest. By reason of the nuptial the Virgin Mary is the Mother of God; because of the royal throne she is the Queen of Heaven; because of the priestly vestments she is the advocate of the human race. (Quoted in Graef 1985, 286–287)

Mary's royal place in heaven rests on two major, related concepts: her unique maternal relationship with Christ the savior and her bodily assumption into heaven, where she is crowned by Christ himself. However, medieval theologians generally concur that Mary's power extends beyond heaven to both earth and hell. As Fulbert of Chartres asserts, "The mother of the Lord rules everywhere in great magnificence, that she can easily send the holy angels to minister to us and cancel the pacts of hell according to her pleasure" (quoted in Graef 1985, 205).

The mingling of these concepts can be seen in the mosaics of Santa Maria Trastevere in Rome, the first church in that city dedicated to the Virgin. Along the base of the apse are six thirteenth-century mosaics by Cavallini of scenes from the life of the Virgin. In the half-dome of the apse a mosaic depicts the Virgin in

Triumph dating from 1140. In this image, Christ and the Virgin sit side by side on an elaborately decorated throne. He embraces her with his right hand, while in his left he displays an open book depicting the Latin text, "Veni, electa mea, ponam in te tronam meam" (Come my chosen one, I shall place thee on my throne, Ps. 45) (Warner 1983, 122).[3] The Virgin herself wears elaborately decorated clothing and a crown. She holds an unrolled scroll on which appears the Latin text, "Laeva eius sub capite meo et dextera illius aplexabitur me" (His left hand is under my head and his right hand embraces me, Cant 2.6). With her left hand, positioned at the top of the scroll, she makes the sign of blessing, her index and middle fingers extended. As Penny Schine Gold (1985, 51–53) points out in her discussion of similar images found carved in French churches, this image is not a coronation of the Virgin. It goes beyond the act of crowning to show Christ and Mary ruling together as equals.

A similar configuration appears in a stained glass coronation of the Virgin in the north choir aisle of York Minster. This panel, dating from the mid-fourteenth century, shows Mary and Christ seated together as they are in the Santa Maria Trastevere mosaic. However, instead of holding a book, Christ holds an orb topped by a cross in his left hand, while he raises his right in blessing. Mary holds nothing; rather she presses her hands together as a gesture of prayer.

Bernard's devotion to the Virgin also inspired Dante's apprehension of the Queen of Heaven and the beatific vision at the end of his *Divine Comedy*. In canto XXXI, the venerable saint replaces Beatrice as the narrator's guide, telling him:

> In order that thou mayst complete thy journey to the very end, for which prayer and holy love have sent me, fly with thine eyes through this garden, for seeing it will prepare thy sight to mount higher through the divine radiance; and the Queen of Heaven, for whom I am all on fire with love, will grant us every grace, since I am her faithful Bernard. (Sinclair 1939, 451)

The imagery of this and the following cantos leaves no doubt in the reader's mind as to the regal nature of Mary perceived by the narrator. She is the "Queen to whom this realm is subject and devoted," "the Lady of Heaven," and the one who enables the narrator to see Christ himself, for as St. Bernard tells him, "Look now on the face that most resembles Christ, for only its brightness can fit thee to see Christ" (Sinclair 1939, 467).

Dante is just one of many great poets to celebrate Mary as queen. Chaucer, in the prologue to "The Prioress's Tale," his rendering of a Mary miracle, describes her as a "blissful Queen." In "An ABC," he calls her "Queen of comfort" and defines her heavenly role:

> He hath thee maked vicaire and maistresse
> Of al this world, and eek governouresse
> Of hevene, and he represseth his justise
> After thi wil; and therfore in witnesse
> He hath thee corowned in so rial wise. (cited in Benson et al. 1987, 639)

Chaucer's contemporary, the Pearl Poet, describes Mary as the "Queen of courtesy" in the dream vision *Pearl*. In this poem the narrator dreams of finding his lost pearl, his dead three-year-old daughter. He sees in the dream the celestial city and his daughter, the Pearl Maiden, explains Mary's unique position there:

> That Queen has all high Heaven's space
> And all dim Earth and Hell in her sway,
> Yet none will she drive from her heritage,
> For she is the Queen of Courtesy.
> . . . . . . . . . . . . .
> But my Lady from whose womb Christ sprung
> Still reigns supreme in royalty,
> And none would ask that throne pulled down,
> For she is the Queen of Courtesy. (Gardner 1965, 113)

Like the narrator of *The Divine Comedy*, the dreamer in *Pearl* receives a vision of Mary in her proper place in heaven that increases his understanding of her regal splendor. As a result, the reader's understanding increases as well, for we learn that all who dwell in heaven are queens and kings.

## Mary as Sovereign

Sometime in the early 1400s, Jan van Eyck painted the Virgin standing in a church, the infant Jesus in her arms. She wears a red dress with a jeweled neckline and gold trim at the hem. Gold edges her cloak, made of the precious color blue. On her head sits a crown, almost as tall as the length of her face, its elaborate filigree studded with large gemstones.[4] In this, as in numerous other visual and verbal descriptions of Mary, she wears the clothes of a queen, but does this make Mary sovereign? Christiano Grottinelli (1987, 8:313ff.) defines the king as the symbolic center around which the state is organized. He enumerates several expressions of the king's role: (1) the monarch and his surroundings represent the cosmos as a whole; (2) the monarch redistributes the wealth of the kingdom, particularly to the poor and needy; (3) the monarch may be a sacrificial victim; (4) the monarch acts as a military leader; and (5) the monarch serves as mediator amongst the three estates (priestly, military, and laboring) as well as between his society and the superhuman powers. One could argue that all of these attributes apply to the figure of Mary as she is constructed in literature, music, and the visual arts during the Middle Ages.

### *Mary and the Cosmos*

*Ave maris stella*, one of oldest known hymns to the Virgin, praises Mary as the Star of the Sea, an epithet that she shares with Venus, Astarte, and other regal predecessors. Another hymn, *Audi cealum*, describes her "as beautiful as the moon, choice as the sun." In the Middle Ages, Mary was also often associated with the woman of the Apocalypse, found in Revelation 12: "And there appeared a great wonder in heaven, a woman clothed with the sun, and the moon under her feet and upon her head a crown of twelve stars" (Rev. 12:1). In her association with the woman clothed with the sun as well as the conventional forms of praise allying her with sun, moon, and stars, Mary reflects the cosmos.

### *Mary as Giver of Goods*

In medieval miracle tales, Mary often provides worldly goods for those in need. In the miracle of "Barns filled at Jerusalem," Mary fills a monastery's barns with grain during a time of famine. In "Mary comes to the Devil instead of the Victim," she provides material wealth to a man who falls into poverty and, in desperation, sells his wife to the Devil to regain his goods. Similarly, in "Christ denied but not the Virgin," Mary rewards a wastrel who has squandered his inheritance but still refuses to deny Mary and thereby obtain wealth from the Devil. Instead of punishing him, Mary provides the young man with a rich bride whose father makes him his heir.

### *Mary as Sacrificial Victim*

The Virgin becomes a sacrificial victim in that she experiences the pain of her son's crucifixion. This motif first appears in the Gospel of Luke, which tells of the infant Jesus's ritual presentation at the Temple. An old man, Simeon, recognizes Jesus as the Messiah and predicts his "rejection." At the same time, Simeon tells Mary, "A sword shall pierce through thine own soul also" (Luke 2:25–35). Many theologians interpreted this as a foreshadowing of the Crucifixion. In depictions of the Crucifixion, Mary's body often mirrors that of her dying son. In paintings showing Christ removed from the cross, Mary frequently swoons and appears herself to have died. In recounting her vision of the Crucifixion, Margery Kempe describes Mary's extreme suffering (Windeatt 1985, 235–240). The Middle English lyric "Stand well, mother, under rood," a dialogue between the Virgin and her dying son, also gives voice to Mary's suffering during Christ's passion.[5]

### *Mary as Military Leader*

Other medieval tales describe Mary's military exploits. In "Julian the Apostate," she revives the dead warrior Mercurius, draws him from his tomb, and sends him to defeat and kill the apostate emperor Julian on the battlefield. "The Siege of Chartres" is won when the bishop displays Mary's shift, which blinds the enemy. The Knight of Kirkby stops by a chapel of Our Lady to hear her mass and misses his tournament, only to discover that the Virgin has fought in his place and defeated all who challenged her.

### *Mary as Mediator*

The devotional rites of city governments, such as those of Siena and Chartres, bear witness to Mary's political involvement. However, the real nexus of her power lies in her role as mediator between God and humans. In manifesting this role, she engages many of the other attributes, as can be seen by examining the concept of Mary Mediatrix.

The hymn *Salve regina* intertwines many of these aspects of medieval Marian piety, including Mary as the mediator who makes Jesus visible, Mary as advocate, and the omnipresent theme of Mary as Queen of Heaven:

> Hail, O Queen, mother of mercy,
> our life, sweetness and hope, hail.
> To thee do we cry, exiles, children of Eve.
> To thee do we sigh, mourning and weeping
> in this vale of tears.
> Therefore, O thou our advocate,
> turn thy merciful eyes towards us.
> And, after this our exile, show to us
> The blessed fruit of thy womb, Jesus.
> O merciful, O kind, O sweet virgin Mary. (Harper 1991, 275)

Written probably in the late eleventh or early twelfth century, *Salve regina* became part of Benedictine, Cistercian, and Dominican liturgical practice (Graef 1985, 229). Not only does it figure in the liturgy, it becomes the pivotal point of several miracles of the Virgin. One legend records the tradition that St. Bernard composed *Salve regina*. According to this tradition, two young monks drown without having made confession. St. Bernard in a dream hears them singing *Salve regina* as they climb up a steep hill toward the virgin (Whiteford 1990, 64). In this miracle, Bernard concludes the drowned monks should be buried in consecrated ground and sets down the hymn he remembers from his dream. One version of this tale is itself composed in verse and intended to be sung.[6] Another legend tells of a miraculous globe of fire that rests on the head of each friar as a community of Dominicans sings *Salve regina* at Compline. In other miracles, reciting *Salve regina* calms storms, puts devils to flight, and, in one instance, occasions the safe delivery of a child.

The rich interplay of Marian attributes that contribute to her role as mediatrix can be seen by examining the parts Mary plays in many of the miracles told to underscore the special aspects of her nature. Over 1,000 instances of these miracles remain extant. They were used as exempla in sermons or to encourage certain liturgical observances. Hundreds made their way into the vernacular languages and were told as stories by writers such as Chaucer and Lydgate.

Of these, one of the oldest is "Theophilus," the story of a man who sells his soul to the Devil to regain his position in the church. This story appears as early as the sixth century (Ward 1893, 2: 595) and reappears in at least fifty manuscripts through the fifteenth century. In most versions of this tale, Theophilus, a well-respected archdeacon, refuses the role of bishop when it is offered to him. The new bishop, resenting Theophilus's popularity, demotes him. Grieved by the loss of his position, Theophilus signs a pact with the Devil in which he renounces his belief in Christ; however, he soon repents and prostrates himself before an image of the Virgin, pleading with her to intecede with Christ on his behalf. Although she lets him know in no uncertain terms that her son is very angry with him, Mary manages to obtain mercy for Theophilus. In addition, she retrieves the contract he's signed with the Devil and leaves it on his pillow (Boyd 1964, 68–87). In this tale, Mary establishes herself as Queen of Hell as well as Queen of Heaven by beating Satan at his own game.

Mary's sovereign nature is overtly displayed in other miracles as well. She functions not only as mediator but as advocate, arguing for those souls she wishes to save from the pains of hell. These are not the souls of the virtuous only. Mary's true sovereignty lies in her attention to those for whom no one else cares. In the *Speculum Sacerdotale* version of "The Drowned Sacristan," she employs her significant linguistic and reasoning ability against the Devil, who claims the soul of a monk drowned on his way home from a night with his mistress. Mary brings Satan, his minions, and the soul before Christ in judgment. The devils begin immediately to accuse the wretch: "He has remained in our service of unchastity and all other vices. He has ever obeyed us and our service until he gave up his spirit." Then says Mary, "False witness rises and shows their lying. If he gave up the ghost in your service as you say, let his lips be opened that we may see what his tongue spoke last upon the point of his death." They open his mouth and find that in his dying he was saying "Ave Maria." She says, "What say you now, Devil? Your stillness shows that you are overcome. Why have you been swollen with pride with such a foul cruelty against this creature? Your own lying and deceit have confounded you" (*Speculum Sacerdotale* 42–45).

Mary displays her courtroom skills in "The Pilgrim of St. James" as well, acting as advocate in some versions, judge in others. The end result in all versions remains the same: The pilgrim, guilty of sinning with a woman before beginning his pilgrimage and persuaded by the Devil in the guise of St. James to castrate himself and then to commit suicide, receives his life back in order that he might atone for his sins and eventually enter into paradise.

In other miracles, the tellers depict Mary as a beautiful queen, surrounded by a retinue of angels and virgin martyrs. One of these, "Purification," presents a dream vision describing Mary and her retinue in much the same way as she appears in both *The Divine Comedy* and *Pearl*. In this miracle, a woman misses mass on the feast of the Purification and falls asleep in her chapel. In her dream she finds herself in another fair church:

> And there she beheld a great company of virgins coming into the church, before whom the fairest of them all was crowned with a diadem. And when they were come, they sat down each one in order. . . . She saw by the altar two candle bearers, a subdeacon and a deacon and a priest, clothed in precious vestments

going to the altar as they would to do mass. And it seemed to this woman that . . . the priest was Christ. (*Speculum Sacerdotale* 28)

Everyone in the congregation receives a candle, including the woman. As part of the feast's ritual, each person is expected to present his or her candle during the offertory, but the dreaming woman refuses to part with hers, even though "the forsaid queen of heaven sent her word by her messenger that she did rudely and ignorantly that she came not to the offering" (28). The woman responds that she would keep her candle as an object of devotion, but "the lady of heaven had her messenger go and pray her to offer her candle or else take it out of her hands violently" (28). The woman scuffles with the angel and the candle breaks in two as she wakes to find the remnant in her hand.

## Celebrating Queen Mary

No queen would be worth her crown without rites and rituals to celebrate her regal nature. Candlemas, or the Feast of the Purification, was just one of the many opportunities in the daily fabric of their lives medieval Christians had to show their devotion to Mary. These occurred not only in the unique, local festivals like the Maestà procession in Siena but in daily and weekly observances fostered by the church. Although the feast of the Coronation of the Virgin was not instituted until 1950, the daily offices of the Virgin; Lady Masses, often celebrated on Saturday, which was held sacred to Mary; and the feasts commemorating the major events in her life—all honor Mary as Queen of Heaven. These feasts, still part of the liturgical calendar, include the Conception of the Virgin, December 8; the Purification, February 2; the Annunciation, March 25; the Assumption, August 15; and Mary's Nativity, September 8. The propers for most of these feasts specifically refer to Mary as Queen and underscore the qualities that contribute to her sovereignty. For example, the sequence hymn for the Feast of the Purification praises Mary as:

> Purest of Virgins, thou alone divine
> Queen of the world; salvation's cause thou art,
> The gate of light and heaven, full of grace. (*Sarum Missal* 348)

Three sequences for the Feast of the Visitation refer to Mary's royal state, including one that mentions the miracle of Theophilus:

> By a miracle new,
> Bread and Shepherd, were born
> of thee, rose without thorn,
> Of all virgins the Queen.
> Of righteousness thou art the city,
> Thou art the Mother, too, of pity:

Theophilus thou didst reclaim
Out of the pit of guilt and shame. (*Sarum Missal* 391)

One of the sequences for the Feast of the Assumption mingles her regal state with her cosmological significance:

Pride of the world, Virgin, thou Queen of Heaven!
Exalted as the sun, fair as the moon,
Behold, how all look up to thee with love. (*Sarum Missal* 430)

Clerics and laypersons alike observed the Hours of the Virgin and the Little Office of the Virgin. The number of surviving illuminated manuscripts of Books of Hours attests to the popularity of this practice, which could be undertaken by anyone without the help of a priest (Harper 1991, 134–136). The Hours of the Virgin contain prayers and responses for all the daily hours: Matins, Lauds, Prime, Terce, Sext, None, Vespers, Compline. Although many of the liturgical references would have been understood only by those educated in Latin, in England many hymns and the daily office had been translated into the vernacular by the fifteenth century.

*The Myroure of Oure Ladye*, which explains the liturgical practices of the Brigittine convent of Syon, just outside of London, sums up the late medieval view of Mary as queen of heaven, listing six "great excellences of our lady." The first is the great joy she gives the blessed Trinity, more than that of all other creatures. The second is the worship given to her by the court of heaven. The third is that she is the spouse of the father of heaven, and fourth, mother of the second person of the Trinity. Fifth, God ordained her without beginning to be Queen of Heaven, and sixth, he ordained her to be Lady over all he made (Blunt 1975, 91–93).

## Summary

From the simple maid of Nazareth found in the gospels to Queen of Heaven, Earth, and Hell, Mary's evolution as a sovereign in Western Christianity rendered her a potent cultural force pervading almost every aspect of medieval culture. Through ritual and celebration, songs of praise, miracle stories, and visual images, Christians expressed their veneration for Mary as Queen, acknowledging her political, military, and salvatory strengths. But of all Mary's attributes, the most potent and revered was that of mediator, for Mary Queen of Heaven, was also Mary, Mother of Mercy, who was willing to intercede for king and commoner, saint and sinner, indeed for all "exiled children of Eve," as the hymn *Salve regina* reminds us.

### NOTES

1. Some scholars believe the Coronation in the Szépmüveszéti Muzeum, Budapest, to be that missing from the Maestà. (See Janella 1991, 73.)

2. The *N-Town Cycle* takes its name from various references in the text to "N-town" (see line 527 of the Proclamation for an example). This allowed presenters to fill in the blank with the name of the town in which the plays were being performed. For many years this cycle was mistakenly referred to as *Ludus Coventriae*, and often can be found under this title in bibliographies and other research tools.
3. Warner points out that this verse was used as an antiphon for the Feast of the Assumption in the Liber Pontificalis, attributed to Gregory the Great.
4. Jan van Eyck, *Madonna in a Church*. Berlin, Staatliche Museen Preussicher Kulturbesitz.
5. This lyric appears in many anthologies of Middle English verse (e.g., Davies 1964, 86–89). Anonymous Four have recorded it on *The Lily and the Lamb* (Harmonia Mundi, HMU 907125).
6. The story of the *Salve regina* has been recorded by Gothic Voices, Hyperion CDA66857.

REFERENCES

Benson, Larry, et al., ed. 1987. "An ABC." Pp. 140–144 in *The Riverside Chaucer* (3rd ed.). Boston: Houghton Mifflin.

Bernard of Claivaux. 1993. *Homilies in Praise of the Virgin Mary*. Kalamazoo, MI: Cistercian Publications.

Blunt, John Henry, ed. 1975. *The Myroure of Oure Ladye* [Early English Text Society, Extra Series 19]. Milkwood, NY: Kraus Reprint. Reprinted, 1981.

Boyd, Beverly, ed. 1964. *Middle English Miracles of the Virgin*. San Marino, CA: Huntington Library.

Clark, Anne L., trans. n.d. *The Complete Works of Elisabeth of Schönau*. New York: Paulist Press (forthcoming).

Clayton, Mary. 1990. *The Cult of the Virgin in Anglo-Saxon England*. Cambridge: Cambridge University Press.

Davies, R. T., ed. 1964. *Medieval English Lyrics*. Chicago: Northwestern University Press.

Gardner, John, ed. 1965. *Pearl*. Chicago: Chicago University Press.

Gold, Penny Schine. 1985. *The Lady and the Virgin*. Chicago: Chicago University Press.

Graef, Hilda. 1985. *Mary: A History of Doctrine and Devotion*. London: Sheed and Ward.

Grotinelli, Christiano. 1987. "Kingship: An Overview." Pp. 313–317 in *The Encyclopedia of Religion* (vol. 8), ed. Mircea Eliade. New York: Macmillan.

Harper, John. 1991. *The Forms and Orders of Western Liturgy from the Tenth to the Eighteenth Century*. New York: Oxford University Press.

Janella, Cecila. 1991. *Duccio di Buoninsegna*. London: Scala.

Pelikan, Jaroslav. 1996. *Mary through the Centuries*. New Haven: Yale University Press.

*Sarum Missal*. 1868. London: Church Press Company.

Sinclair, John. 1939. *Dante's Paradiso*. New York: Oxford University Press. Reprinted, 1972.

*Speculum Sacerdotale*. 1936. Ed. Edward Weatherly. [Early English Text Society Original Series 200]. London: Oxford University Press.

Spector, Stephen. 1991. *The N-Town Play* [Early English Text Society, Supplemental Series 11]. Oxford: Oxford University Press.

von Simpson, Otto. 1962. *The Gothic Cathedral* (rev. ed.). New York: Harper and Row.

Voragine, Jacobus de. 1993. *The Golden Legend*, ed. William Granger Ryan. Princeton, NJ: Princeton University Press.

Ward, H. L. D. 1893. "Miracles of the Virgin." *Catalogue of Romances in the Department of Manuscripts in the British Museum* (2 vols.). London: British Museum.

Warner, Marina. 1983. *Alone of All Her Sex*. New York: Vintage.

Whiteford, Peter. 1990. *The Myracles of Oure Lady, edited from Wynken de Worde's Edition*. Heidelberg: Carl Winter Universitätsverlag.

Windeatt, B. A. trans. 1985. *The Book of Margery Kempe*. New York: Penguin Books.

# Reflections

The essays in this volume increase our knowledge of individual goddesses of sovereignty, their histories, and their relationships with historical rulers. Each goddess is a distinct figure. We read of the ambitious young queen Minatci, who gives battle with the gods. We learn of the wise Cihuacoatl, military strategist and inside ruler. Princess Wen Cheng's long journey to a new home in Tibet contrasts with Mazu's simple life among the fisherfolk of southern China.

Although it is important to keep in mind the uniqueness of each goddess and the differences in their historical situations, four themes do emerge. First, most of these goddesses are related to a ruler through some form of kinship: They are most likely to be the king's ancestor, mother, or beloved. This kinship is expressed in the goddess's loving protection of the ruler and his realm: Health, prosperity, long life, and security from enemies are her blessings. Second, by cultivating moral and ritual propriety, the ruler himself contributes to preserving this relationship. Because he represents the divine order on earth, his own life must share in the integrity of that order. Indeed, often a goddess seeks out one who is thus suited to be king and grants him the power to rule; at the same time, she may withdraw that power if he fails to live up to the demands of his role.

Third, the histories of these deities demonstrates the effect of political change on religious values. When a society comes under foreign domination, its sovereign goddess is reinterpreted by the new rulers: Either she is rendered powerless through demonization or trivialization or she is incorporated into the religious worldview of the conquerors. Finally, in some societies the goddess of sovereignty may expand her support to include others besides the king. A goddess who offers a man eternal life along with kingship may become a guide to immortality for her devotees more generally.

Although these four themes appear here and there in all the essays, we have used them as organizational tools, assigning to each category goddesses who illustrate the theme in an interesting way. We conclude with some reflections on these themes.

## Love and War: Foundations of Sovereignty

Both love and war are foundations of sovereignty, and goddesses of sovereignty can be lovers and warriors. Military strength is an essential ingredient in sovereignty. A defenseless country loses its independence and becomes absorbed into another realm. It is the warrior who expands and protects the boundaries of the kingdom. The role of love in establishing and supporting the kingdom is less obvious. But the histories of these goddesses suggests that it is love that binds together the divine and human realms.

Aphrodite is a good example of a goddess who helps the sovereign determine and safeguard the boundaries of his realm. Again and again she appears as a warrior in the dreams of the Roman rulers. Dreams in which, wearing armor and bearing arms, she actively led the army into battle were interpreted as omens of victory. Aphrodite's Roman career really began, in a sense, after Hannibal and his army defeated the Romans at Lake Trasimene. A state ceremony was enacted to appeal to the twelve most powerful Roman gods for help. On this occasion, Aphrodite, called Venus by the Romans, was included for the first time in this group of guardian deities. Pompey called her Venus Victrix and attributed to her his success in war. Having experienced her help in visions and actual victory, Sulla sent a golden crown and a golden ax to Aphrodite in her city of Aphrodisias. The warrior goddess appeared also to Julius Caesar in his dreams, inspiring him to conquer Gaul.

Minatci too is a warrior. As the young ruler of the Pandya dynasty, she leads her cavalry in a war of expansion. A savage fighter in hand-to-hand combat, she attacks even the gods, sending fear into the heart of the mighty Indra, who flees without a fight. Siva, alone, is able to stop her: As soon as she sees him, Minatci falls in love. The bloodthirsty warrior turns into a bashful, gentle maiden.

Other goddesses of sovereignty are warriors: Cihuacoatl, in her form as Eagle Woman, bore the eagle plumes associated with Mixcoatl, a great warrior. Eagle plumes decorated her shield, and she carried a weapon-like weaving batten. Known for her wise counsel in times of war, Cihuacoatl was a skilled strategist willing to protect individual soldiers on the battlefield. The Chinese goddess

Mazu began her career rescuing seamen in distress, but eventually she became an imperial goddess when the rulers of China experienced her aid in their military endeavors.

Some goddesses of sovereignty lend the ruler their supernatural, or magical, powers for protection in battle. For example, the British queen Boudica invoked the aid of Andraste as she was about to wage war against the Romans. She celebrated her victory by sacrificing the prisoners to the goddess in a sacred grove.

The talisman is a symbolic object that magically protects its bearer. For example, medieval Christian knights often decorated the inside of their shields with the image of the Virgin Mary to secure her protection. In China, the talisman worn by the Yellow Emperor was a gift of the Queen Mother of the West. Three inches wide and a foot long, it was the color of blue jade, with blood-like spots of cinnabar forming a pattern on it. The talisman bore the following inscription:

> Grand Unity is located on the front;
> Heavenly Unity is located on the back.
> He who obtains this will excel;
> When he attacks he will overcome. (Cahill, in this volume, 202)

In addition, the Queen Mother of the West recruited the Mysterious Woman of the Nine Heavens, a goddess of war and sexuality, to teach the Yellow Emperor more about his role as emperor.

Like the Chinese goddess Mysterious Woman of the Nine Heavens, some goddesses are both lovers and warriors. Inanna is a good example; she appears in Sumerian art and myth as a warrior who attacks Mount Ebeh with her spear, boomerang, and battle-ax, setting fire to his forests. At the same time, many of her hymns celebrate her erotic love making with Dumuzi and the ritual of sacred marriage with the king.

Erotic love between the goddess of sovereignty and the king is a motif also in Celtic tradition. The king, by virtue of his *fir flaitheman* ("the truth of the ruler"), serves and protects the kingdom. The presence of these qualities in a man attracts the goddess to him. Often she appears as an old hag, reflecting the sad state of the realm bereft of a proper ruler. The old woman repels all except the one born to be king, who kisses her or lies with her, transforming her into a beautiful young maiden, who grants him and his descendants sovereignty. The accession of a new Celtic ruler was represented as a wedding feast uniting the king and the local goddess of sovereignty: In the kingdom of Tara, for example, the goddess Medb partnered nine kings.

At the heart of the partnership between the goddess and the ruler is a love that is expressed in the gift of majesty, which establishes the king as mediator between the gods and the kingdom. The love that binds them can be of many kinds: The goddess can be the king's wife or consort; she can be his mother, grandmother, or ancestor; or she can be his beloved teacher.

Ancient Egyptian goddesses of sovereignty were often mothers of the king. The Vulture Goddess was called Nekhbet, the hieroglyph for "mother." Nekhbet nursed the king and offered him maternal protection. She acted as a midwife, especially as he was reborn into the realm of the gods. Nut, a sky goddess, was mother of numerous deities, including Osiris and Horus, the dead king and his living counterpart. The Pyramid Texts describe Isis and Nephthys as two sisters of Osiris and mothers of the pharaoh. It is their job to assist him after death as he is reborn an immortal.

Other goddesses of sovereignty are called mother, even when they do not give birth to the king. The Nahua goddess Cihuacoatl was known as Tonan ("Our Mother"). Myths relate how together with the god Quetzalcoatl she created humankind. Cihuacoatl formed the people out of ground bones fertilized by the blood of the god. Likewise, the Chinese nickname *Mazu* means Granny ("maternal grandmother"), but according to legend, this goddess died a young maid without ever bearing children. Nor is there evidence that Minatci, the Mother with Beautiful Fish Eyes, had any children. Her title may be a term of respect, or it may convey a sense that she was an ancestor of the Pandya rulers. Whether or not the Queen Mother of the West originated as an ancestral deity, her name suggests the wisdom and strength of an older woman, one dedicated to the well-being of others.

Finally, although love is most often associated with kinship, other forms of association can manifest this emotional bond. Sometimes a tradition of love exists between teacher and disciple. This is especially apparent in the stories about Xiwangmu and the emperors of China. A meeting with the goddess was considered a sign of the ruler's worthiness. Cahill calls her a "king-making" divinity: She might bestow symbols of imperial legitimacy, maps, calendars, and other magical gifts. She would also try to teach the emperor the religious duties and virtues that are essential to one who is Son of Heaven.

The goddess of sovereignty supports and protects the king and his realm, but nowhere does she act alone. Each of these goddesses belongs to a multitheistic tradition. Thus, her relationship with the ruler brings him into connection with all the deities and the cosmic order to which they belong. The goddess represents the deities, whereas the ruler represents his realm. Their personal bond thus unites the human and the divine, giving the human community an ongoing, dynamic connection to the powers that support a vital and meaningful life.

## Power Bestowed and Power Withdrawn: The Goddess Who Gives and Takes Back Sovereign Power

The theme of power bestowed or withdrawn by a goddess occurs in such disparate places as Ireland, India, Nigeria, and Japan. A goddess usually reveals her power through a ruler who has demonstrated excellence in the realm of moral and ritual actions. The notion of the king's eminence is found in the following stories about the origin of kingship.

In both Hindu and Buddhist texts, we find similar stories about the first king. The great Indian epic known as the *Mahābhārata* relates that originally no king was needed because "all people protected one another by means of righteous conduct" (12.59.5, 13–30, 93–99). However, slowly but progressively the people were overpowered by ignorance, greed, desire, and a lack of correct discrimination. When this occurred, spiritual knowledge perished along with righteous conduct. Because people could no longer protect themselves, the great Hindu god Vishnu was asked to select a person "worthy of the highest eminence" to be their ruler. Vishnu himself brought forth the first king, an illustrious mind-born son called Virajas.

A Buddhist tale found in the *Long Discourses of the Buddha* (*Digha Nikaya* iii 85–92) describes the gradual degeneration of this evolutionary period, or aeon. Initially beings were independent and emanated their own radiance. Made of mind, they had no need for food. However, as these beings slowly degenerated and became dependent on external light and nourishment, they gradually developed into men and women. Greedy for food, they resorted to hoarding, stealing, and violence. To counteract this growing violence and to protect them in the future, the people selected a king, who became known as the great chosen one (*mahasammata*).

In both accounts, the king's role is to live and act virtuously so as to protect people from fear and anxiety. Furthermore, the eminence of the king refers to his greatness in moral terms, both in his personal life and in governing the kingdom. Because both Hinduism and Buddhism began in India, one would expect a common standard for the king. In fact, however, Indian tradition includes two groups of texts that outline the criteria of royalty. The earlier and more idealistic are the royal *Dharmasastras* (texts about the king's duties), which insist that the king's actions must be moral in respect both to their ends and the means to achieve those ends. In contrast, the later and more pragmatic *Arthasastras* (from the early common era) emphasize the attainment of virtuous goals, achieved by any means. Most of the essays in this collection point to a view of kingship that is closer to the older, more idealistic view found in India.

For example, in ancient Celtic tradition, the ruler had to possess royal qualities and his rule depended on his moral behavior. A king did not inherit the kingdom from his father or ancestor; a goddess gave it to him. If he acted improperly after ascending the throne, he jeopardized his reign. As Mac Cana (in this volume) states, a good king secures peace and prosperity for his kingdom, but if "the king is blemished in his person or conduct, the results are correspondingly disastrous" (92). Further, in the Celtic tradition, the goddess of sovereignty was identified with the land; if the land failed to produce a good harvest, the ruler was blamed, because this meant that the goddess had withdrawn her blessings.

A similar notion is found in ancient India. The king's marriage with Sri-Laksmi was essential for the kingdom to prosper. In addition, the king was obligated to live according to prescribed duties, rather than personal whim. If disaster occurred, the king was blamed, because it was a sign that "he had failed in maintaining the blessing of Sri-Laksmi" (Bailly, in this volume, 137). Whenever Sri-Laksmi abandoned a king, the results were the dissolution of the kingdom and a return to political chaos. However, when the king performed the appropriate rituals and lived a virtuous life, not only would the goddess grant the realm prosperity, she would increase it.

In ancient Ireland and India the morality of the ruler was manifest in a long and prosperous reign. In Nigeria and Japan, on the other hand, the emphasis is less on the personal morality of the ruler and more on his ritual behavior. In these traditions, the ruler happens to be a distant relative of the original ancestor, the goddess of sovereignty, whereas in India and in Ireland the king was not a direct descendent of the goddess.

In Nigeria, where many Yoruba goddesses have a direct connection to kingship, a consistent theme emerges: the importance of proper ritual performance in honor of the ancestral goddess at her annual festival. During the festival, the king invokes the deity by offering her sacrifices and by praising her many blessings and her protection of the kingdom. Each goddess, including Osun, Aje, and Orosun, when properly invoked and worshipped, grants her people wealth, longevity, and healthy children. Further, the performance of this annual rite celebrating the goddess renews the king's authority. In the festival of Orosun, she blesses and thereby reinvigorates the king's most powerful symbol of kingship, his sacred *àṣẹ*. If this is not done, "the king's command and authority will come to naught" (Olúpọ̀nà, in this volume, 127). In the Nigerian view, the prosperity and peace of the realm depends on the king's ability to perform rituals of sovereignty correctly.

We find a similar pattern at work in Japan. Originally, the Japanese adopted the idea of having an emperor from the Chinese. However, they do not share the Chinese belief in the Mandate of Heaven, whereby the emperor can lose his right to rule if he fails in the cultivation of virtue. One does not find the Great Goddess Amaterasu withdrawing her favor from the emperor, her descendant. The emphasis is less on the moral standards of the ruler, and more on his performance of the proper rituals. Throughout the centuries, the Japanese have relied on the kinship between the ruler and Amaterasu, believing that all emperors and empresses belong to a "single and unbroken" line of descent from the Great Goddess. In addition, through the emperor Amaterasu becomes the ancestor of all Japanese.

The four essays included in this section consistently stress the two-sided relationship between the goddess of sovereignty and the living ruler. Because the king or emperor is the intermediary connecting the deities and the realm, he must act in ways that meet the needs of the people rather than out of self-serving motives. The two avenues of behavior for the ruler are moral actions and ritual acts. In India and among the ancient Celts the stress lay on the practice of virtue, whereas in Nigeria and Japan the focus is on ritual correctness. Still, all four traditions demonstrate the necessity of showing respect to the goddess in order to receive her blessings for the prosperity of the kingdom.

## Traditions in Collision: Political Change and Perspectives on Sovereignty

Every culture has a worldview that includes certain beliefs, values, customs, and behaviors. If the people of a culture do not encounter people of another culture, they may be unaware of the specific beliefs and values embedded in their worldview. Although variations of these beliefs exist within a particular culture, these are but degrees of difference. People of the same culture unconsciously reinforce the prevailing values and beliefs. It is as if each person is a mirror that reflects the same or a very similar image. Only when people encounter another culture do they realize what values they consider inviolable. This becomes most apparent when others profane one's deepest felt views. The mirror no longer reflects the same image but either distorts or destroys it. Frequently, when traditions are in collision there is violence, trauma, and the uprooting of the conquered. Occasionally, the dominant culture tries to adopt the values of the conquered in order to reduce the degree of confrontation.

The essays in this section describe societies in which violent collisions of traditions prevail. For example, our knowledge of the Celtic Morgan le Fay and the Nahua Cihuacoatl depends on Christian writers, who are interpreting indigenous traditions as inferior and, in many instances, demonic. In Ireland and Mexico, the arrival of Christians determined that the native, or "pagan," values would be destroyed and replaced by Christian ones. Although Cihuacoatl presents a coherent picture of a Nahua matron who advised those fighting in the battles of both birth and military conquest, the Spanish friars pointed to what they saw as inconsistencies in her roles in an effort to undermine her importance and power. While the Nahua people highly regarded Cihuacoatl, the Spanish depicted her as a terrible goddess.

Demonization is apparent also in the Christian treatment of Morgan le Fay. Late Christian writers, such as Malory, claimed the supremacy of Christianity to the detriment of the pre-Christian Celtic culture wherein Morgan le Fay had her roots. For the Celts, she was a goddess with supernatural abilities who granted sovereignty on one who was worthy; by the fifteenth century, when ancient Celtic traditions were nearly forgotten, Malory could describe Morgan le Fay as a decadent and murderous witch. Her power is diminished; her role reversed. She becomes the one who seeks to overthrow the proper ruler, such as King Arthur. Further, at the hands of Malory and others, Morgan takes on the form of a despicable and wayward woman and ceases altogether to be the glorious goddess of sovereignty.

In both ancient Ireland and Mexico the collision occurred between two different religious traditions, the Christian encounter with indigenous cultures. In the case of the Sino-Tibetan Wen Cheng, the clash is between Tibetan Buddhism and the antireligious ideology of Chinese Communism. Certainly for the Tibetans, Wen Cheng's association with Buddhism enhances her status; for the Chinese, on the other hand, this is insignificant. Like the Christians, the Chinese Communists see the conquered people as backward, stupid, and incapable of handling their own lives. In both cases the conqueror looks upon the religion of the conquered as comprising nothing more than superstitions, legends, and other "nonsense." The Chinese see it as their duty to liberate the poor and backward Tibetans from so-called outdated beliefs that prevent them from living a good life. Tibetans are encouraged to marry the Chinese ("older brother"), just as Srong Tsen Gampo married the Chinese princess Wen Cheng. The destruction of Buddhism in Tibet and the attempt at assimilating Tibetans into the Chinese population have resulted only in excessive violence, deaths, and destruction.

Sometimes when traditions are in collision the dominant culture tries to absorb or even coopt a local tradition. *The Story of the Sacred Games* depicts Minatci, a local Dravidian warrior queen worshipped by the people of Madurai, in a subservient role. This text reflects a belief in the supremacy of the national tradition, represented by the powerful pan-Hindu god Siva. Here Minatci appears as nothing more than a dizzy housewife unable to make the simplest decision. She is completely dependent on her puissant husband, Siva, who is in absolute control and can perform amazing miracles. Nevertheless, in the actual rituals dedicated to Minatci in her temple in Madurai, it is she who is supreme. The people of Madurai have successfully prevented the absorption of their beloved queen into the national tradition.

Whereas Minatci remains foremost in local tradition, Chinese Mazu undergoes numerous transformations: Beginning as a sea-goddess worshipped by villagers in southern China, she becomes an empress in the imperial cult, and later still, she is identified with the sovereign claims of Taiwan. When the Chinese rulers moved south they adopted Mazu into the celestial bureaucracy and attributed to her the Confucian values of being filial and loyal to the state. This method must have proven successful because from the Song to the Qing dynasty Chinese emperors elevated her status higher and higher. Even with the collapse of the Qing dynasty, the Republican government persisted in preserving her temples. Today, Mazu survives beyond the borders of mainland China in Taiwan, Hong Kong, and throughout the Chinese diaspora. In Taiwan, Mazu has become associated with Taiwanese national identity as something separate from mainland China. Here in colliding traditions, the imperial culture successfully absorbed Mazu from her local roots, but instead of a reduction in status, Mazu's fame and power have continued to grow over time.

Traditions in collision often result in negative interpretations of the native or local tradition by the dominant or national culture. In an attempt to justify the supremacy and domination of the asserting culture, native beliefs are often condemned as inferior, destructive, and even demonic. Elsewhere the dominant culture may seek to bridge the two worldviews, stressing connections rather than irreconcilable and incompatible differences. This latter, syncretic approach is less destructive and usually creates a more tolerant society.

## Transcendence for All: The Democratization of Sovereignty

Sometimes by virtue of his kinship with a goddess, the king attains transcendence as well as sovereignty. For example, the Romans believed that Julius Caesar was admitted "into the company of the immortal gods" in heaven because of his ancestor Aphrodite (Moon, in this volume, 21). The term *transcendence* appears often in Western philosophy and theology to refer to that aspect of God that exists wholly apart from the world. God is thought to have some kind of unchangeable perfection unlike the mutable creation. We are not using the word in this way. Instead, we find it a useful term to refer more universally to beliefs about any reality that "lies beyond" the realm of ordinary human experience, a "place" where there is no death, no suffering.

The longing for transcendence is not universal. In many societies, it is a matter of course that at death one joins the ancestors in a paradise of some kind. Funerary rites are designed to help the newly dead arrive safely in the abode of the ancestors. For example, the Thompson River tribes of British Columbia describe the journey of the deceased to a place "underneath us, toward the sunset" (Alexander 1916, 147–149). At the end of the trail are found friends and family who have died already. Dancing and singing, they live in a great lodge in a country of warm sunshine where fruits and flowers grow abundantly.

In other societies, the abode of the dead is deemed far from pleasant. For example, Homer depicts the deceased Greeks as unhappy shades floating about in a dark place under the earth. Wherever death is viewed negatively, notions may develop of how to attain transcendence: immortality; liberation from the cycle of birth, death, and rebirth; nirvana; or perhaps salvation from sin and death. The language differs from tradition to tradition, but the goal is one of going to a "place" or "state of being" free from suffering.

As a human who is related somehow to the gods, the king is sometimes thought to be immortal, or capable of rebirth in the world of the gods. In ancient Egypt, the dead pharaoh was identified with the god Osiris. At death, goddesses assisted him as he made the transition to the other world. Nut protected him on this journey, hiding him from his enemy Seth:

> O Nut, spread yourself over your son Osiris the King
> that you may conceal him from Seth . . (Hollis, in this volume, 226)

Isis and Nephthys mourn the dead pharaoh, and then they help revivify him as the god Osiris. What began as a possibility for the king alone, eventually became a goal for others. As Hollis (in this volume) points out, "beginning in the Middle Kingdom, the texts and imagery originally restricted to the king began to be utilized by nonroyal individuals, reflecting the slow democratization of Egyptian afterlife"(226). Persons who were not pharaohs, not even members of the royal family, began to hope for resurrection among the gods. Whereas earlier the deceased pharaoh was identified with the god Osiris, and shared in that god's immorality, now each soul might hope to be reborn as Osiris.

The rather late Egyptian goddess Isis carried this motif with her into the Hellenistic world, where she was known and worshipped all around the Mediterranean as a savior. Initiation into the mysteries of Isis, open to one and all, became a way to attain eternal life. Isis appeared to one devotee, inviting him to worship her and live on eternally in the Elysian Fields, a paradise for heroes, who were partly divine: "You shall live glorious under my guidance; and when you have traveled your full length of time and you go down into death, there also, on that hidden side of earth, you shall dwell in the Elysian Fields and frequently adore me for my favors" (Meyer 1987, 180).

In medieval China a similar pattern occurs. In addition to granting him legitimacy and the emblems of kingship, Xiwangmu participated in the training of the proper king. Less he lose the Mandate of Heaven, the emperor was taught the religious rites of kingship and how to cultivate the virtues pleasing to Heaven. The stories suggest that the Chinese emperors often found the lessons in morality more difficult than other aspects of the job. They tended to disappoint the goddess, losing eventually their grasp on the empire as well.

During the Six Dynasties period, traditional themes of kingship were adopted by the poets and Daoists. Xiwangmu had better success, it appears, with the Daoist adepts, who come to her for advice on how to attain immortality "through ethical behavior, personal cultivation, and religious practice" (Cahill, in this volume, 201). One of her prodigies was Lord Mao, the founder of the Shangqing school of Daoism. Predicting that he would live as long as heaven and earth continued to exist, she described his future heavenly role: "You will control all divine transcendents of the former [southern] kingdoms of Wu and Yue, and all the water sources left of the Yangtze River" (Cahill, in this volume, 211). The Queen Mother of the West, formerly a king maker, became a maker of immortals.

In Christianity, transcendence is often envisioned as eternal life together with God. The coronation of Mary in Christian art points to her identity as Queen of Heaven. No longer limited by a mortal body restricted to an earthly life, the Queen of Heaven is able to help others become children of God, and so find a place in God's eternal kingdom. The *Sarum Missal* even describes Mary as the cause of salvation:

> Purest of Virgins, thou alone divine
> Queen of the world; salvation's cause thou art,
> The gate of light and heaven, full of grace. (Broughton, in this volume, 245)

Mary's passionate concern for ordinary Christians knows no limits: She will fight the very Devil for the souls of sinners, rescuing them from the fires of hell.

In many religions the personal relationship that binds the king and the goddess functions as a model for others. From the goddess of sovereignty the king acquires majesty, the divine power that allows the people and the land to flourish and prosper. Sometimes the king is envisioned as sharing also in the immortality of the goddess. When this kind of relation becomes available to ordinary people, they too become closer to the divine. The goddess of sovereignty then bestows her gifts on all who are worthy, transforming what is limited, mortal, and human into what is beyond death, blessed, god-like.

By focusing on sacred queens and goddesses of sovereignty as an important category of feminine images of the divine, the symbolic nature of sovereignty becomes clear: The human community flourishes when it is governed by values that reflect the divine order. The sovereign serves as a living link between the two realms, and the goddess who rules through the sovereign does so by virtue of a loving alliance. This symbolism expresses the human need for an ongoing and deeply felt relationship with the divine.

REFERENCES

Alexander, Hartley Burr. 1916. *North American Mythology*. Boston: Marshall Jones.

Meyer, Marvin, trans. 1987. "*The Golden Ass*, Book 11, by Apuleius of Madauros." Pp. 176–196 in *The Ancient Mysteries A Sourcebook: Sacred Texts of the Mystery Religions of the Ancient Mediterranean World*. San Francisco: Harper & Row.